MW01134818

Irish Materialisms

Irish Materialisms

The Nonhuman and the Making of
Colonial Ireland, 1690–1830

COLLEEN TAYLOR

OXFORD
UNIVERSITY PRESS

OXFORD
UNIVERSITY PRESS

Great Clarendon Street, Oxford, OX2 6DP,
United Kingdom

Oxford University Press is a department of the University of Oxford.
It furthers the University's objective of excellence in research, scholarship,
and education by publishing worldwide. Oxford is a registered trade mark of
Oxford University Press in the UK and in certain other countries

Published in the United States of America by Oxford University Press
198 Madison Avenue, New York, NY 10016, United States of America

British Library Cataloguing in Publication Data
Data available

Library of Congress Control Number: 2023942449

ISBN 978–0–19–889483–4

DOI: 10.1093/oso/9780198894834.001.0001

Printed and bound by
CPI Group (UK) Ltd, Croydon, CR0 4YY

In memory of my joyful, hilarious, and extraordinary mother,

Joan Burke Taylor.

Acknowledgements

No one deserves my gratitude more than Beth Kowaleski-Wallace, my advisor, mentor, and scholarly role model. Thank you for always sharing your time, your discoveries, your intellectual brilliance and energy, and for being the first reader of all my work. This book would not have been possible without you.

This research received support from the Irish Research Council and the National Endowment for the Humanities. Thank you to my mentors at University College Cork, Clíona Ó Gallchoir and Claire Connolly, for reading early versions of this manuscript and for inspiring me to seek new research discoveries.

I was blessed in my colleagues at the University of Notre Dame, who so generously advocated for my research, especially Barry McCrea, Chanté Mounton-Kinyon, Diarmuid Ó Giolláin, Mary O'Callaghan, Christopher Fox, Mary Hendrikson, and Aedín Clements. I must also thank Timothy LeCain, Rebecca Anne Barr, and Jess Keiser for their comments on the manuscript version of this book, their approval of the project, and for coming all the way to South Bend to say so.

Boston College fostered the early inklings and final stages of this project: thank you to Jim Smith for encouraging me from the very beginning, Marjorie Howes, Joe Nugent, Aeron Hunt, Vera Kreilkamp, Jim Wallace, Guy Beiner, Min Song, the Irish Studies program, and the English Department. The research communities of the American Conference for Irish Studies and the International Association for the Study of Irish Literatures have also bolstered my research from its junior stages.

I have been lucky in the opportunity to share aspects of this book with scholars on either side of the Atlantic. Thank you to the Environmental Humanities program at Venice International University, the Chawton House Library, Peter Gray and the Queen's University Belfast Irish Seminar, David O'Shaughnessy and Aileen Douglas at Trinity for their longstanding encouragement, and the University of Lausanne for graciously inviting me to share my research at their Critical Theory Seminar. Finally, thanks to friends and colleagues Lauren Benke, Rachael Young, Stephen O'Neill, Katie Mishler, Judith Stapleton, Julie Morrissy, Nell Wasserstrom, Matt Scully, and Mollie Kervick.

What a gift it is to have an international support system of friends. I send my appreciation and love to my American friends, especially Lizzy, Keilah, Amber, the Kenny family, the Pennacchias, and my favorite Fordham Rams, Gray and Stephanie. My best Irish pals have kept me laughing and sane while writing this book: my love and gratitude to Cormac, Evgeniia, Orna, Patrick, Niamh, Myles,

Shane, Laura, Nathan, the Slevins, and all the 'chicas' in Dublin who made sure I had some fun too.

My family has always encouraged my research. I'm grateful to cousins Katie, Brian, Meghan, Erin, Brendan, Brett, aunts Wendy, Cindy, Susan, Nancy, uncle Pat, my late uncles Jamie, Bobby, Tom, and my late aunt Mary. Finally, thank you to my wonderful brother Daniel, my dad Joseph Taylor for being my first and forever teacher, my late mother Joan, and my husband Shannon for believing in me and supporting our family, especially our latest addition, Sinéad.

Contents

List of Illustrations

Preface: Retrieving the Colonial Past

In 1875, a young man traveled from Kilballyowen, a farming parish on the western tip of Clare, to Cobh, County Cork, where he set sail for America. His eldest brother had recently led the Fenian Rising at Loop Head Lighthouse and swiftly escaped to New York. Following his brother's oceanic trail, this young man left behind his parents, sisters, brother, cousins, a small mud-walled cabin and thatched roof, some chickens, pigs, and a romantic view of green fields against the Atlantic. Several weeks later, he arrived in the growing town of Danbury, Connecticut, with only a few coins in his pocket.

Danbury was a world of commodities: apartments, markets, railroads, and, most importantly, hat factories. This young man would work in those factories and study the trade by candlelight. In time he would earn a reputation as one of the best hat dyers in the United States and even build a hat factory of his own. Decades later, his eldest son would buy a diamond ring for his fiancé. His Danbury-born children and grandchildren would know Clare only in name—not the mud walls or the thatch or the pigs—but simply that place from the past with the lighthouse, shrouded in mystery. They would never live off the land like their Irish family had. They would buy their houses and their clothes instead. They would be Americans.

The young immigrant who traveled from the earthly environment of Kilballyowen to a marketplace of textiles, dyes, and hats in Danbury, Connecticut, was Michael Francis Delohery, founder of the Delohery Hat Company. He is no longer famous, and his story is not exceptional in the grand scope of history. In fact, this is perhaps the most familiar story in American lore—the dream of rags to riches—and that is exactly the point. I invoke Michael Delohery's story here as a concrete, material example and because he is my great-great grandfather.

In writing this book I have come to know Michael, his lineage, and the material world from which he and his family were descended—a world haunted by famine and the colonial legacy of the penal laws against Catholics, a world of imperial oppression, hardship, and poverty. And yet in that sparse and natural material world, I have found creativity, resistance, and great depth. In my tour through the material world of eighteenth- and nineteenth-century colonial Ireland, Michael Delohery and his ancestors have gone from being names mentioned at family dinners to complex characters.

It is not fashionable to begin a critical academic study with a personal history. It is even less fashionable for a fourth-generation Irish-American to wax lyrical about the old country. But I invoke it here because it *matters*—not just to my family but to this book's methodology. When Michael died in 1927, the Danbury newspapers lauded him as one of Connecticut's finest businessmen, skilled in fine hats, dyes, and textiles, while back home in Clare, his brother, sisters, and cousins were still caricatured as rustic Paddies living in mud and thatch, akin to the way they had been depicted a century prior.[1] Although they contain clues, these periodicals and other written archives ultimately truncate the story of the Deloherys and so many families like them in Ireland and other colonies.

Irish Materialisms seeks to amend some of these omissions, to look closely at materiality in order to texturize and add layers to the history of colonialism and its forgotten, silenced citizens. It contends that we can find further understanding and character in the materiality of the past—the objects and resources that people interacted with on a daily basis, from the average native peasant to the colonial elite that wrote the novels and histories we read today. What follows is about Irish literature and culture of the long eighteenth century, and it is also about the democratizing and narrative power of materiality. It is about how something as small as a coin or pervasive as mud can hold stories that detail the experiences of individuals who did not qualify as protagonists in novels and who were not given the space to record their experiences in the pages of newspapers or travel writing.

What I now know about Michael Delohery comes from stories told (and embellished) by my grandmother and from the Connecticut newspaper archives celebrating the Irish immigrant boy-turned-businessman. But as for Michael's parents, grandparents, and great-grandparents dating back to the eighteenth century, very little documentation exists because the Deloherys were Catholic and spoke Irish. For scholars today, the eighteenth century is an attractive research topic: it witnessed the triumphs of republicanism, the rise of the novel, the Enlightenment, the advent of scientific experiment, industrialization, what we now call the Anthropocene, and of course, the slave trade and imperial expansion.[2] For as loud, discursive, inventive, and destructive as the long eighteenth century was in Britain and the Continent, there is silence across the Irish Sea—things we do not and cannot know about so many people who lived in Ireland after the defeat of the Gaelic Order in the late seventeenth century and before the Great Famine and the immigration of millions of Irish to North America, between 1690 and 1840, roughly.

The decline of native, Gaelic bardic poetry following the Flight of the Earls (1609) and the Wild Geese (1691) from Ireland in the wake of military defeat to British armies means that native, Irish-language records of the colonial experience in this century are sparse, often limited to manuscript circulation or the few

---

[1] 'Michael Delohery Dies in Danbury: Hat Manufacturer, Once an Immigrant Boy, Won Wide Success,' *The Bridgeport Telegram*, 16 April 1927, p. 8.
[2] See Dipesh Chakrabarty, 'The Climate of History: Four Theses.' *Critical Inquiry* 35.2 (2009).

remembered, preserved oral poems from that period, whose lyrical beauty is now accessible to even fewer Irish-speaking scholars.[3] While the late eighteenth century saw a renewed interest in native Irish culture from Anglo-Irish elites sympathetic to Irish nationalism, those literary forms were nevertheless confined to the lucky few who had the means to compose and document their expressions. The cultural life of native, Irish-speaking, Catholic tenants, oppressed under Britain's penal laws, was therefore hidden and lost over the course of this century, submerged in what were known as hedge schools (secret, outdoor classrooms for Catholics) and orally transmitted among other Irish speakers, gradually muffled by the distance of generations, the loss of famine, and the expanse of the Atlantic Ocean.

As with so many other colonies in the eighteenth and nineteenth centuries, Ireland before the 1845 Famine appears hazy now—a strange, different, and more populous island, irrevocably altered by mass emigration and death. Our limited and typically monoglot cultural access restricts our historical understanding to the perspectives and experiences of the English, Anglo-Irish, and imperial elites, who had the privilege and the means to record their lives and ideas. But this book contends that, in the absence of written records, a more comprehensive story of eighteenth-century Ireland and its peoples can be retrieved, piecemeal, through material objects. Although we cannot read their diaries or letters, the disenfranchised, poor, Irish-speaking, and Catholic peoples of eighteenth- and early-nineteenth-century Ireland emerge in shadowed format in English-language writing about Ireland in that long colonial century. And they were material beings; they possessed and handled things. Placed together, the remaining literature and the material objects of eighteenth-century Ireland dialogue and create a new discourse that adds depth and more complex subjectivity to the poor, peasant characters of colonial Ireland, who might otherwise be seen as caricatures in the remaining literature and artwork today.

This book approaches different kinds of matter as cultural remainders of lost experiences in order explore the experience of native, colonial, and peasant characters through the details of local materiality. My research practice of locating narrativity in material facts offers Irish and other cultural studies a means of new postcolonial revision. By reading literature through the material archive—the objects and materials that every average Irish tenant, literate or not, handled—this book seeks a more complete, egalitarian understanding of Ireland, albeit in material fragments. I suggest that these ostensibly 'silent' objects and materials can fill some historical and literary silences, point back to unheard echoes from Ireland's mysterious eighteenth century.

---

[3] One of the most important collections of preserved Irish language poems and their translations is *An Duanaire, Poems of the Dispossessed 1600–1900*, ed. Sean Ó Tuama and Thomas Kinsella, first published in 1981.

In the face of overwhelming loss, unknown pasts, and painful histories, so many of us are left only with materials: keepsakes, a bit of soil, a garment, a portrait. But these are not strictly 'silent' remnants of a once vocal, expressive life. These objects are not mere artifacts or pieces of evidence from which we humans extract clues. They are active meaning makers in their own right. Through interaction and study, we can come to hear and intuit matter's narrativity. The ring snug on my finger now, given by Michael's son, James, to his bride, Rose, in 1914, narrates this: born shortly after the Famine, Michael Delohery inherited colonial subjectivity and found independent success. His eye for color and his knowledge of material texture were rooted in west Clare's bright pigments of blue sea, green grass, and thick, dark soil. In many ways, the following pages began with Michael. As I wrote them, I thought about his legacy: my fearless, proud Irish grandmother and my mother who was crafty with fabrics too and put bright blues and greens in the quilts she made. My family history is bookended by linen and mud on one side, hats and dyes on the other, and now, the pages of this book. These things speak to me, fill in gaps that add depth and detail to the otherwise clichéd immigrant story of Michael Delohery and the running family jokes about the Rising at the lighthouse.

My hope is that what follows can have a similar, deepening, texturizing effect for the study of colonialism, eighteenth-century writing, and national and cultural identities of all colors and materials. This book uses Ireland—that Romantic, so-called ethereal realm of 'saints and scholars'—to ground colonial history back into its material roots. It returns to the resistance and creativity carved out in Irish matter, which has been waiting to tell its story.

Introduction

Postcolonial New Materialism and Nonhuman Narrativity

The main characters in this book are five nonhuman objects: coins, flax, spinning wheels, mud, and pigs, carefully chosen as case studies in colonial culture and thought.[1] These objects were common, everyday items in colonial Ireland, encountered by all classes in Irish society, from dispossessed, nomadic farm laborers to the Anglo-Irish Ascendancy of the 'Big House.' They were also frequently depicted in the pages of eighteenth- and nineteenth-century literature as signifiers of the Irish national character. Some of the objects named here, like linen and spinning wheels, may seem familiar as almost clichéd, quintessential Irish materials, and that is because, as this book will show, these objects helped solidify national characteristics and stereotypes about Irish people in the eighteenth and nineteenth centuries. Chapter 1, for example, discusses the Hibernian coin that impressed the idea of a woman Ireland, while Chapter 3 examines how the spinning wheel facilitated the idea of a disciplined Irish peasant. The fourth and fifth chapters deal in the worst typecast of all: the dirty, piggish Irishman.

This book becomes intimate with its main characters. It digs into the minutiae of each of one of these materials from coin to mud cabin: their scientific properties and processes, how they were handled, assembled, and circulated. Through these details, the objects will begin to 'speak'—not literally of course (except in the first chapter, which involves a talking coin), but more intuitively, through their unique material properties. They also speak through the wider networks of Irish material life and nonhuman interrelations in which they took part. Rather than view these objects in isolation, each chapter addresses other, directly related eighteenth-century Irish objects, like the harp (Chapter 1), the beetle and swingle (Chapter 2), the bog (Chapter 2), and the potato (Chapters 4 and 5), among

---

[1] Bruno Latour defines the nonhuman simply as 'things, objects, and beasts.' More expansively, new materialist historian Timothy LeCain defines the nonhuman as the entire material world 'beyond our human bodies'—a definition by which I abide in this book. Timothy LeCain, *The Matter of History: How Things Create the Past* (Cambridge: Cambridge UP, 2017), p. 16. I use the terms *object, matter, nonhuman,* and occasionally *things* interchangeably in order to avoid redundancy, referring in each case to materiality beyond the human body.

Irish Materialisms: The Nonhuman and the Making of Colonial Ireland, 1690–1830. Colleen Taylor, Oxford University Press.
© Colleen Taylor 2024. DOI: 10.1093/oso/9780198894834.003.0001

others.[2] While this work does not focus on harps or potatoes as case studies, they nevertheless feature as ancillary examples to engage a more complete picture of the fabric of everyday Irish materiality.

Up until now, studies of eighteenth-century Irish material culture have tended (understandably) to privilege available, archived objects owned by the wealthy, such as silverware, chalices, portraits, fine dress, books, printed volumes, and so on—the likes of which are held in Ireland's National Museums and National Gallery today.[3] In contrast, the objects in this book reflect the material life of an ordinary, poor farmer or tenant in eighteenth-century Ireland, from the mud beneath his feet to the coin in his pocket. These common and earthly materials were unlikely or unable to be preserved and archived by curators, which is exactly why they can reveal new cultural histories to us now, giving new significance and respect to the often-erased eighteenth-century Irish peasant.

Of course, coins, flax, spinning wheels, mud, and pigs are very different objects. Organic matter like mud on the ground or a pig's active, moving body may not seem like clearly delineated 'objects' in the same way as a coin or a spinning wheel. Nevertheless, each one of these five nonhuman entities was made into a defined object of scrutiny and sale in the colonialist context, and each one reveals a different insight into Irish experience in the eighteenth century. Together, this book's five organizing objects offer an alternative account of some of the most important events in the study of Irish history and culture, discussed by a wide range of scholars interested in colonization, including: the feminization of the Irish nation, the industrialization of the linen trade, the mud cabin that came to emblematize Irish colonial poverty, and finally, the development of Irish character in literature.

On the page, writers of both colonialist and anti-colonialist persuasions constructed coins, flax, spinning wheels, mud cabins, and pigs as emblems of Irish identity in order to differentiate English character from Irish. At the same time, these objects' features and material processes, such as how a coin was stamped or brown flax bleached white for linen cloth, gradually, subtly instilled ideas in people that both formulated Britain's paternalistic relationship with Ireland and also shaped a nascent, subversive Irish national identity in fiction through the language of material resistance. The deep study of these five objects assembles a new material archive that extends the literary record while uncovering new

---

[2] The potato does not feature as a stand-alone chapter in order to avoid cliché and anachronism: although significant to the functioning of cabin life in eighteenth-century Ireland, the potato's material story is most appropriate for a nineteenth-century account of Ireland.

[3] See: Mairead Dunleavy, *Dress in Ireland: A History* (Cork: Collins, 1989), Toby Barnard, *Making the Grand Figure: Lives and Possessions in Ireland 1641–1770* (New Haven: Yale UP, 2004) and *Brought to Book: Print in Ireland 1680–1784* (Dublin: Four Courts, 2017), and Janice Helland, *British and Irish Home Arts and Industries, 1800–1914: Marketing Craft, Making Fashion* (Dublin: Irish Academic Press, 2007). Most recently, Fintan O'Toole's *A History of Ireland in 100 Objects* (Dublin: RIA, 2013) evidences a popular interest in Ireland's rich material history.

subversive, postcolonial readings that can retroactively change our understanding of colonialism's victims.

Before delving into these material case studies, I want to establish and explain the specific parameters of my methodology and my vocabulary of nonhuman colonial studies, which is designed for the wider humanities at large, not just for Irish or literary studies alone. More specifically, I must explain how new materialism and postcolonial analysis come together in my research, while also reframing the most basic foundational building blocks of rhetorical analysis—object, metaphor, and character—according to what Diana Coole refers to as matter's 'agentic capacity' and what Serenella Iovino and Serpil Opperman call material narrativity, or 'storied matter.' I follow Iovino and Opperman's contention that all material phenomena are part of a vast network of agencies and energies exchanged between human and nonhuman actors, which can be read, literarily, as stories or narratives.[4] In redefining literary devices like object, metaphor, stereotype, and character according to material, nonhuman narrativity, I explicate how bringing new materialist theory together with postcolonial analysis can shift our mode of reading a colonial culture like Ireland's and open up new meanings within a text or archival resource. More precisely, material details and narratives in the following chapters, from coin to mud cabin, highlight new aspects of expressive creativity and resistance within previously overlooked and silenced peasant characters depicted in Irish fiction.

Throughout this book, I aim to demonstrate that new materialist theory is a language available to all human readers on the basis of our lived experience as material, biological creatures. Although many of the new materialist theoretical texts I implement are necessarily complex or abstract, my case studies model how new materialist concepts can be applicable to many academic fields. When presented with a seemingly inert cultural artifact or a limited literary archive, new materialist theory invites us to reread and reorient what we think we know about our social and cultural histories and find new characters in the matter before us.

I.1 Objects, According to New Materialism

I will begin with the most obvious word employed in this book: object. For the past thirty to forty years, postcolonial scholars of British and Irish history have been reading and scrutinizing the library of British imperialism, from Giraldus Cambrensis's *Topographia Hibernica* (1188) to Victorian Britain's *Punch* magazine.

---

[4] Serenella Iovino and Serpil Opperman, *Material Ecocriticism* (Bloomington, IN: Indiana UP, 2015), pp. 1–2. In formulating material ecocriticism—a field which brings the material turn into more stark relief for ecocriticism, and embraces the narrativity of matter—Iovino and Opperman build upon the work of Donna Haraway, Karen Barad, and Wendy Wheeler.

Well-known Irish literature critics like Declan Kiberd, Seamus Deane, Terry Eagleton, Eavan Boland, and Joep Leerssen have enumerated the complex and varying ways that the Irish nation was objectified in political and lyrical writing, abstracted into stereotype, commodified, and used as symbolic ammunition for both imperial and nationalistic projects dating back to the early modern period.[5] Despite this vast and rich array of scholarship, an irony remains: within the postcolonial study of Ireland—a discipline premised on understanding a nation's objectification in the imperialist wheelhouse—objects themselves have been surprisingly underexamined.

This book diverges from previous Irish literary scholarship by beginning with the new materialist paradigm: namely, a more curious approach to the object.[6] New materialist theorists have engaged a concerted effort to free objects and matter from the negative and dismissive connotations of anthropocentric ideas like 'objectification.' Twentieth-century postcolonialism's (and indeed, feminism's) canonical idea of objectification—that is, making colony or colonial citizen into a lesser object, a passive submissive under imperial force and ideology, and a thing to be controlled—is based in the concept of an object as a passive, mute, material item without agency, which humans influence with their will. This definition of object as passive matter, however, is a humanist and slowly eroding myth, which new materialism actively resists. As Jane Bennett writes in *Vibrant Matter,* the idea of a 'dead' object or 'instrumentalized matter' only feeds human hubris and the 'fantasies of conquest and consumption.'[7] New materialists seek to dismantle the subject/object binary and resist the fiction of an either/or approach to human subject and nonhuman object. As Donna Haraway contends, 'We must find another relationship to nature besides reification, possession, appropriation, and nostalgia.'[8] Instead, we must see objects as agential and entwined within a wide network of multiple, complex human *and* material systems.

[5] Declan Kiberd, *Inventing Ireland: The Literature of the Modern Nation* (Cambridge, MA: Harvard UP, 1996); Seamus Deane, *Strange Country: Modernity and Nationhood in Irish Writing since 1790* (Oxford: Oxford UP, 1997); Terry Eagleton, *Heathcliff and the Great Hunger: Studies in Irish Culture* (London: Verso, 1995); Eavan Boland, *Object Lessons: The Life of the Woman Poet in Our Time* (New York: Norton, 1995); Joep Leerssen, *Mere Irish and Fíor-Ghael: Studies in the Idea of Irish Nationality, its Development, and Literary Expression Prior to the Nineteenth Century* (South Bend, IN: University of Notre Dame Press, 1997) and *Remembrance and Imagination: Patterns in the Historical and Literary Representation of Ireland in the Nineteenth Century* (South Bend, IN: University of Notre Dame Press, 1997).

[6] Within the past decade, eighteenth-century English literary and cultural studies have been interested in the role of objects. See, e.g., Jonathan Kramnick's *Actions and Objects: From Hobbes to Richardson* (Palo Alto, CA: Stanford UP, 2020), Jonathan Lamb's *The Things Things Say* (Princeton: Princeton UP, 2011), Julie Park's *The Self and It: Novel Objects in Eighteenth Century England* (Palo Alto, CA: Stanford UP, 2010), and Cynthia Wall's *The Prose of Things: Transformations of Description in the Eighteenth Century* (Chicago: Chicago UP, 2014).

[7] Jane Bennett, *Vibrant Matter* (Durham, NC: Duke UP, 2010), p. ix.

[8] Donna Haraway, 'Otherworldly Conversations: Terran Topics, Local Terms' in *Material Feminisms*, ed. Stacy Alaimo and Susan Hekman (Bloomington, IN: Indiana UP, 2008), p. 158.

The pillar building block of new materialism states that nonhuman matter has agency that we humans, as a different species, cannot always understand. Objects act and communicate in their own unique material and mysterious ways. What appears passive or mute to us may, in fact, be neither, once we resist our own hubris around human knowledge and human senses—that belief in human exceptionalism, that we are separate from or above the material world, that we can investigate and control earthly materials toward our own ends. In contrast to anthropocentrism, new materialist thinkers consider how matter—be it commodity, cultural object, or organic biotic matter—changes or adds to what humans already know, or think they know, about history, society, and other phenomena. Thus, the objects that structure the following chapters must not be approached as artifacts of material culture, but rather, as vibrant, agentic characters with the hidden complexity we would expect of any good protagonist.

Over the past ten years, new materialist thinkers have crafted terms and concepts to dismantle the anthropocentric, conceptual distance between the material object and the human subject. Our language encodes the 'passivity of thingness' as alien to the descriptive language around human action and intent, thus requiring proactive rhetorical shifts.[9] For example, the very concept of anthropomorphism is, for Val Plumwood, an example of 'segregated and polarized vocabularies that rob the non-human world of agency and the possibility of speech.'[10] The rhetorical theft of matter's vibrancy in everyday language is why Jane Bennett coined the now increasingly used term 'thing power.' She redefines the otherwise nebulous, meaningless term of 'things' as material entities with their own forces, agencies, and recalcitrance, attributing a sense of energy to the idea of thingness. The inherent 'thing power' of objects and matter comprises an inexplicable vitality independent from human bodies.[11] To further this philosophy, Bennett asks us to reconceive of historical events as the work of a more-than-human 'assemblage': an interacting, heterogenous collection of bodies, organisms, and vibrant matter, across which agency is distributed in varying degrees. 'There was never a time,' Bennett writes, 'when human agency was anything other than an interfolding network of human and nonhumanity.'[12]

Along with this idea of assemblages and human-nonhuman networks, Karen Barad invites us to substitute interacting with the term 'intra-acting' as a rhetorical reminder that humans are part of and active within the material world. Material and discursive processes, (nonhuman) objects and (human) subjects, coemerge together and intra-act as part of the same world. Another conceptual

[9] Vicky Kirby, 'Natural Convers(at)ions: Or, What if Culture was Really Nature All Along' in *Material Feminisms*, p. 226.

[10] Val Plumwood, 'Journey to the Heart of Stone' in *Culture, Creativity, and Environment: New Environmentalist Criticism*, ed. Fiona Becket and Terry Gifford (New York: Rodopi, 2007), p. 21.

[11] Bennett, *Vibrant Matter*, p. 18.   [12] Bennett, *Vibrant Matter*, p. 31.

solution offered by Karen Barad is 'diffractive reading'—that is, active interpretation that reconfigures the connections between object and subject, nature and culture, science and the humanities, nonhuman and human. Diffractive reading—which is a kind of literary analysis itself—challenges the presumed separateness of the human subject and nonhuman object, and has thus become a main mode of interpretation among new materialists, influencing the readings of literature that follow in this book.[13] As I discuss in more detail later, a diffractive reading method reattributes ideas about national resistance to their origins in matter, challenging the idea that agency is exclusively attributable to human characters. In new materialism, objects re-emerge as co-actors in human life and language—as organisms with which humans 'intra-act' and dialogue as part of the same earthly choreography, which is not always entirely knowable from an empiric sense.

Timothy LeCain has applied the ideas of vibrant matter and diffractive reading to a practical research methodology. His book, *The Matter of History: How Things Create the Past* argues that we must change the way we research and read history to include matter's influence. LeCain calls his research 'neo-materialist' humanism, in which 'we recognize that history, culture, and creativity arise from the things [or objects] around us.'[14] In other words, he presents objects as key, active collaborators in historical events, reconceiving his entire humanist discipline as human-nonhuman cooperative partnerships between humans and minerals, ranchers and cows, traders and silkworms, carbon, copper, and miners. His archive models diffractive reading, moving beyond the written word to incorporate data of the biological sciences. For example, LeCain argues that the unique confluence between humanity's acute sense of touch and the protein molecules in silk helped to create the very idea and practice of class distinctions in relation to dress in Japan and globally.[15] Without knowledge of the material DNA of silk or the human nerve-endings, he argues, we cannot fully understand the historical phenomenon of class distinction. Rather than polarize material culture and material biology, as modern academia's traditional structure typically does, LeCain calls on all disciplines in the humanities to examine how culture, expression, ideas, and social formations emerge from material realities and nonhuman objects, how human cultures are 'intimately embedded in [human] bodies and

---

[13] Karen Barad. 'Posthumanist Performativity: Toward an Understanding of How Matter Comes to Matter.' *Signs* 28.3 (2003): 801–31. Physicist and theorist Karen Barad proposes the term 'intra-action' in place of interaction, which I use intermittently to illuminate my study of object–character intra-action. 'Intra-action' conceptually resists the idea of the individual human subject as existing apart from objects: subjects and objects do not interact as part of separate spheres, Barad argues, but intra-act within the same sphere (p. 815). Both Barad and Donna Haraway advocate for 'diffractive' reading of culture, in which text and world, cultural phenomena and biological nature, are read through one another (p. 811).

[14] LeCain, *The Matter of History*, pp. 16, 15.   [15] LeCain, *The Matter of History*, p. 192.

material environments.'[16] In the same way that LeCain uses silk to analyze classism, *Irish Materialisms* uses what were seen as quintessential Irish objects to analyze colonial relations and the expression of colonial character—how the unjust system of the penal laws or the depreciation of the Irish economy under colonial rule arose, in part, from the impression on the Irish coin or the molecules in flax fibers. In short, human actors and writers mobilized these five pervasive Irish objects, in certain contexts, toward both imperial and nationalist ends, sometimes simultaneously.

I.2 Metaphor and Stereotype, Made Out of Matter

After establishing the material details of coins, flax, spinning wheels, mud, and pigs, respectively, each chapter will examine exactly how these materials influenced the formulation and circulation of Irish stereotypes and colonial policy in writing and visual culture. These object case studies move from challenging the idea of coins, linen, and mud as passive, mute objects in the history of Ireland to examining how these objects were imbricated in common, widely accepted metaphors about Irishness. Even if a coin seems like an insignificant player in the political relationship between Ireland and Britain, the ways in which that coin impacted human rhetoric around Ireland had far-reaching and indeed deadly effects. If objects are the foundation of colonial stereotypes, the resulting metaphor is the ideological currency on which colonial infrastructure and prejudice thrives.

The standard definition of metaphor in the dictionary today ascribes complete control and agency to the human thinker: a person *applies* a figure of speech—an ostensibly human invention—to a material object to which it might not have relation beyond human creativity. But what happens when we shed anthropocentric hubris and approach this cognitive process like a new materialist? The metaphor emerges as more of a collaboration—between the unique properties of the material object and the human thinker who encounters it. In line with a new materialist conception of objects, I approach metaphor in literary representations through the new materialist critical lens that gives matter its due process. In other words, this book analyzes how matter makes the metaphor, rather than how humans miraculously invent metaphors out of matter.

This material idea of metaphor is not a new one. Many critics beyond the field of literary and cultural studies have explored the ways in which the natural, biological world functions semiotically and invites human-made metaphors in response. In the 1980s, psychologist James Gibson defined the idea of 'affordance'

---

[16] LeCain, *The Matter of History*, p. 16.

to describe the complementarity of the material object and the human mind. Affordance, Gibson writes, captures the process by which the environment 'offers, provides, and furnishes' the human being or the thinking animal.[17] Significantly, affordance 'is not a process of perceiving a value-free physical object to which meaning is somehow added' by an observer, but rather, 'perceiving a value-rich ecological object.'[18] Privileging the autonomous, self-definitive materiality of the object, Gibson writes: 'The object offers what it does because it is what it is.'[19] Matter and human being become collaborators in the production of metaphor and social meaning: the object's unique acts and properties 'afford' the human an idea or metaphor. The following chapters trace the details of how certain objects afforded certain concepts: such as how the spinning wheel afforded the notion of a quick-turning mind, sometimes toward subversive ends. In each case study, I regularly use the verbal 'afford' to indicate the agency and influence of the object in the presentation of ideas in literature.

My idea of metaphor directly resists postmodernist theories about an entirely human-constructed, linguistic reality, and instead approaches human thought and expression as what Donna Haraway refers to as a 'material-semiotic' formation—that culture, ideas, and human cognition are both material *and* rhetorical. Haraway coined the term 'material-semiotic' in 1988 as a way to temper the extreme doctrine of postmodernist constructivism, by trying to grapple with both ideological construction *and* a material 'real.' Haraway makes claims for 'embodied knowledges' and argues that knowledge requires a 'material-semiotic technology to link bodies and meanings.'[20] 'Material-semiotic,' Haraway explains, portrays the 'object of knowledge as an active, meaning-generating part of the apparatus of bodily production.'[21] In turn, cultural analysis, history, literary studies must all look at both matter *and* rhetoric to grasp the full effects of a social or scientific phenomenon. Haraway's ideas laid the foundation for many new materialist thinkers that followed in her wake, such as Karen Barad and Stacy Alaimo, whose idea of transcorporeality explores the ways in which the human body is imbricated in a web of meaning with all kinds of environmental and material forces beyond the human form.[22] This book examines Irish character itself as a material-textual formation, as something that emerges from both material and

[17] James J. Gibson, *The Ecological Approach to Visual Perception* (Hillsdale, NJ: Lawrence Erlbaum, 1986), p. 127.

[18] Gibson, *Ecological Approach*, p. 140.

[19] Gibson, *Ecological Approach*, p. 139. Caroline Levine has picked up on Gibson's term and used it in her book, *Forms: Whole, Rhythm, Hierarchy, Network* (Princeton: Princeton UP, 2015), to show how forms—certain patterns, rhythms, and structures—afford certain cultural, social, and political changes and events.

[20] Donna Haraway, 'Situated Knowledges: The Science Question in Feminism and the Privilege of Patrial Perspective.' *Feminist Studies* 14.3 (1988), p. 585.

[21] Haraway, 'Situated Knowledges,' p. 595.

[22] See Stacy Alaimo, 'Trans-Corporeal Feminisms and the Ethical Space of Nature' in *Material Feminisms*, ed. Alaimo and Hekman.

textual realities, as an event wrought by the material environment of colonial Ireland and the rhetorical worlds of British political discourse and national fiction.

Literary critics have begun to elaborate upon the new materialist conception of metaphor that stems from Donna Haraway's material semiotics and, implicitly, Gibson's affordance. Serenella Iovino and Serpil Opperman, for example, established the field of material ecocriticism, which combines the philosophies underpinning ecocriticism and new materialist theory in order to approach 'all physiochemical processes' as capable of 'dynamic articulations.'[23] Every living creature and material organism, Iovino and Opperman explain, tell 'evolutionary stories of coexistence, interdependence, adaptation, and hybridization…whether perceived or interpreted by the human mind or not.'[24] Material phenomena from the melting of metal to the biodegradation of soil can be 'read'—as semiotic, metaphoric, narrative, articulate, and therefore, literary.

The framework of Iovino and Opperman's material ecocriticism is a continuation of biosemiotics as theorized by Wendy Wheeler in *The Whole Creature* (2006), which states that all biological life is semiotic and interpretive.[25] Wheeler puts human poiesis back into nature 'where it belongs.'[26] DNA, for example, is less a mechanical code and more like an expressive language in which cells 'make meanings' that result in a unique text: the body.[27] Wheeler's ideas can be summarized by saying that metaphor and symbiosis are everywhere in the natural, material world—not just in the human mind or human pen. Metaphor is, Wheeler writes, 'a real causal factor in both natural and cultural evolution'—which is, indeed, the claim I make for metaphor in relation to Irish material and colonial evolution.[28] Building upon the biosemiotic idea of metaphor and the discipline of material ecocriticism, my approach to Ireland analyzes the intertwinings of matter and discourse as they 'emerge in material expression' and as they are recreated and constituted in literature and other cultural forms.[29]

Finally, eighteenth-century literary scholar Sean Silver also provides helpful concepts for approaching the materiality of metaphor in literature. Silver's book *The Mind is a Collection* (a metaphor in and of itself) contends that returning to early-eighteenth-century ideas about human creativity offers us useful ways of

---

[23] Iovino and Opperman, *Material Ecocriticism*, p. 34.

[24] Iovino and Opperman, *Material Ecocriticism*, p. 7.

[25] See also Timo Maran, *Mimicry and Meaning: Structure and Semiotics of Biological Mimicry* (New York: Springer, 2017), as well as contributions to the journal *Biosemiotics*, ed. Timo Maran (2008–present). Biosemiotics can be traced to the late nineteenth century in the work of Sanders Pierce and Jakob von Uexkull. For further background on biosemiotics, see: Serenella Iovino, 'Messages from Within: Primo Levi, Biosemiotics, and Freedom' in *Nature and Literary Studies*, ed. Peter Remien and Scott Slovic (Cambridge: Cambridge UP, 2022), pp. 372–90.

[26] Wendy Wheeler, 'Natural Play, Natural Metaphor, and Natural Stories: Biosemetic Realism' in *Material Ecocriticism*, p. 69.

[27] Wheeler, 'Natural Play,' p. 68.   [28] Wheeler, 'Natural Play,' p. 71.

[29] Iovino and Opperman, *Material Ecocriticism*, p. 6.

thinking about how metaphor works. In those days, early Enlightenment thinkers like Thomas Locke and John Reid rightly intuited, Silver argues, that our reality is 'patterned on the world of things.'[30] Early eighteenth-century thinkers offer us a 'materially contingent model of cognition.'[31] Silver explains that metaphor can only emerge through relations between objects, and his book goes on to explore how working with and handling matter historically facilitated human cognition. As Silver so effectively puts it: 'metaphor registers the conviction that arises from our regular experience between objects and effects.'[32] In other words, metaphor is our evidence that everyday thinking, ideology, and of course creative art, respond to the physical world, and vice versa. This is why new materialists are returning to the materiality of linguistic and social constructions: indeed, the very idea of social construction would never emerge without a metaphoric origin in material construction itself.

Irish Materialisms approaches metaphoric affordance and material semiotics in relation to their historical, colonial consequences. It places the conviction that literary expression arises from the material world into the fraught and urgent setting of colonial ideology, where dehumanizing metaphors resulted in powerful, material, and fatal effects. Stereotypes against the poor and native Irish can be traced to semiotic relationships that linked certain aspects of Ireland's material reality—like the fine threads of a flax stalk or the mud composition of a cabin—to colonial concepts about the Irish people's weak, uncivil, or bestial nature. For example, if an English writer likens Irish cottiers living within earthen walls to pigs wallowing in mud, it suddenly becomes all the more defensible to control the Irish, cage them, domesticate them, and perhaps one day, consume them—an idea Swift directly satirizes in 'A Modest Proposal,' when he suggests the rich Ascendancy eat poor Catholic babies like one would eat bacon.

The following journey through nonhuman narrative will show how material processes like minting coins or spinning of flax for linen gave rise to correlating ideas about Ireland that produced resonant, impactful analogies: that national identity could be rebranded, as discussed in Chapter 1, that Ireland, like a woman, could be subdued into domestic industrialization, as discussed in Chapters 2 and 3, or that the Irish were no better than slovenly livestock, as seen in Chapter 4 and 5. Applying the new materialist view of metaphor, I will show that the qualities eighteenth-century writers presented as inherent to the universal Irish national character were in fact cognitive responses to and expressions of the material realities of colonial life. When materiality offers metaphoric ideas and particular

---

[30] Sean Silver, *The Mind is a Collection: Case Studies in Eighteenth-Century Thought* (Philadelphia: UPenn Press, 2015), p. 10.

[31] Silver, *The Mind is a Collection*, p. 8.

[32] Silver, *The Mind is a Collection*, p. 10. For a detailed discussion of the cognitive theorists of new materialisms, see LeCain's chapter 3 in *The Matter of History*, esp. pp 113–21, where he discusses Andy Clark, Benjamin Bergen, and Lambros Malafouris.

avenues of cognition to the writer, it becomes clear that matter is a text in and of itself. Serenella Iovino and Serpil Opperman have effectively expressed this truism: matter everywhere, they write, is a 'mesh of meanings, properties, and processes, in which human and nonhuman players are interlocked in networks that produce undeniable signifying forces.'[33] Studying those same material realities today reveals new, subversive details about the process of characterization itself—the ways in which the objects discussed here buttress as well as challenge colonial metaphor, the ways in which they afforded stereotypes *and* subversive resistance against colonial policy.

I.3 Postcolonial New Materialist Methodology—At a Glance

Before moving to the particulars of Ireland and the literature in question, I wish to highlight the importance of combining new materialist theory with the historical study of colonialism and race for the humanities going forward. This book's convergence of new materialism and postcolonialism—what I call 'nonhuman colonial studies' and describe as a return to postcolonial analysis armed with the tools of new materialist theory—is not a standard cross-disciplinary approach. In fact, these case studies hinge on the intersection of two theoretical fields, new materialism and postcolonialism, whose fruitful integration has yet to be fully realized.

Several scholars have acknowledged the need to expand postcolonial analysis from within the new materialist paradigm.[34] In an article published in 2020, Jerry Lee Rosiek, Jimmy Snider, and Scott Pratt drew attention to the fact that new materialist philosophy has yet to fully engage with indigenous cultures despite clear overlap in relation to the belief in material agency. They call for an integration of indigenous social sciences and postcolonial literatures with new materialist theory, challenging philosophers to resist their Eurocentric training.[35] Similarly, Peta Hinton, Tara Mehrabi, and Josef Barla have criticized new materialists for underrepresenting questions of race, colonialism, and racial bodies despite similar efforts in adjacent fields.[36] It is true that the wider environmental humanities, in

---

[33] Iovino and Opperman, *Material Ecocriticism*, p. 2.

[34] The absence of a postcolonial dialogue within new materialist studies has also been the topic of a recent seminar and podcast: 'What is New about New Materialism: Black and Indigenous Scholars on Science, Technology, and Materiality,' published through University of California Berkeley, https://www.crg.berkeley.edu/podcasts/whats-new-about-new-materialism-black-and-indigenous-scholars-on-science-technology-and-materiality/.

[35] Rosiek et al, 'The New Materialisms and Indigenous Theories of Non-Human Agency.' *Qualitative Inquiry* 26.3–4 (2020), p. 332.

[36] Peta Hinton, Tara Mehrabi, and Josef Barla, 'New Materialisms/New Colonialisms,' https://newmaterialism.eu/content/5-working-groups/2-working-group-2/position-papers/subgroup-position-paper-_-new-materialisms_new-colonialisms.pdf.

which new materialism takes part, have been more attentive to postcolonialism, as in the development of what is known as 'green postcolonialism.' *Postcolonial Ecologies*, edited by Elizabeth DeLoughrey and George Handley, for example, examines the environmental impacts of slavery and imperialism and seeks to place the history of colonialism in dialogue with the landscape. Most famously, Dipesh Chakrabarty bridged the discipline of postcolonialism with ecocriticism through his well-known reflections on the Anthropocene.[37] The dialogue between Irish studies and ecocriticism has begun to germinate recently, as evidenced by Malcolm Sen's collection *A History of Irish Literature and the Environment*.[38] Ultimately, however, while the causality between anthropocentrism and forms of human oppression such as racism, sexism, and speciesism stands as an accepted a priori in the wider environmental humanities, few new materialists have explored the historical mechanics of this relationality as it pertains to nonhuman agency.[39]

One exception to new materialism's general evasion of race and colonialism is Kathryn Yusoff's *A Billion Black Anthropocenes or None*, which effectively analyzes the relationship between human race and geology. Like the previously quoted critiques, *A Billion Black Anthropocenes or None* claims that new materialism has, perhaps unintentionally, 'whitewashed' the history of matter by avoiding the misappropriately defined 'human' issues of race and empire—or, at the very least, by placing the moral, ethical consequences for human life in the background of nonhuman discourse. In response, Yusoff evinces the direct relevance between new materialism and race studies by demonstrating how ideas about matter's agency reverberate profoundly for our ongoing examination of imperialism. Historically, conceptualizations of material events have enacted racial violence and, as Yusoff phrases it, 'operationalize[d] race.'[40] When matter (she uses the example of gold mining) can become property or territory, so can humans, and therefore she views the hierarchizing of matter's properties as a first step toward racializing human beings. Yusoff's analysis of gold mining demonstrates how attending to the material, geological, and biological life of matter inevitably broadens and deepens our understanding of momentous historical and cultural

---

[37] See *Postcolonial Ecologies*, ed. Elizabeth DeLoughrey and George Handley (Oxford: Oxford UP, 2011); Dipesh Chakrabarty, 'The Climate of History: Four Theses.' *Critical Inquiry* 35.2 (2004) and 'Humanities in the Anthropocene: The Crisis of an Enduring Kantian Fable.' *New Literary History* 47.2–3 (2016). See also Upamanyu Pablo Mukherjee, *Postcolonial Environments: Nature, Culture, and the Contemporary Indian Novel in English* (Basingstoke: Palgrave, 2010). For the Irish postcolonial context, John Wilson Foster edited a special issue on Ireland for *The Journal of Ecocriticism* (2013). See also Eoin Flannery, *Ireland and Ecocriticism* (London: Routledge, 2016).

[38] Malcolm Sen, ed., *A History of Irish Literature and the Environment* (Cambridge: Cambridge UP, 2022).

[39] The question of how race is constituted materially in relation to the human body is a more thoroughly explored topic in postcolonial theory and new materialism. See, e.g., essays by Michael Hames-Garcia and Suzanne Bost in *Material Feminisms*, ed. Alaimo and Hekman.

[40] Kathryn Yusoff, *A Billion Black Anthropocenes or None* (Minneapolis: University of Minnesota Press, 2018), p. 4.

shifts, like imperialism. Both LeCain and Yusoff have proven at the methodological and research level that the academic study of human travel, economy, conflict, and culture is *not* strictly human, humanist, or even verbal. Matter has always played a starring role in these colonial events.

Yusoff poignantly writes that 'Material stories are origin stories.' Likewise, the following object case studies in this book offer origin stories for the ways in which the Irish nation and its people have been oppressed, raced, and, significantly, gendered. From coin to flax, the first three chapters in this book illustrate a gendered characterization of Ireland that points back to a physical memory of colonial bloodshed and violent dispossession.[41] Being both subject and object herself, which man claims and subdues, woman and her body became a natural container for Irish character's colonial objectification, as with so many other colonial and enslaved cultures. As the original, aestheticized objects of exchange, traded in wars for peace treaties or riches, women were employed to naturalize the violent objectifying of Ireland and its subjects as ostensibly passive things for English imperialists to control, subdue, characterize, and speak with and for. Thus, my chapters begin with an object (coin, flax, wheel) and often end with a woman, be it a spinner or a fictional heroine.[42]

While coins, flax, and spinning wheels afforded colonial thinkers the imperially advantageous gendering of Irish matter, mud cabins and pigs afforded them the imperially advantageous animalizing of Irish matter on the basis of racialized speciesism. These kinds of bestialized characterizations of natural matter enacted and perpetuated a pervasive colonial infrastructure and ideology that cruelly oppressed poor Irish people. To fully understand a colonial context like eighteenth-century Ireland's, the scholar needs new materialism. One must address matter's potentially racializing and gendering qualities to see the full historical and cultural picture. As I will show, seemingly negligible, pervasive objects like coins, flax, spinning wheels, mud, and pigs powerfully helped imperial actors and writers effectuate colonialism's infrastructural and rhetorical oppression.

My material readings, however, also lead me to more empowered planes than Yusoff's new materialist geology. While the narratives of coins, flax, spinning wheels, mud, and pigs explicate the material foundations of Irish colonial networks, Irish stereotypes, and indeed Irish oppression, they also point, simultaneously, to the agency of colonial Ireland's material world, as it appears, sometimes

---

[41] Yusoff, *Billion Black Anthropocenes*, p. 19.

[42] Some of the early beginnings of new materialist theory emerged in the context of feminism, developed by thinkers like Stacy Alaimo, Susan Hekmann, Karen Barad, and others. The fundamental new materialist principles provide the tools with which to examine and challenge Enlightenment-era binaries that delegate women to the subordinate half of the comparison, such as mind/body, subject/object, active/passive, and of course, empire/colony. New materialist thinking has continued to be been fruitful for feminist critique. See *Material Feminisms*, by ed. Alaimo and Hekman.

surprisingly, in literature. A world of its own self-generating meanings and articulations, nonhuman Ireland is a text in its own right—a text that can now retroactively shift the way we read and interpret colonial literature from this period. It may seem counter-intuitive to turn from the material reality of earthly, colonial life in Ireland to literary representations of that life written by persons far removed from the daily toil of spinning or the domesticity of a mud cabin. However, new materialist critics have argued that literature offers a unique vantage point or privileged site from which to observe sometimes-uncanny material energies and influences. Through literature and art, assumptions about or definitions of the human and nonhuman can become 'newly perceptible.'[43] For critics like Mayra Rivera, literature is a new materialist technology that renders otherwise abstract material forces 'palpable, sensible, and felt.'[44] Val Plumwood argues that literature can give us 'other ways of seeing,' can make visible 'whole new interspecies dialogues, dramas, and projects previously unimaginable.'[45] Because humans inhabit 'material, social, and symbolic worlds,' the material narrative of colonial life must be placed in relationship to the symbolic world of fictional narrative in the long eighteenth century.[46]

By virtue of their unique properties and inherent agencies (what Bennett would call 'thing power'), the objects in this book directly and metonymically point to greater empowerment, resistance, and expression in the oppressed Irish than has been previously recognized, both in the material world and in the symbolic, literary one. Understanding the material realities behind a cultural object, stereotype, or national novel fundamentally shifts the dynamics of colonial agency, and sometimes it does so in favor of the once-silenced colonial subject. Attending to material articulations of these objects necessarily repositions the colonial character in a fictional text as articulate too—even when he or she does not say much in dialogue. The material details of coins, flax, spinning wheels, mud, and pigs will be shown to narrativize a complex inner psychology in the native Irish character, even in literary texts that ostensibly undermine, stereotype, or erase those characters. To read the material articulations of colonial history and colonial texts is to read subversively against the controlled ideological narrative of the human writer and the empire, and as such, new materialism coincides perfectly with subversive postcolonial analysis.

[43] Timothy Clark, *The Cambridge Introduction to Literature and the Environment* (Cambridge: Cambridge UP, 2011), p. 61.

[44] Mayra Rivera, *Poetics of the Flesh* (Durham, NC: Duke UP, 2015), p. 141. See also Tobias Skiveren, 'Literature' in *New Materialism Almanac*, 2018, https://newmaterialism.eu/almanac/l/literature.html.

[45] Plumwood, 'Journey,' pp. 18, 19.

[46] See Samantha Frost, *Biocultural Creatures: Toward a New Theory of the Human* (Durham, NC: Duke UP, 2016), p. 4.

I.4 The Irish Historical and Literary Context

I hope that the ideas and methodology modeled in *Irish Materialisms*—about narrative objects, colonial metaphor, and subversiveness—will be applied to other literatures, cultures, and areas of specialization in Irish, Anglophone, and postcolonial studies. But I have nevertheless had to focus my methodology on a particular subject: in this case, a particular nation at a particular moment in historical (human) time. I have chosen Ireland of the long, eventful eighteenth century as my subject because, first, it is the colonial world with which I am most familiar. More importantly, Ireland offers a unique, compact source of local, material knowledge. It is, after all, a self-contained island and Britain's longest-running colonial project. Within this small geographical space, we can find the story of colonial plantation, military conflict, racism, mass death, mass emigration, and unprecedented ecological and population change within a few short centuries. The eighteenth century is unique in marking the key turning point when Ireland went from being a contentious territory wedged between the old Gaelic Order and the new Protestant Rule to a complete colonial infrastructure under the power of Great Britain—before, of course, the Great Famine brought that version of Ireland to a complete standstill. It is a small, compact, and yet unique, complex case—a suitable testing ground for how reading the material narrative of a colonial past can change the dominant picture of a history and culture we think we know.

I review the story of these five nonhuman objects from around 1690, the time of the Williamite War, which ultimately resulted in the sweeping defeat of Gaelic, Jacobite Irish forces—to around 1830, right after Catholic Emancipation in 1829, which repealed the penal laws and enabled Catholics to serve as MPs in the British Parliament. The year 1830 marks a clear endpoint before the onset of the Great Famine in 1845, which irrevocably changed the course of Irish history, and which was a direct result of the material-semiotic events in the eighteenth century discussed here. To put it simply, this long eighteenth century, from 1690 to 1830, was the century in which Ireland became entirely, effectively, oppressively colonized. During this period, the Irish landscape, economy, writing, national identity, and the Irish people themselves underwent all kinds of material and ideological transformations. The case studies that follow encompass some of the most significant moments in the unique commercial and political history of Ireland, which powerfully impacted the material conditions of everyday life for Irish citizens in the centuries to come.

The dates between 1690 and 1830 include numerous changes in the political status of the island, beginning with the failed Jacobite Rebellion in the late seventeenth century and the Flight of the Wild Geese in 1691, when the last of Ireland's Gaelic rulers and Jacobite forces left for France, solidifying an Anglo-Irish Protestant Ascendancy in Ireland and intensifying the penal laws against

Catholics. Nevertheless, a century later, Henry Grattan earned brief autonomy for Ireland with his independent parliament in 1782.[47] This moment also signaled a change in national allegiance, as Protestant Irish citizens began to identify with a nationalism that had been previously associated with Gaelic Catholics. These nationalist, economic hopes of Irish independence from Great Britain, shared by the Anglo-Irish and Catholic populations alike, led to the establishment of the United Irishmen and their failed, bloody Rebellion in 1798. Two of the most momentous events in Ireland's early nineteenth century include the Act of Union in 1801, which disbanded the Irish Parliament and put the island entirely under the jurisdiction of Westminster, and the campaign for Catholic Emancipation, eventually granted in 1829.

Within these years, there were important shifts in the economic status of Ireland, such as the Wood's Halfpence Affair, 1722–5, the depreciation of Irish capital, the Declaratory Act (1720), which limited the island's economic freedoms by automatically applying laws passed in Britain to Ireland, and the establishment of a flourishing international linen trade, which became Ireland's sole industry for well over a century. The later eighteenth century witnessed a new national movement founded on economic rights, such as the campaign for Irish Free Trade in the 1780s. Following the Act of Union, however, the aim of Irish economic independence became a false hope, emblematized by the disbandment of a separate Irish currency around the 1820s and 1830s, discussed in Chapter 1.

Contrary to popular belief, Ireland did experience a small version of that famous eighteenth-century European phenomenon, the consumer revolution. Stephanie Rains has shown how many of the dominant Irish department stores, such as Todd, Burns & Co. or McSwiney, Delaney, & Co., were established in the early 1800s as draperies. From the early eighteenth century, general stores appeared in Irish provincial towns, as did traveling fairs and markets. Still, these draperies and stores, despite their affordances for the establishment of some Catholic middle classes, do not equate with the far more expansive consumer revolution in England. It remained overarchingly true that eighteenth-century Ireland was seen as an object for England to consume as a luxury, curiosity, or an exotic literary character. While early modern English culture posed Ireland as an armed and dangerous foe, following the Flight of the Wild Geese in 1691, the conquered island became more of a resource than a threatening adversary—an object of consumerism, curiosity, and conundrum, sometimes with the residual undertone of danger. Indeed, the central ideological consequence of Irish travel

---

[47] The Irish Parliament under MP Henry Grattan was considered by many early nineteenth-century nationalists (including Sydney Owenson) as the high point of Irish nationalism in the eighteenth century. Grattan helped found the Irish Patriot Party advocating for greater Irish autonomy and democracy. Most importantly, in 1782, Grattan succeeded in establishing Ireland's Declaration of Rights, forcing the British Parliament to concede Ireland's legislative independence from Great Britain.

writing, culminating in Arthur Young's famous *Tour in Ireland, 1776–1779* discussed in Chapter 4, was to pose Ireland and Irish subjects as a material resource ripe for English development.

In more literal terms, the objects discussed here, such as linen and pork, were popular consumer items bought by English citizens both because of and in spite of their Irishness. Thus, Ireland's position as the consumed rather than the consumer helps to explain the perceived distance between Ireland and the eighteenth-century consumer revolution phenomenon that sparked changes in thinking and literary culture in Britain. The objects of this study will demonstrate that placement and purchase of Irish items in an imperial market afforded a particular rendering of colonial character as feminine and domesticated that served imperial ideology and practice, while only partially disguising the object's violent colonial contexts. As this book will demonstrate, such colonial violence re-emerges when material narrative converses with colonial rhetoric and metaphor in literature.

At the same time that the long eighteenth century witnessed the decline of Gaelic power and increased colonial and economic control from Britain, it also saw a rise of English-language literature about Ireland, often written by Anglo-Irish writers identifying with the Irish nation, dating back to Swift's consciously Irish voice in his political writings in the 1720s.[48] One of the most significant cultural changes in the eighteenth century saw Ireland's printed output transition to being dominated by the English language. There was, of course, a vast amount of literary creativity being expressed in the Irish language orally and through manuscript circulation, but in terms of printed material, Ireland's literacy became English-dominated. My study here focuses primarily on written output in English and novelistic fiction, rather than the oral culture of Irish language storytelling and song, which is extensively discussed in Vincent Morley's *The Popular Mind in Eighteenth-Century Ireland* and collected in *An Duanaire*.[49] While the oral culture of the Irish language informs my close readings, the following case studies spotlight how the materiality of the printed page emerges from the earthly, material pre-text of coins, flax, spinning wheels, mud, and pigs.

In the wake of the Act of Union, there was sharp rise in interest in printed fiction about Ireland. Both ironically and inevitably, when Ireland lost its distinct identity as a separate nation under the Union, the question of national character became a point of departure for writers of both Catholic and Protestant

---

[48] Swift famously critiqued the Declaratory Act (1719), which said any ruling passed in British Parliament immediately applied to Ireland, and Wood's Halfpence (1722), an English patent for Irish coinage, with a new national, indignant voice, addressing the 'whole people of Ireland' as a unified island nation. Almost a century later, many women writers established a new national genre in the Irish tale, aimed at an English readership. Both literary developments are discussed in more detail in Chapter 1.

[49] *An Duanaire, Poems of the Dispossessed 1600–1900*, ed. Sean Ó Tuama and Thomas Kinsella (Dublin: Dolmen, 1981).

backgrounds, engendering a whole subset of English-language romance novels known as the national tale. The onset of the national tale is traditionally traced to Sydney Owenson's *The Wild Irish Girl* (1806), a novel about a prejudiced Englishman who falls in love with a Gaelic beauty and by extension, falls in love with Ireland's native culture too.[50] Owenson, like Maria Edgeworth before her, built upon an eighteenth-century literary trend that openly deployed the synecdoche between national character and literary character, so that the national character became intertwined with the formal concept of literary character in the Irish novel.[51]

As Claire Connolly has documented, the popularity of *The Wild Irish Girl* in England and Ireland, in particular, inspired hundreds of imitations in the first three decades of the nineteenth century, amounting to a hefty 114 Irish titles published between 1800 and 1829.[52] While many authors in the eighteenth century sought to suppress their Irishness, others used 'Irish' as a selling point for publication in Britain (which it remains today, on a global scale) at the turn of the nineteenth century. By the 1810s and 1820s, therefore, England was consuming Ireland as a cultural curiosity with increasing excitement—its romantic tales, its songs like Thomas Moore's famous *Irish Melodies* (1808–34), and its curiosities like the Irish bodkin.[53] Julia Wright has shown how certain locations in Ireland, such as Glendalough and Killarney, became sites of tourist consumption for the romantic English reader and traveler, as advertised in published poems and travel writing.[54] Seizing on her cultural moment, writer Sydney Owenson applied herself as both a product and a player in London's colonial consumer culture, advertising her *Wild Irish Girl* through the performance of her own Irish character,

---

[50] Elizabeth Sheridan's *The Triumph of Prudence Over Passion* (1781) or Jonathan Swift's 'The Story of the Injured Lady' (published 1746) might also be considered earlier iterations of this allegorical Irish national tale.

[51] The definition of a distinct Irish national character dates back to the early modern period, when English discourse used its neighboring island as a foil for its own national identity. Historians often point to Welsh writer Giraldus Cambrensis, royal clerk to Henry II who traveled to Ireland in the twelfth century, as one of the originators of the barbarous Irish character, reiterated famously by Edmund Spenser in *View of the Present State of Ireland*. See Giraldus Cambrensis, *Conquest of Ireland* (1189). For more on the national Irish and Scottish novel, see: Katie Trumpener, *Bardic Nationalism* (Princeton: Princeton UP, 1997).

[52] Claire Connolly defines the national tale genre as 'novels that took Ireland as their topic and setting which often imagined its history via marriage plots that addressed wider issues of dispossession and inheritance, and whose narratives incorporated footnotes and extra-fictional material as spaces of cultural meditation.' The genre gained such popularity that English publishing houses complained of being inundated with Irish titles written by female authors. After Catholic Emancipation (1829), the landscape of Irish literary output and publishing fundamentally changed as the national tale's popularity waned. See 'The National Tale, 1800–1830' in *The Oxford History of the Irish Book*, ed. James H. Murphy, vol. 4 (Oxford: Oxford UP, 2011), p. 399.

[53] Claire Connolly, *A Cultural History of the Irish Novel: 1790–1829* (Cambridge: Cambridge UP, 2012), p. 7.

[54] See Julia Wright, *Representing the National Landscape in Irish Romanticism* (Syracuse, NY: Syracuse UP, 2014).

dressed in Gaelic garb and performing harp tunes for the English elite.[55] In short, as Ireland became more infrastructurally colonial through efforts like the penal laws, the tenancy system, and the linen industry, an emerging, consciously national Irish literature in the English language became a more defined cultural phenomenon.

As part of these new trends toward Irishness in literature, the Irish coin, the spinning wheel, and cabin became useful markers for Irish novel writers wishing to define and signal an Irish character for (usually English) readers. Drawing on popular antiquarianism that celebrated Irish medieval material culture, like those texts written by Joseph Copoer Walker in the late eighteenth century, and travel writing romanticizing Ireland's west, the Irish novel expressed and sharpened national difference through identifiably Irish objects.[56] Critics have often commented on the importance of keynote objects in early Irish fiction: famously, Thady's 'great coat' or Irish mantle in Maria Edgeworth's *Castle Rackrent* (1800) or Glorvina's harp in Sydney Owenson's *The Wild Irish Girl*. Connolly explains that late eighteenth- and early nineteenth-century Irish novels display 'object culture,' in which things considered distinctly Irish generate and frame post-Union Ireland itself as a character in fiction.[57] Indeed, the mantle and the harp, respectively, qualified Thady and Glorvina as characters representative of their native Ireland and its Gaelic history.

My own case studies approach the objects of coin, linen, spinning wheel, mud, and pig not just as 'signifiers,' or passive identity markers, of an Irish character in a literary text, but as characters in their own right, whose details can add new, subversive articulations to the standard literary and historical narratives of Ireland's complicated, contentious eighteenth century. Rather than follow the lead of previously established critical narratives on the national tale or the rise of the novel, I let the objects determine the direction of my close readings of Irish character. Chapter 3, for example, shows how the feminization of Irish linen afforded a particularly feminist version of Irish national character in Sydney Owenson's works, while Chapter 4 traces how the thick walls of dark mud cabins point to a similarly guarded, perhaps rebellious interior within Irish peasant characters in fiction. I contend that the way these objects appear in the fiction *matters*—literally and figuratively—gesturing to wider social and material meanings negotiated between people and objects and thus, readers and characters. Coin, flax, spinning wheel, and mud facilitated the very real, material survival of Irish peasants in

---

[55] See, e.g., Owenson's autobiographical publication, *The Book of the Boudoir*, 1828, where she recalls her first tour of London as a young author, where she was shown off like an exotic creature and played up the Irish role for elite guests, while also critiquing their elitism in her later writing.
[56] Connolly, *Cultural History*, p. 29. See also, e.g., J. C. Walker, *An Historical Essay on the Dress of the Ancient and Modern Irish: Addressed to the Right Honorable Earl of Charlemont. To Which Is Subjoined a Memoir on the Armour and Weapons of the Irish* (Dublin: George Grierson, 1788).
[57] Connolly, *Cultural History*, p. 15.

eighteenth-century Ireland, but they also, through literature and creative language, afforded metaphors and hidden ideas of national resistance. Embracing the object's ability to articulate within a text will inevitably deepen any appraisal of literary and historical documents.

I.5 Toward Future Postcolonial New Materialisms

This book's main argument is its methodology: of reading literature of the colonial period through materiality in order to gain a more egalitarian and varied understanding of otherwise-silenced native experience and subjectivity. It aims to model reading against the grain of dominating narratives about literature and colonial culture while inspiring further, similarly framed case studies. As such, this book is a call to arms—better yet, a call-to-archives—to begin a new materialist postcolonialism for Irish Studies and other ethnic and national humanities fields like it. Reading Ireland's material contexts according to matter's agentic capacity and articulations holds a subversive imperative for the study of all colonial history and culture.

In the eighteenth century's messy materiality of stereotypes and character types, new, subversive, and affirming readings of Ireland come into more active play. Because the metaphors that defined colonial Ireland originated in matter, it also means that these materials, as we can access and understand them now, offer alternate ways of reading and understanding colonial resistance. More specifically, returning to the material roots of characterization allows for more subversive readings of colonial subjects: rather than objectified, stereotyped characters, the unique expressions and agencies of native Irish peoples can come to light through the materiality they handled, which can 'speak' for them now, centuries later.

When one considers the potential agentic capacity of flax plants and pigs in a literary text—what they signify through their material characteristics and particular contexts, often outside of the author's control—the reader can also address the agency of the person who interacts with said flax or pig: a disenfranchised, probably illiterate Irish tenant. Likewise, when one considers the material complexity involved in the biotic ecosystem inside a mud cabin, such as the interaction of dirt's pores with fire kindling or the thermal heat of the earthen walls, greater interior complexity is automatically attributed to literature's simplistic, crude image of that cabin's architects: poor Irish cottiers. My object case studies reveal how the affordances of matter provided colonial thinkers ways of subduing the Irish nation through both material infrastructure and metaphor. They also show how matter afforded the Irish people creative means of asserting their own subjectivity: from expressing national anguish through the metaphor of a false coin, as seen in Chapter 1, to asserting a feminist voice, as in Chapter 3's Florence

Macarthy, who spins her flax and her story together, and finally, to carving out a complex domestic ecosystem inside mud cabins, hidden from prying English eyes, as seen in Chapter 4. This book's coins, flax, spinning wheels, mud cabins, and pigs reveal and foreground Irish character's violent origins and gendered, racialized meanings as well as the creative capacity of Irish subjects to subversively, through materiality, contradict the master narratives of British ideology. Despite the imperial ideologue's efforts to order Irish matter, characterize, and buy Ireland as an object, Irish materiality will be shown to articulate its own histories and stories, shaping characters that are not as flat or stereotypical as they appear.

* * *

The following chapters are both investigations and episodes, a picaresque that moves us, from one object to the next, toward a deeper understanding of colonial culture and character. Each one is divided according to two kinds of material semiotics. First, I engage the nonhuman narrative of the object's own biology and material processes: what metaphors and ideas it affords through its materiality. After establishing the nonhuman metaphors and narratives, I apply them to both canonical and little-known eighteenth- and nineteenth-century texts so that Irish matter's agency evolves into new readings of Irish character on the page. The unique material narrativity of each object illustrates varying models of literary character unique to eighteenth-century Ireland.

Chapter 1 begins with the smallest and most mobile of all the objects: the coin, namely a curious, talking coin that served as the protagonist of a little-known Irish it-narrative, *The Adventures of a Bad Shilling in the Kingdom of Ireland* (1805). This peculiar tale narrated by a coin unites the Irish literary tradition of *aisling* poetry, where Ireland is a kidnapped, abused woman, with the popular genre of the British it-narrative, of which Charles Johnston's *Chrysal* (1760) is the most famous example. The material history of Irish coinage, particularly its iconography of Hibernia dating back to the Williamite War, is essential to understanding this story's crucial rendering of Ireland's colonial subjectivity. The narrative uses the idea of chemical, material transformation, as involved in the process of forging metal coins, to relocate national sentiment *inside* a body forcibly imprinted with Britain's characterization of Ireland as Hibernia. The Irish coin and other *aisling*-like literary characters, such as Glorvina of *The Wild Irish Girl* (1806), intimate the connections between Irish subjectivity under colonialism and bodily violation.

Chapters 2 and 3 explore how the industrial process of manufacturing linen incited thinking that fundamentally changed the characterization of Ireland in colonial ideology. Following a historical overview of the imperial imperatives behind 'improving' Ireland through the linen industry, Chapter 2 argues that the biology of flax facilitated a new Irish national character that was, like fine flax thread, cooperative with industrial mechanism, pliable, and, like bleached flax, unclean but capable of whitening. The unique properties of the flax plant, which fixated the minds of industrialists, tradesmen, English economists, and writers alike, helped to formulate an Irish character that could be seen as other but also feminine and capable of domestication and industrial labor. The violent treatment of flax required prior to spinning, known as beetling and scutching, however, reconfirms the historical violence that informed Britain's rhetorical rendering of a feminine Irish national character, while also insinuating a uniquely feminist form of violent resistance rooted in linen's gendered manufacture.

In Chapter 3, I examine how the mechanics of the most pervasive symbol of the Irish linen industry, the spinning wheel, impacted Irish expression in oral and printed literary forms. The very ontology and activity of the spinning wheel—its motion, its extraction of the flax plant's inner fibers—engineered a concept of a thinking, active mind. The spinning wheel trope in Irish poetry and prose relocates the spinning motion inside the writer or character to visualize an inner, invisible, and busy mind. Because spinners were exclusively women, the spinning wheel also evokes the active mind of a female character in the face of insecure English masculinity—a potential recognized and engineered in the writings of Sydney Owenson, who conceived of a new kind of Irish feminist character with Florence Macarthy. The physical motion of the spinning wheel suggests that, when a national character is feminized and domesticated under imperial rule (as it was in Ireland), a spinner character can also be cognitively subversive against the structures that shape and constrict her.

Chapter 4 addresses what may be the most crudely stereotyped Irish material of the eighteenth and nineteenth centuries: mud. Writers from Edmund Spenser to Arthur Young consistently demeaned Irish character on the basis of its cob architecture, stereotyping so-called 'miserable' mud cabins as 'no better than an English pigsty.' I reframe the cabin according to human-nonhuman cooperation and creative survival, rather than inhuman conditions. Using the biology of soil and the architectural benefits of mud walls, I discuss what the mud cabins offered the dispossessed Irish, rather than what they did not. When seen as a complex and efficient ecosystem of survival emerging from a destroyed landscape, the mud cabin and its dark, smoky interior with two-foot thick mud walls provides a model for reading Irish novelistic character in eighteenth- and early nineteenth-century fiction according to a deep, obscure, and internalized subjectivity. In Henry Brooke's *The Fool of Quality* (1765), interaction with mud makes a character into a hero, but later, in Maria Edgeworth's *Ennui* (1809) and Sydney Owenson's *Florence Macarthy* (1818), the concealed interiors of the Irish cabin directly invite metaphoric comparisons with the unseen, subversive narratives and sensibilities inside the native Irish people. As with the other objects in this book, the articulating power of mud points to an Irish ecosystem and Irish subjectivity that resists the dominant, anthropocentric hierarchies of colonial ideology.

Finally, I conclude this tour of eighteenth-century Ireland with a chapter on the pig as a final case study. Seen through new materialism and posthumanism, the eighteenth-century pig emerges as an active contributor to the domestic eco-system of eighteenth-century cottage life, co-evolving with the Irish people under difficult colonial circumstances and informing modes of Irish language expression, in spite of English rhetoric's swinish racialization of the Irish people. I show how, in the early nineteenth century, the pig helped William Carleton formulate a satiric, anti-colonial form of Irish character in his *Traits and Stories of the Irish Peasantry* (1830), which, for one of the first times in English-language literature, invited readers inside the subversive design of Irish colonial, material resistance. This chapter concludes by linking the two materials that bookend this journey through Irish matter: the pig *and* the Irish coin. In 1926, a century after Carleton published *Traits and Stories*, a Committee acting on behalf of the Coinage Act chose the pig for the reverse side of the new Irish Free State's halfpenny. This pig imprint proved controversial in that it appeared to reprise and condone the bestial, Irish stereotype discussed in Chapter 4. Over a century after the talking coin it-narrator expressed a new, interiorized formula for Irish national loss, the coin continued to serve as a container for the complexity of Irish national identity, its very material presence questioning the residual hold of colonial metaphors predicated on a hierarchical approach to Irish materiality.

*   *   *

In each of the following chapters, the object of focus explicates the sometimes violent and gendered, racialized process by which England gained access to Irish matter and Irish character, while also speaking back, articulating against perceived English control over Irish character as its object and imperial descriptor. The power of the object lies implicitly in the word: an object can object. We have too long severed the noun from the verb, the thing from resistance—but this book seeks to reunite them. Reading the objects of Irish literature, as proposed here, is an act of shifting the discourse around colonialism, Irish character, and creative expression—around who or what we should listen to today in order to better understand all facets of colonial life. By attending to material life, vitality, and properties of Irish matter in relation to textual form, this book reveals and resists the English fiction in which Irish colonial character is an object without depth or agency.

1

Coins

As one of the most universal, ancient human tools for exchanging wealth and signifying national identity, the coin affords a fitting launching pad for this study of Irish materiality and colonial thinking. Coins have often been imbricated in colonial events: imperial wealth, gold mining, native dispossession, the sale of slaves. Indeed, the act of colonization itself involves forcing a foreign currency on a seized land and people. In Ireland, the coin became an important player in the colonial and national events preceding and following the Act of Union, which was passed in 1800 and enacted in 1801. The Union that disbanded the Irish government and made Ireland part of the United Kingdom was a watershed event not just for Ireland but for the question of colonialism across the wider globe. Mere decades before, the American colonies had won independence from Great Britain, while the government was becoming increasingly worried by reports of the republican events in France. The Act of Union seemed to offer the British Empire some control: it disallowed any form of Irish self-governance independent from Great Britain by placing the Kingdom of Ireland entirely under the jurisdiction of Westminster. Moreover, the Act of Union signaled a responsive strategy to extinguish the fiery patriotism of the United Irishman, culminating in the Rebellion of 1798, and any future revolutionary momentum. The Union can therefore be read as a symbolic and swift victory for the British Empire and colonialism at large—a moment that ostensibly signaled the waning end to decades of republican revolution in the Continent, North America, and across the Irish Sea.

In the shadow of this gargantuan political event lies the Irish coin, a material-semiotic formation involved in some of the most important national, literary, and material transitions in Ireland throughout the eighteenth century. This chapter approaches the Irish coin not just as a symbol or signifier, but according to Serenella Iovino and Serpil Opperman's idea of 'storied matter': that objects are capable of articulations through their embedded material relations with people and cultural events.[1] Through the networks of human and nonhuman agents in which they take part, coins express their own, unique material narratives in addition to their rhetorical and symbolic utility in human discourse. Today, critics still turn to the narratives of post-Union literature to understand the Union's impact on Irish identity and the national consciousness, especially Maria Edgeworth's

---

[1] Serenella Iovino and Serpil Opperman, *Material Ecocriticism* (Bloomington, IN: Indiana UP, 2015), pp. 1–2.

Irish Materialisms: The Nonhuman and the Making of Colonial Ireland, 1690–1830. Colleen Taylor, Oxford University Press.
© Colleen Taylor 2024. DOI: 10.1093/oso/9780198894834.003.0002

Castle Rackrent (1800) and Owenson's *The Wild Irish Girl* (1806). I argue, however, that the best means of interrogating the Irish consciousness before and after the Act of Union lies with a lesser-known text and a literary subject who is, in fact, a material object: an expressive, self-consciously colonial character, the Irish forged shilling.

Between June 1805 and April 1806, a story called *The Adventures of a Bad Shilling in the Kingdom of Ireland* was published anonymously in eleven parts in Dublin's monthly periodical, *Ireland's Mirror,* later known in 1806 as the *Masonic Magazine.* In this story, an anonymous author asked his Irish readers to imagine a new kind of character: a talking coin who had witnessed nearly twenty centuries of Irish history and who narrates its long, epic biography to a man walking along Dublin's College Green in an imagined, futuristic 2009 A D. The author justifies the extraordinary conditions of his tale: 'It is necessary for an Author…sometimes to give up the reins of probability…and a reader is not utterly exempted from the same necessity.'[2] For this anonymous author, the material vibrancy of a small coin exchanged between all kinds of Irish citizens throughout history could extrapolate answers to the conundrum of the Act of Union and Ireland's long colonial history in ways that a human protagonist could not.

The Adventures takes part in the popular eighteenth-century it-narrative genre, fiction that gave voice and character to things, rather than people, which flourished in Britain and France between 1730 and 1800. Famous examples in English include Charles Johnston's *Chrysal: or, The Adventures of a Guinea* (1760), which I discuss in more detail below, Tobias Smollett's *History and Adventures of an Atom* (1769), Helenus Scott's *The Adventures of a Rupee* (1782), and *The Adventures of a Pin* (1796). Although it rehearses the tropes of other it-narratives, *The Adventures of a Bad Shilling in the Kingdom of Ireland* also stands out formally because it draws upon the Irish language *aisling,* a traditional poetic genre of the eighteenth century in which the bodies of women functioned as sexualized metaphors for fallen Gaelic nation-states. This bad shilling narrator's story and consciousness are distinct from those of other vocal objects in English literature in that the shilling empathetically enters the psychology of the colonized, detailing the sentiments of Irish national loss from pre-Christian times to the Act of Union. Pertinent to this book's study, this curious, hybridized text will be shown to perform the new materialist ethos of letting matter 'speak' its colonial truth.

In addition to the coin's 'human' voice, *The Adventures of a Bad Shilling* invokes the unique, material text of the Irish coin itself toward powerful national significations. The iconography of the Irish coin from the 1690s to the 1820s afforded very literal metaphors about changes in Ireland's national status, from a partially autonomous kingdom to a subservient colony. As *The Adventures of a Bad Shilling*

---

[2] *The Adventures of a Bad Shilling in the Kingdom of Ireland*, in *British It-Narratives, 1750–1830,* ed. Mark Blackwell, vol. 1 (London: Pickering & Chatto, 2012), p. 140.

makes clear, the material manufacture of coins—melted, forged, and rebranded in fire—paralleled post-Union nationalist sentiments about forced reidentification. Thinking about the exact material make and mint of a coin through a new materialist lens—its metallic compounds and how it was imprinted and circulated— leads to greater insight into the complex multitude of human and nonhuman influences coming together in subversive national thinking at the turn of the nineteenth century. Specifically, a piece of metal physically, forcibly impressed with an external, British value helped to formulate the tension between outside and inside inherent in the defeated sentiments of Irish subjectivity under British colonialism. Through the material text of the coin, *The Adventures of a Bad Shilling in the Kingdom of Ireland* registers a wider shift in the post-Union national consciousness.

This first case study begins by tracing the material history of eighteenth-century Irish coinage though its imposed imprint of Hibernia, a complex and fraught signifier of colonial subjugation dating back to the Williamite War at the turn of the eighteenth century. The material realities of Irish coins and the networks of economic, political, and material relations in which they were involved afford new readings of the Hibernian iconography and allegory throughout the eighteenth century, from Jonathan Swift's *Story of The Injured Lady* to the national tale. I demonstrate how *The Adventures'* coin-narrator combines this fraught character type of Hibernia with the *aisling*'s fallen *spéirbhean* (sky-woman), to create a new character with an inner voice of national sorrow and subversiveness, all constituted through alloyed matter and the imprint of the Hibernian icon.

This chapter spends time close reading *The Adventures of a Bad Shilling in the Kingdom of Ireland* to demonstrate how this little-known text openly, poignantly showcases this book's overarching theme: that Ireland's material history reveals the origins of Irish stereotyping *and* subversive national resistance, as expressed in literature. The narrator's varied material forms and transformations over time—from priceless Gaelic artifacts dating back to pre-Christianity to, ultimately, a debased forged coin—all serve to make it a colonially cognizant and materially resonant protagonist. As a material object and literary narrative, the Irish coin demonstrates how matter contains and remembers key Irish events and experiences under colonialism. To conclude this chapter, I use the material model of character encapsulated in coin narrator—that is, tension between material exteriority and nationalist interiority—to present a reading of one of the most famous Irish characters in the eighteenth and nineteenth centuries: Owenson's Glorvina of *The Wild Irish Girl*. Both characters, Irish coin and Irish girl, intimate a connection between material, bodily violation and Irish colonial subjectivity. In each instance, colonial resistance emerges as a response to forced, material impressions of the colonial character type Hibernia. The coin highlights the gendering of Irish matter and Irish people *and* shows how female characters can nevertheless challenge the imperial gaze.

1.1   Hibernia and the Material History of the Irish Coin

Over the course of the eighteenth century, writers used coins to describe and critique the relationship between Ireland and England. The material facts of Irish currency in that century afforded writers a very clear metaphor of unjust national differentiation. From the sixteenth century onward, Irish currency operated paradoxically as its own separate system but contingent on British currency. For example, in 1805, when *The Adventures of a Bad Shilling in the Kingdom of Ireland* appeared in print, Ireland was using British pounds and pence, but at a devalued rate: thirteen Irish pennies equaled twelve pence in English currency, and twenty-six halfpence made a shilling, while only twenty-four English shillings totaled the same amount.[3] At that time, Ireland was also facing the additional crisis of rampant forgery, which is why the coin protagonist is a 'bad,' or forged shilling. The obvious national implications of a separate Irish currency system and the imperial implications of a devalued rate worsened by forgery made money a contentious material issue *and* an inevitably symbolic matter in eighteenth-century discourse.

The narrative of *The Adventures of a Bad Shilling in the Kingdom of Ireland* draws upon Ireland's monetary context to ironically allegorize the degraded value of the Irish nation following the Act of Union.[4] For example, the coin appears in the first installment at the place where 'the old Irish senate stood,' directly responding to the Act of Union and the loss of local, national representation. Nationally symbolic at each plot twist, this strange tale details a number of different material forms that the protagonist inhabits over the course of his centuries-long life as a way to materially narrativize Ireland's gradual, elemental devaluation under British colonialism. First, the narrator originates, or is 'born,' as a 'daemonic' statue in a pagan temple in pre-Christian Ireland, but when the temple is destroyed, the statue is melted down and remolded into a beautiful Gaelic bracelet worn by the daughter of a Gaelic King in Meath. After being buried in a tomb with his Princess-owner for centuries, the narrator is unearthed sometime in the eighteenth century by a tenant farmer and Catholic ploughboy. The boy gives the narrator (as bracelet) away and it finally winds up in a silversmith's furnace, where it is remolded into a chalice that a Protestant landowner gifts to a local priest and his Catholic tenants. From the Catholic altar, the narrator is stolen again and sold to a manufacturer of base coins, where it is melted into its final and most degraded

---

[3] 'Airgead.' Collins Barracks Museum Exhibition, National Museum of Ireland, 2017. There was a historical precedent for devaluing Irish currency. Queen Elizabeth I deliberately debased the money circulating in Ireland to suppress rebellions from Earl of Tyrone. See Joseph Johnston, 'Irish Currency in the Eighteenth Century.' *Hermanthena* 27.52 (1938): pp. 3–26.
[4] E.g., the coin explains: 'Such was, at that time, the influx of bad silver on the public that many tradesman found it necessary to stamp their initials on the silver they passed,' but those stamps were soon forged as well. *The Adventures of a Bad Shilling*, p. 155.

form: a false shilling. After changing hands for two centuries, the shilling narrator ends up dirty, forgotten, and entirely devalued on the ground 'where the old Irish senate stood' in Dublin city centre, where the reader first meets its narrator in a futuristic 2009. The narrative was either left unfinished, or the author simply ceased publishing installments when the *Masonic Magazine* discontinued in April 1806.

This bad shilling narrator descends from a complex monetary and symbolic history of Irish national events, which contribute to its unique voice and sense of subjectivity under colonialism. Decades before *The Adventures* was published, Jonathan Swift had already set a precedent for coin-based Irish national metaphors. Seven pamphlets written in the voice of a middle-class Irish Drapier, the *Drapier's Letters* (in)famously condemned the royal patent given to William Wood, 'an ENGLISHMAN,' for minting Irish halfpence.[5] For Swift, Wood's patent, awarded by King George, openly solidified Ireland's subordination as a 'dependent kingdom' within an imperial economy. Wood's monopoly was seen as an exploitation of Ireland; it was believed that Wood's copper base, minted far away in Bristol, would devalue the Irish economy. The Drapier thus condemns this copper coin, minted by 'an *Englishman*' at 'a great distance' from Ireland, who 'serves his own interests,' rather than the 'people of the Kingdom of Ireland.'[6]

The *Drapier's Letters* continually exploits the allegedly base, copper metal of Wood's halfpence in order to construct metaphoric coin-based ideas about the state of the Irish nation itself.[7] For example, in the first letter, the Drapier satirically explains: 'if all of Ireland should be put into one scale, and this sorry fellow Wood into the other,... Mr. Wood should weigh down the whole kingdom.'[8] Not long after the Williamite War and the penal laws made clear divisions between a Catholic and Gaelic population and the Protestant, Anglo-Irish Ascendancy, Swift's metaphor reconceived the people living on the island of Ireland as a unified whole by figuring the nation as a single, material unit on one side of the scale, at odds with a common, commercial enemy: an Englishman and his coinage patent. Although some critics have dismissed the central importance of the coin as a material object, arguing the *Drapier's Letters* is primarily concerned with constitutional precedent rather than copper, the metaphor of the scale evinces that Swift's national message relies on the materiality and physical weight of the coin.[9]

---

[5] Jonathan Swift, 'Drapier's Letters' in *Major Works*, ed. David Woolley (Oxford: Oxford UP, 2003), p. 423.

[6] Swift, 'Drapier's Letters,' p. 423.

[7] Suspicion around possible baseness of the copper coins was heightened because Wood was outsourcing the minting to Bristol instead of the Tower of London, where it would have been inspected. *Jonathan Swift's Allies: The Wood's Halfpence Controversy in Ireland*, ed. Sabine Baltes-Ellerman (Peter Lang, 2017), pp. 30–1.

[8] Swift, 'Drapier's Letters,' p. 426.

[9] Sean Moore, *Swift, the Book, and the Irish Financial Revolution* (Baltimore, MD: Johns Hopkins, 2010), p. 134.

The Drapier continues to reference the problematic weight of Wood's halfpence throughout the pamphlets, particularly the early ones, and most famously when he argues that an Irish farmer's one hundred pound rent will be 'at least six hundred pound weight, which is three horse load' while the landlord will need 'two hundred and forty horses to bring up his half-year's rent, and two or three great cellars in his house for stowage' and the bankers, worst of all, will need 'twelve hundred horses.'[10] As with the scale metaphor, Swift uses material imagery and quantitative measurement to impress upon his audience that, for the farmer, the landlord, and the banker with his requisite army of horses, Wood's halfpenny is base, absurd, untenable, and in opposition to the entire Irish nation.

Swift scholars Sean Moore and J. C. Beckett have qualified the inclusivity of the Drapier's intended audience, which, they maintain, was primarily Anglo-Irish.[11] Chris Fox captures the question of Swift's paradoxical nationalism best when he says that Swift's writing in the *Drapier's Letters* marks him as 'a voice of liberty and an originator of the so-called "Patriot"' while, at the same time, others view him as an 'arch defender of the English pale.'[12] From a new materialist perspective, the coin's material prevalence throughout Irish society helped to democratize the Drapier's message, regardless of its original, intended audience, enabling Swift's satire to resonate with a socially diverse audience. When Wood's halfpenny was ultimately revoked in 1725, Swift's Drapier character became a veritable hero among a number of political groups and varied classes in Dublin, from trade workers to shop merchants to the upper classes. The Drapier, who spoke of Irish nationhood through coinage and shared, material economic fate, became the new popular and dominant character of Irish patriotism in the 1720s.[13] Thus, Swift invokes (as some have argued, for the first time in modern, English-language literature) a new idea of Irish national subjectivity founded on economic unity and rallied around a very small, yet important object—the coin—rather than purely on ethnicity or religious affiliation.[14] Thanks to Swift's Drapier, the Irish coin became both a literal and symbolic indicator of Ireland's subjugation to Britain through the metaphor of being 'weighed down.'

[10] Swift, 'Drapier's Letters,' p. 245.
[11] Moore, *Swift, the Book*, pp. 152–3. See also J. C. Beckett, *The Anglo-Irish Tradition* (London: Faber & Faber, 2008).
[12] Christopher Fox, Introduction to *The Cambridge Companion to Jonathan Swift* (Cambridge: Cambridge UP, 2003), pp. 7–8.
[13] *Irish Political Writings After 1725: A Modest Proposal and Other Works*, ed. David W. Hayton and Adam Rounce. Cambridge Edition of the Works of Jonathan Swift, vol. 14 (Cambridge: Cambridge UP, 2018), pp. xxvii–xxx.
[14] See Carole Fabricant, 'Speaking for the Irish Nation: The Drapier, the Bishop, and the Problems of Colonial Representation.' *ELH* 66.2 (1999): pp. 337–72, on Swift's construction of an Irish national voice. Sean Moore argues that the *Drapier's Letters* enabled Swift to extend Anglo-Irish identity while asserting a more modern idea of Irish representation in government. See Moore, *Swift, the Book*, pp. 135, 143.

That Swift and the anonymous author of *The Adventures,* writing a century apart, both turn to the Irish coin as an apt vehicle for unfolding an Irish national message proves the coin's efficacy in signifying the condition of Irishness itself. In both Swift's *Drapier's Letters* and *The Adventures of a Bad Shilling,* a crisis of coin mintage metonymically circles back to wider crises in the state of the Irish nation at large. In *The Adventures of a Bad Shilling,* however, the symbolic imprint appearing on the Irish coin, rather than the quantitative value or weight of the currency, becomes the key detail underscoring the shifting representations of a fictive Irish character. Hibernia, the character appearing on Irish coins through-out the long eighteenth century, is germane to understanding the construction of Irish character in *The Adventures of a Bad Shilling* and the Irish national tales, like *The Wild Irish Girl,* that followed.[15]

From the late seventeenth to the nineteenth century, the Irish coin, from the common halfpenny to the Bank of Ireland six-shilling token, was distinguished by the stamp of Hibernia (a classical female figure personifying the spirit of Ireland) with her harp, a companion to British coin sporting Britannia and the Union Jack (Figures 1.1–2). The Roman name for Ireland dating back to antiquity, Hibernia was used as a sobriquet for the island among English settlers, but it was not until the seventeenth century that the term evolved into an image of the pop-ularized female personification of Ireland, circulated and disseminated via the coin imprint.[16]

When taken together, the images of Hibernia and Britannia on the Irish and English coins' tails, respectively, communicate the economic facts of Irish cur-rency in the eighteenth century: that is, Hibernia as a separate national system weaker than the British. Britannia appears strong, ready for action, armed with a spear and shield, while Hibernia's imprint envisages imperial subjection: she sits unarmed, passively leaning against her harp. This same symbolic construction can be seen a century later in the 1828 political cartoon by William Heath, pub-lished by London-based printer Thomas McLean, where the towering Britannia uses her shield to protect a seated, unarmed Hibernia from the onslaught of a grotesque, papal Daniel O'Connell, who campaigned for Catholic Emancipation in the early nineteenth century (Figure 1.3).

Hibernia signals subservient national status in another, more literal sense: the Greco-Roman figure bears no relationship to the cultural history of pre-modern Ireland. As late eighteenth-century antiquarians like Charles O'Connor, Sylvester O'Halloran, and Joseph Cooper Walker continually emphasized, the island of

---

[15] Swift does in fact imply that the material make of Wood's halfpence is base—copper mixed with other base, brass metals—but this was fabricated for the purposes of Swift's arguments. At the time, there was a widespread concern with issuing copper money in Ireland, as Irish citizens feared it would devalue their currency even more.

[16] One of the earliest examples is the 1654 title page to James Ware's *De Hibernia et Antiquitatibus ejus, Disquisitiones.*

Figures 1.1 and 1.2 Wood's Halfpence, 1723, copper (left) and Bank of Ireland Six Shilling Coin, 1804, silver (right). These images are reproduced with the kind permission of the National Museum of Ireland. Photographs by Paul and Bente Withers, Galata Print Ltd, Llanfyllin, Wales.

Ireland was never part of the Roman Empire. Instead, these patriot scholars promoted the Milesian myth of the Gael's Egyptian/Spanish descent, based on Geoffrey Keating's widely circulated 1634 history *Foras Feasa Ar Eirinn,* in order to dissociate Ireland from the Roman model of imperialism that fueled the

Figure 1.3 William Heath, *March of the Liberator*, 1828, etching, hand-colored on paper. Image courtesy of The Board of Trinity College Dublin.

propaganda of British nationalism.[17] The classical-looking Hibernia, therefore, was an image invented and circulated by a Protestant British Empire to stand as the symbolic 'unfortunate sister' to Britannia and naturalize the idea of Britain's imperial control in Ireland. Despite the fact that Hibernia gained new, empowered, and patriotic connotations in the 1780s, as I discuss below, this original, defenseless persona would prove persistent: the vulnerable, feminine Hibernia in need of British protection would feature in English political cartoons throughout the next two centuries.[18]

The official stamping of Hibernia on Irish coinage can be traced back to an exact and significant historical moment: the Williamite War from 1688 to 1691, which ultimately solidified an English, Protestant Ascendancy in Ireland. From 1689, Jacobite forces defending King James had used bronze and copper gun-money coins—so called because the metal for the coins was obtained from old bronze cannons—in order to pay troops during a chronic shortage of money in

---

[17] Late eighteenth-century British antiquarianism was distinguished for its interest in Roman life, while Irish antiquarians were interested in pre-Christian or early Christian Celtic and Gaelic society—which they sometimes compared to the Greeks, but never the Romans, who were associated with Empire and Britain. See Clare O'Halloran, *Golden Ages and Barbarous Nations: Antiquarian Debate and Cultural Politics in Ireland, c.1750–1800* (Cork: Cork UP in association with Field Day, 2004). Keating's *Foras Feasa Ar Eirinn* was completed in 1634 and widely circulated in manuscript until its publication in 1723, when it became even more widely disseminated in Ireland.

[18] A helpless Hibernia was a common character in nineteenth-century satiric magazines like *Punch*.

Figure 1.4 James II Gunmoney, Thirty pence coin, September 1689. This image is reproduced with the kind permission of the National Museum of Ireland. Photograph by Paul and Bente Withers, Galata Print Ltd, Llanfyllin, Wales.

Ireland (Figure 1.4).[19] Following the Battle of the Boyne and Limerick's fall to William's troops in 1691, the Orange King collected and revalued James's gunmoney coinage, reissuing a new currency that was struck, for the first time, with the image of Hibernia and her harp (Figure 1.5). This Hibernia soon became the standard tails of Irish coins, reverse to an imprint of the Hanover King's profile.[20] Following William's victory, James's copper gunmoney coins were either simply restamped with Hibernia in Limerick (as in Figure 1.5) or melted down, remixed, restamped, and named 'Limerick Money' or 'Brass Money', which led to the common idiom 'not worth a brass farthing', as brass metal did not equal the coin's standard.[21]

The very act of impressing Hibernia over an Irish gunmoney coin is suggestive in an imperial sense. The symbolic and material force of this new impression can almost be seen in Figure 1.5, where underneath Hibernia's harp the trace of James's imprint from 1689–90 remains slightly visible: a small, but clear visualization of conquest and defeat, respectively. By making no reference to Gaelic culture, Hibernia marks the moment when Britain symbolically reimages Ireland with William's influence—an official stamp of control over a Catholic majority population. The metaphoric and symbolic suggestions behind the rebranding of James's coins as William's Hibernia would afford the *Adventures of a Bad Shilling* author a way of thinking about Irish national subjectivity under colonialism over a century later. In fact, there was a lasting affiliation with King William and the symbol of Hibernia in the eighteenth-century cultural mindset: in 1749, a play

---

[19]   Arthur E. J. Went, 'The Coinage of Ireland, 1000 A.D. to the Present Day' in *W. B. Yeats and the Designing of Ireland's Coinage*, ed. Brian Cleeve (Dublin: Dolmen, 1972), p. 65.
[20]   Johnston, 'Irish Currency', pp. 13–14, 'Airgead.'   [21]   Went, 'Coinage of Ireland.' p. 66.

Figure 1.5 Limerick Coinage, 1691, overstruck James II gunmoney. This image is reproduced with the kind permission of the National Museum of Ireland. Photograph by Paul and Bente Withers, Galata Print Ltd, Llanfyllin, Wales.

titled *Hibernia's Triumph* premiered on the Dublin stage to honor King William's birthday.[22] This title reflects the widespread use of 'Hibernia' in English writing on Ireland, seen in Swift's 'A Dialogue in Hibernian Style' and *The Hibernian Patriot*, a 1730 London reprinting of the *Drapier's Letters,* as well as *Hibernia Freed: A Tragedy* (1722), *The Fate of an Hibernian Muse* (1745), *Hibernia Curiosa* (1767), or even the *Hiberniana* that Horatio famously reads in *The Wild Irish Girl.* As early as the turn of the eighteenth century, the new coins themselves were known simply as 'Hibernias,' implying that Hibernia, as both an image and term, became shorthand for a new Protestant and English-dominated Ireland.

Following the Treaty of Limerick, Hibernias continued to be controlled by Englishmen. Swift's outrage at Wood's patent in 1724 was part of a wider pattern of English craftsmen minting Irish coins. Irish coins were typically minted by private patentees, most of them English-born—although some Dublin men held patents for Irish coin mintage.[23] In the early part of the century, Irish money was coined at the Tower of London and sent over to Ireland, further suggesting the metropole's command over Ireland's economic and national status.[24] Even after

---

[22] *Hibernia's Triumph, A Masque of Two Interludes and written in Honor of King William III and performed at the Theatre Royal in Dublin, on the anniversary day of his birth.* (Dublin: Nelson, 1748).

[23] Johnston, 'Irish Currency,' pp. 21–2.

[24] James Simon, *An Essay Towards an Historical Account of Irish Coins* (Dublin: Proctor, 1810), p. 73.

the founding of the Bank of Ireland in 1783—coinciding with a high point in Irish nationalism, when Henry Grattan established brief and novel legislative independence for the Irish Parliament in 1782—no official, national mint was established in Ireland. Instead, Hibernias continued to be minted by private patentees. Thus, for almost a century, up until the Irish coin system was abolished entirely in 1825 as a belated consequence of the Act of Union, the 'character' of Irish national identity, Hibernia, could be regarded as an extant, defenseless image forcibly stamped on Irish subjects by English men.

The synonymity between the Irish coin's Hibernian typeface and a connotation of defeat found explicit literary expression in Swift's 'The Story of the Injured Lady.'[25] Here, much like in the Irish *aisling*, the Hibernia type becomes a vehicle for a nationalist message about England's economic, legislative, and cultural mistreatment of the Irish people. First published in 1745, it is highly likely Swift wrote 'The Story of the Injured Lady' earlier, perhaps around 1707, following the Act of Union with Scotland, later adding the final paragraph, which references the 1720 Declaratory Act.[26] The story operates as a very clear, almost ironically straightforward allegory in which Ireland is the 'injured lady' Hibernia and Scotland the 'rival' married in Union with England, the 'inconstant lover.' Significantly, the story aims to 'give character' to Hibernia, describing her as 'pale and thin with Grief and ill Usage' due to the 'oppressions [she] endures.'[27]

In detailing the injured lady's oppressions, Swift's language frequently invokes money, highlighting the Hibernian character's intrinsic association with coinage. For example, Hibernia regrets that after England 'got Possession' of her and began to play the 'usual Part of a too fortunate Lover,' acting at times like a 'Conqueror,' which can be read as an allusion to the 'Conqueror' William of Orange.[28] The allegory is both economic and sexual: England gets possession of Hibernia and earns fortune *through* her, as one does with money and capital. Continuing her lament, Hibernia points out that England, her lover, had criticized her for she had 'cost him ten Times more than I was worth' and demanded that she 'reimburse him some of his Charges.'[29] Within the context of Swift's allegory, Hibernia self-articulates as money, as cost, as if pointing to her origin on the Williamite coins,

---

[25] Carole Fabricant argues that the Declaratory Act of 1720 figured Ireland as a literary persona constructed by England—a truth that caused Swift to reclaim Ireland's voice in his political writings, from 'Story of the Injured Lady' to 'Universal Use for Irish Manufacture,' to the *Drapiers Letters*. See Fabricant, 'Speaking for the Irish Nation: The Drapier, the Bishop, and the Problems of Colonial Representation.' *ELH* 66.2 (1999): p. 352.

[26] Geoffrey Davies, 'Swift's "The Story of the Injured Lady".' *Huntington Library Quarterly* 6.4 (1943): p. 473.

[27] Jonathan Swift, *The Story of the Injured Lady. Being a true picture of Scotch perfidy, Irish poverty, and English partiality. With letters and poems never before printed. By the Rev. Dr Swift* (London: M.Cooper, 1746), p. 3.

[28] Swift, *Story of the Injured Lady*, p. 4.   [29] Swift, *Story of the Injured Lady*, p. 6.

while drawing distinctions between 'worth' and 'cost' that underscore the Irish coin's devalued currency.

At the very end of 'The Story of the Injured Lady,' coins become a central image again when Hibernia swears allegiance to England, saying that she would 'stand by him against all the world, while I had a penny in my purse.' In the concluding paragraph, which refers to the Declaratory Act, Hibernia hopes her lover will let her manage her 'own little Fortune' rather than 'drain[ing] me and my Tenants so dry that we shall not have a Penny for him or ourselves.'[30] This penny that Hibernia invokes supplies a metonym for the penal laws, the Declaratory Act, trade restrictions and embargos—the economic means of England's imperial control over Ireland.

The coin imagery in Swift's short text intimates a correlation between Hibernia's above quoted 'oppressions' and *im*pression, as of a coin. As discussed by Bonnie Blackwell, some misogynist beliefs in the early eighteenth century—intimated by Swift's Injured Lady—suggested that women retained 'impressions' of the men with whom they had sexual relationships.[31] Like the penny is a metonym for wider economic issues, the impression of a Hibernian coin can be seen as metonymic of Britain's imperial control over Ireland, emblematized and culturally vindicated by the sexual allegory of John Bull and Hibernia. 'The Story of the Injured Lady' is an important precursor to *The Adventures of a Bad Shilling in the Kingdom of Ireland* in that it highlights how the Hibernian typeface transitioned from an imprint on the halfpenny to an imprint on the Irish national and literary imaginary.

Hibernia, however, was not always synonymous with British conquest. In fact, her shifting meanings over the course of the eighteenth century further elucidate why the coin became a central and fitting object for depicting Irish character and national loss in *The Adventures of a Bad Shilling*. In direct contradiction with Hibernia's earlier significations, Irish patriots at the end of the century claimed the Hibernian symbol on the halfpenny as their own national and anti-British banner. The 1770s and 1780s saw a flowering of Irish patriotism, particularly in Dublin, stemming from the establishment of the Dublin Volunteers, local militias founded in 1778, and lobbying for Free Trade, which sought the legislative removal of British restrictions on Irish trade. Padhraig Higgins explains that the Free Trade campaign constituted patriotism as 'shopping for Ireland,' in which middle-class women became the primary vigilantes.[32] Unsurprisingly, the aptly gendered image of this campaign became the same image on the Irish coin:

---

[30] Swift, *Story of the Injured Lady*, p. 10.

[31] Bonnie Blackwell, 'Corkscrews and Courtesans: Death and Sex in Circulation Novels' in *The Secret Life of Things: Animals, Objects, and It-Narratives in Eighteenth-Century England,* ed. Mark Blackwell (Lewisburg, PA: Bucknell UP, 2007), p. 280.

[32] Padhraig Higgins, *A Nation of Politicians: Gender, Patriotism, and Political Culture in Late Eighteenth-Century Ireland* (Madison, WI: University of Wisconsin Press, 2010), p. 100.

Hibernia with her harp, which came to signal local consumer practice as a patriotic exercise.[33] As the Free Trade campaign grew, merchants in Dublin and in some western towns met the commercial desire for patriotic ephemera: merchants sold a diverse array of affordable consumer items, such as jugs, teapots, trade cards, and fabrics, all sporting the image of a more active Hibernia, sometimes standing, sometimes playing her harp (rather than passively leaning back against it as on the halfpenny), and sometimes pictured beside an Irish Volunteer soldier.[34] To display the image of Hibernia amongst your domestic possessions in late eighteenth-century Dublin was to outwardly identify as an Irish patriot and supporter of Free Trade—to affiliate with the patriot's Hibernia, not King William's.

In the late 1770s and early 1780s, the Volunteers and their supporters pressured Westminster into a series of legislative successes for Ireland: the Relief Acts of 1778, which eased the penal laws, Free Trade in 1779, and finally, legislative independence for the Irish Parliament in 1782. When Ireland succeeded in its efforts for Free Trade, Hibernia appeared in a new character: William Hincks's print *Hibernia attended by her Brave Volunteers Exhibiting her Commercial Freedom* (1780) depicts a jubilant, resilient Hibernia surrounded by kneeling colonists representing Europe, Africa, and America offering her their goods. Significantly, Hibernia's harp is abandoned in the foreground as she triumphantly holds a banner reading 'Free Trade' instead (Figure 1.6). At the same time Hincks redraws Hibernia with new independence and strength, however, he also depicts a hierarchy of race in which the classical-looking Hibernia seemingly takes advantage, as an African slave and Native American bow to her, offering goods. Hibernia emerges not only triumphant in economic independence from Britain but also, potentially, problematically dominant in a transatlantic trade network that reminds us of Irish involvement in colonial projects in the Americas.[35]

Whereas for the past one hundred years, the Hibernian body had gestured subordination, vulnerability, and sometimes even complete defeat, in 1780 she emerges a 'new' character type, representing triumphant Irish patriotism, standing like the imperial Britannia rather than the seated, submissive colonial Hibernia. Some writers even sought to rewrite the power dynamic of the 'sisters' Britannia and Hibernia from earlier in the century, representing 'sister kingdoms' on more positive terms during Grattan's parliament in the 1780s. Moyra Haslett argues this positive sister relationality can be seen between protagonists Louisa

[33] Higgins, *Nation of Politicians*, p. 104. See also Elizabeth Kowaleski-Wallace, *Consuming Subjects: Women, Shopping and Business in the Eighteenth Century* (Columbia: Columbia UP, 1997), for a discussion on the gendering of shopping and the idea of female consumerist appetite in eighteenth-century England.

[34] Higgins, *Nation of Politicians*, p. 102.

[35] For a lengthier discussion on Irish imperialism, see Kevin Kenny's introduction to *Ireland and the British Empire* (Oxford: Oxford UP, 2005) and Donald Harman Akenson's *If the Irish Ruled the World* (Montreal: McGill, 1997), a study of Irish slave owners in the Caribbean.

Figure 1.6 William Hincks, *Hibernia attended by her Brave Volunteers, Exhibiting her Commercial Freedom,* 1780. Reproduced courtesy of the National Library of Ireland.

and Eliza in Elizabeth Sheridan's *Triumph of Prudence Over Passion*—although, even here, the loving nature of sister England is called into question.[36]

Toward the end of the eighteenth century, as Irish Catholics and Protestants alike rallied behind the cause of Irish Patriotism, the country, particularly Dublin, was inundated with the newly politicized image of Hibernia, who began to appear on all kinds of Irish print forms as well as ephemera, such as frontispieces, the mastheads of newspapers, trade cards, and so on. In applying the Hibernian symbol, both the Dublin Volunteers and the United Irishmen consciously addressed the shift in her meaning. The *Volunteers Journal* printed in Dublin displayed the image of Hibernia with the subtitle 'Libertas et Natale Solum (Liberty and my native soil),' implying (seemingly without irony) that patriots are newly claiming the typeface of Hibernia as 'native' to Irish national culture rather than an image imposed by Britannia's rule. This awareness is also apparent in the 1770s and 1780s trend of depicting Hibernia with a new protector: not Britannia, but the Volunteer soldier, a conscious rebranding of the earlier trope.[37] Similarly, in the late 1790s, the United Irishmen took up the symbol of Hibernia and her harp along with the phrase 'It [the harp] is newly strung and shall be heard.'[38] That the United Irishmen identify the symbolic typeface as 'newly strung'—that is, has new resonance—points to their awareness of its imperial provenance. On another level, the phrase also acknowledges that Hibernia as a character can be reshaped, rebranded to fit new national contexts, just as she was rebranded on James's gun-money coins in 1691.

Mary Louise O'Donnell argues that the late eighteenth-century deployment of the Hibernia type—a woman Ireland seated at the harp, sometimes referred to as the 'Genius of Erin'—represents a clear fusion of the Anglophone Hibernia and *aisling*'s *spéirbhean* from earlier in the century.[39] Indeed, Irish patriotic applications of Hibernia resemble the nationalist aims of the Jacobite *aisling* mode, and there is even some suggestion that Hibernia began to resonate with the Gaelic national mindset as well. For example, in the *aislingí* of Art Mac Cumhnaigh and Eoghan Rua Ó Súilleabháin written in the 1770s, the speaker initially misidentifies the beautiful *spéirbhean* (the sky-woman or vision of the *aisling*) as Helen of Troy, suggesting that the Anglo-Irish image of Ireland as a classical, Greco-Roman figure may have resonated with the Irish-speaking community. These allusions to Helen acknowledge some conceptual similitude between Hibernia as Ireland and the *spéirhbhean* as Ireland. Padhraig Higgins and Vincent Morley point out that

---

[36] For further discussion of this sisterhood discourse, see Moyra Haslett, 'Fictions of Sisterhood in Eighteenth-Century Irish Writing' in *Irish Literature in Transition, 1700–1780*, ed. Moyra Haslett (Cambridge: Cambridge UP, 2021), p. 298.

[37] Higgins, *Nation of Politicians*, p. 188.

[38] Mary Louise O'Donnell, 'A Driving Image of Revolution: The Harp and its Utopian Space in the Eighteenth Century.' *Utopian Studies* 21.2 (2010): p. 255.

[39] O'Donnell, 'Driving Image,' p. 272.

Irish-language writers engaged rhetorically with the nationalist efforts of the Anglo-Irish Volunteers, such as by celebrating England's imperial misfortunes in America.[40] What's more, some of the Hibernian prints supporting Free Trade were reprinted with Irish-language captions, or at least included phonetic spellings of Irish-language phrases, suggesting a bilingual exchange of the Free Trade Hibernia between Irish-speaking patriots and English-speaking ones.[41]

Hibernia's material form—the gestures of her body in art and insignia—proved malleable to the changing sentiments of Irish citizens toward the British crown over the course of the eighteenth century, paradoxically signifying both British conquest and Irish patriotism at once. Maria Edgeworth's *Castle Rackrent* (1800) captures Hibernia's intrinsic irony as an Irish coin typeface when Sir Condy Rackrent, torn between a shallow love for Judy McQuirk and a shallow desire for Isabella Moneygawl's fortune, flips a coin to choose his wife:

> said [Sir Condy] I was never fonder of Judy than at this present speaking, and to prove it to you, (said he, and took from my hand a halfpenny, change I had just got along with my tobacco); and to prove it to you Thady, says he, it's a toss up with me which I shall marry this minute, her or Mr. Moneygawl of Mount Juliet's Town's daughter...'and by this book (said he, snatching up my ballad book, mistaking it for my prayer-book, which lay in the window)—and by this book (said he)...I'll stand or fall by the toss, and so, Thady, hand me over the pin out of the ink-horn,' and he makes a cross on the smooth side of the halfpenny—'Judy M'Quirk (said he) her mark, x.'[42]

Here, the sexual and economic resonances of Hibernia as a national symbol satirically come together as either side of an Irish halfpenny—as either Judy's body or Isabella's fortune, respectively. The very presence of the coin in this equation, with two women on two sides of the Irish halfpenny, inserts a subnarrative into the text about the divided nature of eighteenth-century Irish society—between Anglo-Irish Protestant and Irish Catholic identities—represented by the divided imagery of the Irish coin itself (on one side the English King, on the other, Hibernia). That, at the moment of the toss, Judy, the Irish Catholic woman, is literally defeated by the coin itself, and by the rich Anglo-Irish woman Isabella, can be linked back to the Swiftian representation in which Hibernia connotes defeat by an imperial system that economically benefits Britain. Whether intended by Edgeworth or not, the complex material history and iconography of Irish halfpennies enters this scene and inserts its own material-semiotic narrative, satirizing the ideological work Hibernia effects. This double-edged Irish halfpenny,

---

[40] See Vincent Morley, *The Popular Mind in Eighteenth-Century Ireland* (Cork: Cork UP, 2017).
[41] Higgins, *Nation of Politicians*, pp. 16, 94.
[42] Maria Edgeworth, *Castle Rackrent*, ed. George Watson (Oxford: Oxford UP, 2008), pp. 44–5.

which is both real and literary, highlights the interchangeability of coin for woman and the process by which women are turned into one-dimensional, one-sided symbols for political ideas while their bodies are deployed as tokens of exchange.

Most importantly, *Castle Rackrent* details the process by which Hibernia transitions from being a typeface on a coin to a 'thing' of fiction that carries its own external, material narratives into the fictional setting. When Condy places the mark of Judy McQuirk—the x—on the smooth side of the coin, the text renders the process by which Hibernia, a nonverbal image, becomes language. As Judy's signature, the x that marks the spot, replaces the coin's typeface, Hibernia becomes associated with a native character in Irish fiction, Judy. However, that the coin can be impressed with an x implies it may be a forgery, insinuating an alternative material narrative: that Hibernia is a 'false' surrogate for native Irish woman Judy. Furthermore, on top of specifying that Sir Condy flips a halfpenny, which of course bore the image of Hibernia on the tails, Edgeworth also includes the detail about Thady's ballad book, which Condy mistakes for a Bible. Such ballad books were often decorated with images of Hibernia, as was the case with one ballad book of the period, *Paddy's Resource, or the Harp of Erin*.[43] When Condy mistakes the ballad book for a Bible, he swears allegiance to the image of Hibernia, rather than God, and ironically renders his oath to 'live by the toss' as a romantic gesture for Judy false as well. Underneath the comic scene of a nuptial coin toss, the materiality of the soft, impressed halfpenny and nationalist ballad book create an alternative material subnarrative that points to the irony and disconnect between Hibernia's classical, Anglicized image and the fact of a 'real' Irish woman appearing in literature, Judy.

These late eighteenth-century applications of the Hibernia character type, from the Free Trade movement's Hibernian consumerism, to the insignia of the Volunteers and United Irishmen, and the coin toss in *Castle Rackrent,* reveal the transition in Hibernia's meaning and function—from being, in Swift's writing, an allegorical signifier of Ireland's depreciation in the British imperial economy to, sixty years later, a non-quantifiable symbol of Irish national representation itself. The coin toss scene in *Castle Rackrent,* begins to point to the process by which Hibernia, the complicated and layered symbol of Ireland, is no longer just a type, but rather exists suspended somewhere in the air between an exterior imprint and a new kind of emerging Irish fictional character. Just five years after the publication of *Castle Rackrent,* the Irish coin would become a fully fledged subject in its own right in *The Adventures of a Bad Shilling in the Kingdom of Ireland,* linking

---

[43] O'Donnell, 'Driving Image,' p. 260. Edgeworth seems to have been interested in Hibernia's symbolic, perhaps even comic, resonance. In a letter to Miss Charlotte Sneyd, dated 2 April 1799, she writes, 'Tell Sneyd that there is a political print just come out, of a woman, meant for Hibernia, dressed in orange and green, and holding a pistol in her hand to oppose the Union.' *The Life and Letters of Maria Edgeworth,* ed. Augustus Hare (Boston: Houghton Mifflin, 1895).

the material memory of Hibernia's colonial imprint with a burgeoning, new, colonially subversive character in Irish fiction.

1.2 Coins, the English It-Narrative, and *Chrysal*

Coins played an important role in eighteenth-century English fiction as well, helping readers to navigate a changing economic landscape brought on by consumerism and colonial expansion. Scholars like Crystal Lake, Barbara Benedict, and Brad Pasanek have traced the coin's widespread cultural and rhetorical value in eighteenth-century England. Both Lake and Benedict show how, in the early eighteenth century, coins came to be seen as important, collectible artifacts that preserved human history.[44] Writers like Joseph Addison defended the eighteenth-century pastime of collecting coins as a means of cultivating memory and identity in the absence of other historical artifacts. Brad Pasanek has catalogued the numerous ways in which the coin proved an apt material vehicle for the metaphoric mind in eighteenth-century discourse: by furnishing the metaphors of impression, being newly minted, counterfeit or false representation, base metal versus the sterling standard, and the idea of man's imagination as coin mint or coin store.[45] As Lake points out, however, a rise in counterfeit coinage in the eighteenth century also meant that coins' material fallibilities put them at the center of debates around history, circulation, and social corruption.[46]

In the second half of the eighteenth century, coins became the focus of the popular it-narrative genre as a result of significant economic changes emerging at the time. James Thompson's important monograph, *Models of Value,* traces how material changes in British mints directly incited transitions in the rhetoric around human representation in English print culture at large. Thompson calls it a 're-representation of money, as it passe[d] from realist to nominalist conceptions of value, in a dematerialization from metal to paper medium; and the reconceptualization of money as such from wealth itself to capital.'[47] As economic and imperial changes gave rise to investments in global capital, rather than minted silver, Adam Smith's *Wealth of Nations* (1776) redefined money as imagined capital rather than a material standard. In other words, by the late eighteenth century, the signifier of money supersedes its material composition. Mark Blackwell's

---

[44] See Crystal B. Lake, *Artifacts* (Baltimore, MD: Johns Hopkins University Press, 2020) and Barbara Benedict, 'The Moral in the Material: Numismatics and Identity in Evelyn, Addison, and Pope' in *Queen Anne and the Arts,* ed. Cedric D. Reverand II (Lanham, MD: Bucknell, 2015), pp. 65–83.

[45] Brad Pasanek, *Metaphors of Mind: An Eighteenth-Century Dictionary* (Baltimore, MD: Johns Hopkins University Press, 2015).

[46] Lake, *Artifacts*, p. 107.

[47] James Thompson, *Models of Value: Eighteenth Century Political Economy and the Novel* (Durham, NC: Duke UP, 1996), p. 43.

work on it-narratives argues that the genre developed as a response to these eighteenth-century changes in the English economic landscape, from the rise in consumerist culture and the concept of capital to general communal anxieties about ephemerality, class, and market value. Coin it-narratives, in particular, expose Britain's social anxieties about the economic and emotional significance of money. These coin narrators are both players in a consumerist system and moral critics of it: objects in bribery, corruption, prostitution, and colonial exploitation, yet they also democratically reveal 'the function of money in binding together diverse members of society.'[48]

Perhaps more than any other genre, the coin it-narrative literalizes the changes in value described by Thompson, turning the means of purchase in the market-place into a subject with interior, expressive value. It-narrators, Blackwell explains, offer an 'inside view' of a material object, while also possessing the unique it-narrator ability to have a close inside look at their owners via physical proximity.[49] Hats, petticoats, coins in a person's pocket, or any other small possession are spatially close to their owner's body and thereby analogize closeness to that person's inner thoughts. When coin-narrators describe their owners' emotional depths, they literally convert their commercially valuable bodies into sentimental voices. Despite Thompson and Blackwell's important frameworks for reading coin it-narratives, we have seen that the history of Irish coinage, like the history of Irish literature, is different and distinct from the English model. To better contextualize an *Irish* coin it-narrative like *The Adventures of a Bad Shilling*, therefore, we must look to a coin it-narrative that has been categorized as both English and Irish literature, which deals in the eighteenth-century English themes of consumerism and capital described by Blackwell, but bears the authorship of an Irishman.

Charles Johnston's popular first novel, *Chrysal, the Adventures of a Guinea* (1760–5), is credited with launching the it-narrative genre.[50] Within two years of its publication, *Chrysal* went through three editions, and, in the decades that followed, inspired many other it-narratives about coins, hats, petticoats, and animals.[51] In addition to its importance for the it-narrative genre at large, Johnston's Irish connections—born in Limerick and educated at Trinity College before moving to England, then Calcutta—make *Chrysal* an essential precursor to *The Adventures of a Bad Shilling*. In fact, the bad shilling character seems to be a direct response to, or Irish nationalist rewrite of, Johnston's text. There are many undeniable parallels: for example, Chrysal originates as sentient Peruvian gold,

[48] Mark Blackwell, Introduction. *British It-Narratives,* ed. Blackwell, vol. 1, pp. xiii, xli.

[49] Blackwell, Introduction, p. xviii.

[50] I use the spelling 'Johnston' rather than the more common 'Johnstone,' following Daniel Sanjiv Roberts's argument for the more accurate Johnston. 'Johnstone' appears to have been a later variant circulated by Walter Scott's edition of *Chrysal*. See Daniel Sanjiv Roberts, 'Biographical Note' in *The History of Arsaces* (Dublin: Four Courts, 2014), p. 227.

[51] Aileen Douglas, 'Britannia's Rule and the It-Narrator.' *Eighteenth-Century Fiction* 6.1 (1993): p. 65.

while the Bad Shilling begins its life as a sentient pagan Celtic statue. Later, Chrysal is transformed into a crucifix made by a Jesuit, while, similarly, the Bad Shilling becomes a Catholic chalice. Of course, the final form for both it-narrators is the coin: a British guinea and a forged Irish shilling, respectively. *Chrysal*, however, enjoyed much more popularity and circulation than *The Adventures of a Bad Shilling*, perhaps because of its varied, transatlantic setting (Chrysal travels from Peru to Portugal, Holland, and London, while the bad shilling remains in Ireland) and its wider British readership. By the end of the eighteenth century, just before *The Adventures of a Bad Shilling* appeared in *Ireland's Mirror*, *Chrysal* had been through twenty-four editions.[52]

Like all it-narratives, *Chrysal* is a text about value, circulation, marketplace, and also, crucially, about British identity and empire. Criticism on *Chrysal* has shown continued interest in material culture as a pillar of the story's cultural significance. Marta Kvande and Emily Grover, for example, discuss the text's various 'material' preoccupations: the materiality of manuscript circulation (the text is presented to the reader as a manuscript that has passed through several hands until the current editor), the growing output of eighteenth-century print culture, and the significance of the material form of the guinea itself.[53] Johnston wrote *Chrysal* during the Seven Years' War (1756–63), an event that ensured British control over markets in North America, the West Indies, and Africa, while asserting consumerism itself as an emerging, central feature of English identity. In the form of a well-traveled guinea, Chrysal seems to embody the perfect medium for interrogating a newly commercialized Britishness, its materiality, and its far-reaching empire.

Chrysal self-identifies as a distinctly British character, despite being 'born' in a gold mine in Peru, much in the way the bad shilling proudly self-identifies as native, Gaelic Irish. (The bad shilling, however, *was* 'born' in Ireland.) As such, Chrysal seems to affirm, symbolically, and literally through its travels, that economic influence in distant, resource-wealthy colonies is inherent to a new emerging British identity and patriotic sentiment, which Chrysal regularly voices as pride in his patriotic shape as guinea. Chrysal also reflects the empire's financial verve through its rapid, continued exchanges between people. It even warns the reader of this new mobility as a guinea: 'I am now entering upon a stage, where the scenes are so various, so quickly changed, that it will require your strictest attention to keep pace with my relation.'[54] While *Chrysal* is critical of the private greed of its owners, it supports English war efforts to the point where, according

---

[52] Joe Lines, *The Rogue Narrative and Irish Fiction, 1660–1790* (Syracuse, NY: Syracuse UP, 2021), p. 141.

[53] Marta Kvande and Emily Gilliland Grover, 'The Mediation is the Message: Charles Johnstone's *Chrysal.'* *Eighteenth-Century Fiction* 32.4 (2020): 535–57.

[54] Charles Johnston, *Chrysal; Or the Adventures Of a Guinea*, 2 vols (London: T. Beckett, 1760), vol. 1, p. 93.

to Aileen Douglas, 'empire cleanses trade,' narratively.[55] *Chrysal's* overarching message seems to suggest, Douglas explains, that a virtuous British Empire is the solution to market greed—that imperialism can morally correct commerce by generously spreading English culture. Douglas traces this same moral yet imperial theme in a later coin it-narrative, *The Adventures of a Rupee* (1782).

Although *Chrysal* concerns itself with Britishness and ostensibly offers an apology for the British Empire's mission, signified by its praise of George III and the novel's dedication to William Pitt, it is essential to note, as Moyra Haslett, Daniel Roberts, and Joe Lines have, that Charles Johnston was an Irish author often sympathetic with Irish affairs.[56] There is but one brief, shaded reference to Ireland in *Chrysal's* narrative: the coded knowledge, for an Irish reader, that William Johnson, born in Meath, meets a 'native of his own country' in North America, which Moyra Haslett argues demonstrates 'how an Irish dimension is always a possibility in this fiction [*Chrysal*].'[57] Johnston engaged with Irish topics and Irish characters more directly in his later works, like *The History of John Juniper* (1781), which Joe Lines argues, contrary to *Chrysal*, 'sympathizes with the colonized poor' and 'critiques British misrule' while positively characterizing Irish men in line with 1780s Irish patriotic discourse.[58] Similarly, Daniel Roberts implies that Johnston's explicit 'ancient-regime critique of empire' in his later works may help explain why they were less popular than *Chrysal*.[59]

Johnston's Irish origins, therefore, demand a reassessment of Chrysal's keynote transformation from Peruvian gold to Spanish doubloon to, finally, its 'rightful' state as a British guinea. Chrysal explains his transformation into a coin thus:

> I here came into the possession of a new master, and immediately after changed my Spanish appearance for the fashion of the country, and in the shape of a guinea, entered into the most extensive state of sublunary influence, becoming the price of every name that is respected under heaven.[60]

The text then mentions the mint where Chrysal 'put on the shape of a guinea' before being sent to a bank.[61] For Chrysal, Britishness is a 'shape' associated with global respect and generosity, rather than a mere 'appearance,' as the Spanish doubloon is described, perhaps reflecting those eighteenth-century social anxieties about untrustworthy external class and market signifiers described by Mark Blackwell. By its own words, the guinea assumes Britishness through its own

---

[55] Douglas, 'Britannia's Rule,' pp. 75, 78.
[56] Daniel Sanjiv Roberts, Introduction to Charles Johnston, *History of Arsaces*, p. 17.
[57] Moyra Haslett, 'Experimentalism in the Irish Novel, 1750–1770.' *Irish University Review* 41.1 (2011): p. 75.
[58] Lines, *Rogue Narrative*, p. 159.
[59] Daniel Roberts, 'A "Teague" and a "True Briton": Charles Johnstone, Ireland, and Empire.' *Irish University Review* 41.1 (2011): p. 148.
[60] Johnston, *Chrysal*, vol. 1, p. 93.   [61] Johnston, *Chrysal*, vol. 1, p. 95.

agency, as if the machinery at the mint had no role in its reidentification. This British 'shape,' which Chrysal admires as 'the beauty of my figure,' is explicitly praised at several points in the novel for its virtuous signification, rather than its monetary value, reflecting Thompson's discussion of the eighteenth-century transition from monetary to nominal value.[62] Liz Bellamy describes how Chrysal's new imprint is described like a soldier 'impressed by the sight of himself in his uniform,' underscoring the text's correlation of globalized, deployed money with British patriotism.[63] In the novel's second volume, a Bulgarian king spies Chrysal's 'shape' in a pile of other foreign coins and praises the 'munificence' of Britain for 'diffusing' its riches far and wide, which he equates to 'true wisdom!' in leadership.[64] However, when read alongside the material history of Irish coinage and Johnston's own Irishness, this quoted passage detailing Chrysal's 'shape' as a guinea can be seen to carry a double, subversive narrative.

Despite the novel's ultimate affirmation of British global influence, Chrysal's language as he details his transformation questions the security of British identity, implying that it is malleable, easy to adopt, or 'put on' (using Chrysal's own words) as a superficial exterior. Even if one's narrative or inner 'spirit,' as Chrysal is defined, originates elsewhere, an object or a person can nevertheless 'put on' the 'shape' of Britishness as if a uniform or disguise. This resonates with contemporary cultural anxieties around defining Britishness. Kvande and Grover connect *Chrysal* with the increasing eighteenth-century anxiety about 'who belonged' to Britain in response to developments in colonial acquisition, consumerism, and international conflict from the mid to late century.[65] Chrysal seems to, perhaps unconvincingly, assuage this fear about who or what belongs to Britain when it describes its beloved guinea shape as 'mutilated' like a soldier's body (in reality, 'clipped' by a Jewish man, part of the tale's anti-Semitism), and yet acknowledges Britain is the only nation in the world that would 'receive their own coin under the disgrace of such diminishing.'[66] Again, the coin converts material value into moral value when money appears in the context of service to Britain's global mission, dedicated to 'its own' Britons. Chrysal's patriotic hope is soon dashed when 'no one in London would accept me at my original value,' again implying a subversive questioning of the text's overarching British imperial affirmations.[67] As an Irish-born writer, Johnston, like Swift before him, would have been keenly aware of the contentious and important role coins played in both nationhood and economic rights. The material history of Irish coinage at the turn of the eighteenth century, from William's reissued gunmoney Hibernias to Wood's halfpence, would

---

[62] Johnston, *Chrysal*, vol. 2, p. 240.
[63] Liz Bellamy, 'It-Narrators and Circulation: Defining a Subgenre' in *The Secret Life of Things*, ed. Blackwell, p. 126.
[64] Johnston, *Chrysal*, vol. 2, p. 169.
[65] Kvande and Grover, 'Mediation is the Message,' p. 537.
[66] Johnston, *Chrysal*, vol. 2, p. 240.   [67] Johnston, *Chrysal*, vol. 2, p. 264.

teach any Irishman to be suspicious of the exterior of a coin while remaining vigilant about coins' potential to devalue nationhood, at least in Ireland.

Whereas *Chrysal* presents the coin as a medium of British identification *and* a medium of so-called 'benevolent' British imperialism through trade, *The Adventures of a Bad Shilling in the Kingdom of Ireland* uses the materiality of the coin to take its reader inside the perspective of the colonized instead. Another key difference lies in the fact that Chrysal verbally chooses his British identity and shape, whereas the narrator in *The Adventures* is forcibly forged into a British shilling but retains its invisible Irish identity in a scene, discussed in more detail below, that links with the *aisling* poem's trope of bodily violation. Chrysal speaks from a position of power as a guinea where the bad shilling speaks from a place of victimization and defeat as an Irish false shilling. As a guinea, Chrysal gains purchase on an international market, literally, as it moves about Europe as an acknowledged, valuable object, whereas the bad shilling winds up debased and forgotten on the ground of Dublin's streets. These key departures add credence to the idea not only that the author of the *Adventures* was responding to the British messages of *Chrysal* but that he or she was also intentionally working within the it-narrative genre to reinvent it as a fiction with anti-Unionist and anti-colonial possibilities, subversively realized through the material make and voice of the false coin who allegorizes the Irish nation.

1.3 A Hybrid Genre: The It-*Aisling*

Having established the important contexts of Hibernia, Irish coinage, and the it-narrative, I can now turn, in detail, to the fascinating world of *The Adventures of a Bad Shilling in the Kingdom of Ireland*. What makes the Irish shilling distinct from other English it-narratives, even *Chrysal,* is its immediate evocation of the Irish-language *aisling* or vision poem, which would have been a familiar reference for the eighteenth-century Irish reader. A Jacobite genre with Irish nationalist and anti-British tendencies, the *aisling* allusions enable the author of *The Adventures* to clearly, polemically depart from *Chrysal*'s pro-Britain message and speak to an Irish readership. Furthermore, the bodily imprint of the female Hibernia on the Irish coin inevitably afforded the anonymous author a way of rethinking the longstanding, traditional *aisling* allegory of Ireland as exploited female body for a modern, post-Union Ireland under the jurisdiction of a commercialized British Empire.

The *aisling* genre of Irish oral poetry was one of the most popular forms of cultural expression in mid-eighteenth-century Ireland, developing in the wake of the failed Irish uprising of the Williamite War in the late seventeenth century. Its basic formula is an allegory in which a beautiful, ethereal woman representing Erin, or Ireland, comes to the poet in a dream or vision and mourns her 'true'

Jacobite husband and, in some cases, the poet then witnesses her rape by the British imposter(s). As Daniel Corkery argued in his twentieth-century recovery work on Irish-language poetry, the *aisling* was distinguished from early modern bardic poetry not only because it responded to a contemporary historical event (the failed Jacobite Uprising) but also because it was delivered in stressed meter that was stylistically more akin to ballads than court poetry.[68] This was lyric, decorative, rhythmic poetry, Corkery explains, whose vision stirred the poor cottiers that first heard it.[69]

Munster poet Aogán Ó Rathaille (1675–1729) famously pioneered the *aisling*, which soon became the standard form for traveling poets in the wake of the Flight of the Wild Geese. Ó Rathaille's 'Mac an Cheannaí' (c.1719), for example, introduces the allegory as 'Aisling ghear' (a bitter vision) of 'an ainnir shéimh darbh ainm Éire' (the maiden mild whose name was Ireland).[70] In the second stanza, the *spéirbhean* is described as 'céile Bhriain,' or wife to Brian—alluding to Brian Boru the High King of Ireland and thus a fallen, Gaelic nation. The *spéirbhean* mourns and waits for her lover, 'Mac an Cheannaí,' or the Stuart Pretender, a name with connotations relating to savior or redeemer.[71] Similarly, in Ó Rathaille's more visceral 'Gile na Gile,' the *spéirbhean* is betrothed to 'an duine ba ghile ar shliocht chine Scoit' (a man most fine of Scottish blood)—the Stuart King—and the poet then watches her rape by goblin brutes or 'slibire,' alluding to English settlers or perhaps Williamite soldiers.

The *aisling*'s allegory of stolen Ireland/kidnapped woman is inflected with the poet's and woman's shared sorrow, and tropes like the word *brónach* (sorrowful) and imagery of the *spéirbhean* weeping permeate the poems from Ó Rathaille's time to later in the century, with the *aislingí* of Eoghan Rua Ó Súilleabháin or Art Mac Cumhnaigh, who composed from around 1750 to 1780. Although Ó Rathaille and many of his successors were Munster natives, his mode spread north to his followers among the Ulster poets, such as Art Mac Cumhnaigh, whose *aisling* 'Úr-Chill an Chreagáin' (The Churchyard of Cregan) is considered one of the most beautiful in the genre. Whereas in the seventeenth century, Irish poetry had been clan-based and aristocratic, after Ó Rathaille popularized this poetic mode in the early 1700s, many folk poets like Rua Ó Súilleabháin, Seán Clárach Mac Domhnaill, and Eoghan Mac Cárthaigh repeated the conceit, and gradually the *aisling* became a communal, national form of Gaelic expression in Ireland.

---

[68] Daniel Corkery, *The Hidden Ireland: A Study of Gaelic Munster in the Eighteenth Century*, 2nd edition (Dublin: Gill, 1956). p. 126 One of the most important early books on Irish language literature, *Hidden Ireland* praises *aisling* poets like Aogán Ó Rathaille and Eoghan Rua Ó Suilleabháin.
[69] Corkery, *Hidden Ireland*, p. 134.
[70] Seán Ó Tuama, ed., and Thomas Kinsella, tr., Poems of Ó Rathaille, Ó Suilleabhain, Mac Curtaigh, etc. in *An Duanaire 1600–1900: Poems of the Dispossesed* (Dublin: Foras na Gaeilge, 2002), p. 157.
[71] Ó Tuama and Kinsella, *An Duanaire*, p. 155.

As Joep Leerssen has argued, the *aisling* played a crucial role in the creation of an Irish national identity in the eighteenth century. The mode's poetic ideology, he explains, qualifies as national not only because it transcended province and class but also because it brings 'cultural identity and political aspiration together.'[72] This process parallels Hibernia's role in galvanizing middle-class Anglo-Irish citizens toward the Patriot cause of Free Trade in the 1770s and 1780s. Over time, the *aisling* mode found its way into English-language iterations as well—bilingual folk songs and poems, broadsides, and, as I argue in this chapter, the British it-narrative. Vincent Morley's research on the popular consciousness of middle-class Irish speakers in the eighteenth century has proven that the *aisling* was an alive, versatile literary formula throughout the long eighteenth century, recycled in many Jacobite songs and poems critiquing the penal laws and Protestantism.[73] Over time, the popular *aisling*'s political aspirations even broadened beyond strict Jacobite sectarianism to include Anglo-Irish political concerns like the United Irishmen and the Rebellion of 1798 in the latter part of the century, and Catholic Emancipation in the early years of the nineteenth century, with some of them addressed directly to Daniel O'Connell.[74] The repetition of this mode and its endurance, despite the decline of the language and the suppression of Jacobite politics, helped create the idea of what Leerssen calls an 'eternal Gaeldom'—a constructed Gaelic identity that was seemingly immune to historical change and inherent to the idea of a universal Irish national character.[75]

Evidence proves that over the course of the eighteenth century, Ireland became increasingly bilingual, as a majority of the poor rural population gradually adopted English words. Bilingual ability was necessary for the day-to-day functioning of landed estates and commercial transactions across the country.[76] Eighteenth-century Irish-language writers regularly accessed and read English-language print culture, and even engaged with the political concerns of Anglophone Ireland in their own writing, such as the Free Trade campaign in the late 1770s and early 1780s.[77] Eighteenth-century Irish writers like Aodh Buí Mac Cruitín, Liam Inglis, and Peadar Ó Dóirín wrote in both languages. Peadar Dubh

---

[72] Joep Leerssen, *Mere Irish and Fíor-Ghael: Studies in the Idea of Irish Nationality, its Development and Literary Expression Prior to the Nineteenth Century* (Cork: Cork University Press, 1996), p. 241.

[73] See Vincent Morley, *The Popular Mind in Eighteenth-Century Ireland* (Cork: Cork University Press 2017), which studies manuscript versions of popular works in Irish, including many *aislings*, over the long eighteenth century. Morley responds to and updates Corkery's *The Hidden Ireland* (first published 1924).

[74] Leerssen, *Mere Irish*, p. 249.   [75] Leerssen, *Mere Irish*, p. 251.

[76] The interchange between English and Irish language cultural forms in eighteenth-century Ireland continues to be a gray area for scholars, but recent works like the *Irish and English* collection edited by James Kelly and Ciarán Mac Murchaidh suggest a greater cultural overlap between the two languages than has been previously believed. See James Kelly and Ciarán Mac Murchaidh, eds, *Irish and English: Essays on the Irish Linguistic and Cultural Frontier 1600–1900* (Dublin: Four Courts Press, 2012), p. 218.

[77] Higgins, *Nation of Politicians*, p. 7.

Ó Dálaigh even wrote a bilingual *aisling* in alternating English and Irish lines, such as 'Agus éirigh, Ghrainne Mhaol [And rise up, Grainuaile] / And exterminate this hearsay.'[78] Although the permeation of English into Irish writing exceeded that of Irish into a growingly Anglophone world, by the second half of the eighteenth century, the Protestant elite in Ireland no longer viewed the Irish language as the threat they had considered it to be in the seventeenth century.[79] The Ó Neachtain language circle in Dublin served as a stronghold of the language in Anglophone Ireland, and, in turn, members of the Protestant elite came into possession of Irish-language manuscripts.[80] Anglo-Irish writers like Charlotte Brooke and antiquarians like Joseph Cooper Walker translated Irish writing for an English-speaking audience. Significantly, Brooke's *Reliques of Irish Poetry* printed the original Irish typeface alongside the English.

The Adventures of a Bad Shilling in the Kingdom of Ireland is yet further evidence of this cultural interchange between English and Irish language forms in the popular writing and mindset of the long eighteenth century. Although written in English prose, *The Adventures of a Bad Shilling in the Kingdom of Ireland* self-consciously presents as an *aisling*. At times, the text's satiric voice may seem to cohere more readily with the parodic, sometimes whimsical tone of the it-narrative genre than it does the intensely dramatized sorrow of the standard *aisling* poem. Mark Blackwell, for instance, has noted how the tale's deployment of asterisks in the text pay homage to Laurence Sterne's satiric style. Nevertheless, *The Adventures* takes its allegorical message seriously. At the same time as the anonymous author opens with tongue-in-cheek jest, he also invokes the standard *aisling* request for the reader's acceptance of his vision, however fanciful:

> If it is necessary for an Author, who rides the trotting-horse of the Muses through the following region of Romance, sometimes to give up the reins of probability...a reader is not utterly exempted from the same necessity. I must therefore entreat my reader (or he will never be able to understand a syllable of which I am *now* writing) to imagine himself dead and buried, at least two centuries—to inhabit a new body—to live in a new Dublin—and to purchase a new Ireland's Mirror. These premises being granted to the imagination, I proceed to detail.[81]

Like an *aisling*, the narrative opens under the mutual agreement between writer and audience that realism will be suspended for the purposes of 'understanding' the meaning of what will follow.

---

[78] Leerssen, *Mere Irish*, pp. 284–5.   [79] Kelly and Mac Murchaidh, *Irish and English*, p. 34.
[80] Kelly and Mac Murchaidh, *Irish and English*, p. 27.
[81] *The Adventures of a Bad Shilling*, p. 140.

The opening contractual logistics of the narrative are followed by an appari-
tion, when the coin seems to emerge out of nowhere from the symbolic 'spot on
which the old Irish senate stood' near College Green in Dublin.[82] Likewise, in
Rua Ó Súilleabháin's 'Creo Draíochta' (Magic Mist), for example, the *spéirbhean*
suddenly appears on the bough of a tree in the wood where the speaker is walking. Furthermore, the author of *The Adventures* first identifies the shilling as a
member of the *sídh,* colloquially known the Good People: 'Whether I had picked
up the Devil or one of the Good People I was alike unable to determine.'[83] The
coin's fantastical appearance on the grounds of the former Irish Senate building,
rather than a mystical wood, engages contemporary politics—namely, the 1801
Act of Union.[84] The fact that this futuristic *aisling* vision is a coin emerging on the
grounds of the former Senate building (today, ironically, a Bank of Ireland) may
satirically comment on the fact that the British government enticed Irish
Members of Parliament to vote in favor of the Union with the bestowal of honors
or payments. *The Adventures* updates the *aisling's* formula and material personification in order to connect the story's meaning to its immediate post-Union context. Finally, like the metaphoric *aisling* mode, the penultimate installment of *The
Adventures of a Bad Shilling in the Kingdom of Ireland* involves sexual assault. The
bad shilling's owner in these final chapters is the young granddaughter of an Irish
Jacobite soldier who fought bravely at Culloden. At the time the narrator resides
with her, the young girl's cruel guardians in Dublin force her into prostitution, a
moment that alludes to the sexual violence of the *aisling* mode.

Of course, the 'dark round substance'—that dirty piece of metal—found in
College Green looks nothing like the beautiful, ethereal *spéirmhná* (sky-women)
of Ó Rathaille's or Mac Cumhnaigh's *aislingí*, but it performs analogous nationalist and material significations. As the shilling explains, it did not begin its life as a
shilling at all, but rather, a statue in a pagan temple, followed by its longest incar-
nation as a bracelet, or Gaelic torc, worn by an Irish hero. Its identity as a torc is a
symbolic phase within *The Adventures* not only because the shilling remembers
this particular form most fondly—as a pre-imperial, indigenous Gaelic cultural
artifact—but also because it reflects the ideological framework of the *aisling*
mode. In its heyday, the bracelet played a central role in an ancient Gaelic marriage and military victory:

[82] *The Adventures of a Bad Shilling*, p. 140.   [83] *The Adventures of a Bad Shilling*, p. 140.
[84] Aside from the Rebellion of 1798, the Act of Union was arguably the most impactful and con-
flicted political issue in Anglo-Irish affairs in the eighteenth and into the nineteenth century, pre-
Famine. Kevin Whelan notes how Parliament's 114 commissions and sixty committees sitting on Irish
issues between 1800 and 1833 evince British anxiety over the unstable Union and the 'Irish Question.'
Kevin Whelan and Daire Keough, eds, *Acts of Union: The Causes, Contexts, and Consequences of the
Act of Union* (Dublin: Four Courts Press, 2001), p. 24.

[I was] worn as a bracelet / on the arm of the brave youth who in female disguise avenged insulted Ireland on the Danish Appiust [Turgesius].[85] The youth who wore me was, for his valour and intrepidity, rewarded with the hand of the fair princess of Meath: who prized me so much, as the ornament won by her lover and husband in this perilous adventure, that, in compliance with her dying request, I was the bracelet that fastened her funeral vestments.[86]

The bracelet mediates an Irish marriage exchange—a marriage which itself represents political reward for militaristic Irish victory against Viking conquest (and the threat of forced sex between Viking leader and Irish princess). The material body of the it-narrator, therefore, like the *spéirbhean*, codifies both romantic and political ideas: that of a 'true' marriage between Gaelic princess and Gaelic hero, rather than an imperial invader. Its material existence as an artifact of both a nuptial and political covenant enacts the metaphorical duality of the *aisling* form, where the *spéirbhean's* sexual relationships analogize a nationalist message.

Despite these happy beginnings, the narrator soon suffers the typical *aisling* violation: like the *spéirbhean* in Ó Rathaille's 'Gile na Gile' who is kidnapped away from her Jacobite fiancé (King James), the narrator is continually stolen away from its 'rightful' Irish owners. For instance, after living in the Princess's tomb for centuries, the protagonist (as bracelet) is found by Teddy O'Shaughnessy, a young Catholic ploughboy from Meath, who is morally superior, if socially inferior, to the man who takes it off him: the greedy, Anglo-Irish landowner McAlister.[87] Then, the it-narrator just misses being saved by a priest who recognizes it for its true worth, who can read its value as an 'old Irish' artifact 'worth one hundred guineas or more'—a coded reference, perhaps, to *Chrysal,* that implies the material culture of Gaelic Ireland is one hundred times more valuable that the modern, commercial British guinea.[88] A silversmith permanently ruins the bracelet's Gaelic craftsmanship by putting it into his furnace, and the priest leaves, dejected. Finally, the silver piece, which has now become a chalice, is stolen away from its 'patriotic' (to use the shilling's own words) place on the Catholic altar, and sold to a manufacturer of 'base coins,' where it is truly violated, irrevocably subjugated into its subaltern metallic form as a 'bad

---

[85] The story contains a long, detailed footnote explaining this quasi-mythic historical anecdote about the Danish Viking Turgesius, who built a castle in Meath and fell in love with King Malachy's daughter, demanding her hand. The Princess, however, was saved from this fate when Malachy's men, dressed in female attire, caught Turgesius and his men unaware and killed them. The author of *The Adventures* lifts this historical anecdote from Geoffrey Keating's *Foras Feasa Ar Eirinn* (1634), book 2, chapter 1, a subsection titled 'Maelsechlainn's Daughter—Death of Turgesius.' Given that history's popularity among both Irish and Anglo-Irish scholars and antiquarians in the eighteenth century, the story would likely have resonated with readers as an allusion to Keating's work (Kelly and Mac Murchaidh, *Irish and English*, p. 101).
[86] *The Adventures of a Bad Shilling*, p. 144.   [87] *The Adventures of a Bad Shilling*, p. 145.
[88] *The Adventures of a Bad Shilling*, p. 150.

shilling.'[89] This final form as coin signals the ultimate commercial and colonial defeat: its original identity materially eradicated via melting and rebranded with the Hibernian, monetary impression.

Like the *spéirbhean* of Eoghan Rua Ó Súilleabháin's 'Ceo Draíochta,' who is 'by horned tyrants daily devoured,' the narrator is repeatedly adulterated by greedy Irishmen, who serve their own avarice, rather than a national ideal.[90] That one of the shilling's last owners in 'modern Dublin'—that is, the author's contemporary moment—is the young, beautiful granddaughter of a former Jacobite hero, who is raped by a successful Dublin tradesman, affirms the it-narrator is a *spéirbhean* in commercialized form. At one stage, the narrator reads the granddaughter's mind, explaining how he 'traced back those disastrous events that led to her present unfortunate condition,' thus blending his own life and subjectivity with hers.[91] This moment is microcosmic of the it-narrative at large, which is, after all, an account of the 'disastrous events' that led to the narrator's own 'present unfortunate condition' as a base coin in a futuristic, nationally degraded Dublin. Bookended by two *spéirbhean*-like owners, the Princess of Meath and Jacobite Colonel's granddaughter, the it-narrative presents the before and after of a fallen, erased Irish culture coded through female embodiment and metallic shape.

1.4 Material Impression and Colonial Consciousness in *The Adventures of a Bad Shilling*

The Adventures is preoccupied with the mechanics of the coin's national consciousness, providing a series of explanations for its emotive abilities throughout the narrative. The coin details how it first developed a consciousness, and then, how that consciousness was preserved throughout his many material alterations—from statue to bracelet to chalice to shilling. These anecdotes are part satire and part fancy, but they nevertheless demarcate a developing and self-consciously Irish subjectivity, which, crucially, stems directly from colonialism's material effects. The bad shilling it-narrator turns these one-dimensional, fraught national character types, *spéirbhean* and Hibernia, into a talking, thinking, feeling character, which is worth examining for its material and metaphoric narratives. (Of course, the transformation from woman to money has gendered implications, to be addressed at the end of this chapter.[92])

---

[89] *The Adventures of a Bad Shilling*, p. 155.

[90] Ó Tuama, Ó Tuama and Kinsella, *An Duanaire*, p. 189.

[91] *The Adventures of a Bad Shilling in the Kingdom of Ireland*, in *Ireland's Mirror, or The Masonic Magazine* [Dublin] 3 (Jan. 1806): p. 21.

[92] The narrator is not exact about the date of its formation into a bad shilling. Throughout the eighteenth century, the reverse side of shillings circulating in Ireland could sport anything from Britannia or Hibernia, to the imperial sun surrounded by insignias of England, Wales, Scotland and

If, as Mark Blackwell explains, the it-narrative 'literalizes the figurative,' then this small, talking shilling repeatedly literalizes the relationship between Irish subjectivity and material violation at the turn of the nineteenth century.[93] For example, the speaking coin, like the typical *aisling* poet, serves as the expressive voice and 'lone witness' to a vision of a glorified Irish past, which it details.[94] When buried in the tomb with the Princess of Meath, the shilling describes the experience of his spectatorship and self-identifies as sole witness:

> Here *I witnessed* the tremendous decay of mortality. The sweet form of beauty, the prey of worms and corruption!…at last, reduced to a heap of dust, and mingled with the parent earth, *I alone remained* entire of all that was committed to the tomb, with the beautiful daughter of the renowned Malachy. Empires die alike with men—and rival or inferior states rise on their ruins![95]

As Mark Blackwell has commented, the shilling's language is grandiose and overly sentimental like a Sternean satire, but such emotional grandiosity and emphatic sorrow are also, as discussed previously, identifying traits of *aisling* poetry. In this passage, *The Adventures* literalizes the figurative metaphor of national decay implied by the *aisling* lament: he watches Gaelic Ireland disintegrate, the decay of the Princess's beauty offering the metaphor of a once sovereign Gaelic order's own historical decay.

The physical decay traumatically recalled by the it-narrator points to the unspoken violent history playing out above ground: the land being plundered and colonized by Vikings, Normans, and the New English over the course of several centuries. Toward the end of this passage, the it-narrator announces the political, anti-imperial significance of the *aisling* mode: that Empires die and new 'inferior states rise on their ruins,' like the House of Hanover rising on the body of the decaying, *spéirbhean*-like Gaelic Princess of Meath. The complexity of *The Adventures*' literary form lies in the fact that as the coin-narrator recites his own *aisling* vision of the decayed Princess/Ireland, it is also a bodily metonym of decaying Ireland itself: a ruined Gaelic artifact mourning a glorified past. *The Adventures*, then, is an *aisling* within an *aisling*, making the shilling both metaphor and national orator at once, object and subject in a national and material narrative.

The Adventures' narrator both speaks on its own behalf and vocalizes the inner experiences of other native Irish characters—sensing, describing, and visualizing their otherwise silenced subjective experiences under the conditions of British

Ireland (Ireland's being the crowned harp), or the words 'one shilling.' If it bore the image of Britannia, that might suggest the erasure of Hibernia/Ireland under the Union. Regardless, that the narrator is Irish, a *spéirbhean*, a coin, and a patriotic symbol nevertheless invokes Hibernia in the story.
[93] Blackwell, *British It-Narratives*, p. xli.   [94] O'Donnell, 'Driving Image,' p. 415.
[95] *The Adventures of a Bad Shilling*, p. 144, my emphasis.

colonialism. This kind of narrative omniscience is characteristic of the British it-narrative, where the object-narrator senses and describes its human owners' emotions, but uniquely in the *Adventures,* the Irish it-narrator is particularly attuned to the thoughts of poor Irish people oppressed by colonial conditions, otherwise silenced or overlooked in British fiction.[96] For example, during its time with the young Catholic ploughboy Teddy O'Shaughnessy, the narrator empathizes with a poor beggar on the street who is being harassed by an Anglo-Irish landlord named McAlister. McAlister says, 'You are all thieves or idlers,' demonstrating an anti-Catholic, anti-Irish prejudice. Ironically, although McAlister is the only person in the scene who recognizes the bracelet as a Gaelic artifact, the it-narrator feels subjective affinity with the beggar instead, entering his thoughts: 'Anger swelled in the beggar's soul [at these insults]—but his almost bursting heart sent a tear into his eye—and it relieved him.'[97] Here, the it-narrator goes *inside* the Irish beggar's soul, views his bursting heart, and thereby projects the material proof of beggar's emotive depth in contrast to McAlister's voiced, racist elitism.

The shilling traces the material mechanics of its own consciousness to a pre-Christian, pagan, and quasi-mythic Ireland: 'When Meibhe reigned Queen of Connaught... the silver that is contained in me formed part of a colossal statue in the palace of Eumania, which was dedicated to Bel,' or the Sun God in Celtic mythology.[98] But after Christianity came to Ireland, the shilling explains, the temple was destroyed and the silver statue melted down into 'some female ornaments worn by the ladies of the court of Malachy of Meath.'[99] In explaining this transition, the shilling details the material preservation of his own subjectivity: 'the principle of demoniac consciousness adhered to a small portion of the idol which was melted down into some female ornaments.'[100] By its own description, the shilling bears a subjectivity—what it calls 'the principle of consciousness'—that is a Celtic, pre-Christian, supernatural consciousness. Other it-narratives like *Chrysal* similarly explicate their object protagonists' human-like consciousness, but uniquely in *The Adventures,* this human subjectivity correlates to an antiquarian ideology of Irishness, where Irish national character is predicated on Celtic antiquity—an idea purported by Sylvester O'Halloran, Charles O'Connor, J. C. Walker, and later, Sydney Owenson.[101] Most importantly, the author of *The Adventures* announces, via the vehicle of a coin, that Ireland contains its own pre-imperial consciousness that endures, *literally,* in materiality. The author/

---

[96] Blackwell, *British It-Narratives,* p. xvii.   [97] *The Adventures of a Bad Shilling,* p. 145.
[98] *The Adventures of a Bad Shilling,* p. 141. This information was probably taken from Sylvester O'Halloran's *A General History of Ireland* (1778) or the contemporary works of Charles O'Connor. Queen Meibhe was a pre-Christian heroine figure from Celtic Ireland, who married an Ulster chieftain, explaining the reference to Palace of Euamania (sometimes used for Ulster in these writings about pre-Christian Ireland).
[99] *The Adventures of a Bad Shilling in the Kingdom of Ireland,* p. 143.
[100] *The Adventures of a Bad Shilling in the Kingdom of Ireland,* p. 143.
[101] See O'Halloran, *Golden Ages and Barbarous Nations.*

scribe of *The Adventures*, the man that hears the shilling speak, calls it 'My invisible,' privileging the shilling's unseen pre-imperial Celtic and Gaelic consciousness, rather than its British embodiment, as its defining characteristic.

Although the shilling identifies the original source of its consciousness as demoniac, pagan Celticism, it traces the roots of its current, speaking subjectivity— the narrative of *The Adventures* as such—to the moment when it becomes a symbol of dual nationality as a Catholic chalice gifted to a priest by his Anglo-Irish landlord, akin to the dual political resonance of the late eighteenth-century Hibernian icon. Before the shilling relays the transformation, it pauses to detail its own consciousness again:

> It will be recalled that I was once imprisoned in a Pagan idol—that the power of making my observations and communicating the varied series of my eventful history, was derived from infernal agency—Had I continued till the present moment *solely* under that influence, the reader would have been presented with a far different narrative.   (p. 151)

Here, the shilling acknowledges that its own subjectivity is completely changed by and conditional on its material form as a chalice, its third bodily form (the first two being demoniac statue and Gaelic bracelet). It explains that the Anglo-Irish nobleman who ordered his commission 'felt, most sensibly, the sad distractions of a hapless Ireland. He lamented the perversities, the fatal bigotry dextral and sinistral that divided the country. He wished every Irishman to consider his countryman as his brother in this life.'[102] This patriotic sensibility, which articulates the ethos of both late century Anglo-Irish antiquarians and United Irishmen who desired a unified Irish 'brotherhood' across sectarian divide, inspires his Lordship to offer the chalice/shilling as a 'peace-offering,' which the shilling labels a 'patriotic' gesture.[103] Although the narrator's exterior form changes almost constantly in the narrative, this marks one of two moments where the shilling acknowledges an interior conversion. He calls it 'a complete change of heart and manners': 'I stood completely different from all I ever was before.'[104] This symbolic ritual—in which an Anglo-Irish landlord demonstrates patriotic sensibility for Ireland's colonial history and the oppression of Catholics—transforms the shilling's consciousness and creates the subjectivity that enables the narrative he speaks: the hybridized text of *The Adventures*, both English and Irish in literary influence.

The strangest and most significant account of the narrator's subjectivity, however, comes during its reformation into its most debased form as a bad shilling. Unlike in *Chrysal*, where the narrator simply announces that it 'entered' into the

---

[102]   *The Adventures of a Bad Shilling in the Kingdom of Ireland*, p. 151.
[103]   *The Adventures of a Bad Shilling in the Kingdom of Ireland*, p. 151.
[104]   *The Adventures of a Bad Shilling in the Kingdom of Ireland*, p. 152.

shape of a guinea, as if of its own volition and without any detail of its material alteration at the mint, the bad shilling narrator describes his material *and* subjective transformation into a coin in depth.[105] Whereas before the shilling explained how its consciousness 'attaches' to certain substances and 'becomes resident' within it, here the consciousness spreads and multiplies rather than just relocating:[106]

> The whole [degrading mixture] was formed into a large metallic sheet, which was presently cut into round pieces like button-tops. The Principle of consciousness had extended itself through the whole mass, during the boiling operation in the crucible. I therefore found myself now, for the first time during my existence, surrounded by a number of companions. We endured the torment of being filed round our edges, scraped, and reduced to some resemblance of the wretched coin that then passed current in Dublin.[107]

The shilling's subjectivity is cloned via the material viscosity of the consciousness, which visualizes subjectivity itself as a malleable, molten metal. Only when the narrator becomes a coin does the consciousness spread—to identical coins, or 'companions' as it calls them. It is no coincidence, therefore, that at the end of this passage, the shilling echoes Swiftian sentiment about shared, national humiliation-by-coin-mintage: the experience of 'being reduced' to a 'wretched coin' is no longer the shilling's own solitary misfortune but a shared experience of both bodily and commercial degradation, acknowledging, as in the *Drapier's Letters,* the interconnectedness between coins and a shared, communal Irish national consciousness.

As with the forced stamping of William's Hibernia on James's gunmoney coins, the humiliating violation of the shilling's alloy quoted above signifies new English control over Ireland. That a once-precious Irish artifact is restamped as a forged British shilling and forced to circulate within an imperial economy satirically comments on the Union's erasure of Irishness after 1800, while also implying that the Union has irrevocably imprinted on the Irish national consciousness at large. As displayed by the creative mind of the anonymous author of *The Adventures,* the material act of minting of coins could furnish a cognitive coping mechanism around the disorienting Act of Union. When the beautiful Gaelic bracelet-turned-chalice becomes a forged shilling, *The Adventures* expresses anxiety about the erasure of Irish culture and identity under the Union, but, crucially, offers an expressive, metaphoric, 'invisible' subjectivity as a consolation. As the narrative visually represents the coin forger stamping the narrator, it also insinuates that

[105] Johnston, *Chrysal*, vol. 1, p. 93.
[106] *The Adventures of a Bad Shilling in the Kingdom of Ireland,* p. 155.
[107] *The Adventures of a Bad Shilling in the Kingdom of Ireland,* p. 155.

the *spéirbhean* becomes the national consciousness residing underneath a false and forced British insignia. In this final, dramatic reformation, the shilling reveals how post-Union Irish subjectivity is compressed under exterior imprints of Britain's Irish stereotype—and also, how that former national subjectivity can *endure* invisibly, despite external material pressures, and even spread throughout a community.

One aspect of late-century it-narratives, Mark Blackwell explains, is the means by which the genre can visibly demonstrate *how* fiction might depict interiority. In *The Adventures,* our narrator illustrates how the it-*aisling* mode might reflect a new Irish national subjectivity in post-Union Ireland, where, without a Parliament, the nation has no clear external signifier of nationality, and all that remains is the physical spot 'on where the Irish Senate stood' and the invisible consciousness of a lost Gaelic age. *The Adventures* presents a clear, modern understanding, in a colonial context, about how material realities are linked to the human consciousness, about how material change—like the erasure of a Parliament, the decay of material culture, or the rebranding of a national symbol—fundamentally impacts the subjectivity inside Irish character. Ultimately, this strange and multifaceted tale realizes a new materialist pillar: that matter affords humans new lanes of cognition, as described by James Gibson, as well as new modes of creativity. In *The Adventures,* these new ways of thinking appear in the coin's resilient subjectivity and in the story's wider, material metaphor for the shape of post-Union national consciousness.

1.5 Allusions to Gendered Violence in the Irish Coin Narrative and National Tale

At the start of this chapter, I suggested that a deeper understanding of the coin's material narrative would lead to a more nuanced analysis of the national tale genre, specifically Sydney Owenson's *The Wild Irish Girl* (1806). In the two decades following 1801, many Irish and English writers took to the page to respond to the sudden reidentification of Ireland under the Union. They reacted in prose, plays, novels—even Jane Austen's *Emma* alludes to societal confusion around Union of Great Britain and Ireland.[108] Almost immediately, the popular genre of the Irish national tale began to take shape: a quasi-novel distinguished by cultural and historical footnotes that defended the Irish language and culture, and which sought to sympathetically depict the native Irish people for the English reader. Many of these tales, *The Wild Irish Girl* most notably, were an amalgamation of novelistic,

---

[108] See 'Austen Answers the Irish Question: Satire, Anxiety and *Emma*'s Allusory Ireland.' *Persuasions* 38 (2016): pp. 218–27.

allegorical, and poetic literary forms.[109] As critics like Ina Ferris, Mary Campbell, Joseph Lennon, and Claire Connolly have argued, national tales, like *The Adventures,* alluded to the *aisling* through their beautiful, Irish female protagonists and their allegorical love stories.[110]

Just like the it-narrator of *The Adventures of a Bad Shilling,* Glorvina, the Princess of Inismore, heroine of Owenson's *The Wild Irish Girl,* is a character in which *spéirbhean* and Hibernia coalesce. She is ethereal, fairy-like like the *spéirbhean,* and yet she is frequently pictured with her harp like Hibernia, consciously representing the allegorical and gendered similitude between the two types. Regularly in Horatio's letters, Glorvina stands in for the Irish national character at large, referred to as an 'emblem' and even, at one instance as the 'Genius of Erin' herself, the name given to the United Irishmen's Hibernian insignia from ten years earlier.[111] Owenson regularly and self-consciously references Glorvina's 'character' as 'both national and natural.'[112] Because of Horatio's excessively romantic descriptions, it is easy (perhaps natural) to classify Glorvina as a two-dimensional character, but critics like Ina Ferris, Julia Wright, and Claire Connolly have explored Glorvina's complexity. Ina Ferris, for instance, explains that even though Glorvina provides Horatio with a primeval, romanticized vision of Ireland, she also 'makes apparent the way in which this reading is in large part a function of his own modern desire.'[113] Ferris characterizes Glorvina as a vision and foil through which Horatio shapes his own subjectivity, and yet she clearly 'possesses a more knowing and adult consciousness than Horatio is willing to grant the "wild Irish girl."'[114]

Adding to Ferris's reading, I argue that Glorvina's 'national and natural' character stems from her material connection to the Irish coin's typeface, which manifests when she is read alongside *The Adventures of a Bad Shilling.*[115] Glorvina's character in *The Wild Irish Girl* exists in relation to clichéd typecasts forced on her by Horatio's outside English impressions:

---

[109] *The Wild Irish Girl* soon became what Claire Connolly has characterized as a 'media event' that resulted in Owenson's celebrity and seven reprints in just three years. Women in Dublin and London began to dress like the 'wild Irish girl,' wearing imitation red mantles and matching Irish hairpins dubbed 'glorvinas,' while men fell in love with the charms of the heroine's alluring creator, sometimes writing Owenson love letters addressed to 'Glorvina.' See Connolly, ' "I accuse Miss Owenson:" The Wild Irish Girl as Media Event.' *Colby Quarterly* 36.3 (2000): pp. 98–115.

[110] See: Ina Ferris, *The Romantic National Tale and the Question of Ireland* (Cambridge: Cambridge UP, 2004), Mary Campbell, *Lady Morgan: The Life and Times of Sydney Owenson* (London: Pandora, 1988), and Joep Leerssen, *Remembrance and Imagination: Patterns in the Historical and Literary Representation of Ireland in the Nineteenth Century* (Cork: Cork UP, 1996).

[111] Sydney Owenson, *The Wild Irish Girl,* ed. Kathryn Kirkpatrick (Oxford: Oxford UP, 1999), pp. 52, 79.

[112] Owenson, *The Wild Irish Girl,* p. 120.   [113] Ferris, *Romantic National Tale,* p. 55.

[114] Ferris, *Romantic National Tale,* pp. 55–6.

[115] Bonnie Blackwell argues that, rather than criticize the lack of depth and complexity in female characters of the long eighteenth century, we must read them as it-narrators in order to better understand their novelistic purpose: i.e. as a device that lends inside access to a variety of characters, like in a picaresque. 'Courtesans and Corkscrews,' pp. 87–9.

> Conceive for a moment a form full of character, and full of grace, bending over an instrument singularly picturesque—...The expression of the divinely touching countenance breathed all the fervor of genius under the influence of inspiration, and the contours of the face, from the peculiar uplifted position of the head, were precisely such, as lends to painting the happiest line of feature, and shade of colouring.   (p. 97)

A paradox emerges in Horatio's account: that Glorvina's form is 'full of character' suggests her character exists *inside* her, hinting at her private, inner consciousness, and yet, he describes Glorvina as if her body is a painting, obsessing over her 'form,' the exterior look of her gestures and 'countenance.' As the English artist gazing on a 'real' Irishwoman, Horatio cannot help but turn Glorvina into Hibernia, the one-dimensional, gesturing figure of Ireland, pictured with clichéd harp.

Glorvina's response to seeing the picture—a response that is illegible to Horatio—crystallizes her own subjectivity in relation to his Hibernian copy in the same way the coin narrator expresses its inner, humiliated subjectivity in contradistinction to the external, forced imprint of the Hibernian mint:

> the colour did not rush to her cheek (as it usually does under the influence of any powerful emotion), but rather deserted its beautiful standard, and she stood with her eyes riveted on the picture, as though she dreaded by their removal she should encounter those of the artist.   (p. 100)

That the color drains from her face upon viewing the image and that she avoids meeting Horatio's gaze suggests not, as he reads it, shyness, but potentially disgust at his depiction of a Hibernian stereotype. Because Horatio's family dispossessed Glorvina's of their land during the Williamite War, when he turns her into Hibernia, the text consequently creates a fraught symbolic reminder of Horatio's ownership over Glorvina's ancestral land, and, allegorically, her body (both *spéirbhean* and Hibernia are, after all metonyms for Irish land). Later, we learn that Glorvina avoids Horatio and demonstrates a 'cold reserve' toward him, reaffirming her distaste at the image.[116] Yet Horatio continues to turn Glorvina into a Hibernian typecast: for example, in a later letter, he confesses to closing his book of '*Hiberniana*' and riveting his eyes on Glorvina instead 'who, not unconscious of the ardent gaze, sweeps with a feathery touch the chords of her harp, or plies her fairy wheel with double vigilance.'[117] He substitutes a scholarly study of Irish

---

[116] Owenson, *The Wild Irish Girl*, p. 116.
[117] Owenson, *The Wild Irish Girl*, p. 161. A parody of *The Wild Irish Girl* titled 'Glorviniana' was published in the periodical journal *The Anonymous* in 1807. It mocks Owenson's effusive descriptions of Glorvina and the contemporary obsession with Glorvina as a popular character, as discussed at the start of this chapter. The title, 'Glorviniana,' is a spin on Horatio's Hiberniana, quoted above.

history and culture for a voyeuristic gaze on his own personal, idealized Hibernian body. In this self-consciously symbolic moment, the text demonstrates how men like Horatio reduce 'real' Irish people to a series of uniform, eroticized impressions.

Significantly, in both instances, when Horatio turns Glorvina into the Hibernian emblem, readers also get a glimpse of another, more subversive Glorvina, who is not what Horatio represents. The color draining from her face quoted above and, in this last example, perhaps anxiously making herself busy at the spinning wheel under the discomfiting pressure of his gaze both suggest Glorvina's reluctance toward these Hibernian replicas. We might see these clear bodily signals as Glorvina's sieged subjectivity, briefly surfacing from under the suffocation of Horatio's characterization and first-person narrative. Just like the Irish coin it-narrator, Glorvina's deep and hidden consciousness emerges when Horatio's pen imposes imprints of Hibernia upon her. The alienness of Glorvina's almost Gothicized characterization in the final, third-person chapter of the novel, when she screams 'Which of you murdered my father?' further exposes the falsity of Horatio's idyllic, docile Hibernian imprints by alluding to the seventeenth-century origins of both the *spéirbhean* and Hibernian character types: violence and English dominance in Ireland.[118] A darker reading of the novel would suggest that Horatio sees Glorvina as his own personal Hibernia *because* that stereotypical image alludes back to the Williamite War, when his ancestors won his right to own her. This is why Mary Jean Corbett reads the conclusion to *The Wild Irish Girl* as forced marital embrace or rape, rather than a 'marriage solution' like Robert Tracy.[119] If we read the final section of the novel according to rape rather than romance, then Glorvina mirrors the coin it-narrator, embodying the same character model of an inner *spéirbhean* residing underneath and resisting a Hibernian imprint imposed by Horatio and his ancestors.

My reading of *Castle Rackrent* earlier insinuated native Irish character comes into literary focus via Hibernian irony and the gendered, false image of Ireland, and the same can be said of Glorvina. The irony in Horatio's account boils down to the fact that, for all the time he spends observing Glorvina's body, his own personal *Hiberniana*, he still cannot *read* her. The reader of his letters, therefore, can only locate Glorvina's genuine subjective feelings through the recognition of narrative irony—that is, the opposite of what is written. Like irony itself, Glorvina's real character exists apart from the surface-level meaning of Horatio's words: her 'true' subjectivity, which is more tragic than romantic, exists in an invisible fictional space outside the epistolary exchange. As such, Glorvina

---

[118] Owenson, *The Wild Irish Girl*, p. 242.
[119] Mary Jean Corbett, 'Allegories of Prescription: Gendering Union in *The Wild Irish Girl.*' *Eighteenth-Century Life* 22.3 (1998): pp. 92–102; and Robert Tracy, ' "Maria Edgeworth and Lady Morgan: Legality versus Legitimacy.' *Nineteenth-Century Fiction* 40.1 (1985): pp. 1–22.

encapsulates the irony of late eighteenth-century Irish national representation at large: despite being her own character, Glorvina's subjectivity transforms and appears in response to English representations of Hibernia.

Although Horatio delights in his eroticized descriptions of the coy and child-like Glorvina, by end of the novel, Glorvina's status as a distraught, dispossessed, and orphaned figure at the mercy of her English landlords potentially removes the delight in the previous titillation of his letters. *The Wild Irish Girl*'s erotic fantasies cannot be separated from the material power structures in which they take part—of money, property, colonialism, and perhaps even, as Mary Jean Corbett suggests, forced sex. Both Glorvina and the shilling it-narrator are characters whose depth emerges through stereotypical impressions of a feminized Irish image and a history of colonial violence. Indeed, all the characters involved in this material study of the Irish coin—the *spéirbhean*, Hibernia, the Judy/Rackrent coin, the Irish coin it-narrator, and now Glorvina—share the obvious characteristic of femininity, often in a problematically sexualized context, thereby linking femininity and material force in the representation of Irish character.

In her essay 'Courtesans and Corkscrews,' Bonnie Blackwell argues that it-narrators must be read as female because the material experience of the it-narrator—being constantly circulated and regularly devalued—is a female experience. She equates it-narrators with female characters in the eighteenth-century novel by pointing out that they 'achieve allegorically what *Roxana* achieves literally: a representation of the rapid diminution of a woman's value as she is fondled and possessed by many consumers.'[120] Likewise, the bad shilling it-narrator, a modernized *spéirbhean*, suffers regular bodily violation within the Jacobite analogy, making it physically female. Indeed, almost all of the narrator's bodily forms are feminized ones: as bracelet, chalice, and even coin (the word *shilling* is a feminine word in Irish—*scilling*). If, as Blackwell argues, the it-narrative highlights that commodities are like women, the Irish nationalist perspective in a post-Union era on display in *The Adventures* adds another layer to the comparison: associating the feminized diminution of the object with the rapid diminution of the Irish nation (and a flourishing Irish patriotism) following 1798, bringing nation, woman, and object together. It is no coincidence that the patriotic shilling's most degraded form is when it is literally imprinted with the image of the female body (Hibernia).

Unlike the constant sexual innuendo in Sterne's *A Sentimental Journey* or, later, *Tristram Shandy*—works that, stylistically, *The Adventures of a Bad Shilling in Ireland* mimics—sex is never lightly addressed in the Irish it-narrative.[121] Our coin it-narrator does not objectify the female body with titillating metaphors but

---

[120] Blackwell, 'Courtesans and Corkscrews,' p. 287.
[121] The text contains many series of asterisks in place of some of the shilling's thoughts, referencing *Tristram Shandy*, which also contains the same satiric deployment of asterisks.

empathizes with it subjectively, even describes the 'humiliation' of its own, analogous bodily degradation. Significantly, toward the end of the penultimate installment, when the Jacobite's granddaughter is raped, the narrator decries her situation, reflecting on systemic violence against women: 'our streets afford lamentable proofs of numbers, who…are too young to share in the guilt—although they endure all the horrors of Female Infamy.'[122] This critical empathy marks a profound departure from the bawdy innuendos of other it-narratives, concluding that the feminization of the Irish object and subject is more fraught than in the English it-narrative tradition. What Blackwell's argument underscores for an Irish context, through hybridized texts like *The Wild Irish Girl* and especially *The Adventures of a Bad Shilling*, is the troubled gendering of Irish matter and Irish character in colonial culture at large.

*   *   *

Coins were frequent features in eighteenth-century Irish literature, from Swift to Edgeworth to *The Adventures*. The complications and depreciation of the Irish currency system following the Williamite War impacted the way that Irish nationalists thought and wrote about Ireland, from the Irish scale weighed down by Wood's Halfpence to the Irish coin it-narrator who invisibly held the long history of the Irish nation inside its false coin body. The inherent sense of identity erasure afforded by melting and rebranding a coin proved a perfect metaphor for articulating a post-Union interiorized national sensibility in the face of a new outward-facing country. Ultimately, *The Adventures of a Bad Shilling in the Kingdom of Ireland* literalizes a key fact for Irish literature and for this book: that matter details the physical pain and colonial injustice inherent in the emerging Irish consciousness in the eighteenth and nineteenth centuries. Finally, the substitute of coin for woman in *The Adventures of a Bad Shilling, Castle Rackrent*, and, allusively, *The Wild Irish Girl*, satirically demonstrates the ways in which Irish identity, Irish people, and Irish land—whether represented by the *spéirbhean* or Hibernia on a coin—are bought property in an English market, much like a woman in a man's economy, perhaps shortening the distance between the battlefield and the marketplace. In conclusion, therefore, our it-*aisling* narrative establishes a pattern that I explore in the following chapters on the linen trade: the causal relationship between the feminization of Irish objects in consumer culture and the formulation of a new, colonial characterization of Ireland.

---

[122] Blackwell, 'Courtesans and Corkscrews,' p. 75.

2

Flax

Jonathan Swift's first published work on Ireland, *A Proposal for the Universal Use of Irish Manufacture in Cloaths and Furniture for Houses etc. Utterly Rejecting and Renouncing Every Thing wearable that comes from England* (1720), stirred up trouble in eighteenth-century Dublin, leading to the arrest of his printer, Edward Waters of Essex Street. In court, Waters refused to name the author while, behind the scenes, Swift used his influence with the Lord Deputy to have Waters acquitted.[1] A short pamphlet supporting the purchase of Irish textiles would not typically be cause for prosecution, but Swift's defamatory treatment of English commercial practice bordered on seditious. Most damning of all, perhaps, was the *Proposal's* satirical perversion of Ovid's Arachne myth, executed in Swift's quintessential sardonic tone:

> [Pallas and Arachne] both met upon a Tryal of Skill; and *Pallas* finding herself almost equalled in her own Art, stung with Rage and Envy, knot her *Rival* down, turned her into a Spyder, enjoyning her to *Spin* and *Weave* for Ever, *out of her own Bowels*, and *in a very narrow Compass*. I confess, that from a Boy, I always pity-d poor *Arachne*, and could never heartily love the Goddess on account of so *cruel and unjust a Sentence*; which however is *fully executed* upon *Us* by *England* with further Additions of *Rigor* and *Severity*. For the greatest Part of *our Bowels and Vitals* are extracted, without allowing us the Liberty of *Spinning* and *Weaving* them.[2]

Swift's invocation of Ovid demonstrates the longevity of the spinning trope in literature. It also suggests that by 1720, there was something distinctly and recognizably Irish about spinning and weaving—a consequence of the era's burgeoning Irish linen industry. Over the next one hundred years, as the linen manufacture quickly became Ireland's sole substantial industry, writers, businessmen, and scientists alike would continue to characterize linen-making as a naturally Irish proclivity.

Swift's application of the trope is unique for its irreverence, scatological imagery, revision of Ovid's Pallas as a jealous, spiteful (English) woman, and apt

---

[1] Irvin Ehrenpreis, *Swift: The Man, his Works, and the Age*, vol. 3. *Dean Swift* (Ann Arbor: University of Michigan, 1962), vol. 3, pp. 123–30.
[2] Jonathan Swift, *A Proposal for the Universal Use of Irish Manufacture in Cloaths and Furniture of Houses, etc.* (Dublin: E. Waters, 1720), pp. 8–9.

Irish Materialisms: The Nonhuman and the Making of Colonial Ireland, 1690–1830. Colleen Taylor, Oxford University Press.

satirical analogy of Ireland as an endlessly spinning, weaving, disemboweled Arachne.[3] In the eighteenth century, Irish women all over the nation *were* endlessly spinning as part of an imperial economy that took advantage of Ireland's textiles or 'vitals' and limited the country's trade to a 'narrow compass.'[4] But what makes Swift's disemboweled Arachne dangerous, even criminal, can be captured in his equation of Irish textile with gruesome bowels. As I will demonstrate throughout this chapter, such grisly imagery attacks the very material foundation of Ireland's new characterization as a domesticated woman, whose fine, white flax and soft, clean linen helped model an ideology of British paternalism.

In these next two chapters, I delve into the material details of the linen industry in Ireland to see how linen's unique material composition and manufacture contributed to ways of thinking about and expressing Irishness over the course of the eighteenth century. I consider the linen industry in terms of its material affordance, as defined by psychologist James Gibson, who emphasizes the complementarity of the material object and the human mind. Affordance, writes Gibson, is 'perceiving a value-rich ecological object' that then furnishes, via its unique values and properties, the thinking animal with an idea or function.[5] In line with this, I analyze linen like I did the coin: as a material-semiotic formation, as reflecting both its own material stories that afforded human thinking while also partaking in ideological constructions designed by writers to affirm colonial power structures.[6] Because of the vast reach of Irish linen and its complex manufacturing process, I have divided its material-semiotic affordances into two chapters: one on the literal seed and origin of linen cloth, the flax plant, and one on the most iconic symbol of the trade, the spinning wheel. Establishing flax's affordances for gendered colonial ideology in this chapter will lead me to connect the spinning wheel with a particularly feminist type of subversion in the next.

The biological nature of fibrous, viscous flax discussed here and the physical motion of the spinning wheel discussed in the following chapter are germane to our understanding of Irish national identity and fictional character. Flax and spinning wheels, more than any other objects, were agents that linked the linen industry with Irish subjects across the whole island, from poor cottiers in Connaught to the Scots-Irish weavers and bleach mill owners in Ulster and, eventually, British consumers across the Irish Sea. I will show how the material

[3] In Ovid, Arachne is the arrogant, jealous character while Pallas is the more subdued character who meets the young, prideful woman's challenge. Swift clearly alters these characterizations for the benefit of his English-Irish allegory—making Arachne an innocent victim to Pallas's (England's) greed.

[4] Swift is referring to a series of legislative measures dating back to the Navigation Acts of 1660 that limited Irish exportation to England. Only after initial exportation to England could Irish goods travel to the English colonies in the Americas.

[5] James Gibson, *The Ecological Approach to Visual Perception* (Hillsdale, NJ: Lawrence Erlbaum Associates, 1986), p. 140.

[6] Donna Haraway, 'Situated Knowledges: the Science Question in Feminism and the Privilege of Patrial Perspective.' *Feminist Studies* 14.3 (1988), p. 585.

experience of linen manufacture provided new ways of thinking that consequently reshaped imperial ideologies into a more clearly coherent paternalism. This is why a writer like Swift could best critique British imperial policy by defiling the idea(l) of the Irish spinner's fine, feminized product: because it had helped formulate political archetypes of eighteenth-century Anglo-Irish relations in the first place.

This chapter's case study homes in on the smallest yet most fundamental unit of the Irish linen industry. Flax was not a passive canvas on which Britain outlined its new Irish character, but rather, a complex organism and deserving subject of isolated study in its own right, whose unique characteristics actively contributed to the development of Irish character. I focus on two particular stages of the linen manufacture—the early steps of flax dressing, which involved what was known as beetling and scutching, and the later stage of flax bleaching—as directly involved in the wider ideological idea of improving Irish industry, which could (and did) extend to ideas about improving the Irish people through domestication (i.e. gendering) and purification. In this material-textual formulation of 'improvement' in Ireland, industry (ostensibly) replaced violence, and the uncouth Irish character could be refined, cleaned, and made useful, just like the flax plant. To phrase all of this another way: the new eighteenth-century reformulation of Irish character in national and literary terms, from something barbarous in the sixteenth and seventeenth centuries into something useful and nonthreatening in the eighteenth, descended from and disseminated through the material process of altering the flax plant.

Refiguring eighteenth-century linen according to new materialist concepts like Gibson's affordance and Karen Barad's 'intra-action' highlights the symbiotic relationship between the flax plant, the Irish people, and British ideology. Intra-action is particularly useful concept for this case study in that, by replacing interaction, the term conceptually undoes the bifurcation of human body and nonhuman matter, emphasizing a dynamism of shifting forces between people and other organisms.[7] In this case, the intra-action of flax, Irish bodies, and English writing in their varied, changing agencies resulted in particular, ideological characterizations of Ireland. The fine, soft features of flax thread helped to characterize Ireland as a feminine, economically productive, and, as my discussion of bleaching will reveal, ethnically altered colonial subject.[8] At the same time, remembering Jane Bennett's 'vibrant matter,' or the recalcitrance of objects, means that flax's biology could also insinuate subversive ideas into the rhetorical

---

[7] Karen Barad, *Meeting the Universe Halfway: Quantum Physics and the Entanglement of Matter and Meaning* (Durham, NC: Duke University Press, 2007).

[8] Karen Barad. 'Posthumanist Performativity: Toward an Understanding of How Matter Comes to Matter.' *Signs* 28.3 (2003): p. 811.

and visual depictions of Irish linen, despite the industry's attempts to subdue and purify both flax and Irish character.[9]

2.1   A Brief History of the Irish Linen Industry

The turn of the eighteenth century was a turning point for the Irish economy and Irish social life, when spinning and weaving flax went from being a standard domestic task to a national industry and international trade. In 1700, Ireland produced one million yards of linen cloth per year; in 1800, annual exports amounted to forty million yards.[10] This did not happen 'naturally,' but through imperial policies of development and the organized importation of machines, techniques, and people to Ireland. Jane Gray associates eighteenth-century Ireland's fast-growing linen industry with Franklin Mendels's term 'protoindustrialization'—not quite the urban factory systems we associate with Dickens, Gaskell, and nineteenth-century England (even today, Ireland is seen as unique for not experiencing that level of nineteenth-century industrialization), but a form of organized commercial development all the same, including working-class formation, household production, and market-organized rural industries.[11] Rather than factories, Irish households 'lay at the heart of the Irish linen industry.'[12] Husbands would grow flax, wives and daughters would spin that flax into yarn and sell it to weavers, who would then sell their woven cloth to bleachers for final polishing before exportation.[13]

Ireland's protoindustrialization as a linen country was the brainchild of four men: the Earl of Strafford, the Duke of Ormonde, William Temple, and Samuel-Louis Crommelin. In the early seventeenth century, the Earl of Strafford and Lord Deputy to Ireland, Thomas Wentworth, applied a heavy-handed policy that sought to suppress Irish woolen manufactures which, in his words, threatened to 'trench' on the clothing of England, 'their staple commodity.' Instead, as he explains in a 1636 letter, 'I have endeavoured another way to set [the Irish] on work, and that is, by bringing the making of linen cloth.'[14] Strafford argued that the Irish soil and climate were suited to growing flax and the women 'naturally bred to spinning,' as many others would reiterate for decades to come.[15] Following Strafford's return to England as an advisor to Charles I, James Butler, Duke of

---

[9] Jane Bennett, *Vibrant Matter* (Durham, NC: Duke UP, 2010), p. ix.

[10] W. H. Crawford, *The Impact of the Domestic Linen Industry in Ulster* (Belfast: Ulster Historical Foundation, 2005), p. 87.

[11] Jane Gray, *Spinning the Threads of Uneven Development: Gender and Industrialization in Ireland during the Long Eighteenth Century* (Lanham, MD: Lexington, 2005), p. 3.

[12] Gray, *Spinning the Threads*, p. 5.   [13] Gray, *Spinning the Threads*, p. 5.

[14] Qtd. in Edward Wakefield, *An Account of Ireland: Statistical and Political*, vol. 1 (London: Longman, Hurst, Rees, Orme, & Browne, 1812), p. 681.

[15] Wakefield, *An Account of Ireland*, vol. 1, p. 681.

Ormonde and viceroy of Ireland, continued to foster the Irish linen scheme and thereby suppress England's competition in the woolen manufacture. Ormonde brought Dutch workers over from Holland to teach the Irish techniques in flax dressing (preparation), spinning, and weaving.[16] Former diplomat William Temple insisted that the Irish soil and Irish women were particularly suited to a linen industry and encouraged participation from 'each Member of a [Irish] Family (women as well as men).'[17] Most crucially, Temple emphasized governmental support for the Irish linen trade.[18]

By the late seventeenth century, Temple's vision had been realized: in 1696, English parliamentary policy guaranteed the burgeoning linen industry in Ireland with the removal of import duty on Irish linens, meaning they sold more cheaply in England than those from Europe—Holland and France, for example. King William III appointed Samuel-Louis Crommelin, a French Huguenot living in Holland and then England, as royal overseer of the Irish linen industry, which he expanded throughout Ulster. Several other Huguenot weavers immigrated to Ulster at the turn of the eighteenth century, while Crommelin founded the country's first mass bleaching establishment in Lisburn and published a detailed essay on the best methods of sowing, dressing, and bleaching flax: *An Essay Towards the Improving of the Hempen and Flaxen Manufactures in the Kingdom of Ireland* (1705). Lisburn, Belfast, and the surrounding counties of Down, Armagh, and Antrim became the core of the British Empire's linen manufacture, and would remain so for two centuries. In 1702, Queen Anne awarded Crommelin the royal patent—a moment that highlights the increasing value of Irish linen in the world market and a growing association between good Irish linen and British consumerism.

As Crommelin's royal endorsement suggests, the history of the linen industry in Ireland is tied up with the country's religious and imperial conflicts, particularly the history of the Ulster Plantation, dating back to 1609. Following the Flight of the Earls in 1607, when Hugh O'Neill, Rory O'Donnell, and one hundred of their followers fled Ulster for mainland Europe, the Crown sanctioned the organized, Protestant colonization of Ulster, which had formerly been the province most resistant to English control, thus marking an end to the Gaelic Order in Ireland. The plantation required that immigrants be Protestant and English-speaking, making Ulster an ideal place for members of the Protestant elite like Ormonde and Crommelin to successfully execute their scheme for the linen industry. Of course, the cultivation of flax of had been practiced throughout

---

[16] Brenda Collins, *From Flax to Fabric: The Story of Irish Linen* (Lisburn: Lisburn Museum Publication, 1994), p. 10.

[17] William Temple, 'An Essay Upon the Advancement of Trade in Ireland, written to the Earl of Essex, Lord Lieutenant of that Kingdom. July 22, 1673' in *Miscellanea in Two Parts* (London: Tonson, 1697), pp. 114, 116.

[18] Temple, 'Essay,' p. 118.

Ireland long before the Ulster plantation: there is evidence of at-home flax dressing for fabric making as early as the eleventh century.[19] But the establishment of the Ulster plantation helped to augment Britain's successful attempts to (proto) industrialize Ireland and also explains the localization of the linen manufacture in Ulster.

The 1690s was a time of notable growth in the establishment of the linen industry, coinciding with a wave of immigration to Ulster, when many Scottish Presbyterians fled famine in Scotland. By 1720, the Scots-Irish Presbyterians were the majority population in Ulster and comprised the weavers, bleachers, and merchants that expanded the Irish industry. Wealthier Scots-Irish landholders and farmers would employ their undertenants in service of the linen business, providing spinning, weaving, or bleaching work.[20] Typically, weaving families in the north would employ young men to weave and young unmarried women or widows to spin (the origins of the term 'spinster'), so that even the small farms would involve several employees.[21] Land ownership was a prerequisite for a bleaching business, making it a typically Anglo-Irish, Protestant enterprise, as Catholics rarely owned land in eighteenth-century Ireland. R. F. Foster's history of modern Ireland contends that the linen industry further separated Ulster from the rest of island: the linen tradesmen, interacting with Britain on an industrial level in ways the rest of Ireland did not, entrenched a separate, Protestant settler identity in the North. This identity partition would go on to intensify throughout the next three hundred years of Irish history.[22]

The linen manufacture in Ulster involved many intricate stages of flax treatment, from planting to bleaching to sale at the linen halls. First, after a flax crop was planted (from seeds saved from the previous crop or purchased imported seeds from places like Riga, Latvia or Nerva, Spain), sown, and picked, the stalks were soaked or 'retted' in water for ten days or more so that the hard wooden stem could later be removed. The Irish landscape, with its many rivers and bogs, was particularly conducive to soaking mass quantities of flax—another reason Ormonde and Temple viewed Ireland as suited to the linen manufacture.[23] Next, the soaked flax was dried, and because of Ireland's wet climate, this was often done with fire and smoke inside a heated barn. Once dry, the flax would be beetled (beaten), scutched (struck with a knife to remove the wooden stem), and hackled (combed) in order to single out the long, pliable fibers for spinning. From the 1740s, scutching in the North of Ireland was often done with a scutch mill, but in the west and south, it was exclusively done by (female) hands, a fact I will return to later in this chapter.[24]

---

[19] Collins, *From Flax to Fabric*, p. 1.   [20] Gray, *Spinning the Threads*, p. 64.

[21] Crawford, *Impact*, p. 122.

[22] R. F. Foster, *Modern Ireland 1600–1972* (New York: Penguin, 1989), p. 217.

[23] Crawford, *Impact*, pp. 30–1.   [24] Collins, *From Flax to Fabric*, p. 15.

Spinning came next, twisting the uneven flax fibers into long, fine, uniform thread, followed by the boiling of the yarn in water with added plant ashes to soften the thread and aid in the subsequent bleaching process. In the late eighteenth century, there was a concentrated effort to use domestic, rather than imported, plant ashes in the boiling process: Irish farmers Rockeric O' Connor (Roscommon) and James Breakey (Cavan), for example, wrote to the Linen Board to describe their ash-making procedures and encourage the use of Irish vegetable weed ashes.[25] Next, weavers, who were most often men, would work the yarn into cloth on their looms (although some yarn from the west and south was exported as it was), then bring their finished fabric to brown linen markets in Belfast or Dublin, where bleachers would check the unwhitened cloth (bearing the official brown linen seal distributed by the Linen Board) for quality and send their purchases to their bleaching mills in the North.[26] In the early part of the century, linen was bleached with buttermilk and the process could take up to six weeks, but by mid-century, the incorporation of alkali solutions, such as dilute sulfuric acid, revolutionized bleaching in Ireland, shortening the time needed to whiten the fabrics. The Irish industry was the first to employ sulfuric acid, helping to advance its commercial growth and international reputation over other national manufactures.[27] Bleached cloths meeting the Linen Board's requirements would then travel to Dublin's White Linen Hall, established in 1728, for sale and exportation to England. However, by the late eighteenth century, some bleachers began to bypass the Linen Hall and sell to England directly, while Northern bleachers established their own linen halls in Belfast and Newry, eventually making Belfast the new center of linen trade by the 1780s.[28]

Although the linen manufacture was concentrated in the counties of Down, Armagh, and Antrim, the industry also relied on the mostly female labor of western and some southern counties to transform the flax plant into yarn. While those provinces to the south were mostly spinning wool for the English market, flax was increasingly incorporated into domestic industry across Ireland, especially because, as the Irish linen trade grew, flax proved more lucrative than spinning wool. Weaving linen required an almost endless supply of yarn, so while spinners were the most numerous and, as I will show, undervalued laborers in the linen industry, they were also the most crucial. The majority Protestant and Presbyterian weaving districts in the north were dependent on the labor of poor, Scots-Irish

---

[25] See *To the Right Honourable and Honourable Trustees of the Linen and Hempen Manufacture.* Containing: Roderick O'Connor, Esquire's Letter and Observations on Ashes and James Breakey's Process and Affidavit, as also his Remarks, Dublin 1783, held in Queen's University Belfast Special Collections.

[26] Brown and white linen seals would display the weaver or bleacher's name, respectively, and county of origin. In terms of imagery and design, these stamps often included a spinning wheel or the crowned harp as their insignia. The Irish Linen Centre and Museum in Lisburn, Northern Ireland exhibits several of these eighteenth-century seals.

[27] Crawford, *Impact*, p. 31.   [28] Collins, *From Flax to Fabric*, p. 18.

women as well as the Catholic spinning districts in the west of Ireland, especially west Ulster and north Connaught, and even some southern counties. Small profits earned from the sale of flax yarn were often a poor rural, tenant family's main source of income—the means to pay rent to Anglo-Irish landlords.[29] Some areas followed a putting out system, in which landlords or middle-men would buy raw flax materials to distribute to female laborers in return for wages.[30] According to W. H. Crawford, the linen industry was only able to expand at the impressive speed it did in the 1730s and 1740s because of increased yarn supply from counties like Roscommon and Sligo.[31] Irish yarn was uniformly the cheapest on the market and even became a kind of currency in Ireland, used for purchasing power and bartering.

Of course, eighteenth-century linen was not an exclusively Irish product: after all, many of the Ulster farmers and merchants had initially learned their trade from the Dutch. What is more, many of the ideas discussed in this chapter with regard to the material and cultural ramifications of linen manufacture are applicable to Scotland, especially because many weavers and businessmen in the north of Ireland were of Scottish descent. Yet, by the mid-eighteenth century, Irish linen had surpassed the Scottish industry in growth, quality, circulation, and reputation, doubling the Scottish output by the late eighteenth century.[32] Flax grown in Ireland had a different feel to the Scottish, its fibers smoother and finer, and therefore farmers and merchants believed that flax was better suited to Irish soil than Scottish.[33] In fact, as the industry grew, Ireland had to import flax seed less frequently, making the linen production more self-sufficient in Ireland from farm to market.[34] Another factor that catalyzed Irish linen's fast success had to do with bleaching techniques. By the late eighteenth century, many linen drapers became bleachers, increasing the number of bleach mills in the country, while the incorporation of alkali solutions improved the white bleaching stage of the manufacture. Thus, Irish linens quickly earned a better reputation than the Scottish in terms of refinement and execution: simply put, Irish linens were considered finer and whiter, while Scottish linens were more often labeled as 'coarse.'[35]

Specialized Irish linens were used to make sailcloth for the British navy throughout the eighteenth century, and Irish linen was regularly exported to the American colonies, sometimes Jamaica. In fact, 20 percent of Irish linens exported to England were re-exported to North America, especially New York and Pennsylvania, where advertisements for 'Irish Linens' in the *Pennsylvania Gazette*,

---

[29] Gray, *Spinning the Threads*, pp. 42–5.   [30] Gray, *Spinning the Threads*, p. 118.
[31] Crawford, *Impact*, p. 87.   [32] Gray, *Spinning the Threads*, p. 282.
[33] (Anon.), *A View of the Present State of Ireland* (London: Faulder, 1780), p. 12.
[34] Anne McKernan, 'War, Gender, and Industrial Innovation: Recruiting Women Weavers in Early Nineteenth Century Ireland.' *Journal of Social History* 28.1 (1994): pp. 110–11.
[35] Gray, *Spinning the Threads*, p. 136.

for example, evince the national product's strong reputation.[36] As linen merchant and expert Robert Stephenson wrote in 1784, 'Americans seek for and prefer our linens.'[37] By the Georgian period in the United Kingdom, Irish linen more than any other was desired as bedding in England.[38] As part of the growing refinement and expertise of Irish linen makers, some merchants in Ulster specialized in expensive damask or handwoven patterned linens: a Mr Coulson of Lisburn was the damask manufacturer for Queen Charlotte, wife to George III, and the then Prince of Wales, George IV.[39] The Coulsons continued to manufacture damasks for the royals up through William III's reign.[40]

As Swift's *Proposal for the Universal Use of Irish Manufacture* would suggest, the material reality of widespread linen production offered a means of discursively asserting Ireland's economic rights. In 1754, Robert Stephenson, who later became the Linen Board's official Inspector General and traveled all over the country observing the industry, wrote the following: 'the Linen Merchants and all Traders in this Kingdom...have severely experienced the general Neglect shewn to our Trade by the Board of Admiralty, which not only check our Exports and Imports, and oppress the Merchant.'[41] Stephenson often associates patriotic pride with Irish linen, discussing the 'high Estimation of Irish flax for Ages past' and asserting 'there is no Part of the World where superior Flax is raised.'[42] In 1784, he published a long tract rejecting the observations of John Arbuthnot, who had replaced Stephenson as Inspector for the Linen Board, on the grounds that he was English and not Irish, much like the Drapier regarded William Wood: a 'stranger to our climate, lands, people, employment, and abilities.'[43]

As linen became Ireland's main industry, it buttressed the discourse on economic nationalism throughout the eighteenth century, much like Hibernia in Chapter 1. In fact, Irish linen also provided the very paper on which economic treatises by Swift and Stephenson were written. Eighteenth-century paper was

---

[36] Gray, *Spinning the Threads*, p. 24.

[37] Robert Stephenson, *Observations on the Present State of the Linen Trade of Ireland: in a series of letters addressed to the Right Honourable trustees of the Linen Manufacture. In which the Reports, Libel, and British Examination of Mr John Arbuthnot, Inspector General of Leinster, Munster, and Connaught, are considered and refuted* (Dublin, 1784), p. 34.

[38] Sara Pennell, 'Making the Bed in Later Stuart and Georgian England' in *Selling Textiles in the Long Eighteenth Century: Comparative Perspectives from Western Europe*, ed. Jon Stobart and B. Blondé (London: Palgrave Macmillan, 2014), p. 31.

[39] Collins, *From Flax to Fabric*, p. 28. When damask linen was popular in the late eighteenth century, craftsmen like Coulson would make and distribute pattern books each season, and customers would visit the various draperies to view these books. See Ada K. Longfield, 'Notes on the Linen and Cotton Printing Industry in Northern Ireland in the Eighteenth Century.' *Belfast Natural History and Philosophy Society* 4.2 (1950–5): p. 57.

[40] 'Flax to Fabric: the Story of Irish Linen.' Permanent Exhibit, Irish Linen Centre and Lisburn Museum, Lisburn Northern Ireland.

[41] Robert Stephenson. 'Considerations on the Present State of the Linen Manufacture, Humbly Addressed to the Trustees of the Linen Board, 1754.' *An Inquiry into the State and Progress of the Linen Manufacture in Ireland* (Dublin: Powell, 1757), p. 207.

[42] Stephenson, *Observations*, pp. xi, 7.   [43] Stephenson, *Observations*, pp. xi, 7.

made from linen rags, a fact that, James Ward argues, provided writers the material means of rhetorical play on the page. Swift, for example, utilized paper's origins in linen to both associate the act of writing for Ireland with the patriotic purchase of Irish manufactures, as in *A Universal Use for Irish Manufacture*, and also to titillate readers with the bawdy link between bed clothes and printed paper, as in his *Journal to Stella*.[44]

With the rise of the Dublin Volunteers and the Free Trade movement, Irish linen gained even greater currency as an emblematic sign of patriotic support and pride. Luxury items of Irish workmanship like damask linens were a means of signifying a family's support of Free Trade, eventually granted in 1780. A respectable household was expected to possess and maintain domestic linens: table linen, in particular, should be Irish, and properly made, laundered, and stored.[45] Some aristocratic Anglo-Irish patriots publicly lauded Irish linen, such as the Countess of Moira who, in 1770, held a fancy dress ball to encourage the linen industry, attended by six hundred of the country's gentry.[46] Toward the end of 1773, the Countess even conducted her own personal experiments with flax and presented them to the Royal Dublin Society so as to, in her own words, be of 'service to Ireland, by opening a Door to a greater Consumption of Home Manufactures, and a farther Employment for the Indigent of this Kingdom.'[47] In 1809, one W. Steel Dickson published an article in the Belfast magazine arguing that if Anglo-Irish ladies encouraged their tenants' industriousness and bought their linen craftwork, they would 'add dignity to their titles.'[48] Consumerism of Irish goods could generate patriotic fervor and societal respect at the same time that the manufacture of such goods endorsed the Anglo-Irish elite's reign over their Irish tenants.

As any trip to an Irish tourist shop will demonstrate, Irish linen remains a desired commodity today, but by the mid-nineteenth century, the industry's growth tapered, particularly for laborers in the south of Ireland. The mechanization of flax dressing in the 1830s further concentrated the linen manufacture in the North, ending the domestic yarn-making industry and, as some argued, inadvertently contributing to further poverty in the rest of the country.[49] Young women in the north of Ireland who would have dressed and spun flax at home were forced to migrate to cities like Lisburn or Belfast to work in factories, like Barbour's water-powered Hilden Mills near Lisburn, which employed three hundred

[44] James Ward, 'Pamphlets into Rags: Swift on Paper' in *Reading Swift: Papers from the Sixth Munster Symposium on Jonathan Swift*, ed. Kirsten Juhas, Hermann J. Real, and Sandra Simon (Munich: Wilhelm Fink, 2013), pp. 341, 343, 349.

[45] Toby Barnard, *Improving Ireland? Projectors, Prophets, and Profiteers 1641–1786* (Dublin: Four Courts Press, 2008), p. 260.

[46] See *Dictionary of National Biography*, s.v. Countess of Moira.

[47] *Proceedings of the Dublin Society* 10 (Dublin: S. Powell: 1773–4), 27 January 1774, p. 326.

[48] Qtd. in Wakefield, *An Account of Ireland*, vol. 1, p. 688.

[49] Collins, *From Flax to Fabric*, p. 21.

workers in 1823.[50] Barbour's Flax Thread of Lisburn grew into an internationally streamlined business, with another factory in Patterson, NJ, and shops in New York, London, Paris, Hamburg, Sydney, Milan, and many other capital cities.[51] The historical pattern of an Irish industry dependent on romanticized, domestic female labor finds a later iteration in Victorian Ireland's lace making and home textile manufactures. Post-Famine relief projects established for the poor rural Irish and stimulated by Ascendancy philanthropists developed into a handmade lace business intended for the English urban marketplace.[52] Moreover, the Arts and Crafts Movement of the late nineteenth century celebrated textiles and embroidery handmade by rural Irish women, while Victorian elites like Lady Aberdeen followed the tactics of Lady Moira and supported the Irish home industries with balls, parties, and sponsored exhibitions that displayed the fashions of handmade Irish lace and dress.[53]

2.2   Improvement: Linen and Colonial Ideology

The remaining pages of this chapter turn from a traditional history of linen to flax's material semiotics, examining, in detail, how transforming a bundle of flax into linen cloth impacted eighteenth-century ways of thinking and writing about Irish character. The natural starting point for this query is the most commonly discussed objective among the Irish linen manufacturers: 'improvement.' Although improvement existed as a common term in the English language long before the linen manufacture took root in Ireland, the period's fixation on constantly improving linen points to the ways in which its manufacture furnished an ideological framework for how to improve Irish character itself. By applying a new materialist approach that focuses on the material origins of human language and semiotics, it becomes clear that the discourse on how linen should be handled gave rise to ideas about how the Irish people should be handled as well. Of course, 'improvement' is an obvious, perfectly justifiable term to use in relation to industry and commerce, but in Ireland, it directly connects to the nation's history of violent colonial conflict over land.

---

[50] 'Flax to Fabric,' exhibit.

[51] Barbour's Prize Needlework Series. A Treatise on Lace Making, Embroidery, and Needlework with Irish Flax Threads (Barbour, 1894).

[52] See Janice Helland, 'Caprices of Fashion: Handmade Lace in Ireland 1883–1907.' Textile History 39.2 (2008): pp. 193–222, and '"A Delightful Change of Fashion": Fair Trade, Cottage Craft and Tweed in Late Nineteenth-Century Ireland.' Canadian Journal of Irish Studies 36.2 (2010): pp. 34–55. See also Mary Burke, 'The Cottage, the Castle, and the Couture Cloak: "Traditional" Irish Fabrics and "Modern" Irish America, 1952–1969.' Journal of Design History 31.4 (2018): pp. 364–82.

[53] See Janice Helland, British and Irish Home Arts and Industries, 1880–1914: Marketing Craft, Making Fashion (Dublin: Irish Academic Press, 2007).

A few examples can demonstrate the ubiquity of improvement in eighteenth-century discourses on Irish linen. In 1673, Sir William Temple said that Ireland's natural resources, including good soil and capable female workers, 'may certainly be advanced and improved into a great Manufacture of Linen' to serve the purpose of 'draw[ing] much of the Money which goes from England to [France and Holland]…into the Hands of His Majesty's Subjects of Ireland, without crossing any interest of Trade in England.'[54] Here, Temple suggests that improving linen will result in profit for England, and so England should make use of, or improve upon, Ireland's natural resources. In 1705, Crommelin published his essay *An Essay Towards the Improving of the Hempen and Flaxen Manufactures in the Kingdom of Ireland* to 'rectifie the mistakes which the people of this Kingdom have hitherto lain under in relation to those [linen] Trades.'[55] A century later in 1774, writing on behalf of Ireland rather than England, Lady Moira reported to the Royal Dublin Society that 'great Improvements may easily be made in this Branch of [Flax] Manufacture; its Utility can only appear by farther Trials,' referring to a special flax yarn she manufactured to answer the purposes of cotton.[56] David Ramsay, author of *The Weaver and Housewife's Pocket-Book* (1750), hopes his 'little book' may help 'every Houswife' to 'contribute to the Improvement of our Linen Trade,' emphasizing the female individual's role in the national economic project.[57]

Our modern use of improvement as 'making better' came into the English language in the seventeenth century through a very particular historical context involving monetary profit and the enclosure of land. From the fifteenth to nineteenth centuries, 'improvement' could either mean to make use of something for financial gain (by the seventeenth century, this definition simply became profit) *or* a piece of land made profitable by enclosure and cultivation.[58] The second definition indicates a historical connection between improvement and the Enclosure Acts—a series of fifteenth-to-eighteenth-century laws that confiscated land previously considered common or public for entitled ownership and thereby contributed to a landless laboring class in England. In the seventeenth century, the term 'improvement' moved beyond its rootedness in the land through analogy, but as Helen O'Connell explains, there has always been a 'complex underlying connection between improvement and profit.'[59] In the seventeenth and eighteenth centuries, the term was most commonly applied to technological advancement, as the

[54] Temple, 'Essay,' pp. 114–15.
[55] Samuel-Louis Crommelin, *An Essay Towards the Improving of the Hempen and Flaxen Manufactures in the Kingdom of Ireland* (Dublin: R. Owen, 1734) [originally printed Dublin, 1705], pp. 1–2.
[56] *Proceedings of the Dublin Society*, 4 January 1774, p. 324.
[57] David Ramsay, *The Weaver and Housewife's Pocket Book, containing the Rules for the right Making of Linen Cloth* (Edinburgh: Ramsay, 1750), p. vi.
[58] *Oxford English Dictionary*, s.v. 'improvement' (n.).
[59] Helen O'Connell, *Ireland and the Fiction of Improvement* (Oxford: Oxford UP, 2006), p. 3.

focus shifted from the local to the wider commercial market. 'Improvement' discourse in the eighteenth century typically sought to pave the way for modernization, and the words of Temple, Crommelin, and Lady Moira quoted above clearly correspond to this standard arc of modernizing via technological improvement.[60]

Arthur Young's *Tour in Ireland, 1776–1779* negatively correlates industry, land, and economic improvement with native Irish character. Damning the graziers in Ireland, he writes that they 'pass nine tenths of the year without any exertion of industry' and claims 'works of improvement would be mortifying to their sloth.'[61] Following Young, English statistician and agriculturalist Edward Wakefield makes the rather ironic argument that the Irish people need outside (i.e., English and Anglo-Irish) inducement to improve their industry: 'A spinner, to become industrious, must be presented with a wheel.'[62] This indicates, he argues, 'something very singular in the Irish character; and one is almost inclined to believe that it is deficient in energy.'[63] In these latter two examples, there is a quick, perhaps unconscious slippage between improving the material conditions of Ireland— farming, industry—and changing the perceived core characteristics of the Irish people. For Young and Wakefield, the discussion of improving Irish linen immediately invokes the (British) project of improving Irish character at large. In these examples by Young and Wakefield, improvement becomes a loaded term perniciously linked with elitist characterizations of the poor Irish as backward, slothful, and unable to help themselves.

Young and Wakefield's dual conversation about improving industry and simultaneously disciplining the Irish nation descends from an early modern history in which improving Ireland meant controlling Irish land and Irish character. From the sixteenth century, the mission of improving Irish husbandry justified colonization. As indicated by Spenser's *View of the Present State of Ireland* (1596), British culture in the sixteenth century recast Ireland as a savage people and land in need of cultivation (i.e., English influence and improvement). Spenser's Irenius, for example, insists that Catholics in Ireland must first be taught husbandry, the 'enemy to war' and the 'nurse of thrift and the daughter of industry and labor,' so as to 'increase' the 'good conditions' of the Irish soil.[64] Here, 'increase'—linked to an earlier definition of improve as growth—implies the cultivation of Irish land for English dominion and control, revealing the powerful, imperial implications of apparently innocuous suggestions for economic development. As Toby Barnard's research has shown, many new Protestant landholders in seventeenth-century

---

[60] O'Connell, *Ireland and the Fiction of Improvement*, p. 3.

[61] Arthur Young, *A Tour in Ireland*, 2 vols, ed. Arthur Wollaston Hutton (London: G. Bell & Sons, 1892), vol. 2, p. 30.

[62] Wakefield, *An Account of Ireland*, vol. 1, p. 698.

[63] Wakefield, *An Account of Ireland*, vol. 1, p. 698.

[64] Edmund Spenser, *A View of the Present State of Ireland*, ed. W. L. Renwick (Oxford: Clarendon, 1970), pp. 157–8.

Ireland became so-called 'improvers' of Irish land, cartography, husbandry, and industry—a mission understood as benevolent and so pervasive as to be rarely challenged.[65]

The term improvement also connects to counter-revolutionary literature in the early nineteenth century. Not long after Young's *Tour*, the Rebellion of 1798 engendered a reactionary genre of Irish "improving fiction": didactic, realistic prose that offered peasants and landowners practical schemes for improving post-Union Ireland's squalid conditions.[66] According to Helen O'Connell, the project of improvement in early nineteenth-century Ireland sought to curb the excess and hedonism associated with the Irish peasantry and those involved in 1798.[67] O'Connell's argument is also applicable to discourses around linen a century earlier: interest in developing Ireland's industry spiked around the time of the Williamite War, when the failure of Jacobite Catholic forces supporting James II to rebel against William's rule solidified British, Protestant control in Ireland in 1691. Thus, when the British and Protestant elite expelled the leading Gaelic Irish forces and intensified the penal laws, these measures also indirectly encouraged a Protestant-controlled linen industry that could improve flax and, perhaps, the native Irish who remained.

This association between improving the linen manufacture and anti-revolutionary strategy becomes starkly clear in a 1756 letter Robert Stephenson wrote to the Linen Board. He writes to petition more funds for the industry that, he argues, will 'effectually restrain the Working People from forming themselves into Combinations, which always precede Idleness and Rioting.'[68] Stephenson places the increase of a linen industry workforce in explicit, antipodal opposition to rebellious behavior in Ireland, along with that stereotype of the odious 'idle' Irish character. What's more, in his 1765 report to the Linen Board, Stephenson implies that establishing charter schools to teach the trades of spinning, weaving, and other linen manufactures in Catholic counties like Kerry will result in greater religious conversion rates, and thus a more Protestant Ireland. He writes that the trade schools 'will induce the lower class to get into the Linen Manufacture, as by this means the Children are prepared to be more useful to Masters and Mistress's, and are easily completed in those Branches of Business, which lay a foundation for establishing Colonies of Protestants, supported by a Staple Manufacture.'[69] Here, Stephenson spells out the imperial connotations of 'improving' the linen manufacture, underscoring the proselytizing, theocratic, and Anglicizing impulse behind spreading the trade across southern Ireland.

---

[65] Barnard, *Improving*, p. 40.   [66] O'Connell, *Ireland and the Fiction of Improvement*, p. 1.

[67] O'Connell, *Ireland and the Fiction of Improvement*, p. 6.

[68] Robert Stephenson, 'A Letter to the Right Honourable and Honourable the Trustees of the Linen Manufacture' (Dublin: James Hunter, 1759), p. 4.

[69] Stephenson, *Observations*, p. 99.

The etymological, religious, and territorial contexts in Young, Wakefield, and Stephenson demonstrate the connections between linen and a more sinister version of 'improvement' that serviced colonial ideology. The very process of industriously manufacturing linen furnished these writers with ideas about cultivating and perhaps 'conquering' Irish materiality. After all, the steps of the manufacturing process, as they improved, turned the coarse conditions of the Irish land into a flax crop that became a luxurious, profitable commodity for Britain. The transformation of land into profit could then proffer British and Anglo-Irish landholding thinkers the idea that Irish people might also be improved toward England's benefit as well, if they diligently applied themselves to linen-making work.

2.3   From Improving Fine Flax to a Feminized Irish Nation

A woman's hands, more than any other part of the linen manufacture, focused the attention of those seeking to improve Irish linen. According to writers, industrialists, and businessmen, the way to improve linen was to improve the yarn, and the way to improve yarn was to make it finer. Fine yarn—meaning thin, smooth, and delicate—came to evidence refined technique in Irish craftswomen and thereby signify improved industry and domesticity in the Irish people at large. In the same way improving linen extended to improving Ireland, the fineness of the flax plant or thread facilitated an increasing association of Irish character with femininity in that flax's fineness and delicacy easily extended to the Irish flax dressers who made it fine in the first place. Thus, an acutely biological, molecular reading of flax can deepen our understanding of the material origins of Irish character's gendering in the eighteenth century.

Most discourses on flax in the eighteenth century interchange the figurative meaning of fine—as of a superior quality—with the more literal, material meaning of small or thin. Edward Wakefield emphasizes the importance of fine yarn in his *Account of Ireland*: 'The quality of the linen depends on the fineness of the yarn'—the finer and thinner the yarn, the better (and more profitable) the linen.[70] Another publication, also reprinted by the Dublin Society, *Some Considerations on the Improvement of the Linen Manufacture in Ireland*, probably by Robert Ross, likewise insists a finer flax crop will 'save the Spinner a good deal of Trouble [and] occasion the Thread to take the Twist readily...and makes the Linen whiten evenly without Stripes or Rows.'[71] In other words, by making the flax finer, both

---

[70] Wakefield, *An Account of Ireland*, vol. 1, p. 688.
[71] Robert Ross, *Some Considerations on the Improvement of the Linen Manufacture in Ireland, Particularly with Relation to the Raising and Dressing of Flax and Flax-Seed* (Dublin: printed by R. Reilly, 1735), p. 124.

farmer and spinner will help improve the entire linen manufacture at large. Irish linen manufacturer Robert Stephenson expresses a similar fixation with flax's inherent fineness, writing: 'Irish flax, in every Degree of Operation, is remarkable for its Silkiness and kindly manner of working'—referring to both the texture of the crop and its gentle handling.[72] Both Ross and Stephenson also suggest agency, or cooperation, in the flax fiber: its 'kindly manner of working.'

From a new materialist perspective, the production of high-quality linen is contingent on the *collective intra-action* between flax fiber, hands, and spinning wheel. Fine, thin yarn is achieved when a spinner, having dressed her flax and isolated the fibers, feeds them into the spinning wheel, twisting the flax fibers between her (often moistened) forefinger, which creates resistance against the spinning wheel's pull so that there are multiple rotations happening at once, on the wheel and in the hands, in opposite directions. As an organism, flax's DNA makes it particularly responsive to this twisting motion. The pectic substances in flax afford a viscosity and gel-like property that makes it pliable as it enters the spinner's hands.[73] Biologists Sharma and Sumere explain that flax cellulose is one of the most 'longitudinally ordered forms,' meaning it is particularly conducive to fineness in comparison with other plant fibers or wool, for example.[74]

Almost all writers on the industry, including Stephenson, Wakefield, and the Dublin Society, emphasize the need for gentle, female hands in making fine flax yarn—an idea that can be traced back to William Temple's 1673 essay on Irish linen in his *Miscellanea*. The idle Irish character so harshly described by Arthur Young was, for Temple, an opportunity to improve Ireland through female hands: 'Besides no Women are apter to spin well than the Irish, who laboring little in any kind with their Hands, have their Fingers more supple and soft than other Women of the poorer condition among us, and this may certainly be advanced and improved.'[75] Classifying native Irish women as a natural resource, Temple's prejudiced and, indeed, sexist outlook suggests English industry can harness and rechannel the defective disposition of the lazy native Irish character, who 'labor so little,' by taking advantage of the supple, unworked hands of Irish women. For two hundred years, manufacturers would echo Temple's perception of good linen as rooted in soft, female hands. Ross, for example, argued that flax dressing and spinning requires the 'Gentleness of Hand [of] a weak Girl.'[76] Likewise, Wakefield insists that fine yarn cannot be achieved by a mill: 'female labour has certainly the advantage over machinery, as the yarn produced by the former may attain to a degree of fineness which cannot be given to the latter.'[77] Such intricate work also involves patience, stillness, and in Wakefield's eyes, 'diligence'—qualities associated

---

[72] Stephenson, 'Considerations,' p. 10.
[73] H. S. Shekhar Sharma and C. F. van Sumere, *The Biology and Processing of Flax* (Belfast: M. Publications, 1992), p. 12.
[74] Sharma and Sumere, *Biology and Processing*, p. 30.   [75] Temple, 'Essay,' p. 114.
[76] Ross, *Some Considerations*, p. 11.   [77] Wakefield, *An Account of Ireland*, vol. 1, p. 686.

with women in the eighteenth century and, at the same time, generated as feminine through the delicate, microscopic craftwork.[78]

The gendered values emphasized by Temple, Ross, and Wakefield are reflective of a wider, nascent British commercial phenomenon in which, Kate Smith and Claire Walsh have shown, shopping became an active, sensual experience associated with touch.[79] This is, in part, why writers emphasized that the finer the flax thread the better, as thin, high thread counts ultimately yielded a higher gross in market thanks to the tactility associated with luxury and British consumerism. Similarly, Chloe Wigston Smith and Serena Dyer emphasize British shoppers' increasing 'material literacy', or proficiency in detecting high-quality, female handiwork in domestic and foreign textiles—handiwork that Wigston Smith has elsewhere shown was sexualized, especially in the novel.[80] It follows then, that the English writers quoted above would view Irish female hands as a valuable resource that could facilitate a rising commercial value for Irish linen predicated on tactile, shopping pleasure.

Despite the rhetorical feminization of flax through emphasis on dexterous female hands, biology tells us it is not so much the texture, size, or gendering of the hands but the interaction of plant molecules and moistened fingertips that results in fine thread. Flax fibers respond to water so that, when moistened, the cellulose molecules in flax freely move, meaning the hydrated flax can more readily lend itself to being stretched out into thin thread, which is why women spinning flax often wetted their hands with spit or a nearby bowl of water as they handled the flax fibers. The dampening of the fibers makes them more ductile, viscous, and therefore thinner and longer as they enter spinning wheel's motion.

Although the science behind fine flax threads emphasizes the mutual collaboration between water, hand, and flax, eighteenth-century publications fetishized fine yarn as the product of the government's improvement efforts, visible in Irish women's deft, delicate hands. In 1809, a publication celebrating a spinner from Castlereach, County Down, named Anne M'Quillin praises her 'superfine yarn'— the 'extraordinary' product of Irish women's 'ingenuity.'[81] The magazine's report

---

[78] Wakefield, An Account of Ireland, vol. 1, p. 684. In Desire and Domestic Fiction (Oxford: Oxford UP, 1987), Nancy Armstrong shows how conduct books construct the idea of the new modern subject as a supervisory, diligent, domestic woman. The new modern middle-class femininity, she argues, is a combination of invisibility and vigilance, qualities the labor of the spinning wheel would also seem to inculcate as feminine, even though that work was more working class than middle class. Nevertheless, middle-class women in Ireland also spun flax—more as a pastime than a means or earning wages.

[79] See Kate Smith, Material Goods, Moving Hands: Perceiving Production in England, 1700–1830 (Manchester: Manchester UP, 2014) and Claire Walsh, 'Shop Design and the Display of Goods in Eighteenth-Century London.' Journal of Design History 8.3 (1995): pp. 157–76.

[80] See Serena Dyer and Chloe Wigston Smith, eds, Material Literacy in Eighteenth-Century Britain: A Nation of Makers (London: Bloomsbury, 2020) and Chloe Wigston Smith, Women, Work, and Clothes in the Eighteenth-Century Novel (Cambridge: Cambridge UP, 2013).

[81] Qtd. in Wakefield, An Account of Ireland, vol. 1, p. 686.

explains that some may be 'incapable of estimating the fineness of Anne's yarn'—suggesting it is so thin as to be unfathomable, perhaps even invisible.[82] Anne's yarn reaches one hundred miles per sixty hanks compared to German spinning of the same weight, which reaches only twenty-three miles.[83] M'Quillin's yarn was so fine—in both size and quality—that it was used to make lace for Lady Dufferin, 'far superior to any thing of the kind which was ever seen in this country.'[84] This account presents M'Quillin and her fine thread as objects of national pride, perhaps even figuring M'Quillin as a technological, national advancement herself. But there is a more cynical reading to be gleaned in the praise of Anne M'Quillin. Thanks to orchestrated efforts to improve and expand Ireland's linen industry, patronized by the likes of her landlady, Lady Dufferin, the young worker has 'improved' and mastered her skill with almost mechanized precision. However, according to the biology of viscous flax discussed above, the crop is not mastered as such, but rather, *yields*—to the water, to the hand, to the whole linen-making process. Thus, a new materialist reading that incorporates flax's biological nature into this picture of Irish character demonstrates how flax was deployed as a micro-material agent serving a wider imperial project. After all, Anne M'Quillin, like the flax plant, had to actively yield to that imperial apparatus of improvement for it to work.

Flax, by virtue of its unique biological makeup and proclivity for fineness, contributed to a material-semiotic process that reframed the native Irish character as submissive, cooperative, and crucially, feminine—rather than the Gaelic aggressors of the early modern period, whose menacing presence and violence symbolically justified English oppression. Although technically speaking a worker's hands need not be female or 'gentle' to make fine flax thread, keeping flax in the hands of so-called gentle yet industrious and 'improving' Irish women held sociocultural advantages for eighteenth-century British ideology. The incorporation of a woman's supposedly gentle hands as a necessary organ of the linen manufacture creates a template that naturalizes the incorporation of a new (supposedly) docile, feminized Irish character into an imperial economy. As such, Stephenson's previously quoted words about flax's 'kindly manner of working' and Ross's discussion of flax 'taking the twist readily' perhaps unconsciously say the same of the new Irish character—that it is compliant and amenable, that it takes to the industrial process 'kindly,' without resistance.

When circulating in Britain, therefore, handmade Irish linen—the product of fine thread spun by docile, dexterous female fingers in Irish cottages—afforded material evidence that helped to impress this gendered, paternalistic model of

---

[82] Wakefield, *An Account of Ireland*, vol. 1, p. 687.

[83] One hank is twelve cuts, and one cut is 300 yards, meaning one hank is 3,600 yards of thread (Collins, *From Flax to Fabric*, p. 16).

[84] Wakefield, *An Account of Ireland*, vol. 1, p. 688.

English–Irish relations where Ireland is a woman in need of British and Anglo-Irish patronage (and consumerism). As early as 1735, Robert Ross's *Some Considerations on the Improvement of the Linen Manufacture* presents the manufacture of linen as a 'Relief' project for Ireland, as 'No nation ever stood in greater need of assistance.'[85] Ross goes on to celebrate how the linen manufacture 'affords great employment to the People, especially to weak women,' and he congratulates the north of Ireland, where Irish daughters who were once 'a burthen to the poor Farmer' have become, through the 'Spinning Trade,' a 'treasure to him and the country.'[86] In turn, the superfine thread that became the bedrock of improving the linen industry could simultaneously offer English buyers both the experience of handmade luxury and the gratification of their national charity—the false comfort of providing for Ireland's livelihood articulated through the physical, tactile comfort of fine, soft bed dressings.[87]

Whereas porous human hands—feminine or not—were useful for making flax fibers fine, the feminine image of handmade flax thread was absolutely essential in symbolic and ideological terms for the successful orchestration of a new British imperial machine in Ireland. The fixation on and fetishization of (super)fine spinning could materially minimize Ireland as a kingdom and a threat, potentially thin out its nationalist danger from a century before into near invisibility. This feminized, unthreatening new industrial Irish character found symbolic resonances in the artwork and literature of the eighteenth century. One of the most well-known texts on Irish linen is William Hincks's *The Linen Industry*, twelve plates depicting and describing the stages of the Ulster linen industry, taken from his drawings during time spent in the linen counties of Tyrone, Armagh, Antrim, and Down, and published in London in 1783. Almost every plate in the series features a beautiful, idealized, pastoral woman at its center (see Figures 2.1–2.3).[88]

This idyllic sylph-like trope serves to romanticize the industrial labor of a new, diligent Irish (male) subject, usually positioned in the background of the scene, like the men working with a new scutching mill in Plate V (Figure 2.1) or the

---

[85] Ross, *Some Considerations*, p. 2.   [86] Ross, *Some Considerations*, p. 24.

[87] Touch was an important aspect of eighteenth-century Britain's shopping culture. Kate Smith argues that the interaction with texture constituted 'evidence of production' and therefore caused the shopper to consider the ways an item had been manufactured, which was a crucial mediation in the shopping process. See Smith, *Material Goods*, p. 18.

[88] William Hincks, a self-taught artist born in Waterford, completed twelve drawings documenting the steps of the linen industry while still in Ireland. His drawings are 'from the life' in the Linen Triangle, counties of Down, Armagh, and Antrim. He converted the drawings to engravings in stipple and had them published in London in 1783, following his immigration to England. No official commission for the prints is known but Hincks does dedicate the plates to various members of the Anglo-Irish gentry in the North of Ireland, such as Randal William McDonell, Earl of Antrim (Plate IV), Earl of Hillsborough (Plate V), Early of Moira (Plate VI), and Lord Bangor (Plate IX), perhaps seeking patronage. They were later published by printer Robert Pollard, London, in 1791. Hincks is known for a number of other engravings, after his drawings, including portraits and *Hibernia attended by her Brave Volunteers, Exhibiting her Commercial Freedom*, discussed in Chapter 1 (Figure 1.6). He died in London in 1797.

Figure 2.1 William Hincks, 'This Plate representing a Perspective View of a Scutch Mill, with the Method of Breaking the Flax with grooved Rollers, and Scutching it with Blades fixt on a shaft, both turn'd by the main Wheel. Great Improvements in the Method of Breaking and Scutching of Flax', Plate V, *The Irish Linen Industry*, 1783, paper print, etching and stipple. Reproduced from the original held by the Department of Special Collections of the Hesburgh Libraries of the University of Notre Dame.

bleach mills of Plate IX (Figure 2.2). Hincks's plate on yarn making is, notably, an all-female idealized domestic scene: a visual imprint capturing that pointed gendering of the rural Irish (Figure 2.3).

Hinck's visual texts link to fictions and other prints that use linen to characterize Ireland as a woman. An ironic pamphlet supporting the bounty on Irish linen by Anglo-Irish author William Chaigneau, for example, personifies industry itself as an enchanting female character: 'Linen gave rise to industry in Ireland— Industry soon shewed her alluring charms and diffused her baneful influence over the land...and consequently enrich[ed] England by an addition of some millions of useful and faithful subjects.'[89] Chaigneau allegorically invokes the

---

[89] William Chaigneau, 'Three Letters to the Fool,' in *History of Jack Connor*, 2nd edition (Dublin: Hulton Bradley, 1766), p. 356.

Figure 2.2 William Hincks. 'This Plate representing a complete Perspective
View of all the machinery of a Bleach Mill, upon the Newest and Most approved
Constructions, Consisting of the Wash Mill, Rubbing Boards moved by a Crank,
and Beetling Engine for Glazing the Cloth, with a view of the Boiling House,' Plate IX,
The Irish Linen Industry, 1783, paper print, etching and stipple. Reproduced from
the original held by the Department of Special Collections of the Hesburgh
Libraries of the University of Notre Dame.

ideological significations of flax: that the new Irish subject born of the linen manufacture is industrious, 'useful' to England, and significantly, female. Thus, the
Irish women who produce superfine, luxurious thread naturalize the eighteenth-
century model of Anglo-Irish relations discussed in Chapter 1, where Ireland/
Hibernia is the smaller, feminine kingdom that works to serve the Crown. This is
nowhere more apparent than in the political cartoon *Suitors to Hibernia on her
having a Free Trade* (1780) (see Figure 2.4). In this satiric print, published by
J. Mills in London, Ireland is the standard seated Hibernia character, discussed in
the previous chapter, who identifies herself as the 'wife to John Bull' and greets
four male suitors/tradesmen representing France, Spain, Holland, and Portugal.
Significantly, a roll of linen lies in the foreground, as the four suitors offer gold,
herring, wine, and other goods in exchange for some of Hibernia's linen—none of
these men, however, it is implied, will offer what her husband England can. The
cartoon simplifies and affirms a material fact: linen's signifying role in the

Figure 2.3 William Hincks, 'Representing Spinning, Reeling with the Clock Reel, and Boiling the Yarn,' Plate VI, *The Irish Linen Industry*, 1783, paper print, etching and stipple. Reproduced from the original held by the Department of Special Collections of the Hesburgh Libraries of the University of Notre Dame.

feminization of Ireland, Anglo-Irish relations, and Irish industry, while other national types and commodities remain masculine.

Understanding flax's gendering and its rhetorical and symbolic extensions in artwork can also enhance our readings of canonical Irish texts, such as *Gulliver's Travels* (1726). As indicated in *A Proposal for the Universal Use of Irish Manufacture*, quoted at the start of this chapter, Swift was all too aware of the imperial implications of fine Irish textiles. Clement Hawes outlines how *Gulliver's Travels* applies the most conventional topoi of the eighteenth-century colonial project in order to satirize colonial modernity.[90] As he explains, 'The satiric effect of *Gulliver's Travels* depends on Swift's ironizing, literalizing, and above all, reversing the commonplace tropes of seventeenth and eighteenth-century British colonial discourse.'[91] As the four books move from the perspective of the colonizer to

[90] Clement Hawes, Introduction and 'Three Times Round the Globe: Gulliver and Colonial Discourse' in *Jonathan Swift: Gulliver's Travels and Other Writings*, ed. Clement Hawes (Boston: Houghton Mifflin, 2004), p. 4.
[91] Hawes, 'Three Times Round,' p. 439.

Figure 2.4 *Suitors to Hibernia on her having a Free Trade*, 1780, published by J. Mills, paper print, etching. © The Trustees of the British Museum.

the colonized, Swift manipulates scale to recast the hubris of the imperial project as absurd rather than natural or charitable. In books 1 and 2, in particular, linen provides the material with which Swift can effect this distortive imperial spectrum.

When Gulliver arrives in Lilliput, for example, 'Two hundred Sempstresses were employed' to make him shirts and 'Linnen for my Bed and Table, all of the strongest and coarsest kind they could get; which, however, they were forced to quilt together several Folds for the thickest was some Degrees finer than Lawn.'[92] It is not a stretch to read this scene through an Irish context, especially given Swift's earlier satire of the Irish Arachne's never-ending spinning labor. That hundreds of women must engage in intensive labor to make Gulliver (i.e., Britain) gargantuan amounts of cloth satirizes the Irish female exertion behind fine British textiles. Moreover, that the thickest, coarsest fabrics in Lilliput are finer than lawn—an ultrafine, thin linen—to Gulliver literalizes the material-semiotic thread I have been tracing: that superfine, luxurious linen in Britain is the work—both materially and symbolically—of many tiny Irish female hands. Gulliver's

---

[92] Jonathan Swift, *Gulliver's Travels* (Oxford: Oxford UP, 2005), pp. 56–7.

sensory response reframes luxury as illusion: to Gulliver the fabric is ultrafine lawn, but for the women who make it, that lawn is coarse, hard work. All these tiny seamstresses—who are almost invisible to Gulliver—visualize and, in the process, denaturalize a metaphoric ideology of Ireland as the smaller, feminized kingdom. Later, Swift seemingly invokes the typically male Irish weaving farms and bleach mills in Ulster: 'Five hundred Workmen were employed to make two Sails to my Boat...by quilting thirteen fold of their strongest Linnen together.'[93] Again, Swift satirizes Britain's seemingly endless consumption of Irish linen, which was used for British sail cloth, particularly during the Napoleonic wars.[94]

Next, when Gulliver is in Brobdingnag and becomes the colonizer's exotic pet, Glumdalclitch sews him 'seven Shirts, and some other Linnen of as fine Cloth as could be got, which indeed was coarser than Sackcloth.'[95] Swift continues to denaturalize luxury and satirize the idea of superfine linen through a tactile imperial scale, making the obsession with small thread appear ridiculous when the cloth literally cannot be made fine enough for Gulliver's/Britain's comfort. He also adds that Glumdalclitch 'constantly washed [his linen] with her own Hands,' highlighting the fetishization of female touch embedded in fine linen cloth.[96] In contrast to book 1, a correlation emerges between Gulliver's feminized, disen-franchised status in Brobdingnag, where he is handled like a sex toy among the giant women at court, and the fact that he cannot feel the luxury of their fine linen, inversing the typical association of sumptuous textiles with sexualized female worker discussed previously.[97] With each book, the size, fineness, and amount of linen available to Gulliver serve as a tactile semiotics of Swift's satire on imperial bigness. More specifically, *Gulliver's Travels* places a magnifying glass over the material foundations of a new imperial ideology on Ireland: that is, fine, luxurious linens and female handiwork. In doing so, *Gulliver's Travels* questions what pliable, fine flax helped legitimize: the seamless incorporation of a colony, or colonial subject, into an empire.

2.4 Flax Dressing (Beetling and Scutching): Fine Linen's Violent Pretext

In facilitating allegories of a feminine, passive, and domesticated Irish character, viscous, pliable flax seems to obscure, perhaps even erase, the history of Anglo-Irish violence from a century before, as poeticized in the *aisling* poetry of Chapter 1. However, a new materialist approach to flax suggests that the plant and feminine versions of Irish character were not as cooperative or docile as they

---

[93] Swift, *Gulliver's Travels*, p. 69.   [94] McKernan, 'War, Gender,' p. 109.
[95] Swift, *Gulliver's Travels*, p. 86.   [96] Swift, *Gulliver's Travels*, p. 86.
[97] See Smith, *Women, Work, and Clothes*, for more on the sexualization of the female textile worker.

appeared in Hincks's images, or in the other tracts and images referenced above. When it comes to the material intra-action of the flax plant and the female worker in the steps required immediately prior to spinning, neither the procedure nor the discourse around flax dressing could be characterized as 'fine' or docile. The methods needed to prepare flax for spinning—beetling and scutching—returned the discussion of improving linen to deep-seated, historic fears about Ireland's violent character. Yet again, a discussion of the material process of handling flax in the linen manufacture yields a deeper, inherently more complex understanding of both 'improvement,' British ideology, and the potential subversions of Irish character in connection with Irish materiality.

Beetling and scutching were inherently brutal. Beetling involved the physical beating of the retted and dried flax crop with a wooden mallet known as a 'beetle,' so as to break the plant's exterior wooden stem. Etymologically, from the seventeenth century on, beetling was defined as 'to beat in order to thresh, crush or flatten,' usually in reference to flax.[98] Then, scutching entailed holding the bundles of beetled stalks over a sharp-edged scutching board and striking them with a long, wooden blade, known as a scutch or swingle, in order to remove the woody particles from the soft fibrous materials needed for thread (see Figure 2.5 for Crommelin's drawings of scutch board and two swingles). Like 'beetle,' the verb 'scutch' entered the English language in the early seventeenth century and meant to strike or slash (sometimes slice), as well as to strike *at* someone with a stick or whip.[99] As the definitions suggest, the flax dressing was a laborious and *violent* process, requiring physical strength and destructive, potentially harmful instruments.

Although scutch mills were introduced in Ulster in the 1740s, both scutching and beetling were most often domestic tasks executed manually by women. Unlike in the previous chapter, where male violence was allegorically coded through the female body, in the case of linen, women literally and regularly engaged in the violent work of preparing flax from within the ostensibly docile space of the humble Irish home pictured in Hincks's images. What's more, women often beetled and scutched in groups, gathering in local barns with their mallets and blades to work on the flax together.[100] In the southern spinning districts and small rural farms throughout the country, female spinners performed flax dressing at home or in a local barn.[101]

The improvement discourse approached dressing of flax by focusing on the containment of violent action. A letter submitted to the Dublin Society in the 1730s, for instance, underscores the destructive nature of beetling and scutching and registers genuine alarm at Irish practices of flax dressing. As R.M., the signed author of the letter, explains, beetling and scutching are inherently dangerous, even 'pernicious,' but such destructive methods are 'eminently hurtful' in Ireland,

---

[98] *Oxford English Dictionary*, s.v. 'beetle' (v.).   [99] *Oxford English Dictionary*, s.v. 'scutch' (v.).
[100] Gray, *Spinning the Threads*, p. 116.   [101] Gray, *Spinning the Threads*, p. 145.

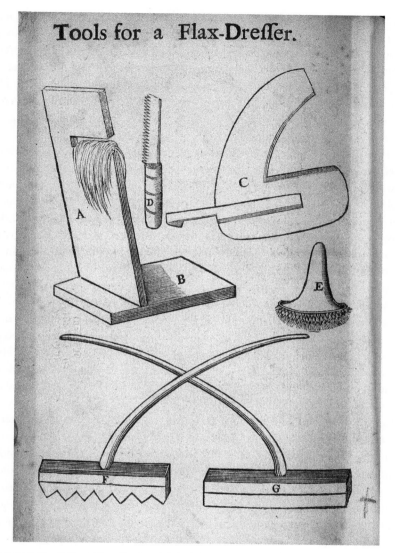

Tools for a Flax-Dreſſer.

Figure 2.5 Tools for a Flax-Dresser Including A & B, 'Scutching-Board,'
C, 'Scutching-handle...made four times larger' and D 'The Knife,' 1734, Appendix
to Samuel, Louis Crommelin, An Essay Towards the Improving of the Hempen
and Flaxen Manufactures in the Kingdom of Ireland, p. 56. Reproduced courtesy
of the National Library of Ireland.

where 'they are attended with additional disadvantages from bad instruments or
the unskillful use of them.'[102] R.M. pleads for caution and care among flax dressers but he laments that when it comes Irish scutchers, in contrast to the careful

---

[102] *Essays by the Dublin Society* (London, reprinted 1740), p. 155.

Dutch, very 'little of Caution…appears…among us.'[103] To vindicate his argument, the author describes the detailed violence of scutching with fixated horror: 'the Scutch is destructive in the highest sense…Every stroke tears the scattered Threads it meets with,' continuing, 'Some part indeed of that Destruction may be ascribed to the excessive Violence with which our Scutchers lay about them.'[104] In other words, R.M. identifies a disastrous combination: the naturally dangerous work of scutching and the seemingly innate 'excessive Violence' of the Irish flax workers.

Furthermore, R.M. seems to equate scutching with bodily assault, anthropomorphizing the resourceful plant as if human flesh: 'a few unguarded strokes…bruise the Harle [fibre].'[105] Although these strokes actually "improve" the plant toward human ends, in the hands of "unguarded" Irish peasants, scutching may point to potential human-on-human violence—a fear which R.M. then projects onto the plant itself. The central threat is not the act of scutching or even the tools used, but rather, the inner, violent Irish character that manifests in the physical practice of scutching. Crommelin's essay for improving the linen manufacture also described the Irish manner of preparing Flax as 'extremely pernicious and ruinous,' the 'first' reason being that the steps are 'manag'd by Women altogether ignorant' who 'over-labour' the flax.[106] Finally, Samuel Martin Stephenson, likely a relative of Linen Board Inspector Robert Stephenson, expresses his own concern over the violence of these manual labors, and he calls for improved beetling machinery, criticizing the 'expense, tediousness, and painfulness of this [beetling] operation.'[107] Even though the linen industry had ostensibly tamed and domesticated the Irish character through the cultivation of fine thread, it would also seem its origins in flax's natural, grown state simultaneously resurrected deep-seated seventeenth-century fears about Irish brutality.

William Hincks attempted to depict beetling and scutching in the standard idyllic, feminine light of his other eleven prints on linen, but not quite with the same efficacy, failing to romanticize the work's subtextual, violent undertone. *A Plate Representing the common Methods of Beetling, Scutching, and Hackling the Flax*, depicts five women and one man dressing flax in a rustic barn (Figure 2.6) and displays a spattering of bucolic icons: the young girl and puppy at play, the two birds perched on the beam, and the window open to sunlight. Like Hincks's other female characters, the women at work in this image are all neatly dressed and ideally figured with soft features, even a hint of blushed cheeks. With her exposed bosom and flowing hair, the standing scutcher, in particular, epitomizes

[103] *Essays by the Dublin Society*, p. 156.   [104] *Essays by the Dublin Society*, p. 156.
[105] *Essays by the Dublin Society*, p. 156.   [106] Crommelin, *Essay*, p. 156.
[107] S. M. Stephenson, *On the Processes and Utensils Employed in the Preparation of Flax, and in the Manufacture of Linen in Ireland* (Belfast: Transactions of Belfast Literary Society, 1811), p. 9.

Figure 2.6 William Hincks, 'A Plate representing the common Method of Beetling, Scutching, and Hackling the Flax,' Plate IV, *The Irish Linen Industry*, 1783, paper print, etching and stipple. Reproduced from the original held by the Department of Special Collections of the Hesburgh Libraries of the University of Notre Dame.

the beautiful virgin maiden—except, of course, for the fact that she wields a sharp and menacing weapon high above her head.

The instruments depicted here—beetles and swingles—insert significations of threat and violence throughout the image. The two scutchers mirror one another, holding large, sharp, imposing, machete-like swingles high above her head, as if ready to strike in unison. The beetles are less overtly menacing, but the fact that they are wielded by the two small girls in the foreground marks a potentially more alarming, if less obvious, feature. Furthermore, the stool tipped over in the right foreground indicates commotion, some sense of an event: that the beetling or scutching may have agitated the dog and birds, who are active figures in the scene. No doubt unintended by Hincks, the comely and innocent portrayals of the women serve to underscore the contrasting, threatening material subtexts of their instruments and the violent reality of their work—and, potentially, their innate Irish character. It is also possible to read emasculating undertones in Hincks's image: the flax stalks awaiting the swingle resemble phallic shapes. Read in this light, the violence cultivated by Irish women in the practice of flax dressing directly undermines gendered archetypes the linen industry ostensibly affirmed for masculine, paternal British ideology.[108] The imagery of Hincks's plate on scutching and beetling unintentionally envisages the idea that, by encouraging women to practice the physical exertion of flax dressing, the linen manufacture affirms *and* challenges the imperial, improvement model that positioned Britain as a paternal figure presiding over a delicate, feminine Ireland. That linen required such physical assault to be manufactured in the first place directly undermines the ideological comfort provided by soft, handspun flax, which disseminated a pacified picture of Irish female domesticity throughout consumerist Britain. Flax, in its original state as a picked crop, is not so easily amenable to refinement as the improvement discourse on linen would suggest. Instead, then the physical realities of flax dressing intimate that Irish character only becomes domesticated and fine *after* violent alteration.

Flax's material subversions add yet another layer of subversion to the footnotes in Sydney Owenson's *The Wild Irish Girl* (1806), presented in the voice of a scholar who supplements protagonist Horatio's impressions of Ireland. Early on in the text, when Horatio comes across linen-workers in Ireland, Owenson tactically inserts a couple footnotes about flax dressing. First, she cites a personal memory of being welcomed into a cottage in Sligo by 'an old woman and her three granddaughters; two of the young ones engaged in scutching flax.'[109] More pointedly, the following footnote quoting antiquarian General Charles Vallancey presents female communities of flax workers as a long, honored Irish tradition inherited from pre-Christian tribes:

> These conventions of female industry so frequent in many parts of Ireland are called *Ouris*...foreigners, who came from very distant countries...taught the Irish the art of...the management of flax...The word *Ouris* now means a meeting of women or girls at one house or barn, to card a quantity of flax, and sometimes there are a hundred together[110]

Owenson recharacterizes flax dressing from an Anglicized industrial process used to 'improve' Ireland into a partly fictional ideal of an ancient and mythical Irish craft. Together, these two footnotes imbue the novel's romantic travel narrative with an undercurrent of nationalist, physical threat. The second footnote's image of one hundred women beetling and scutching flax together—Hincks's plate (Figure 2.6) multiplied by twenty—assails the foundations of an English

---

[108] The fear of castration appears in some eighteenth-century colonial texts like Tobias Smollett's *The Expedition of Humphry Clinker* (1771). In that text, Lismahago tells of his comrade, the Irishman Murphy, who is 'mangled' by Native American women to the point of 'render[ing] him unfit for the purposes of marriage' (vol. 2, p. 170). The moment signifies both native savagery in North America and the failed manpower of British colonizing forces. See *The Expedition of Humphry Clinker*, 3 vols. (London: Johnston, 1771).

[109] Owenson, *The Wild Irish Girl*, p. 20.   [110] Owenson, *The Wild Irish Girl*, p. 21.

male character codified through the eighteenth-century allegory of Ireland as the pacified, subservient wife to John Bull. Subliminally, these small footnotes on scutching and flax dressing intimate a material scenario in which Horatio, newly transplanted to Ireland, is potentially in danger of bodily harm, especially when read inter-textually with Hincks's ominous image of the same flax dressing tradition. The dynamic style of *The Wild Irish Girl*, which consistently undermines Horatio's observations through editorial footnotes, reveals how female Irish characters engaging with flax—even when they are underdeveloped or marginalized into footnotes—actively extract allusions to and memories of violence. The material semiotics of flax biology and literary text ultimately articulate this: even if flax and the Irish subject/text eventually cooperate with external pressures, the Irish character, like the freshly picked flax stalk, does not yield without a challenge that demands exterior force.

2.5   Bleaching and the Stain of Irish Nature

In addition to the fineness of flax thread, the whiteness of linen cloth proved a topic of extended consideration in discourse on improving eighteenth-century Irish linen, in large part because bleaching techniques helped to expedite the expansion of the industry in Ireland and its international reputation. The establishment of large bleach greens (large-scale bleaching companies with acres of fields or 'greens' where the white cloth would be laid out to dry) in Ulster and, second, the incorporation of sulfuric acid in the bleaching process, which could more effectively 'whiten' the fabric, augmented Irish linen's success in a global market. Adopting new materialism's focus on material details sometimes invisible to the human eye, this section explores how a chemical reading of bleached linen extends to Irish people—their relative whiteness, cleanliness, and thereby their ethnic 'nature.' Whiteness is, of course, a heavily loaded, oftentimes malignant concept, especially in the context of eighteenth-century British history. In discourses on linen making, 'whiteness' generally meant the absence of color—specifically the brown color made by the flax oil. Nevertheless, I will suggest that material-discursive process of bleaching linen instigates a racist conceptualization of the Irish as a dirty people—a dirtiness that can nevertheless be cleaned, even purged, through sometimes destructive methods and techniques. In the same way spinning fine flax thread provided the material conditions for a new British imperial ideology as paternalism over a small, nonthreatening, feminized Ireland, bleaching provided the conditions in which imperialists could discuss the ethnic superiority of the English in terms of whiteness and cleanliness versus Irish dirt and stain.

In its natural state, flax is a brown, tawny color, but existing cultural values of white cleanliness, stemming from values of purity—both racial and

sexual—demanded that linen 'look' clean. Unlike with fine yarn, when flax's biological nature as a longitudinal and malleable fiber created metaphors of Irish
cooperation and docility, flax in this instance had to meet pre-existing cultural
demands for purity, both metaphoric and material. As Beverly Lemire has shown,
from the mid-eighteenth century, there was a growing interest in the whiteness of
textiles, especially linens, which linked to an increasing anxiety about cleanliness
that had become 'emblematic of respectable family life' in Britain.[111] As part of
this culture of cleanliness, eighteenth-century conduct books and instructional
household manuals stress the maintenance of a pristine house and provide directions on how to starch linens and preserve that increasingly desired domestic
whiteness. For example, *Madam Johnson's Present, Or Every Young Woman's
Companion in Useful and Universal Knowledge* details how to remove stains from
linen with starch and how best to keep bed dressings clean.[112]

Linens, more so than other cloths, came to carry the cultural weight of British
cleanliness, and this was no coincidence: flax fabric is more easily cleaned than
any other plant fiber. As mentioned previously, flax is excessively porous, and
thereby easily washed due to its absorbency and quick drying, giving it the advantage over wools and silks in this regard.[113] In the hands of people who cleaned
domestic spaces, linen became expressive of cleanliness itself. Madam Johnson's
manual, for example, instructs maids to clean and dust with a 'linen cloth' or
'linen duster' specifically.[114] In line with this correlation between white linen, the
appearance of cleanliness, and social standing, the Dublin Society professed in
the 1740s that: 'No flax crop will be a good one which is not at the same Time a
clean one.'[115] Hincks's depiction of bleaching scenes document the gentrification
inherent in whitening. Plate X, for example (Figure 2.7), features the big
Ascendancy house on the bleaching green, a bucolic river, and two lovers of
leisure—a definite shift from the lower classes manually preparing flax in cottages
or factories in earlier plates. As the plates chronologically trace the linen industry's
steps of manufacture, they also document a shift from lower classes in cob
cottages, as in the beetling and spinning scenes (Figures 2.6 and 2.3) to the wealth
of the industry bleachers, further associating bleaching and whiteness with higher
social value and erasing any sense of manual labor.

In turn, a cyclical material-semiotic pattern appears: flax must be bleached in
response to cultural mores of cleanliness and white purity, and, in turn, white
linen comes to solidify and circulate those same mores and metaphors of

---

[111] Beverly Lemire, 'An Education in Comfort: Indian Textiles and the Remaking of English Homes
of the Long Eighteenth Century' in *Selling Textiles in the Long Eighteenth Century: Comparative
Perspectives from Western Europe*, ed. Jon Stobart and B. Blondé (London: Palgrave Macmillan,
2014), p. 14.

[112] Mary Johnson, *Madam Johnson's Present; or Every Young Woman's Companion in Useful and
Universal Knowledge* (Dublin: Williams, 1770), pp. 172–7, 180.

[113] Kathleen Curtis Wilson, *Irish People, Irish Linen* (Athens, OH: Ohio UP, 2011), p. 176.

[114] Johnson, *Madam Johnson's Present*, p. 166.   [115] *Essays by the Dublin Society*, p. 185.

Figure 2.7 William Hincks, 'This Perspective View of a Bleach Green, taken in the County of Downe.' Plate X, *The Irish Linen Industry*, 1783, paper print, etching and stipple. Reproduced from the original held by the Department of Special Collections of the Hesburgh Libraries of the University of Notre Dame.

domestic purity. If, however, white linen signifies cleanliness and, potentially, English racial superiority, it follows that the Irish land and the Irish flax crop that make brown flax would be viewed as unclean.

The obverse to English domestic cleanliness is, of course, colonial contamination. Dirt and filth are common tropes ascribed to colonial subjects in imperial tracts, and disgust at dirty domestic scenes regularly justified British paternalism.[116] English influence in Ireland, it was believed, could clean the colonial subject. Young's *Tour in Ireland* infamously explains that the lower Irish 'have no idea of English cleanliness.'[117] Although dirt is a common trope across all kinds and means of social differentiation, especially class, Young's words nevertheless clarify that, in his eyes, there is something distinctly, perhaps ethnically Irish about dirt and mud, which I discuss at greater length in Chapter 4. In 1798, a dirty face became an even more dangerous sign of Irish otherness. During the Rebellion,

[116] Hawes, 'Three Times Round,' pp. 442–3.
[117] Arthur Young, *Tour in Ireland (1776–1779)*, 2 vols, ed. Arthur Wollaston Hutton (London: George Bell & Sons, 1892), vol. 1, p. 20.

rebels would practice blackening their faces with charcoal to avoid detection in the night. In 1798, Maria Edgeworth joked that she was vigilantly looking for Irish rebels with dirty faces: 'If I am to have my throat cut, it may not be by a man with his face blackened with charcoal.'[118] In irony, she claims that a 'very clean face' is a 'strong symptom of guilt,' continuing that 'clean nails ought to hang a man'—implying that the Irish are not habitually clean, only when removing evidence of rebellious activity.[119] Despite surface-level humor, her words suggest genuine fear of a charcoal-faced United Irishman and a general aversion to Irish dirtiness. Arthur Young's—and, to some extent, Maria Edgeworth's—implied belief in the dirtiness of the Irish character links to a cultural precedent for ultra-white linen, when the material process of bleaching extended to ethnic characterizations of the native Irish as unclean.

Bleaching—whitening with sunlight or chemicals—has always been historically associated with the whitening of linen specifically, dating back to the twelfth century.[120] Unlike cotton, which is naturally white, flax requires extensive chemical treatment to achieve that white absence of color, or the removal of the flax oil. The bleaching of flax fiber is, in this sense, inorganic: oxidizing agents must be added to the flax plant to whiten it. Before the addition of chemicals like sulfuric acid in the later eighteenth century, bleaching was done with lye—an alkaline solution made from weed ashes—or buttermilk and was a long, tiresome, and damaging process, involving at least ten rounds of bleaching and resulting in the extraction of all cellulose matter from the flax plant in order to achieve whiteness.[121] Each of these two different methods of bleaching—first, using what might be called 'natural' oxidizing agents such as buttermilk and, second, applying sulfuric chemicals in more modernized bleaching methods introduced in Ireland in the later eighteenth century—helped shape ideological concepts around if and how Irish character might be 'whitened.'

Despite the energy and time exerted in whitening flax the 'organic' way with buttermilk, no amount of time or whitening agents, some believed, could counteract the stains Irish nature might inflict on white linen. The Irish human nature and the terrain in which flax grew was seen as black, boggish, dirty, and thereby resistant to cleanliness. For example, in 1705, Samuel Crommelin rebukes the Irish for retting their flax crop in 'Any Ditch or Hole where they can get but Water,' which, he explains, 'dyes or tinges the Water black as Ink: This discolours their Flax in the first Instant, to such a degree, that all the Bleaching in Nature can

---

[118] Qtd. in Susan Egenolf, 'Maria Edgeworth in Blackface: *Castle Rackrent* and the Irish Rebellion of 1798.' *ELH* 72.4 (2005): p. 850.

[119] Maria Edgeworth, *Life and Letters of Maria Edgeworth*, ed. Augustus J. C. Hare (London: Arnold, 1894), vol. 1, p. 44.

[120] *Oxford English Dictionary*, s.v. 'bleach' (v.).

[121] Crommelin, *Essay*, p. 38; Sharma and Sumere, *Biology and Processing*, p. 343.

never bring their Cloth to a good Colour.'[122] Crommelin's metaphoric language is suggestive: the so-called blackness of the Irish earth indelibly stains the cloth so that no gift of 'Nature' can clean it again. Furthermore, Crommelin is happy for fish and other natural environments to become collateral in the service of clean retting: his essay is unalarmed at the concerns expressed by farmers who claim flax retting harms the indigenous fish population and rivers.

A 1737 essay submitted to the Dublin Society also emphasizes the need for clean, clear water in retting, discouraging the use of bog water, which 'gives the Flax a tawny colour.'[123] According to this essay, the flax dresser should at all costs avoid 'Bog-Holes and Rivers' and build his own reservoirs instead.[124] The British mindset held an underlying disquiet about the Irish bog, that unknown feature of the Irish landscape associated with the concealed, dangerous Irish native since the early modern period. Anglo-Irishman Thomas Amory's 1756 novel *The Life of John Buncle*, for example, openly admits this genuine fear of bogland: 'I have seen in Ireland the arches of several of those bogs broken, and a deep unfathomable water at some distance from the arch. They are very dangerous, frightful places.'[125] Moreover, during the Rebellion of 1798, rebels would often conceal themselves in bogland, taking advantage of the British soldier's ignorance of and aversion to such terrain.[126] The bog, through its 'unfathomable' depths and black, unpredictable subterrain—the domain of the rebel—comes to metaphorically signify perceived unknown danger in the Irish people in literature. In turn, flax retted in bog water becomes embroiled, through color and stain, with all the bog represents in regard to Irish character: violent rebellion against British rule. Such (dis)colorings, of course, do not belong in the white, purified English domestic household. Therefore, we can correlate aversion to bogwater retting, metonymic of an overarching fear of Irish nature (both topographical and human), with the impulse to improve bleaching in Ireland.

Aversions to Irish nature were also localized in the Irish domestic space. The same essay concerned with tawny bog water submitted to the Dublin Society takes issue with the Irish method of drying flax indoors because 'the Smoke in its Passage through the Flax must infallibly discolour it.'[127] According to linen experts in the Dublin Society, the stain of the flax cloth's origins in an Irish household may make it unfit for English expectations of whiteness. Similarly, the vegetable ashes used by Irish cottiers to treat their flax thread at home were known to

---

[122] Crommelin, *Essay*, p. 11.   [123] *Essays by the Dublin Society*, p. 122.
[124] *Essays by the Dublin Society*, p. 139.
[125] Thomas Amory, *The Life of John Buncle, Esq.*, vol. 2 (London: Johnson, 1766), p. 262. Bogs are porous wetlands, with deep rivets of water underneath what appears to be solid land. They are commonly occurring across Ireland, especially in the midlands and the west, and peat or turf—dried square pieces of bogland—were used as fuel to warm Irish fireplaces for centuries.
[126] Clare O'Halloran, 'From Antiquarian Text to Fiction's Subtext: The Extended Afterlife of Spenser's "View of the Present State of Ireland".' *Spenser Studies* 31–2 (2018): p. 517.
[127] *Essays by the Dublin Society*, p. 143.

stain the flax yellow, as in the traditional early modern, 'saffron-colored shirts' of the Gaelic Cheiftains—meaning that anything less than pure white linen could potentially allude to a rebellious Ireland of the Elizabethan era.[128]

To address these kinds of bog-based fears, linen manufacturers encouraged cottiers to proactively clean brown flax threads at home by boiling newly spun yarn. As early as 1705, Crommelin had insisted that Irish spinners should buck, or soak, newly spun yarn with lye—a vital step to cleanse the yarn in the service of later bleaching procedures.[129] In 1790, the Trustees for Promoting the Linen and Hempen Manufactures of Ireland began to heed such suggestions, offering bounties on 'high white Yarn.'[130] Unlike the discolored Irish cabin, the Anglo-Irish domestic space became, in one instance, a laboratory for new bleaching techniques. In 1773, Lady Moira completed an experiment on manufacturing special flax yarn that would mimic the properties of white cotton, which she reported to the Dublin Society, who then reprinted her findings. One of the merits of her special flax yarn, her report argues, is that it is 'capable of taking the clearest White, if long and properly bleached.'[131] The Countess uses her influence to reconfigure the domestic scene as helping to improve Irish linen's whiteness, rather than discolor it, as with the poor Irish cabin. Also implicit in this shift is the idea of modernized technology: synthetic flax-cotton thread or new, more effective chemical compounds.

In relation to these fears about the Irish environment's potential stains or contaminations, concerns arose in relation to the accepted agents of naturally bleaching linen. For instance, there were punitive legislative measures taken against improper bleaching: a merchant could be banned from bleaching for two years for using 'improper materials' such as 'pigeons dung' or 'soap-dregs.'[132] In particular, the pigeons-dung suggests that same disgust with dirty bodily habits as intimated by the stereotype of slovenly, piggish Irish domesticity, which I discuss in Chapter 5. Similarly, when Swift's metaphoric analogy of the spinning Arachne, with which this chapter began, turns flax and textiles into spider 'bowels,' he invokes a very essential fear around Irish materiality by turning that base nature—bowels and dung—back onto the British consumer. As James Ward and Seamus Deane have argued, Swift regularly used the material semiotics of the body's excrement to dramatize the consequences of a *political* body that has no control,

---

[128] A. Hume, 'Historical Notices of Spinning and Weaving.' *Ulster Journal of Archaeology* 5.1 (1857): p. 181.

[129] Crommelin, *Essay*, p. 36.

[130] *Trustees for Promoting the Linen and Hempen Manufactures of Ireland, Broadside* (Dublin: Williamson, 2 March 1790).

[131] *Proceedings of the Dublin Society*, 27 January 1774, p. 325.

[132] *An Abstract of the Acts of Parliament now in Force, Relating to the Linen Manufacture.* Published by order of the Commissioners and Trustees appointed by his Majesty for Improving the Linen Manufacture of Scotland. (Edinburgh, 1751), p. 11.

like Ireland.[133] Using shocking anatomical imagery, Swift discerns and accesses this fear around dung, dirt, contamination, and textiles in order to (negatively) advocate for Ireland's domestic economic rights and underscore the perversion of the 'dependent Kingdom' economic model he criticized.

Over the course of the century, anxieties around bleaching linen in Ireland began to abate as bleach greens improved and quickened the bleaching process with new whitening agents: chemical compounds of sulfuric acid. In fact, by the latter part of the century, writers on the Irish industry came to celebrate the increasingly improving whiteness of Irish linen. Robert Stephenson, for example, claimed that Irish bleaching 'surpasses the whitest Display of Nature.'[134] Indeed, by the turn of the nineteenth century, Irish linens 'bleached on grass'—meaning linens whitened in large-scale Ulster bleach greens that used the best whitening agents, methods, and machinery—became a strong selling point for Irish merchants in London.[135] Whereas earlier whitening with buttermilk damaged the flax over the course of the lengthy process, the new addition of sulfuric acid could quickly, chemically alter flax to make it more readily responsive to whiteness.

Ostensibly, on the surface, the whitening process seemed to improve painlessly with the addition of sulfuric acid, but at a more microscopic level, the compound altered flax's natural color through a damaging chemical reaction. When flax is bleached, when it sheds its brown oils in response to an oxidizing agent, it loses some of its matter and is permanently, irrevocably altered—a fact that implicitly extends to ideas about white fabric's correlative cultural ideal: purity. Etymologically, the associations between bleaching and purity emerged in definitive terms in the late eighteenth century.[136] Language used in household manuals and letters containing advice for domestic bleaching reveal this synonymity between 'bleached' and 'pure' and illuminate the material and metaphoric violence of bleaching. The Weaver and Housewife's Pocket Book, for instance, instructs spinners to 'purge [their yarn] from its filth' so it may 'stand the Trial of Bleaching better; because there is nothing left in the Yarn but the pure stuff.'[137] The same manual insists that yarn must be boiled because if 'not well purged' the yarn will thin the cloth in bleaching.[138] The language perhaps unconsciously discloses the violent subtext in the chemical bleaching of flax: the wording is suggestive, even evangelist, and affirms a belief in the impurity of the natural—that is, untreated with chemicals— state of the brown flax crop.

[133] See James Ward, 'The Political Body in Jonathan Swift's Fiction.' *Irish University Review* 41.1 (2011), p. 42. Also, Seamus Deane, 'Classic Swift' in *The Cambridge Companion to Jonathan Swift*, ed. Christopher Fox (Cambridge: Cambridge UP, 2003).
[134] Stephenson, *Observations*, p. 77.   [135] *The Observer*, classified ads, 1808, p. 1.
[136] *Oxford English Dictionary*, s.v. 'bleach' (v.).
[137] Ramsay, *The Weaver and Housewife's Pocket Book*, p. 41.
[138] Ramsay, *The Weaver and Housewife's Pocket Book*, p. 41.

Cavan farmer James Breakey, hoping to promote the use of domestic Irish vegetable ashes in bleaching, uses violent language to describe the effect of foreign, fast-whitening ashes: 'the sharp saline nitrous Quality...eats, or as I may use the Expression, enervates the Thread.'[139] Significantly, in the eighteenth century 'enervate' meant both to weaken and, as an adjective, unmanly or effeminate, further invoking—whether consciously or not—the dual characterizations of Ireland as docile (through violent physical treatment) and feminized.[140] Most importantly, as both texts suggest, bleaching intensifies, perhaps even brutalizes, mere cleaning: the acid incites a transformation in the flax's molecules, resulting in permanent whitening effects that were understood socially as purification.

The severe material reality of chemically altering flax's color reveals the violent undertones implicit in the idea of Irish character's transformation. The flax plant surrenders to the extant, 'purifying' force of sulfuric acid and readily, *permanently* sheds its brown oil and color, sheds the so-called stains of Irish nature (the bog water, dirt, and cabin smoke). Happily for British consumers and bleach mill owners, flax is, in Lady Moira's words, 'capable of taking the clearest White,' capable of visual transformation through the reactive addition of external forces, such as sulfuric acid (or British influence).[141] What the chemical facts of bleaching reveal to us now, on a material-semiotic level, is that whiteness is not achievable without violent treatment and alteration—that Irish character, like Irish linen, cannot be seen as purified, cleansed, changed, without some extant interference that is inevitably, if invisibly at the molecular level, brutal. Bleaching, as a material process and desired aesthetic, helped to affirm imperial ideology and action in Ireland: namely, the belief that Irish character could not meet English domestic standards without undergoing a (violent and permanent) transformation of its natural state.[142]

With these chemical and biological details, then, it is possible to see how metaphors around Irish contamination issue from a material process: how bleaching stimulates cultural ideals of cleanliness, whiteness, and alteration in damaging ways for native Irish culture. For example, Young's idea of the Irish as fundamentally lacking English standards of cleanliness, discussed in more detail in Chapter 4, are directly connected to the prejudiced implications behind Edward Wakefield's later observations on linen bleaching at the turn of the century, when

[139] James Breakey, 'Process and Affidavit, as also his Remarks' in *To the Right Honourable and Honourable Trustees of the Linen and Hempen Manufacture* (Dublin, 1783), pp. 11–12.
[140] *Oxford English Dictionary*, s.v. 'enervate' (v. and adj.).
[141] *Proceedings of the Dublin Society*, 27 January 1774, p. 325.
[142] See Rajani Sudan, *The Alchemy of Empire: Abject Materials and the Technologies of Colonialism* (New York: Fordham UP, 2016), for a discussion of 'technologies of colonialism and empire' in India. Sudan analyzes the imperial ambitions of transforming native substances toward an English standard, reflective of making an impure colonial land lucrative. For example, she discusses how methods of making ice in India were deployed ideologically to transform the warm Indian climate into more English and acceptable conditions.

he writes, 'In England, great suspicions are entertained in regard to the arts practiced by the bleachers in Ireland, and on that account, large quantities of linen are imported, either in a brown or a half bleached state.'[143] Wakefield does not explain what these 'suspicions' are exactly, but in all probability they link to the previously discussed fears about the stains of Irish nature—the black bogs and smoky cottage. At the same time the Irish are encouraged to continually improve their process of whitening linen, English ideology and consumer practice characterizes their product, and perhaps their ethnicity, as insufficiently white. Perhaps paradoxically, half-bleached linens imported from Ireland distribute an image of the Irish as dirty and unclean while bright, white linen imports offer the comforting idea that the Irish people can be transformed and domesticated, purged of their incivility, violence, and natural habits of filth.[144]

I mentioned earlier that whiteness is an inherently malignant concept and category, particularly in the context of eighteenth-century culture. An exploration of the linkages between material bleaching and cultural whiteness is incomplete, therefore, without mentioning bleached linen's implications for racial discourse. Humanist, cultural variations of 'bleach' in relation to human skin tone reveal the ethnic implications of whitening the flax plant: the idea of a 'bleached face,' meaning a pale or pallid cheek, appeared mid-century.[145] As early as the sixteenth century, 'linen cheeks' appeared in Shakespeare's *Macbeth*, a metaphoric phrase used to signify white, pale skin.[146] From around 1780 to 1820, discourses on race and ethnicity began to shift as physical attributes increasingly defined a coherent, modern ideology of race. Before that, Jane Ohlmeyer explains, England's classification of civilized versus barbarous, or clean versus dirty, especially in relation to Ireland, was the language of ethnic superiority.[147] Angela Rosenthal has convincingly shown how whiteness as a racial category and value emerged in the late eighteenth century, regularly signified through the visual trope of woman's fair skin and blushing check in portraiture, blending with her all-white clothing.[148] Even Irish national tales written as a response to racist travel writing seem to consciously link English treatment of the native Irish people as dirty or uncouth with a burgeoning nineteenth-century ideology of racial superiority. In *The Irish Recluse* (1809), for instance, a national tale by Sarah Isdell, the sardonic heroine

---

[143] Wakefield, *An Account of Ireland*, vol. 1, p. 692.
[144] In *Imperial Leather* (London Routledge, 2013), Anne McClintock makes a similar argument about the Victorian soap industry, which, she argues, distributed evolutionary racism, expressed by the likes of Charles Darwin, to the illiterate (p. 208). She also argues that white powder cosmetics dating back to the eighteenth century can be seen as commodity racism (p. 209).
[145] *Oxford English Dictionary*, s.v. 'bleach' (v.).
[146] A. Hume, 'Spinning and Weaving: Their Influence on Popular Language and Literature,' *Ulster Journal of Archaeology* 5.1 (1857): p. 105.
[147] See Jane Ohlmeyer's essay, 'Colonization within Britain and Ireland, 1580s–1640s' in the *Oxford History of the British Empire*, vol. I (Oxford: Oxford UP, 1998).
[148] Angela Rosenthal, 'Visceral Culture: Blushing and the Legibility of Whiteness in Eighteenth-Century British Culture.' *Art History* 27.4. (2004): p. 578.

introduces a beautiful Catholic Irish girl, Emma Summers, to a lovestruck Englishman by ironically saying, 'This is one of our female ourang-otangs... but perfectly harmless,' drawing on the racial discourse in travelogues that described native peoples, like the Hottentotts, as apes.[149] Thus, we have to consider how, in the context of the Irish linen industry, the rising capital value of 'clear' whiteness, that desired aesthetic of 'high white linen,' might have helped to inculcate a congealing white racial category as a secondhand effect.

Counter-revolutionary, post-Union improving fictions, such as Mary Leadbeater's *Cottage Dialogues* (1811) and Anna Maria Hall's *Sketches of Irish Character* (1829) explicitly employ white linen as a semiotic sign of an idealized Union, where female practice helps to purge Ireland from its violent, chaotic past. First, in Leadbeater's *Cottage Dialogues*, the central theme of diligent cleanliness assembles an image of what Irish domesticity should look like and how Irish characters should act. Rose and Nancy are archetypes of how and how *not* to behave, respectively. Rose, for example, uses the money from her spinning (fifteen shillings a month) to buy a new dress, emphasizing the importance of looking 'clean and smooth,' while Nancy claims she would rather idle away at the fair. Their choices in this earlier sketch correlate with the state of their households in a later sketch, when Nancy praises the whitewash and cleanliness of Rose's cottage, the linen Rose bleached herself at home, and the curtains she spun for the windows.[150] Nancy, whose contrasted house is in financial and physical disrepair, asks Rose how she has achieved these standards of economic frugality and cleanliness, and Rose's replies emphasize the importance of making and bleaching one's own linen: 'We don't pretend to much dress, but we strive to be clean... if you take my advice, you'll always keep a bit of wool, and flax, and spinning in the house. ... We made all that linen as I told you and bleached it ourselves.'[151] Rose is, in this case, both an average, everyday Irish peasant and an idealized, allegorical Irish woman who cleans and bleaches of her own volition—the antithesis to the uncleanly Irish rural character described by Arthur Young thirty years before.

Anna Maria Hall's similar work, *Sketches of Irish Character* (1829), shows how British standards of improvement are signified, via cleanliness, on the female body:

> Mick Leahy looked affectionately at his wife [Norah]—and well he might. She was clean and industrious—cheerful and contented—the mud walls of her cabin were whitewashed—a glass window—small but unbroken—looked but on a little garden... [his clothes] of his wife's spinning.[152]

[149] Sarah Isdell, *The Irish Recluse*, 3 vols (London: J. Booth, 1809), vol. 1, p. 245; Hawes, 'Three Times Round,' pp. 443–4.
[150] Mary Leadbeater, *Cottage Dialogues Among the Irish Peasantry*, Introduction and notes by Maria Edgeworth (London: Johnson, 1811), p. 175.
[151] Leadbeater, *Cottage Dialogues*, pp. 192–3.
[152] Anna Maria Hall, *Sketches of Irish Character* (London: How & Parsons, 1842), pp. 345–6.

Here, the ideological work of the linen manufacture—the feminization of the improved Irish subject and the cleansing of Irish nature—is spelled out in stark, plain English on Norah's clean body and white walls. The didactic characterizations of Hall's Norah and Leadbeater's Rose are, like flax and sulfuric acid, elements contributing to a wider ideology of Irish improvement. These kinds of improving fictions were distributed as study texts for non-denominational schools and delivered directly to rural households. As Helen O'Connell explains, it was hoped that improving fictions would replace the native Irish tradition of fireside storytelling.[153] In turn, we might see the pages of these sketches, made from linen rags themselves, as mimicking the cultural work of white linen cloth in England—distributing the ideal image of a newly improved Irish subject and a clean, feminine Ireland throughout society.

As in the footnotes of *The Wild Irish Girl*'s flax dressers, a final, subversive postscript to this material narrative of clean linen can be found in poetry written by a young Irish woman. Ellen Taylor, daughter of an Irish cottier and a domestic servant, published her *Poems* in Dublin in 1792. Although relatively unknown, Taylor's collection is nevertheless an important example of Irish laboring-class eighteenth-century poetry that had number of well-connected subscribers from the Dublin literary scene at that time, including a Mrs Lefanu, Countess Mt. Cashell, and Elizabeth Griffith.[154] The introduction, written by an unidentified advocate, overemphasizes her poverty and surprising 'genius' given her modest background as the daughter of 'an indigent Cottager, in a remote part of the Queen's County [Laois].'[155] Taylor's 'Written by the Barrow Side, Where She was Sent to Wash Linen' associates the labor of cleaning and whitening linen with internal emotion and reflection. The poem alludes to the unwieldiness of her emotion, which surfaces through contact with flax linen:

> I feel more sensibly each blow,
> Dealt by relentless fate...
> With fluttering heart, I lay me down,
> And Rife with aching head.[156]

The speaker regrets that, because of her work as a maid, she cannot 'indulge without control, / Each thought that flows' from her soul.[157] For Prescott, the poem 'plays on the tension between her position as a local servant, the menial and physical task before her, and the life of the mind, a luxury usually only afforded to the

---

[153] O'Connell, *Ireland and the Fiction of Improvement*, p. 19.
[154] Sarah Prescott, 'Ellen Taylor (years unknown; one extant publication, 1792)' in *Irish Women Poets Rediscovered*, ed. Maria Johnston and Conor Linnie (Cork: Cork University Press, 2021), pp. 25–6.
[155] Ellen Taylor, *Poems by Ellen Taylor, the Irish Cottager* (Dublin: Grafton, 1792), p. A2.
[156] Taylor, *Poems*, p. 8.   [157] Taylor, *Poems*, p. 9.

wealthy and educated.'[158] Adding to Prescott's analysis, the material presence of
the linen Taylor was sent to wash becomes an important mediator in this rela-
tional, social tension. The linen's porous flax threads, opening to the water of the
river, contrast the speaker's impermeable emotive depth, which she must close off
and discipline to effectively do her work. The poet's physical, tactile contact with
flax produces a poem from the depths of her own subjectivity, while she, through
writing the poem, releases her unwieldy thoughts and feelings into the porous
flax itself. Given linen's pre-text of beetling, Taylor's line about 'feeling each blow'
of misfortune in her life potentially alludes to that violent disciplining of Irish
character for industry or, in this case, domestic work. Yet Taylor reframes cleaning linen as an act of her own poetic resistance to the structures of class she has
been forced obey, rather than an affirmation of Anglicized hierarchies of social
status, race, and nationality. Her poem acknowledges that, despite ostensible passivity, resistance can express itself through the material intra-action of flax, female
hands, and water.

*   *   *

The linen manufacture of the flax plant provided the material conditions for fundamental changes eighteenth-century thinking and writing about Irishness. It
incorporated Ireland into British society: materially, through industrial expansion and consumer practice and, ideologically, by facilitating the perceived feminization, domestication, and cleansing of the native Irish character. We should
not see flax or linen cloth as mere objects in an imperial machine, but as partici-
patory actors who by virtue of their unique characteristics and Irish contexts contributed to the construction of a new, ostensibly non-violent Irish subject that
was, like flax, cooperative with industrial advancement and a new paternalistic
model of Anglo-Irish relations. On the other hand, the next chapter will show
how, in the Irish national novel, the spinning wheel's kinetic agency afforded a
feminist critique of the imperial policy that flax thread ostensibly served.

---

[158] Prescott, 'Ellen Taylor,' p. 24.

3

Spinning Wheels

In the explanatory notes for Mary Leadbeater's *Cottage Dialogues* (1811), editor
Maria Edgeworth identifies 'The Spinning Match' as her favorite sketch. This particular dialogue details a spinning contest patronized by a local landlady—a custom in which Irish peasant women would travel to the local Anglo-Irish estate
and compete to win the prize for the best and most quickly spun yarn. Edgeworth's
editorial endnotes praise this fictionalized spinning contest because 'Nothing…is
more exquisitely affectionate, natural or touching than this simple account.'[1]
Edgeworth commends Leadbeater for her 'exact representation of the *manner of
being* of the lower Irish' and highlights the spinning wheel as a particularly realist
and resonant signifier of native Irish life.[2] *Cottage Dialogues* is an endless cycle of
spinning wheels, which appear repeatedly throughout the text to represent
'authentic' rural Ireland for the English reader and narrate the benefits of Irish
domestic industry to Irish cottiers. Indeed, the sheer ubiquity of spinning wheels
in Leadbeater's text captures something of Edgeworth's promised 'exact representation': by the mid-eighteenth century, the spinning wheel had become a widely
disseminated fixture of Irish life and literature, linking the apparatus with Irish
cultural expression.[3]

The number of spinning wheels in eighteenth-century Ireland proliferated at a
rapid pace thanks to concerted political and economic efforts. In the mid-
seventeenth century, the Duke of Ormonde, serving as Lord Lieutenant in Ireland,
imported the Dutch spinning wheel, which eventually became the low Irish
wheel, to Ireland in order to augment the linen industry's growth. Over the course
of the eighteenth century, the Board of Trustees of Linen Manufacturers, established in 1711, distributed thousands of spinning wheels to women in poor rural
households across Ireland and established spinning schools in nearly every
county.[4] At the turn of the nineteenth century, Thomas Campbell and Arthur
Young, among others, would recount seeing spinning wheels in nearly every cottage they visited in rural Ireland.

---

[1] Mary Leadbeater, *Cottage Dialogues Among the Irish Peasantry*, Introduction and notes by Maria
Edgeworth (London: Johnson, 1811), p. 323.
[2] Leadbeater, *Cottage Dialogues*, p. iv.   [3] Leadbeater, *Cottage Dialogues*, p. iv.
[4] Robert Stephenson, *Observations on the Present State of the Linen Trade of Ireland: in a series of
letters addressed to the Right Honourable trustees of the Linen Manufacture. In which the Reports, Libel,
and British Examination of Mr John Arbuthnot, Inspector General of Leinster, Munster, and Connaught,
are considered and refuted* (Dublin, 1784), pp. v–vi.

Irish Materialisms: The Nonhuman and the Making of Colonial Ireland, 1690–1830. Colleen Taylor, Oxford University Press.
© Colleen Taylor 2024. DOI: 10.1093/oso/9780198894834.003.0004

As domestic Irish yarn exports grew, particularly after 1750, more and more women were impelled to spin for their families' (and Ireland's) survival.[5] Government leaders, economic developers, the Anglo-Irish elite, and individual family units expected virtually all laboring class Irishwomen in Ulster and Connaught, including girls, to spin flax thread in service of the national production of linen cloth. In the south of Ireland, women typically spun wool, rather than flax. Mary O'Dowd has counted some 30,000 rural Munster women employed in spinning wool for the English market in the 1760s.[6] Whether they spun wool or flax, laboring women were almost always engaged in spinning work: single women were often hired by a middle-class households as spinners who contributed to general household work, while married women and young girls more often spun on their spinning wheels at home, combining domestic tasks with money-making work.[7] Even in noble houses, female servants would not only be well versed in caring for fine linen but also be expected to spin flax themselves.[8] The linen manufacture's support of domestic spinning among poor tenants across Ireland fit neatly with Anglo-Irish views on paternalism discussed in the previous two chapters: that landholders and gentlewomen must take responsibility for their poor Catholic or Scots-Irish tenants, encourage their industry and 'improvement,' and thereby support the national good.

Long before linen became Ireland's main industry, and long before it helped construct a new version of Irish national character, the spinning wheel had been associated with creativity in antiquity. Using new materialism, this chapter explores the physicality underlying this trope's resonance—how people who interacted or, as Barad would have it, intra-acted with these wheels, responded to its materiality in their thinking and writing. Barad's idea that the human individual and material apparatus are intra-active and inseparable in terms of their shifting, dynamic agencies is especially fitting for the eighteenth-century spinning wheel, which materially and culturally melded both the spinner's foot with the treadle (foot peddle) and the spinner's mind with the turning wheel.[9] Adopting the new materialist idea that human cognition is the result of both material and semiotic forces according to Gibson's affordance (in which an object provides the human with a thought), I argue that the experience of the wheel's motion, which elongated flax and wool's fibers through quick, rotational movement, helped to augment the very concept of an active, interior human consciousness: a subject

---

[5] W. H. Crawford, *The Impact of the Domestic Linen Industry in Ulster* (Belfast: Ulster Historical Foundation, 2005), p. 31.

[6] Mary O'Dowd, *A History of Women in Ireland, 1500–1800* (London: Pearson, 2005), p. 141.

[7] O'Dowd, *History of Women*, pp. 139–40.

[8] Edward Wakefield, *An Account of Ireland, Statistical and Political*, vol. 1 (London: Longman, Hurst, Rees, Orme, & Browne, 1812), p. 690.

[9] Karen Barad, *Meeting the Universe Halfway: Quantum Physics and the Entanglement of Matter and Meaning* (Durham, NC: Duke UP, 2007).

that can be developed from within, its mind and thoughts drawn out and refined.[10] As Serenella Iovino and Serpil Opperman argue, all physiochemical processes are capable of their own dynamic articulations through their embedded materiality.[11] In this case, spinning wheel's physics, which ordered the loose flax fibers into uniform thread and demanded a spinner's patience, held particular resonance for Britain's pervasive paternalism in relation to Ireland by supporting bodily discipline and introspection. At the same time, the object's rhythmic, cir-cular physics actuated ideas about generative, creative human thought outside of Britain's ideological parameters.

Whereas flax was a material-semiotic text that contributed to the gendering of Irish character, here the activity of the spinning wheel is more polemically aligned with a feminist mind and ethos. Traditionally, spinning might be completed in pairs at home or larger groups of women, occasionally in private. Either way, the wheel's steady revolutions afforded a rhythmic substructure to the work, and thus spinning wheels occasioned communal singing and composition among women, as well as colloquial phrases that affirmed women's spinning work as the mind's work as well. By the early nineteenth century, the spinning wheels in national tales by Sydney Owenson, and later the linen chest in the Banim brothers' novel, *The Croppy*, afforded the cultivation of a subversive mind within Irish female characters. The Irish novel's rotating spinning wheel narratively actuates the opaque but active mind of the peasant spinner and mobilizes the eighteenth-century oral tradition of women's spinning songs to insinuate cognitive resistance to Britain's gendered framework of colonial relations. Intentionally reading the spinning wheel's materiality—its physics, functioning, and material semiotics—reveals textual threats of female knowledge, autonomy, and even castration of the British male character.

3.1 Spinning Wheels as Pre-existing Signifiers for Creativity and National Identity

Although this chapter deals in the Irish material reality underpinning the historic spinner trope, it is useful to review a few central examples from literary history dating back to Greek mythology. The association between spinning, weaving, and literary productivity can be traced to classical texts like the *Odyssey*, where Penelope's weaving and unweaving marks the epic's passage of time and signifies her fidelity. The idea of the female spinner figure is most ancient and prolific in

---

[10] James J. Gibson, *The Ecological Approach to Visual Perception* (Hillsdale, NJ: Lawrence Erlbaum, 1986), p. 127. Also, Barad, *Meeting the Universe*.

[11] Serenella Iovino and Serpil Opperman, *Material Ecocriticism* (Bloomington, IN: Indiana UP, 2015), p. 34.

the image of Greek and Roman mythology's three Fates, who spun and cut the thread of a person's life.[12] Perhaps because of these mythic origins, spinning has long been associated with both bringing to life and bringing to death—the ultimate omniscient power over a person's narrative and fate, which, coincidentally, mirrors the position of the author over his or her character. Centuries later, in the early modern period, when the production of cloth became an international industry, images of the spinning woman abounded across cultures and media— on printed pages, in stained-glass windows and paintings both religious and secular.[13]

Feminist critics have been attracted to this longstanding spinner trope in folklore, fables, art, and classical literature, exploring how the gender-determined female task of spinning has long been seen as the work of life and death. For example, Ann Rosalind Jones and Peter Stallybrass argue that, throughout the Renaissance, when classical figures like Penelope and the Fates reemerged in art and folklore, 'the making of life and death was powerfully inscribed' in spinning.[14] Like Jones and Stallybrass, Frances Biscoglio charts how these powerful significations of female spinning endured from antiquity to the Middle Ages: the distaff, spindle, and later, the wheel served as metaphors for female power in medieval art.[15] Varied folk tales such as those recorded by the Grimm Brothers in the nineteenth century 'register the power of spinning women.'[16] However, this metaphorical power incurred negative connotations for spinners as well. For example, Biscoglio shows how Eve was reinvented as the disobedient spinner wife in the Middle Ages, while Jones and Stallybrass examine a seventeenth-century satirical broadsheet from the Netherlands belittling the clergy by depicting them as spinners and featuring demonic figures in the foreground.

In a British cultural context, since at least the early modern period, the spinner signified song, folk memory, and, as seen in *Twelfth Night*, ancient cultural preservation. In that play, Osario says:

> O, fellow, come, the song we had last night.—
> Mark it, Cesario. It is old and plain;
> The spinsters and the knitters in the sun
> And the free maids that weave their thread with bones
> Do use to chant it.[17]

[12] Frances Biscoglio, '"Unspun" Heroes: Iconography of the Spinning Woman in the Middle Ages.' *Journal of Medieval and Renaissance Studies* 25.2 (1995): pp. 163, 171.
[13] Biscoglio, '"Unspun" Heroes,' p. 163.
[14] Ann Rosalind Jones and Peter Stallybrass, *Renaissance Clothing and the Materials of Memory* (Cambridge: Cambridge UP, 2000), p. 133.
[15] Jones and Stallybrass, *Renaissance Clothing*, p. 168.
[16] Jones and Stallybrass, *Renaissance Clothing*, p. 106.   [17] *Twelfth Night*, 2.4, lines 48–52.

As implied here, female spinners, knitters, and weavers produce their craftwork and (re)produce ancient songs: make thread and weave with 'bones'—a pun that potentially means both the weaving shuttle tool, made of bone, and remains of a cultural time long past. As noted in the previous chapter, Swift used the spinner Arachne to analogize an oppressed Irish character in *A Proposal for the Universal Use of Irish Manufacture* (1720), much as he did with Hibernia in *The Story of the Injured Lady*, discussed in Chapter 1. A century later, Thomas Moore would adopt a similar conceit in his *Memoirs of Captain Rock* (1824), depicting Ireland as another cursed, classical character: 'the destiny of Ireland remains still the same— that here we still find her, at the end of so many centuries, struggling like Ixion, on her wheel of torture, never advancing, always suffering—her whole existence one monotonous round of agony.'[18] Less explicitly than in Swift, Moore's characterization nonetheless signifies Ireland's national state through the impact and impression of a woman enslaved to a wheel, its monotonous rounds, and unchanging results—much like the poor, rural Irish spinner who, with such low prices paid for Irish yarn, had to constantly spin to survive.[19]

In patriotic depictions of Irish national character, the spinning wheel encoded economic, colonial grievance, but it was also a familiar feature in English economic satires. The same year Swift wrote of Arachne and Irish textiles, Daniel Defoe adopted a homologous model on behalf of the English woolen manufacture, *The Female Manufacturers Complaint: Being the Petition of Dorothy Distaff, Abigail Spinning-Wheel, Eleanor Reel, and Spinsters* (1720). The pamphlet is written in satiric, ironic format, assuming the voice of English spinners petitioning a fictitious elite woman, Lady Rebecca Woolpack, to buy English wool rather than foreign calicoes. Like Swift with Hibernia, Defoe ventriloquizes three female characters, Dorothy Distaff, Abigail Spinning Wheel, and Eleanor Reel. These personas are equated with their industrial tools in name, grievance, and signature, so that the idea of their respective character identities amounts, in literal terms, to the parts of the spinning wheel apparatus. This becomes a visual fact at the end of the letter/pamphlet, when Abigail Spinning Wheel, illiterate, signs the faux-petition with the sketch of the wheel (Figure 3.1).

Because Abigail's mark (typically an x or cross for the illiterate) is the spinning wheel itself, the boundary between human subject and industrial object collapses on the page, literalizing the wheel as the identifying impression of her character type. Perhaps significant, the mark also mirrors the seal used by the Linen Board to brand brown and white Irish linens as authentic and official, intimating that Defoe's fictive spinner holds the mark of an authentic textile. Defoe's application

---

[18] Thomas Moore, *Memoirs of Captain Rock* (London: Longman, Hurst, Rees, Orme, Brown, & Green, 1824), p. ix.

[19] Jane Gray, *Spinning the Threads of Uneven Development: Gender and Industrialization in Ireland During the Long Eighteenth Century* (Lexington: Lanham, 2005), p. 45.

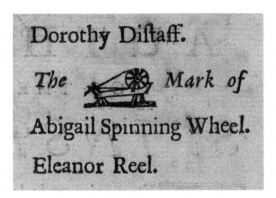

Figure 3.1 Dorothy Distaff, Abigail Spinning Wheel, Eleanor Reel, 1720. The Female Manufacturer's Complaint, Being the Humble Petition of Dorothy Distaff, Abigail Spinning-Wheel, and Eleanore Reel, &c, Spinsters, to Lady Rebecca Woollpack (London: Boreham, 1720), p. 19. Rare Book & Manuscript Library, University of Illinois at Urbana-Champaign.

of this ventriloquized spinner-character acknowledges and ironizes the ways in which the national character in the early eighteenth century is dependent on the legible 'characters' of industrious materiality—both the spinning wheel typeface and the spinner trope.

Like Defoe's spinning wheel mark, a moment in Mary Leadbeater and Elizabeth Shackleton's later publication *Tales for Cottagers* (1814) continues to associate national character with the 'impression' made by a spinning wheel. In 'The Scotch Ploughman,' a Scottish farmer named Andrew comes to Ireland to work and falls in love with a local Irish girl, Honor Kenagh. Both Honor's character and spinning 'impress' upon Andrew: 'The character of Honor, more than her beauty, made an impression on Andrew's heart; he never saw her but she brought his sister to his recollection, and as he listened to her singing at her wheel, he thought the Irish songs were almost as sweet as the Scotch.'[20] As with the mark of Abigail Spinning Wheel, this sketch conceives of the spinning wheel as an impression of female character, but here the imprint is an interiorized mark on Andrew's heart, rather than a literal, visible mark on the page. Andrew's spinning-impressed heart correlates with the imprinted coin it-narrator in Chapter 1, specifically the connection between physical imprint, as on Andrew's heart, and interior emotion, as in his affection. In this case, Honor's singing at her wheel also gives Andrew the impression of Irish national character at large. He later reflects on her songs in the Irish language and decides 'the Irish and Scotch had originally been one nation';

[20] Mary Leadbeater and Elizabeth Shackleton, *Tales for Cottagers, accommodated to the present condition of the Irish Peasantry* (Dublin: Cumming, 1814), p. 161.

her spinning practice projects the idea of Irish national character as intrinsically Gaelic, potentially incorporating Ulster's Scots-Irish population.[21]

Honor, Abigail Spinning Wheel, and Swift's Arachne are universalized, simplified national types whose characters are rendered through the impression made by the spinning wheel, underscoring the connection between character in nationalized fiction and material object. And yet, as material apparatuses, spinning wheels do not impress; rather, they extract, extend, and rotate. Spinning is, by definition and action, a *drawing out* of a suitable material.[22] The spinning wheel takes what is inside the flax stalk—the soft, hair-like fibers—and draws them out, literally, into thin, neat lines by swiftly moving them from the spinner's hands, around the wheel, and onto the bobbin or pirn. The spinning wheel deals in refining something from the inside and thereby its material process more fittingly applies to late eighteenth-century conceptions of interior subjectivity drawn out and refined, rather than a passive mark or signifier of national identity.

3.2 The Material Roots of an Active, Thinking Mind

I propose to explore this long-established cultural association between spinning, creativity, and national character in greater material depth, looking at something we think we already know about this trope with 'new eyes' that foreground the materiality of the spinning wheel as contributing to the epistemology of human thought and subjectivity. In making these connections, I draw from the work of Sean Silver, particularly how he originates the English etymology of epistemology in the weaving of wool. Silver locates the conceptual origins of the idea of complex thinking in the loom as an object, noting how 'complicated' and 'complication' are words that emerge in discussions on weaving.[23] From this, Silver argues, we can begin to understand how the ideology of the mind's work connects metaphorically to the act of perpetual, extended weaving—the constant, complicated crisscrossing of barely visible fibers.[24] But spinning, by virtue of its distinct material process, generates its own unique epistemological concepts, particularly, as discussed later on in this chapter, in relation to the rendering of a woman's inner subjectivity in literature.

In 1661, scientist William Petty provided a detailed, mechanistic account of the spinning wheel for the Royal Society of London. The language of his report denotes how the physics of spinning came to engender metaphysical ideas about the human mind. According to Petty, to spin is to transform a figure, to twist and

---

[21] Leadbeater and Shackleton, *Tales for Cottagers*, p. 161.

[22] *Oxford English Dictionary*, s.v. 'spinning' in 'spin' (v.).

[23] Sean Silver, 'Production and Practice' in *A Cultural History of Hair in the Age of Enlightenment*, ed. Margaret Powell and Joseph Roche (London: Bloomsbury, 2021), p. 82.

[24] Silver, 'Production and Practice,' p. 88.

to connect or unite: 'Spinning is a sort of connected parallel bodies by changing their figures alike, from strait to screws.' He elaborates that: 'this series of continual twistings and interposings...is the very essence and ratio formalis of spinning.'[25] Petty's choice of words here about the 'essence' of spinning is significant given that spinning extracts the 'essence'—that inside, core matter—of a fiber and develops it into a human product. As a term, 'essence' evokes the idea of the immaterial spirit alongside the physical attributes of twisting thread, intimating an embryonic link between subjectivity and spinning.[26] Petty's concepts of drawing out or getting at the essence of something evoke the creative, writerly work of representing human consciousness. Like the spinning wheel that connects various fibers into a neat whole, draws out the inner nutrients, and refines the flax plant's interior, the novel writer connects various events into cohesive plots and develops a protagonist's interior mind through plot twists and complications, descriptions, and dialogue.

Spinning's essential function is also, for Petty, 'unit[ing] distant threads'— material language that points to the mind's work of metaphor, that is, linking disparate ideas into one concept. Metaphors, of course, as discussed in the introduction, are the basic building block of colonial ideology. Read in correlation with an Irish context, Petty's words carry a double-edged metaphor that subtly aligns with Britain's desired imperial control over Ireland. Significantly, in Petty's account, spinning is a *disciplined* process, twisting unruly flax into uniform thread: that continual twisting and pulling that 'changes' multiple 'screws' or entanglements into straight lines of thread. Despite the patient repetition required for spinning, it is nevertheless, at the microscopic level, a forceful act of imposing control: tightly twisting the fibers then coercing those twists into neat, straight lines that force the flax into a certain shape.

The microscopic twisting discussed by Petty intimate connotations of forced configuration that resonate with the idea of improving Ireland as a means of disciplining native Irish character. In fact, as an object and mechanism, the spinning wheel stimulates the early modern definition of improvement: it actively cultivates a piece of Irish land (the flax fibers) into a profitable product (saleable yarn). In line with British standards of organized, cultivated land (and organized, cultivated colonies), spinning was seen to improve on the hard, raw nature of flax and wool and Irish people by spinning them out into organized, regimented segments that could be made useful to the economy. Because of its material link to the semiotics of human epistemology, the context in which a discussion of the spinning wheel's mechanization appears *matters*, literally. By correlating with the work of the human mind, the Irish spinning wheel can also potentially carry

---

[25] William Petty, 'Of Making Cloth with Sheep's Wool' (1661) in *The History of the Royal Society of London For Improving of Natural Knowledge, from its Rise* (London: A. Millar, 1756), p. 56.

[26] *Oxford English Dictionary*, s.v. 'essence' (n.).

covert, sometimes insidious double meanings that point back to linen's overarching colonial value for Britain.

Andrew Gray's *Treatise on Spinning Machinery* (1819), a more modern supplement to Petty's seventeenth-century report, identifies motion, rather than twisting, as the essence of the spinning wheel. Tracing a history from ancient distaff to modern-day two-handed spinning wheels, Gray continually emphasizes the way in which the spinning wheel 'conveys motion.'[27] Gray's emphasis on motion, in conjunction with spinning wheel's long-established cultural ties to creativity, creates a particular material-semiotic trajectory: that quintessential, rotating activity of the spinning wheel relocates the idea of motion inside the person who sits still and works diligently with it, conceiving subjectivity itself as a silent, invisible, internal motion—the many revolutions of thought and feeling. The spinning wheel visualizes the idea of a person's inner life or thought process as active, in motion, constantly circular and turning. Once stimulated by the foot pedal or treadle, the spinning wheel rotates of its own accord: it suddenly responds to an external stimulus, as a thought might, and generates a new product or idea through quick rotation.

This metaphoric affordance—the conceptualization of consciousness as a spinning wheel at work inside person's mind—can be traced in our contemporary vernacular, which regularly evokes spinning in relation to an active thought, such as 'my mind was spinning' or 'I was turning the idea around in my head.' The latter idiom, which seems so obvious to us now, clearly captures and links back to both Petty and Gray's understanding of spinning's ratio formalis—both a twisting of thought and an active, turning mind. The former phrase dates to at least the early nineteenth century.[28] In his 1820 poem, 'Letter to Maria Gisborne,' for example, Percy Bysshe Shelley, compared thinking to spinning: 'So I...Sit spinning still...From the fine threads of rare and subtle thought.'[29] As another more explicit example, American writer Augusta Evans Wilson writes in her novel *Vashti* (1869): 'Your mind exhausts and consumes itself, like fabled Arachne, spinning itself into filmy nothings.'[30] The material and imaginative interconnectedness of wheel and thinking mind is so fixed as to remain in everyday colloquialisms centuries later.

In 1857, scholar Abraham Hume, writing for the *Ulster Journal of Archaeology*, celebrated the links between spinning, weaving, and everyday linguistics in Ireland and Scotland. Hume's two essays for the *Ulster Journal* explore the ways in which, in his words, the English language has been 'enriched' by the material practices of spinning and weaving, 'how our commonest expressions would

---

[27] Andrew Gray, *A Treatise on Spinning Machinery* (Edinburgh: Constable, 1819), p. 57.
[28] *Oxford English Dictionary*, s.v. 'spin' (v.).
[29] Percy Bysshe Shelley, *The Poetical Works of Percy Bysshe Shelley*, ed. Mary Shelley (London: Moxon, 1840), p. 266.
[30] Augusta Evans Wilson, *Vashi* (New York, 1869), p. 220.

require to be altered, if we can suppose that the spinning-wheel and the loom had never existed.'[31] Intuiting the material basis of human metaphor long before Gibson wrote about affordance, Hume uses 'afford' to reflect the complementarity of the object of the spinning wheel and local language. His first essay 'observes the subjects of spinning and weaving influencing the habits of thought and expression...giving form and shape to sentences, affording expressiveness to thoughts by the appropriateness of the similitudes.'[32] His words seem to depict the spinning wheel according to the new materialist's idea of vibrant matter. Rather than characterize Hume as an extraordinary, anachronistic new material-ist, his essay affirms that Scots-Irish and Irish people were self-aware of the ways in which the apparatus had shaped their minds and mouths.

Together, Hume's two essays document the eighteenth- and nineteenth-century phrases and songs that deploy spinning metaphorically, including 'the sailor "spins a long yarn;" the orator follows "up the thread of his discourse." '[33] Hume even explains how a spinster came to signify an unmarried woman: 'a woman was considered unfit for marriage until she had spun a set of napery...a set of bed, table and personal linen.'[34] The idea that women should be engaged in making this napery until they were married, even long after they acquired the skills to do so, and even if they might never wed, shows how spinning came to inform and name social status in Scotland and Ireland. Most of the phrases referenced by Hume associate threading with conversing or spinning with productivity, such as 'a goin' foot's always getting something' referring to the treadle of the spinning wheel, which the spinner presses with her foot to make the wheel turn.[35] Hume's essays illustrate a vibrant, material Irish consciousness inundated by the activity of spinning wheel. As such, the physics of spinning draws out the metaphysics of interiorized subjectivity, as it is preserved in colloquial and literary metaphor.

With its continual twistings, revolutions, and evidentiary activity, the spinning wheel was an effective means of conceiving and rendering cognition in a novel or poem. Thus, the Irish spinner character type is not just a familiar rustic ideal in Mary Leadbeater's writing, but a thinking subject that actually holds, via its mate-rial, etymological origins, much more depth than meets the eye. As I will explore throughout the rest of this chapter, these contrasted yet simultaneously coexisting valences of spinning's essence—disciplined inner nature and rotating thought—show that the Irish spinner character might yield to imperial stereotypes of Irish national identity discussed in the previous chapters or signify an invisibly active mind that subversively resists those ideologies.

---

[31] A. Hume, 'Spinning and Weaving: Their Influence on Popular Language and Literature.' *Ulster Journal of Archaeology* 5.1 (1857): p. 104.
[32] Hume, 'Spinning and Weaving,' p. 94.   [33] Hume, 'Spinning and Weaving,' p. 104.
[34] A Hume, 'Historical Notices of Spinning and Weaving.' *Ulster Journal of Archaeology* 5.1 (1857): pp. 175–6.
[35] Hume, 'Spinning and Weaving,' p. 106.

3.3 Spinning Wheels and Subjectivity in
Irish Song and Poetry

Before Petty and Gray wrote their treatises on spinning, Irish minds and voices had long been at work behind the spinning wheel. Throughout the seventeenth and eighteenth centuries, women in Ireland and Scotland were known to complete their spinning as a choral community, singing songs to pass the time and reinforce the rhythm of the work.[36] One extant, printed example of this culture is an inexpensive booklet titled *The Spinning Wheel's Garland*, published in 1775: a collection of five Irish folk songs in the English language. As the title intimates, these songs were composed and circulated specifically to accompany spinning work. A number of these small booklets were published throughout Britain and Ireland in the late eighteenth century, containing songs about spinning wheels such as 'The Spinning Wheel's Glory,' 'The New Spinning-Wheel' and most frequently, a number of different tunes simply titled 'The Spinning Wheel.' These booklets reflect an English, printed iteration of what was typically an Irish-speaking or Ulster-Scots vernacular oral tradition. While eighteenth-century Irish rural culture was characterized by these choruses of female spinners, by the turn of the nineteenth century—a time when the novel became interested in the individual—the figure of the lone Irish spinner rhyming at her wheel superseded the trope of the singing, spinning community, at least in published poetry coming from Ulster.[37]

Famous tune and song collectors like Edward Bunting, George Petrie, and Patrick Joyce have preserved fragments of this once-rich and very much daily custom: the Irish spinning song genre. Breandán Ó Madagáin maintains that the custom of women singing while spinning was as universal in eighteenth- and nineteenth-century Ireland as the spinning wheel itself.[38] He references a local history of Kerry which recalls a well-known and professional spinner, Máire Ruadh, who sang all day to keep time with her wheel.[39] One of the most famous recordings of the Irish genre appears on the album *Songs of Aran*: 'An Túirnín Lín' (The Flax Spinning Wheel), which is a cheerful song whose quick rhythm clearly matches the movement of a spinner's foot on the treadle, keeping time with the regular rotations of her wheel. Rhythm, rather than melody or verse, was in many ways the most important aspect of these songs. George Petrie, discussing the

---

[36] Emma Robertson, Michael Pickering, and Marke Korczynski, ' "And Spinning so with Voices Meet, like Nightingales they Sung Full Sweet:" Unraveling Representations of Singing in Pre-Industrial Textile Production.' *Cultural and Social History* 5.1 (2008): p. 21.

[37] Robertson et al., 'Unraveling Representations,' p. 21.

[38] Breandán Ó Madagáin, 'The Functions of Irish Song in the Nineteenth Century.' *Béaloideas* 53 (1985): p. 204.

[39] Ó Madagáin, 'Functions of Irish Song,' p. 204.

spinning song 'Óró a chumain ghil,' recalls that the spinner/singer, so engrossed in the rhythm, as if a trance, becomes unaware of the length of her verses.[40]

While women like Máire Ruadh often sang on their own at their wheel as if in a private reverie, most traditional spinning songs required at least two spinners to create a melodic dialogue. The song 'Luirín ó lurtha,' 'A spinning wheel song,' requires two songstresses, for example, and most songs took the form of a 'question and answer' structure between *an chéad chailín* and *an dara cailín*, or larger numbers of female participants. In eighteenth- and nineteenth-century Ireland, rural communities were known to hold spinning parties, which inevitably involved song as the main form of entertainment, and would even be attended by men in some cases, as recorded in Henry Coulter's *The West of Ireland* (1862). Older references to these dialogic spinning songs show how they take the form of a confrontational conceit about potential suitors. In reality, Sorcha Nic Lochlainn argues, this 'confrontation' was likely a light-hearted conflict designed for the entertainment of nearby listeners at a spinning party, as if a comic opera. The call and response nature of these matchmaking spinning songs gave occasion for comic retorts that derived their humor from emasculating descriptions of men, what Nic Lochlainn calls 'ritual dispraise,' such as descriptions like 'he's a walking wisp, he staggers at the knees.'[41] Comedy was clearly a function of the communal spinning songs, serving, as Ó Madagáin writes, to lighten the labor and relieve the monotony of the work.[42] The ephemerality of these songs, oftentimes composed on the spot during the spinning or clothmaking work, other times scripted orally beforehand, gave these spinner-composers the security to express comical retorts that otherwise might irreverently and dangerously undermine Irish masculinity. As Galway and Mayo song collector Eileen Costello writes in 1923, the attraction of these humorous spinning songs lay in the fact that they could be 'insulting with impunity.'[43]

On a more serious note, many of these clothmaking songs associated the production of yarn and linen with reproduction. The connection between clothmaking songs and rituals of human fertility is of 'considerable antiquity' in the Gaelic traditions of Scotland and Ireland, where there was a direct overlap between making clothes and clothing babies.[44] The song 'Cuach mo lon dubh buí,' which is an Irish spinning song associated with Ulster traceable to both Donegal and Limerick, offers a unique insight into how these spinning songs might also empower women with the license of free sexual expression. The song is a

---

[40] Ó Madagáin, 'Functions of Irish Song,' p. 159.

[41] Sorcha Nic Lochlainn. ' "Out of a Reverie, and as if Giving Unconscious Expression to a Deep Internal Feeling": Women's Clothmaking Songs in the Gaelic Tradition' in *Oxford Handbook of Irish Song, 1100–1850*, ed. Conor Caldwell (Oxford: Oxford UP, 2021). https://doi.org/10.1093/oxfordhb/9780190859671.013.3.

[42] Ó Madagáin, 'Functions of Irish Song,' p. 198.

[43] Eileen Costello, *Amhráin Mhuighe Seóla* (Dublin: 1923), p. 97.

[44] Nic Lochlainn, 'Out of a Reverie.'

narrative about a young woman forced to marry an old man and one day comes upon a *gruagach*—a young, supernatural, golden-haired man—with whom she has a sexual encounter. The contrast between the young sexual partner and the old, moral husband, Nic Lochlainn writes, 'is almost certainly an emblem of fertility' while permitting, relatively speaking, some sense of bawdiness that might not otherwise be acceptable in public society, suggesting that such songs were sung for female ears alone.[45] As Nic Lochlainn maintains, even when operating in the standard rhythmic formula and matchmaking conceit, Irish female songs could nevertheless make space for some sense of quiet, coded subversion or 'contained protest', as in the Irish keening and lament tradition, through the themes of emasculating description and female virility.

There is also a thread of eighteenth-century music that correlates spinning with nationalism and Irish patriotism. For example, a song commemorating the Flight of the Wild Geese, the last of Gaelic Chieftains, written around 1700, metaphorically correlates the spinning wheel with national devotion to Gaelic leadership and Jacobite resistance. The character of the spinner songstress gives voice to national sentiment: 'I'll sell my rock, I'll sell my wheel, / I'll sell my only spinning wheel, / For to but buy my love a sword of steel.'[46] This song exchanges the material value of the spinning wheel for the symbolic value of dedication to the Jacobite cause in Ireland. The spinner connects wheel with sword—romantic love with love for a Gaelic Ireland and desire to defend it against the English colonizers. In selling her spinning wheel, the singer pledges her own sacrifice to the national cause. Sorcha Nic Lochlainn argues that other kinds of spinning songs emphasized pride of place, further intimating the nationalist potentials or opportunities within the genre of this fleeting, oral spinning song.[47] From emasculating jokes to fertility narratives to nationalist symbolism, the material rhythm of the spinning wheel gave rise to a subversive form of communal and individual expression among women. These songs and themes freed them, temporarily, through rhythmic contact with their spinning wheels, from the discipline of society's gendered expectations, quite the opposite of the ideological work the spinning wheel ostensibly served within the linen manufacture's colonial project: that is, to pacify and discipline the Irish subject.

If spinning women utilized the *ex tempore*, ephemeral nature of song to voice themes not typically accepted in wider society, Ulster weavers, on the other hand, saw the spinning wheel as a creative vehicle for published poetic works that engaged with their local community. From the late eighteenth into the nineteenth century, Ulster country poets—names like James Campbell, James Orr, Alexander MacKenzie, and Thomas Beggs, among others—began to write and publish short books of poetry featuring verse in the local Ulster-Scots vernacular. Themes were

---

[45] Nic Lochlainn, 'Out of a Reverie.'   [46] Hume, 'Spinning and Weaving,' p. 97.
[47] Nic Lochlainn, 'Out of a Reverie.'

typically pastoral and often localized around the imagery of making linen, the 'everyday' experience of cottage life in Ulster. John Hewitt's 1974 collection of these Ulster poets, what he called the *Rhyming Weavers*, was the first comprehensive study to reclaim and reintroduce this provincial lyric tradition, which has since garnered increased interest from scholars. Critics like Frank Ferguson have pointed out that not all the poets writing in the Ulster pastoral identified by Hewitt were actually weavers. Instead, some of these ascribed rhyming weaver poets came from other classes and merely adopted the voice of a laboring weaver, as was common in British and Irish pastoral writing. It was only in the late eighteenth century that linen weavers from the laboring class began to be published as poets.[48]

Jennifer Orr has recently argued for greater aesthetic, nascent-Romantic merit in this Ulster pastoral tradition, particularly through its founding poet, Antrim cottier Samuel Thomson, whose verse paved the way for the Ulster weaver tradition at large.[49] Orr argues that, despite their ostensibly simplistic, quaint country verse, many of the poems in this local tradition sympathized with more radical ideas through coded messages. Some of these poets, like James Orr, for example, identified as United Irishmen.[50] David Gray has expanded Hewitt's genre of the Ulster pastoral to earlier poems by the likes of Anglo-Irishman William Starrat in the early eighteenth century and Donegal clergyman Matthew Draffen in the mid-eighteenth century.[51] What is most important for my purposes here is that many of these poems taking part in the Ulster rhyming weaver tradition assume the voice and character of the lone spinner who is contemplative at her wheel. Invoking laboring, solitary spinning women of the turn of the nineteenth century, these male weaver poets capture a more maudlin, self-reflective monologue stemming from the spinning wheel, as opposed to the humorous, rhythmic dialogues performed by the actual spinners at work throughout Ireland.

In *Desire and Domestic Fiction*, feminist historian Nancy Armstrong argues that eighteenth-century discourse constructed women as the first modern psychological individuals in literature—individuals through whom political ideologies of class and gender played out. This modern woman's self-discipline, romantic desire, and domesticity, as it appeared in writing, formulated a new social order of the middle class where political power moved from the visible aristocratic body to the quieter politics of literary representation of the inner self. Armstrong's model is relevant for the material semiotics of the spinning wheel, especially as it

---

[48] Frank Ferguson, 'We wove our ain wab: The Ulster Weaver Poets' Working Lives, Myths and Afterlives' in *A History of Irish Working Class Writing*, ed. Michael Pierse (Cambridge: Cambridge UP, 2017), p. 90.

[49] Jennifer Orr, ' "No John Clare": Minute Observations from the Ulster Cottage Door.' *John Clare Society Journal* 29 (2010): pp. 52–3.

[50] Orr, 'No John Clare,' pp. 58–9.

[51] David Gray, ' "Stemmed from the Scots"? The Ulsters-Scots Literary "Baird" and the Pastoral Tradition." *Eighteenth-Century Ireland* 32 (2017): pp. 30–1.

emerged through a new Irish poetic character: the contemplative, disciplined female individual at her wheel. The spinning poems of the rhyming weavers use the motion of the spinning wheel to give individuation and emotive consciousness to the spinning woman, while also encoding the object with the idea of a static human body supplanted by an active mind. Whereas the oral culture of spinning songs composed by women subverted society gender norms within the space of the song's conceit, the poetic version of spinning verse more often affirmed Irish character's idealized portrait as an industrious woman with a disciplined mind that emerges from the feminized industrial body.

It would seem the linen discourse's fetishization of Irish women as necessary machinery for fine thread, discussed in the previous chapter, provided rich metaphorical fodder for folk and satiric poets throughout the century, not just the Ulster weaver poets. In particular, English writer Henry Baker's early eighteenth-century poem, 'The Spinning Wheel' (1725), openly sexualizes the spinning wheel when the speaker, hoping to seduce her husband, brings her spinning wheel into their bed:

> But finding it was all in vain
> To sigh, to reason, or complain,
> She from his side did softly steal
> And fetch'd to bed her spinning wheel.[52]

The end of the poem implies the spinning wheel will participate in their erotic play:

> The Doctor, smiling, guessed what she meant
> His blushing spouse's compliment,
> And took the Thing by its right Handle,
> Laid down his Book: Blow'd out the candle.[53]

The substitution of 'thing' for wheel in the penultimate line could be read as phallic innuendo or a surrogate for eroticized, objectified female body parts, as the spinning wheel's function becomes sexual, rather than industrial. Such innuendo can be located in the improvement discourse on linen: manufacturer and linen inspector Robert Stephenson, writing of the yarn from the southern spinning districts, explains, 'There is a Plumpness and Fullness in the Pound Yarn made in the

---

[52] Henry Baker, 'The Spinning-Wheel.' *Original Poems: Serious and Humorous* (London: Roberts, 1725), p. 44.
[53] Ibid., p. 45.

southern Provinces.'[54] As if taking cue from Baker's 'The Spinning Wheel,' Stephenson's language, although likely unconsciously sexualized, nevertheless equates voluptuous yarn with the spinner's female body.

The theme of inactive wheel and inactive female body can be seen in eighteenth-century ballads. In the 1775 broadside folk song titled 'The Spinning Wheel,' the active wheel is again a substitute for the youthful, sexualized female body:

> My spinning wheel runs smooth and light
> and swift links off my five hank Dozen...
> But when I get the parting Kiss...
> Oh then the Heart and Wheel grows heavy.
>
> ...
>
> By the absence of my youthful Swain
> There's Cuts and some odd threads a wanting[55]

The song correlates the speaker's quick, fine spinning with sexual stimulation, and the absence of the latter begets the failure of the former. The Ulster weaver poets furthered this sexual metaphor, but in a way that was distinguished by a contemplative, nostalgic, and individual mind—a kind of disciplined reflection. For example, Antrim bleach mill worker Thomas Beggs wrote a spinner poem that associates fine thread with the speaker's red-cheeked healthy maidenhood: 'An' when I was rade, an' hale, an' young / My thread cam' level, an' fine as a hair.'[56] The fine thread is equated with female youth and beauty, which the speaker, now old, impoverished, and unable to spin on her wheel, nostalgically laments. Such metaphoric analogy is not arbitrary, but a response to a material fact of Beggs's surrounding linen country. Spinster is, as Hume documents, a term that originated in the spinning wheel: unmarried women or widows were the main employees in spinning mills in Ulster.[57]

The wheels in Ulster weaver poems become an extension of the speaker's contemplative mind as well as her body. In Beggs's 'The Auld Wife's Address to her Spinning Wheel,' the eponymous wife addresses her wheel as her own memory: 'An' since the first day she came into my shielf, / We aye had something to keep an' to spare.'[58] The wheel and wife share the goods of their creative labor: the speaker

---

[54] Robert Stephenson, 'Considerations on the Present State of the Linen Manufacture, Humbly Addressed to the Trustees of the Linen Board, 1754.' *An Inquiry into the State and Progress of the Linen Manufacture in Ireland* (Dublin: Powell, 1757), p. 18.

[55] *The Spinning Wheel's Garland, Containing Five Excellent New Songs* (London, 1775), p. 1.

[56] John Hewitt, ed., *Rhyming Weavers* (Belfast: Blackstaff, 2004), p. 169. 'Rade' means red, as in red-cheeked or blushing, and 'hale' means healthy in the Scots dialect.

[57] Brenda Collins, *From Flax to Fabric: The Story of Irish Linen* (Lisburn: Lisburn Museum Publication, 1994), p. 16.

[58] Hewitt, *Rhyming Weavers*, p. 168.

'sung [her] sang, an' [her] wheel [she] plied.'[59] The poem is begotten of the wheel itself, spinning out the wife's reflection on her personal decline and the overarching decline in Ulster's domestic spinning industry following the introduction of industrial machinery. Even the form of the poem reflects the object of the spinning wheel: like the wheel, Charles Armstrong argues, 'the rhymes of the poem create a circular motion of departure and return' as the poem comes to replace the spinning wheel as a work of art.[60]

David Herbison, considered one of the last and most prolific Ulster weaver poets, wrote 'The Auld Wife's Lament for her Teapot,' which also adopts the voice of a spinner and laments the loss of the youthful female body and lifestyle through the silent, still spinning wheel. Reflecting on how she'll no longer entertain suitors in her home, the speaker cries, 'My auld wheel now sits silently / Aboon the bed.'[61] Somewhat paradoxically, in Herbison's poem as well as Beggs's, the silent, unmoving wheel draws out the speaker's internal reflection, as motion transfers from the once busy wheel (and body) to the turning thoughts and emotions of the speaker's own interior life. Therefore, the spinning wheel that domesticated the Irish female body becomes a visible, material fact of an invisible, *immaterial* subjectivity in verse. These individual spinners of the rhyming weaver poems track the textual transition from the disciplined female body at the wheel to the disciplined inner mind as a rationalized response to a formerly active sexuality—a mind that is reflective in its emotion, rather than embodied in sensibility.

Earlier in the eighteenth century, when ideas about individual subjectivity were beginning to appear in sentimental fiction and the English novel, the conscious human mind and the spinning wheel began to coalesce in the Irish novel in addition to Irish verse. Anglo-Irish writer Thomas Amory's second installment to his novel *The Life of John Buncle*, published in 1766, depicts contemplative spinner characters like those in the later poems of the Ulster weaver poets. Although *The Life of John Buncle* does not technically take place in Ireland, critics like Ian Campbell Ross have noted that Amory's novel is consciously about Ireland and Irish experiences, including spinning.[62] At one point in the text, the main character comes upon an idealized pseudo-convent and spinning community:

The [women] were all together in a large handsome room: they sat quite silent, kept their eyes on their work and seemed more attentive to some *inward meditations* than to any thing that appeared or passed by them. They looked contented

[59] Hewitt, *Rhyming Weavers*, p. 168.
[60] Charles I. Armstrong, 'Poetic Industry: The Modernity of the Rhyming Weavers.' *Review of Irish Studies in Europe* 2.1 (2018): pp. 143–4.
[61] Hewitt, *Rhyming Weavers*, p. 171.
[62] For a longer discussion of Amory, see Ian Campbell Ross, 'Thomas Amory, John Buncle, and the Origins of Irish Fiction.' *Eire-Ireland* 18.3 (1983).

and happy. They were all extremely handsome, and quite clean, their linen fine and white.[63]

This passage engages a number of the literary linen themes discussed thus far: the emphasis on fine, white linen, the association of the wheel with feminine beauty, and significantly, the additional association between spinning and interior thought. Although these women are not developed characters, or characters at all, really—more like passing figures in the text—this moment nevertheless redirects the motion of the spinning wheel inward toward the idea of subjective thought and 'inward meditation' in the Irish character. Significantly for the Irish context, this interiorized character is located inside the still, passive, and disciplined female body, who keeps her 'eyes on [her] work' and her mind's eye turned inward, indifferent to potentially distracting (or dangerous, rebellious) surroundings.

Mary Leadbeater's *Cottage Dialogues* also tries to capture the authenticity of native Irish women with 'The Spinning Match,' referenced at the start of this chapter. In the sketch, Leadbeater's young Betty beats twenty other competitors for the top prize—the gift of a 'wheel, cloak and cap,' but most prestigious of all is 'the Lady's commendation' who is, in Betty's words, 'so grand, and so beautiful, and so good' and who even, at the time of the match, 'walked round by the spinners, and spoke to everyone there, so free, and so pleasant.'[64] Betty epitomizes the disciplined Irish female character type that served ideas about improving Ireland. Through her spinning wheel, this gentle, girlish peasant responds positively to industrialized labor and the class system that keeps her at work. Perhaps in a reverse trajectory to Amory's earlier text, Leadbeater's overarching ideology reassociates the spinner's inner feeling with affection for the Anglo-Irish Ascendancy, which she expresses through the material productivity of her spinning wheel.

Both *Cottage Dialogues* and a later publication, *Tales for Cottagers, accommodated to the Present Condition of the Irish Peasantry* (1814) co-authored by Leadbeater and Elizabeth Shackleton, emphasize a mother's duty to teach her girls how to spin efficiently. In Leadbeater's 'The Spinning Match,' Betty thanks her mother for her prize: 'it is you I am obliged to for my cloak, my wheel, and my cap. If you had not taught me to spin, and watched to make me spin an even thread, I might have been ashamed to go [to the match] at all.'[65] In *Tales for Cottagers*, another ideal cottier stereotype, Kitty, shares a maternal filial bond with her daughter through spinning, while Mary's father thinks happily about the increased production of the household: 'Richard longed as much as Mary to see her spinning and thought how delightful it would be to hear the noise of the two

---

[63] Thomas Amory, *The Life of John Buncle, Esq,*. vol. 2 (London: Johnson, 1766), pp. 55–6 (my emphasis).

[64] Leadbeater, *Cottage Dialogues*, p. 205.   [65] Leadbeater, *Cottage Dialogues*, p. 205.

wheels together, and the young voice of his daughter as she sung at it.'[66] In both these cases female labor is sentimentalized and made personal though maternal and paternal affection, as the spinning wheel becomes a locus of familial sentimentality as well as female maturation into young adulthood. Meanwhile, those Irish women who do not spin, like Susy in *Tales for Cottagers*, go into debt.

Finally, poems written by (rather than about) an Irish spinner can deepen our understanding of this disciplined, inwardly directed literary subjectivity. For example, a young Irishwoman and writer, Sarah Leech, was published and marketed specifically as a spinner-poet and can be linked with the Ulster rhyming weavers of a few decades prior. The introduction to Leech's *Poems on Various Subjects* (1828) emphasizes the poet's 'humble sphere of life' as a 'peasant orphan girl' whose only means of 'subsistence' is spinning flax, making her poverty the enigma of her verse while also typecasting her as the idealized, humble, domestic Irish spinner.[67] Significantly, before this introduction, the collection features a frontispiece of Leech at the wheel, simultaneously spinning, reading, and thinking (Figure 3.2). Beside her wheel rest a quill and paper, while her hand moves the flax on the distaff into the wheel's circulation. Like the poems that follow it, the frontispiece uses the central placement of the wheel to construct an idea of moving thoughts rotating within Sarah's own mind. The spinning wheel interiorizes Sarah as a poet-character, implying the busy motion of her inner life while her body remains still and diligent at the wheel or the page. Furthermore, the introduction following this image specifies that the man patronizing her collection's publication first discovered Leech 'busily plying her spinning wheel in a humble cabin,' associating her domestic production with her poetic production.[68] This frontispiece continues a visual theme appearing in William Hincks's 1783 sketch of spinning women in Ulster (Chapter 2, Figure 2.3), in which the profile angle of the spinning woman at the center of the image renders her contemplative, looking off into the distance in thought as she spins.

Leech's collection includes a poem written in her honor that, much like the introduction, identifies the distinctive attribute of Leech's character (and Ireland's) as spinning itself. Richard Ramsay of Letterkenny, the guest poet, praises Leech:

> The Sappho of our Emerald Isle;
> The Useful distaff we may trace
> Back to the happy 'olden times';
> Hence spinning can be no disgrace.[69]

---

[66] Leadbeater and Shackleton, *Tales for Cottagers*, p. 97.
[67] Sarah Leech, *Poems on Various Subjects, by Sarah Leech, a Peasant Girl. With a Biographical Memoir* (Dublin: J. Charles, 1828), pp v, 16.
[68] Leech, *Poems on Various Subjects*, p. 15.
[69] Ramsay, in Leech, *Poems on Various Subjects*, p. 53.

Figure 3.2 *Sarah Leech*, 1828. Frontispiece to Sarah Leech, *Poems on Various Subjects* (Dublin: J. Charles, 1828). Reproduced courtesy of the National Library of Ireland.

Ramsay evokes the ancient trope of the spinner-thinker by referencing Sappho and the figurative ancestral distaff that links Sappho to Leech. He also deliberately nationalizes spinning and thereby feminizes Ireland throughout the poem: 'Such lovely maids are seldom seen, / As at the Irish wheel appear.'[70] Finally, Ramsay's poem suggests that Sarah's special verse, like his characterization of her, comes

---

[70] Ramsay, in Leech, *Poems on Various Subjects*, pp. 53–4.

from the spinning wheel: 'Sweet orphan of the tender lyre / Whose rural verses smoothly flow.'[71] This imagery blends the acts of thinking, writing, and spinning as threads that come together on the spinning wheel and 'smoothly flow' into one motion, one thread, and one verse.

Leech wrote a response to Ramsay's poem, 'Epistle to Mr. Richard Ramsay on purusing his beautiful Address to the Author,' in which she works within the spinning wheel trope imposed on her by his paternalistic verse—compliant, like thread, with the shape he has attributed to her. Like Ramsay, she figures the spinning wheel as the generator of her thoughts:

> Wi' heck weel-teeth'd and spit renew'd
> I sat me down to spin contended
> And your address o me reviewed
> Which set my head amaist demented.[72]

The heck and spit, parts of the spinning wheel apparatus, are renewed like her 'spirit,' so that the spinning wheel itself gives motion to both the thread and her own interior life. As these poems reveal, the work of the spinning wheel naturally lends itself to the conceptualization and invocation of an individual's interiority while constructing the idea of quiet, affectionate feeling as invisibly active in a poor, hardworking, and passive Irish girl.

Like the linen industry itself, some of Leech's poems (re)generate a Protestant, loyalist ideology of Irish politics. Leech wrote anti-Catholic emancipation poems, such as 'The Brunswick Clubs,' which reads, 'Ye British Protestants awake, / The rebel trumpets sound alarm,' as well as pro-Union poems like 'Epistle to Editor of the Londonderry Journal,' which praises those men not 'terrified by Munster pike' in 1798.[73] As we saw in the previous chapter, the linen industry helped to affirm a Protestant-controlled industrialization of Irish domestic life, and in this particular case, so does the spinner-poet and her creative activity. Leech's verse, like the twisted, disciplined thread on her wheel, is compliant with British sovereignty. The wheel's revolution, contrasted with the stationary spinner, seemed to redirect the essence of Irish character inward, inside the spinner. We might surmise, therefore, that published spinning poems like Leech's *had* to lend themselves toward the idea of a disciplined female body and poetic voice because of their public nature, whereas the oral nature of the Irish spinning songs chorused at home allowed a greater freedom of political expression in both the spinner's body and voice.

---

[71] Ramsay, in Leech, *Poems on Various Subjects*, p. 54.
[72] Leech, *Poems on Various Subjects*, p. 55.   [73] Leech, *Poems on Various Subjects*, pp. 62, 44.

3.4 From Linen's Misogynist Discourse to
Owenson's Feminist Characters

Although the spinning wheel seemed to encourage docility in women at an industrial level and actively tame the Irish subject in printed, poetic accounts of the spinning woman, it did something entirely different for Irish novelist Sydney Owenson. Unlike the weaver poets, Owenson responded to the spinning wheel's materiality by figuring a more agential and subversive version of inward-facing Irish character than the disciplined, contemplative subject seen thus far. Owenson therefore moves the potentials of female spinning's subversiveness, otherwise dissolved into the air in the moment of spinning song's completion, into permanency on the printed page. In two of her novels in particular, *The Wild Irish Girl* and *Florence Macarthy*, Owenson uses the spinning wheel's motion to destabilize the English gaze (and the reader's) and challenge the authority of English masculinity. Owenson's novelistic spinning wheels responded to a wider masculine discourse in Ireland, which attempted to control the gendered freedoms the spinning wheel enabled for Irish women.

While the eighteenth-century Irish spinner seemingly affirmed a new imperial model of docile Irish character, her character was shadowed by a continental, cultural history in which female spinning posed a symbolic threat to patriarchal and paternal orders, as seen in the character of the disobedient spinning Eve, discussed earlier. Moreover, in a more material, lived sense, the linen industry enabled new social and economic freedoms for Irish women. Mary O'Dowd has documented that, among the middle classes in eighteenth-century Ireland, many women were able to establish their own businesses in the clothmaking trade.[74] In urban settings, she explains, the Irish textile industry 'provided [urban] women with the most common way of making a living', particularly single women.[75] One of the most successful examples is the McCracken sisters (siblings of the United Irishman Henry McCracken) of Belfast, who ran a muslin manufacture for twenty years.[76]

Focusing on the social changes the linen industry held for spinners of the peasant class, historian Jane Gray argues that the quick expansion of the Irish linen industry was built upon seemingly limitless, undervalued female labor. Nevertheless, despite the injustice of this overall conclusion, spinning also, Gray acknowledges, provided poor women forms of independence, autonomy, and economic self-agency that would have otherwise been unavailable. In spinning districts in Connaught and Munster, women's labor was often a main source of income, giving women greater economic value over their husbands or fathers. Poor Catholic tenants, Gray writes, maintained their 'precarious grip on the land

---

[74] O'Dowd, *History of Women*, pp. 121–2.   [75] O'Dowd, *History of Women*, p. 125.
[76] O'Dowd, *History of Women*, p. 128.

through their women's labor in spinning.'[77] At the same time, Irish spinners experienced greater economic independence outside of the traditional family structure. With her spinning earnings, an unmarried or widowed woman might provide for herself for longer periods of time before having to remarry or move into a weaving household that employed spinners.[78] Moreover, the rural commercialization of flax gave women greater movement and social interaction outside the home. Women traveled to markets to sell their own handspun yarn, encountering new places, people, and experiences along the way. Local women regularly gathered together to prepare flax and spin in a community, creating an all-female network throughout the countryside.[79] Paradoxically, at the same time the linen industry grew rich on the poverty of female spinners by undervaluing their product, it also created a female population on which it was entirely reliant.

It is no surprise, therefore, that the economic and political tracts that praise the Irish women 'naturally bred to spinning' also communicate patriarchal anxiety about women's influence over the industry. One of Robert Stephenson's main concerns in 'Considerations on the Present State of the Linen Manufacture' (1754) is spinning schools organized and run by women, which he seems to want to abolish. He informs the Linen Board that they have put too much focus on establishing spinning schools—that there is generally too much spinning in Ireland at the expense of weaving. Given that spinning was exclusively done by women and weaving by an overwhelmingly male population, there is a gendered implication in his concerns, implying unease with growing networks of female self-sufficiency and authority. Similarly, Arthur Young claims in his *Tour of Ireland* that employing more city men as weavers and increasing landlord patronage of weaving 'will in a few more years do more good for their country than all...their spinning wheels will do in a century.'[80] If the spinning wheel increased female independence, then Stephenson and Young's desire to decrease the amount of spinning wheels in Ireland consequently signals a desire to restrict female autonomy.

Naturally, Stephenson's critiques take particular issue with women placed in positions of authority through spinning. He lampoons spinning school mistresses for teaching students to 'draw flax beyond the staple' in the service of fine spinning: that is, to stretch a spun thread longer than the average length of a collection of fibers, which could result in splintered thread. He claims such methodology slows the process of learning: 'the Prejudice [drawing flax beyond the staple] must naturally do the Manufacture is of the worst Consequence, and the spinning School-mistresses have been rather more culpable in this...than any others in the Kingdom.'[81] Stephenson positions these female spinning authorities as a direct

---

[77] Gray, *Spinning the Threads*, p. 45.   [78] Gray, *Spinning the Threads*, p. 115.
[79] Gray, *Spinning the Threads*, p. 116.
[80] Arthur Young, *A Tour in Ireland*, 2 vols, ed. Arthur Wollaston Hutton (London: G. Bell & Sons, 1892), vol. 2, p. 217.
[81] Stephenson, 'Considerations,' p. 16.

threat to the manufacture at large, both undermining their expertise and also acknowledging their wider, far-reaching influence within the industry. As another example, he takes issue with a spinning school in Dublin that employs two-handed spinning wheels, which, Stephenson claims, produce thread so uneven as to 'destroy all our Manufactures.'[82] What is at issue here, for Stephenson, is not so much destruction as control—that a spinning school could initiate new technologies and techniques outside the jurisdiction of male authorities like himself. As a final insult, Stephenson's 1765 report to the Linen Board advocates for abolishing yarn halls, or yarn-selling markets, which are, he claims, 'improper articles of expense' given that yarn is, in his words, 'only a material.'[83] Here, Stephenson's budget plans undercut Irish female autonomy: disbanding the yarn halls, a space where Irish spinners sell their wares directly, would consequently limit their mobility outside the home, their autonomy within the trade, and the individual value of their refined flax product.

William Carleton, whose own mother was a spinner and regularly sang at her wheel when he was a child, published his *Traits and Stories of the Irish Peasantry* in 1832, which gives some insight into Irish middle-class and peasant reservations about female spinning. Carleton's incorporation of local Irish folk tales implies that some of the anxieties around spinning may have been linked to a fear of female earning. 'The Lianhan Shee,' for example, tells of a peasant character named Mary, knitting alone in her cottage, who is visited by a woman under the curse of the Lianhan Shee, a fairy mistress who confers wealth on a person then leeches upon his or her body and soul. Likewise, John and Michael Banim's *Tales of the O'Hara Family* (1825), involves a short anecdote about a character named Christien Moore and her blind mother, both 'tireless spinners,' who make their fortune by spinning 'coarse blankets...[and] sheets' to furnish their lodging enterprise.[84] These women literally make their independence and capital by spinning and knitting, but they are also presented as teetering on the edge of social norms, such as Christien who had 'three obedient' husbands, a fact that constitutes both comic oddity and her own social deviation.[85]

In line with this perhaps subconscious fear of female earning facilitated by spinning, various writers sought to promote the linen industry through misogynist rhetoric—an ironically self-sabotaging tactic, given that, as Jane Gray has shown, the linen industry relied on female labor and cooperation. Most famous of all, Jonathan Swift's *Proposal for the Universal Use of Irish Manufacture* attacks Irish women for wearing foreign brocades rather than Irish gowns and petticoats.

---

[82] Stephenson, 'Considerations,' p. 185.

[83] Robert Stephenson, 'Report of the State of the linen Manufacture of Ireland for 1765.' *The Reports and Observations of Robert Stephenson made to the Right Honourable and Honourable Trustees of the Linen Manufacture for 1764 and 1765* (Dublin: Printed by the order of the Linen Board, 1766), p. 143.

[84] John and Michael Banim, *Tales of the O'Hara Family* (Duffy, 1865), p. 319.

[85] Banim and Banim, *Tales*, p. 319.

Similarly, Robert Stephenson condemns the new Linen Board Inspector Mr Arbuthnot's reports on the Irish industry by using 'old woman' as a repeated, belittling insult. For example, he writes, 'there is not an old woman in Ireland but has better adapted implements than any he has yet produced.'[86] On another occasion, he says Mr Arbuthnot's so-called 'conclusions' about linen are obvious facts that 'every old woman in Ireland knows' already.[87] In other words, Arbuthnot is so amateur, so unaware of the complex workings of the linen industry that he is on par with an ignorant old Irish woman, a linen laborer of the lowest standing and least education, dissociating the act of spinning from its afforded metaphor of active deep thinking. Nevertheless, it is those old Irish women who, in congress with flax, furnish and stimulate the national industry that Stephenson seeks to champion.

From a new materialist perspective, the active Irish spinning wheel, generating ideas about subjectivity, could both reconstruct the idea of the disciplined, passive yet contemplative Irish subject while also—by virtue of its very activity—suggest that female spinners might have as much control over their own minds as the spinning wheel had over the flax. It is this very material-semiotic implication that Sydney Owenson seizes upon to challenge any masculinized rhetoric that devalued spinning. Famous in her own lifetime for retaliating against misogynist rhetoric from her male critics, Owenson was well aware of Ireland's longstanding spinning and song tradition and thereby capitalized on the wheel's affordance female self-assertiveness in Ireland.[88] Owenson reconfigured the spinning wheel's materiality and kinetic energies toward a novelistic concept of subjectivity that was not just inward but explicitly subversive in the face of English paternalism. Chapter 1 discussed how Owenson's *The Wild Irish Girl* bridged the Irish literary tradition of the *aisling* lament with the English novel, extending the parameters of what an English-language novel and its heroine could look like. I suggest Owenson does something similar with the English novelistic tradition of representing subjectivity, using the spinning wheel to figure a different kind of Irish literary character, who holds inaccessible depth that challenges the standard novelistic definition of a deeply personalized protagonist, who the reader peruses like an open book. Coincidentally, reading the spinning wheel's feminist implications for Irish character unfolds a more nuanced critical reading of Sydney Owenson as a writer.

---

[86] Robert Stephenson, *Observations on the Present State of the Linen Trade of Ireland: in a series of letters addressed to the Right Honourable trustees of the Linen Manufacture. In which the Reports, Libel, and British Examination of Mr John Arbuthnot, Inspector General of Leinster, Munster, and Connaught, are considered and refuted* (Dublin, 1784).

[87] Stephenson, *Observations*, p. 31.

[88] For a discussion of Owenson responding to her critics, such as John Wilson Croker, see Claire Connolly, '"I accuse Miss Owenson": The Wild Irish Girl as Media Event.' *Colby Quarterly* 36.3 (2000): pp. 98–115, or Mary Campbell's literary biography of Owenson, *Lady Morgan: The Life and Times of Sydney Owenson* (London: Pandora, 1988).

Within the past two decades, Sydney Owenson has been praised by a number of notable literary critics—Terry Eagleton, for example—for her staunchly Gaelic, nationalist, and anti-Union politics, as well as her charming character, bold symbolism, and performative social appearances where she played the 'wild Irish girl' to her own personal advantage in English aristocratic drawing rooms filled with Tory politicians.[89] However, despite her merits as a representative of liberal thinking in early nineteenth-century Ireland, Owenson has rarely been distinguished for her aesthetic abilities as a novelist. Since the beginning of the nineteenth century, Owenson's more famous and celebrated contemporaries, Jane Austen and Maria Edgeworth, have stood as the accomplished pioneers of the novel with whom Owenson does not compare. Austen and Edgeworth themselves spurned Owenson's writing style. In the winter of 1809, Austen wrote the following in a letter after perusing Owenson's recent publication, *Ida of Athens*: 'the Irish Girl does not make me expect much. If the warmth of her Language could affect the Body, it might be worth reading in this weather.'[90] Similarly, Edgeworth wanted to be publicly disassociated from her fellow Irish novelist and asked friends and family to confirm the two authors had never met socially.[91]

Owenson's style came under fire frequently in her lifetime, and not just in private correspondence. For example, a parody of *The Wild Irish Girl* titled 'Glorviniana' appeared in 1807 in a short-lived Dublin periodical, *The Anonymous*. The short piece quotes and attacks 'The Owensonian manner' of writing and even, at one stage, implies Owenson cannot speak English.[92] In particular, the mock editor lampoons Owenson's ornate descriptions of Glorvina: 'Glorvina is really delightful. Her manners are "the result of natural intuitive coquetry" mixed up, as I have said before, with the primeval innocence, Rouseauishness, Werterism, and the Lord knows what.'[93] Owenson was also regularly, viciously attacked by male reviewers at the *Quarterly* and *Edinburgh Review*—a challenge she met by publishing responsive retaliations.[94]

Many critics have since echoed these thoughts on Owenson's flowery language. Joep Leerssen, for instance considers it a 'flaw': 'The hybrid vacillation of Morgan...between a novelistic and a romantic register seriously flaws [her] Irish

[89] See Terry Eagleton, *Heathcliff and the Great Hunger: Studies in Irish Culture* (London: Verso, 1995).

[90] Jane Austen, *Jane Austen's Letters*, ed. Deirdre Le Faye, 4th edn (Oxford: Oxford UP, 2011), pp. 173–4.

[91] Marilyn Butler, *Maria Edgeworth: A Literary Biography* (Oxford: Clarendon, 1972), p. 258.

[92] 'Glorviniana' in *The Port Folio*, vol. 7, ed. Joseph Dennie (Philadelphia: Dennick & Dickins, 1812), pp. 227, 230. According to Joseph Dennie, the satire was probably written by Anacreon Moore and a Mr Curran. See Dennie, *The Port Folio*, vol. 7, pp. 228–241.

[93] Dennie, *The Port Folio*, vol. 7, p. 234.

[94] Ina Ferris, *The Romantic National Tale and the Question of Ireland* (Cambridge: Cambridge UP, 2004), pp. 68–71.

tales, often to the point of ludicrousness.'[95] More recent feminist criticism, however, has championed Owenson's value for the Irish canon. Ina Ferris deliberately defends Owenson as an author worthy of increased critical engagement, and her book, *The Romantic National Tale and The Question of Ireland*, began the work of seeing a complex creative model at work in Owenson's hybridized, deterritorialized heroines.[96] Despite Ferris's compelling arguments, the author's aesthetic contributions remain undervalued in comparison to her national ones.

I propose that this de-emphasis on Owenson's aesthetic accomplishments correlates to an Anglocentric and anthropocentric understanding of literature—a lack of material imagination when it comes to thinking about the rendering of subjectivity beyond the English standard of Austen's intimacy between protagonist and reader. This is where new materialism can intercede: by highlighting creative, material aspects of Owenson's formulation of Irish character that have been underplayed and overlooked. Her application of the spinning wheel's motion suggest that Owenson did not necessarily set out, like Austen, to develop a perfectly coherent, personalized, deep-thinking character that the reader could get to know intimately through his or her private reading experience. Rather, in the act of politicizing her female characters and their spinning wheels, as in *Florence Macarthy* (1818), Owenson changes the parameters and expectations of the novel's protagonist, adapting to the colonial dynamics of Anglo-Irish relations.

Owenson's spinner characters in her novels, of which the eponymous Florence Macarthy is most iconic, encapsulate an Irish mindset that coheres with Owenson's own anti-Union and bluestocking politics. Florence Macarthy offers the pinnacle example of a self-consciously feminist character engineered in tandem with the physical materiality of the spinning wheel. In that novel, Owenson intentionally blends her own identity as author with eponymous Florence Macarthy, who, as Ina Ferris explains, is deliberately both abstract personification of woman Ireland and also a 'fully developed' feminist, nationalist individual.[97] In one of the novel's keynote moments, Florence Macarthy (known in this moment as Lady Clancare) actively spins flax while the novel's male protagonist watches her, declaring the work of her spinning wheel as the work of writing her own narrative:

> With Ireland in my heart, and epitomizing something of her humour and her sufferings in my own character and story, I do trade upon the materials she furnishes me, and turning my patriotism into pounds, shillings, and pence, endeavor at the same moment, to serve her and support myself. Meantime my

[95] Joep Leerseen, *Remembrance and Imagination: Patterns in the Historical and Literary Representation of Ireland in the Nineteenth Century* (South Bend, IN: University of Notre Dame Press, 2010), p. 52.

[96] Ferris, *Romantic National Tale*, p. 76.   [97] Ferris, *Romantic National Tale*, pp. 72–3, 76.

wheel, like my brain, runs round. I spin my story and my flax together; draw out a chapter and an hank in the same moment; and frequently break off the thread of my reel and of my narration under the influence of the same association.[98]

This is one of the first instances where Florence speaks openly in the text, suggesting that the spinning wheel has transformed a shadowy, enigmatic figure into an assertive, expressive character. When Florence Macarthy boldly declares 'I spin my story and my flax together,' Owenson reworks the spinning wheel's energy from quiet subjectivity kept in check, like that in the Ulster weavers' spinning poems, quoted earlier, toward outward proclamations of patriotism. In almost ironic contradiction with the spinners who seemingly complied with British policies of industrializing Ireland, Owenson's novelistic spinning wheel in *Florence Macarthy* is defiant, almost rebellious, resisting the controlling male gaze of Florence's male, Anglo-Irish onlooker, Fitzwalter, and of England itself. The character's tone, like her spinning wheel, is combative: she 'breaks off' the thread and narrative with assertive force, positioning wheel and word as modes of defending herself (and by proxy, her author) and her nation.

What's more, Florence tells Fitzwalter that she spins on the same wheel as her grandmother, 'who had the blood royal of Ireland in her veins,' adding that, 'our grandmothers of the highest rank in Ireland were all spinners.'[99] Here, Owenson reshapes the spinning industry in Ireland as native tradition rather than imperial improvement, replacing the recent history of British and Anglo-Irish industrial ambition with her own 'order'—an idealized and matrilineal Gaelic past. Thus, at the same time the spinning wheel develops the formerly mysterious Florence Macarthy into a bold, self-assertive character, it also signifies and constructs an idea of collective female agency in Ireland. She redirects the agentic capacity of the wheel's spinning motion toward female agency that imagines and extracts women's history from a dominant male narrative, resists the gaze and constraints of imperial ideologies, and spins it into something new: a subversive Irish woman in fiction.

Florence's words quoted above envision a narrative process in which the spinning wheel (and Irish novel) can transform Ireland's 'sufferings' into female and economic gain. If, as Macarthy claims, the spinning wheel 'furnishes' the work of self-narrative, it follows that any spinner can wield and craft her own mind toward national or personal advantage—a bold feminist conviction. Through Florence's wheel, Owenson also constructs a meta-reflection on the novel itself, self-consciously describing the work of making an assertive, individualistic Irish character like Florence Macarthy as the spinning of flax fiber into hanks, or

---

[98] Sydney Owenson, *Florence Macarthy: An Irish Tale*, ed. Jenny McAuley (London: Routledge, 2015), vol. 3, p. 274.

[99] Owenson, *Florence Macarthy*, vol. 3, p. 274.

chapters. Ferris sees this scene as a metaphor for Owenson writing Irish tales for the English market—an extratextual allusion that justifies Owenson's own efforts to turn 'national injury into economic gain.'[100] In that reading, Florence signifies an updated national allegory of Union that invokes the modern commercial and marketing context of Anglo-Irish relations within the linen and Irish tale trades. However, Florence's declaration is not simply metaphor or an allegory, but also a literal, physical demonstration of the power the spinning wheel holds—how it can exert its own kinetic force and give shape to the active, vibrant interior mind of the female character and female author, whose thoughts 'run round' like wheels.[101]

Owenson associates subversive and nationalist politics with deep-seated inner convictions, so that even when Florence is silent the spinning wheel reminds us of her strong inner life, particularly, her patriotic feminism. A few years later, Sarah Leech would practice Macarthy's philosophy, using her spinning wheel to make money from her published poems and publicly express her personal, loyalist opinions on Ireland (although very different from Owenson's anti-Unionism). *Florence Macarthy*, therefore, corroborates the process in which a character's subjective thought in Irish fiction develops in relation to the physicality of the spinning wheel as apparatus. Owenson's imagery of the symbolic wheel literally spins the trope of female spinners into subjects who possess, among other thoughts and sentiments, their own political convictions. This is different than the dominant model Nancy Armstrong locates in the English novel, where the new ideal of domestic, disciplined, female individual disguises the political power structures she encodes. However, at most stages throughout the text, Florence is, like many of Owenson's other heroines—Glorvina of *The Wild Irish Girl* and Beauvoin O'Flaherty of *The O'Briens and the O'Flahertys* (1824), for example—in the shadows of the narrative, either wearing a disguise, pretending to be her cousin rather than herself, or elusive in the narrative's plotting. Therefore, the spinning wheel becomes an active, physical affirmation of Florence's moving thoughts at the same time that Owenson removes the heroine from the reader's familiarity, keeping her aloof and inaccessible.

An earlier version of Florence's spinning subjectivity appears in *The Wild Irish Girl* (1806), where the wheel resists imperial, male authority as well as alludes to physical violence. Early in the text, Horatio, newly arrived in Ireland, finds himself 'attracted towards a ruinous barn by a full chorus of females.'[102] Inside the barn he discovers 'a group of young females seated round an old hag who formed the centre of the circle...all busily employed at their wheels, which I observed went merrily around in exact time with their song.'[103] The reader inhabits

---

[100] Ferris, *Romantic National Tale*, p. 72.   [101] Owenson, *Florence Macarthy*, vol. 3, p. 274.
[102] Sydney Owenson, *The Wild Irish Girl*, ed. Kathryn Kirkpatrick (Oxford: Oxford UP, 1999), p. 21.
[103] Owenson, *Wild Irish Girl*, p. 21.

Horatio's perspective on the scene as the wheels convey motion—'went merrily around in exact time with the song'—encapsulating the correlation between the spinning wheel's revolution and the interior, active deep subjectivity of the protagonist Horatio, stimulated by new and exotic sights. Owenson awards the spinning wheels their own active agency as they keep time with the women's song, and thus acknowledges the cooperative relationship between flax, wheel, and woman I have been tracing throughout this chapter.

Despite the vividness of this gendered colonial encounter, it is not strictly an original one. As Jones and Stallybrass explain, 'depictions of sexually promiscuous scenes in the spinning room, when men entered a woman's world' were common in European writing from the fifteenth to seventeenth centuries, particularly in Dutch and German culture.[104] As mentioned earlier, Irish author Thomas Amory depicted this voyeuristic trope in an Irish context half a century before Owenson, when his protagonist John Buncle enjoys watching a group of 'extremely handsome' women as they spin. The image of the singing spinner was a long-established trope, a 'pleasing evocation of pre-industrial labor,' when Owenson wrote this scene.[105] At the same time, however, the tradition of bantering melodic exchanges among spinning women in Ireland, discussed previously, can easily destabilize this pleasing, feminine image of 'pre-industrial labor.'

The coded, female awareness of the potentially emasculating humor in the Irish spinning song tradition *is* what makes Owenson's depiction of scene particularly original and uniquely Irish in its feminist implication. Unlike John Buncle, Horatio's voyeurism is detected and ridiculed:

The whole was sung in Irish, and as soon as I was observed, suddenly ceased; the girls looked down and tittered—and the old woman addressed me sans ceremonie, and in a language I now heard for the first time...I explained with all possible politeness the cause of my intrusion on this little harmonic society. The old woman looked up in my face and shook her head; *I* thought contemptuously—while the young ones, stifling their smiles, exchanged looks of compassion, doubtlessly at my ignorance of their language.

So many languages a man knows, says Charles V, 'so many times he is a man,' and its certain *I* never felt myself less invested with the dignity of one, than while I stood twirling my stick, and 'biding the encounter of the eyes,' and smiles of these 'spinners in the sun.'[106]

Horatio stands outside a physical circle of spinners and a figurative circle of female knowledge, secret communication, and craft. His inability to understand

<hr/>

[104] Jones and Stallybrass, *Renaissance Clothing*, p. 5.
[105] Robertson et al., 'Unraveling Representations,' p. 11.   [106] Owenson, *Wild Irish Girl*, p. 21.

the spinners and their song emasculates him; by his own words, he is emptied of the 'dignity' of man, realizing the fears implied by Hincks's symbolically emasculating plate on flax dressing discussed previously (Chapter 2, Figure 2.6). In *The Romantic National Tale and the Question of Ireland*, Ina Ferris offers a perceptive reading of the scene's gendered implications: the spinners who look back into Horatio's gaze, she argues, make him 'aware of the existence of another world in which his usual (English, masculine) identity no longer quite sustains itself.'[107] That 'other world' is not just the world of women or the Irish language, but also of spinning wheels, the harmonized chorus of human-nonhuman rhythm, which a baffled Horatio observes go 'round in unison' with the 'strains' of their chorus.[108]

Horatio's masculine presence, and thereby his English paternalism, becomes a joke shared among the spinners, who 'titter' and 'hide their smiles,' while all he can do is 'twirl his stick.' With this final image of the unintelligible Horatio, face to face with feminine, Irish ridicule and contempt, foolishly twirling his impotent stick (a sign of his English gentility and status), Owenson seems to laugh at masculinity itself, both its social and anatomical authority. Whereas Amory's *The Life of John Buncle* depicts the spinning women as objects to view, Owenson adds vocal, subversive expression to the spinning room trope, renders the wheels and women into subjects that can respond to and actively challenge a man's voyeuristic objectification. In Owenson's take, the English traveler becomes the textual object of the song's humor, rather than Horatio turning the women into Irish stereotypes in his letters, as would have been common in English travel writing.

Because this scene is told from within Horatio's interior perspective, it also demonstrates an adversarial relationship between an Irish, female spinning wheel and English subjectivity. These moving, secretly communicating spinning wheels intercede in Horatio's sense of self—the most basic maleness of his own character and identity. What bothers Horatio most, what causes him to truly feel the effects of social emasculation, is that he cannot understand the women's material and physical language—that he cannot know how the wheels move in time with their song or what the spinners are thinking behind what he supposes are a contemptuous look from the old woman and compassionate smiles from the young ladies. Thus, the spinning wheel's melodic motion in the scene alerts us to how these responsive women have seized and stalled Horatio's English subjectivity by undermining its foundation in the male gaze and English speech. Equally important, the spinning wheels also signal the women's own indecipherable interior narratives—a legible sign of their unreadable thoughts. In particular literary contexts like Owenson's, the spinning wheel's movement nonverbally articulates both an active mind *and* a threat to the paternalistic order that, in other contexts, the spinning wheel corroborated. Owenson's writing shows us that, despite

[107] Ferris, *Romantic National Tale*, p. 53.   [108] Owenson, *Wild Irish Girl*, p. 21.

ideological attempts to discipline the woman and her instrument, the spinning wheel nevertheless makes Irish female subjectivity readily apparent and visible, alarming characters like Horatio, writers like Robert Stephenson, or, potentially, the perceptive English reader. The turning wheel visualizes the turning thoughts and sentiments of the woman beside it, which might otherwise be buried under layers of ideological constructions that figure women as Hibernia or docile, disciplined instruments in a male-run industry.

Whereas Horatio, the English character, is a 'traditional' novelistic protagonist who shares his inner thoughts intimately with the reader, Owenson's texts award Irish female characters interior minds without divulgence. Rather, the material process of the spinning wheel affirms that these characters contain their own private thoughts and languages outside the discursive domain of the text, which, as we have seen in the past chapter and this one, attempts to ideologically characterize Ireland as feminized, subdued, and disciplined. Owenson's spinning wheels, signifying thought and subjectivity without detail, both undermine the text's authority and thwart the ability of the reader, placed in the position of English onlooker, to read the 'real' Irish character that lies underneath the language of literary representation and national stereotypes. In texts like *The Wild Irish Girl* and *Florence Macarthy* the spinning wheel articulates a subversive narrative for Irish character that opposes the improvement discourse that instigated the circulation of spinning wheels throughout Ireland in the first place.

3.5 Feminist, Material Subversion in *The Croppy, A Tale of 1798*

Following Owenson's lead, a later novel by writing team John and Michael Banim, *The Croppy; A Tale of 1798* (1828) openly explores the subversive potential of Irish, female subjectivity. The old woman character trope, which *The Wild Irish Girl* invokes through the disproving old spinner in the barn, becomes a fully developed, deep character in the Banims' Nanny the Knitter, an old *sean bhean bhocht* character who savvily makes money by knitting and matchmaking. Nanny the Knitter's handicraft parallels her narrative technique, and, as with Florence Macarthy, her mind, speech, and hands are always in parallel motion. As the narrators explain: 'however employed in talking, [Nanny's] hands were never idle' for she 'knit[s] her stockings and her narrative together.'[109] This line recalls the earlier feminist character Florence Macarthy, who spins 'her story and her flax together.'[110] Knitting, of course, is different from spinning, although the two craftworks have

---

[109] John and Michael Banim, *The Croppy; A Tale of 1798*, 3 vols (London: Colburn, 1828), vol. 1, pp. 30, 105.

[110] Owenson, *Florence Macarthy*, vol. 1, pp. 30, 105.

been historically feminized and associated with one another, particularly regarding the spinning of woolen yarn for home-made knitting in southern and western Ireland. Sorcha Nic Lochlainn groups spinning and knitting songs together in her discussion of the sometimes-subversive clothmaking song tradition, explaining that women's work with knitting, just like spinning, was often accompanied by communal music in eighteenth- and nineteenth-century Ireland.[111] Although Nanny is characterized as a knitter, rather than named 'Nanny the Spinner,' her character nevertheless invokes that old woman spinner trope common in eighteenth-century Ulster weavers' poetry—an allusion that is further affirmed by the fact that she narrates her story from inside a linen chest.

In *The Croppy*, the starring object is the linen chest. This chest furnishes the authors with a whimsical and pointed opportunity to explore the interchangeability between Irish subject and material object and stage a material model of colonial subjectivity. The novel's blending between material object and human subject (the linen chest and the character Nanny) enables the subversive, feminist interiority developed by Owenson to flourish on a successfully satiric level when the unlikely characters of Nanny and the linen chest dupe some Irish villains. The narrative of *The Croppy* does not enter Nanny's interior life until the third volume, when the criminal Bill Nale and his gang come to ransack the 'Big House,' and Nanny locks herself inside a linen chest to hide from them. A large linen chest, which the narrators tell us 'may yet be found in the possession of Irish housewives of the middling class,' is a consumer byproduct of the eighteenth-century Irish linen industry.[112] Thus, when Nanny enters the chest, laying down upon her 'couch of linen,' both she and the reader literally enter and inhabit the material contexts of the linen-making industry.[113]

Significantly, Nanny's contact with that cushion of linen instigates the novel's inward turn to her thoughts, and her character transforms into an it-narrator like the coin of Chapter 1. The following pages of the novel are told from inside Nanny's perspective *inside* the linen chest, literalizing the interiority of novelistic character through the sensory experience of being inside the hollow material object. All the sensations and experiences of the scene are rendered from inside the chest: for example, Nanny hears the approaching 'clamour of voices and the stamping of feet... closer and closer they came,' giving her 'sensations almost of dissolution' in fear at the approaching gang.[114] When Nanny gets an inside view of the material object, readers get an inside view of her character.

Akin to Horatio who could not make sense of the Irish spinners' thoughts and words, Bill Nale and his gang fail to realize that Nanny, an Irish subject, hides

---

[111] Nic Lochlainn, 'Out of a Reverie.' 'Cuach mo lon dubh bhí,' for example, was sung during both knitting and spinning in the Donegal Gaeltacht.
[112] Banims, *The Croppy*, vol. 3, p. 68.   [113] Banims, *The Croppy*, vol. 3, p. 69.
[114] Banims, *The Croppy*, vol. 3, p. 70.

inside the chest when they steal it from the Big House: one asks 'What's in this big chest?' to which the other replies 'Only some linen.'[115] This simple reply, 'only some linen,' comically underscores how, by underestimating a domestic item like a linen chest, these men consequently underestimate the perspective hiding inside. Unable to unlock the chest, they steal it and carry it across the Irish countryside and the ransacked battlefields of 1798, as Nanny becomes an accidental spy to their murderous plotting. She hears conversations in 'very low tones' interspersed with jolting and loud bangs as she 'concludes that the [road] became still more difficult, for Nanny could feel that she traveled very slowly.'[116] A series of ten or eleven pages are told in this style, a complete fictional immersion in how a series of events—even important historical events like the Rebellion of 1798— might feel from inside a domestic interior and inside a subliminal female perspective. What's more, as Nanny continues to listen to Nale's plots of kidnap and murder, the text openly collapses the distinction between materiality and female subjectivity in wordplay: 'Nanny felt no increase of comfort in her chest.'[117] Here, 'chest' means both the literal chest she is locked inside and her own chest—the feelings and anxiety she experiences within her mind—a syntactic, intra-active blurring of material object and human subject.

The perspective of this chapter, which is both the linen chest's and Nanny's, signifies material and female agency. As the episode unfolds, albeit farcically— interspersed with Nanny's absurd Stage Irish phrases like her 'ould heart riz up to the root iv her tongue' in fear—the perspective facilitated by the linen chest awards Nanny greater power of knowledge over her adversary, Bill Nale, who had long wanted her dead for knowing too many of his secrets.[118] The literal subversiveness of the chest/Nanny's point of view and the powerful implication of her physical access to Nale's thoughts emerge in the following description:

> She caught...the continuation of a dialogue held between Nale and Sam, as they sat at different sides of the chest, and spoke in loud accents over it. From the free and confidential manner in which they interchanged some important opinions and allusions, Nanny concluded that they were now alone...and alas! Unsuspicious of [her] near espionage.[119]

The image is a provocative one: two men discuss the events of the Rebellion over a linen chest which they erroneously presume to be a passive, negligible object— in the same way as women were seen as passive objects of national symbolism and industrial economy. Thus, the creativity and humor of the Banims' scene coincidentally highlights how men like Bill Nale underestimate both the material

[115] Banims, *The Croppy*, vol. 3, p. 71.
[116] Banims, *The Croppy*, vol. 3, pp. 75–6.
[117] Banims, *The Croppy*, vol. 3, p. 78.
[118] Banims, *The Croppy*, vol. 3, p. 73.
[119] Banims, *The Croppy*, vol. 3, p. 76.

and feminine worlds, failing to notice what is right underneath his nose as he speaks across the linen chest and across Nanny. In fact, during the journey inside the chest, Nanny bears witness to Bill's misogyny when he says, 'Them women are the divils—out-an-out…ever since the day I [Nale] was born one woman or another crowed over [him].'[120] Ironically, the chest/woman listening *underneath* Bill's voice poses the real threat to his fate. By failing to consider what might be inside an object, and likewise, inside a woman, Nale makes himself vulnerable.

Most importantly, the passage above effectively blurs the material and figurative narratives when a linen chest containing a feminine, subversive interiority is literally situated in the middle of a male discourse. That this entire episode takes place within the wider context of the Rebellion of 1798 points to the feminized subversion potentially lying within the material world across all kinds of masculinist narratives, histories, and imperial ideologies. In a sense, then, the Banims use the linen chest to imagine and furnish the undivulged feminist, material narrative lying within the unreadable interior of an Irish female character like Owenson's spinners or old woman tropes like Nanny. One might even see these hidden and unreadable characters depicted by the Banims and Owenson, respectively, as a fantasy that, in the wake of failed rebellion and Act of Union, subversively reasserts Irish national meaning inside ostensibly inert and unagentic things and people.

As with the other Irish characters traced so far in this book, Nanny's interior experience, as developed inside the linen chest, originates in violence. Her escape into the chest is initially motivated by the fear that Bill Nale will murder her, and her subjective experience inside the chest is characterized by the anxiety he will discover her. As with the shilling it-narrator of Chapter 1, Nanny's interiorized experience is bookended by the memory of violence and the fear of its return. Moreover, wartime violence literally surrounds the interiorized episode, as the chest/Nanny travels through the battlefields of 1798. Violence also resides in the very material constitution of the linen on which Nanny lies—in the flax that was beetled and scutched before becoming the fine stuff of middle-class bedding locked away in a chest. The material narrative of linen underscores the fact that violent action and dangerous labor are the material foundation of Nanny's journey.

These first three case studies—coin, flax, and now spinning wheel—have narrated a material and cultural phenomenon in which Irish objects are feminized to cover up a violent colonial past. However, new materialist readings that privilege matter's agency, nonhuman-human intra-action, and the affordances of material processes can nevertheless peel back that rhetorical disguise of a pacified, submissive Ireland. The Banims' linen chest episode literalizes the new materialist

[120] Banims, *The Croppy*, vol. 3, p. 79.

readings of the previous two chapters: that subversive feminine subjectivity can emerge out of Ireland's violent contexts. Characters like Florence Macarthy, the spinning women in the barn in *The Wild Irish Girl*, and Nanny the Knitter remind us that what is feminized in the wake of colonial oppression also necessarily bears feminist potential, be it spinning wheel, literary character, or the Irish nation.

*   *   *

Spinning wheels and the flax they spun were some of the most pervasive, powerful, paradoxical objects in eighteenth-century Ireland. At the same time that they created the material subculture for new imperial formulations of Irish character as docile, feminine, and industrial, they also afforded the literary imaginary with an Irish peasant character that was subversive and potentially feminist—a threat that could emasculate the codified British, male subject. The production and sale of Irish linen does not displace or conceal the violent gendered history of British–Irish relations but rather continually regenerates its memory through the literary communion of Irish women and the spinning wheel. One might even be tempted to say that the material and domestic practices of the eighteenth-century linen industry put the possibility of violent Irish reaction into the hands and minds of women.

The spinning wheel's material and metaphoric connection to Irish subjectivity can also change the way we read the cultural implications of Irish linen's international circulation in the century that followed. By the mid-nineteenth century, Barbour's Linen Thread, a company founded in 1784, had replaced domestic spinners as the main manufacturer of Irish flax yarn. One hundred years after its establishment, Barbour's opened stores in New York, Boston, Chicago, London, Paris, Hamburg, Montreal, Sydney, Milan, Madrid, and many other cities. Celebrating their international reach and reliable 'durability,' Barbour's 1894 advertisements utilized that familiar eighteenth-century trope of the Irish spinner at the wheel, but this time, with a roaring lion at her side, tangled up in her newly spun flax threads (Figure 3.3). The lion signifies the advertised 'strength and durability' of Barbour's thread through the symbolic heraldry of England's national animal. What the advertisement also demonstrates is that, even when commercialized on a global scale, the commodity of Irish linen still relies on the visual currency of the domestic Irishwoman hand-spinning flax.

However, the spinning wheel's connection to feminist subjectivity, as traced throughout this chapter, can be seen to reframe the image's intended marketing. The object's material narrative reminds us that Barbour's spinner possesses her own invisible subjectivity, which may scheme to tether the English lion rather than disentangle it. Together, the natural strength of flax as a robust fiber and the quick movement of the spinning wheel communicate resistance and implacability, and in this context also invoke the physical opposition between British

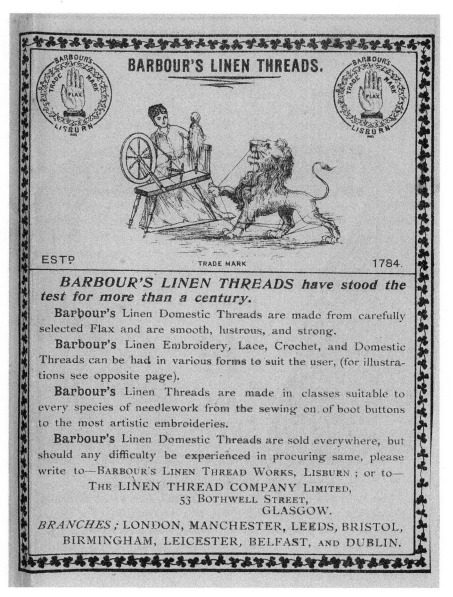

Figure 3.3 *For Strength and Durability, Barbour's Linen Thread*, 1894, advertisement, *Barbour's Prize Needlework Series*. Reproduced courtesy of the National Library of Ireland.

symbolism and Irish spinner nearly a century after Horatio's English identity was threatened by Irish spinning wheels.

This postscript to the history of Irish linen, therefore, proves the subversive potentials of the Irish spinning wheel and flax fiber were as durable as Barbour's own threads claimed to be. In fact, shortly after Barbour's Thread circulated this image of the English lion entangled in strong Irish flax, Irish embroiderers like Evelyn Gleeson and Lily Yeats helped to establish the Dun Emer Guild and Cuala Industries, which patronized Celtic Revival crafts, including textiles displaying politicized Celtic images from Ireland's pre-colonial history, later associated with the Irish War of Independence and the Irish Free State. In J. M. Synge's photographs and writings documenting his time on the Aran Islands in 1898, the spinning wheel continued to signify and celebrate an 'authentic,' rural Irish culture and character.[121] Thus, even at the turn of the twentieth century, on the eve of the Easter Uprising, spinners continued to steward Irish character's violent material history. After all, Barbour's advertisement sends a clear, if unintended, message: that even a small domestic commodity, even a woman, can contain a subversive, material message and halt the British lion in its tracks.

---

[121] See J. M. Synge, *My Wallet of Photographs* (Dublin: Dolmen, 1971) and *The Aran Islands* (Dublin: Mansuel, 1907).

4

Mud

One of the most ubiquitous slights leveled against Ireland in the modern colonial era centered on its mud-walled homes. Personifying misery in an 1842 letter to the editor of the *Morning Chronicle*, Charles Dickens decried the 'roofless [Irish] cabin...pig in the parlour, a fever in the dungheap, seven naked children on the damp earth floor.'[1] To modern eyes, this characterization of the dirty, over-crowded Irish hovel reads as an infamous cliché—one that could have easily been written by any number of English writers from the seventeenth century onward. In 1596, Edmund Spenser wrote in his *View of the Present State of Ireland* that the Irishman's habitations were 'swine-sties' rather than houses, and marked 'the chiefest cause of his so beastly manner of Life, and savage Condition, lying and living together with his Beast in one House, in one Room, in one Bed; that is clean straw, or rather a foul Dunghil.'[2] Writing almost two hundred years later, Arthur Young similarly maligned mud cabins, referring to them in one instance as 'the most miserable looking hovels that can well be conceived.'[3]

By the mid-eighteenth century, the mud cabin had become a visible and symbolic locus for emerging semiotics on Irish racial identity and stereotyping of the Irish peasant, vindicating the British Empire's civilizing mission in Ireland. Despite attempts by nationalist writers like Sydney Owenson to humanize poor cottiers oppressed by colonialism, English commentators could rarely see past mud's constructed connotations of filth and bestiality. Clean, industrious, and Enlightened English culture was portrayed as the solution to the dirty, lazy, and barbarous Irish subject living in a mud cabin. Improvement fictions at the turn of the century, including Maria Edgeworth's *Popular Tales* (1800), encouraged Irish tenants to build and inhabit English-style stone cottages in place of their dire mud cabins—a domestic advancement that authors claimed would advance the Irish character by making tenants more industrious, clean, and civil. Later in the nineteenth century, well-meaning Anglo-Irish landlords like Charles Cobbe of

---

[1] Charles Dickens, 'To the Editor of the Morning Chronicle, 25 July 1842' in *The Selected Letters of Charles Dickens*, ed. Jenny Hartley (Oxford: Oxford UP, 2012), p. 107.

[2] Edmund Spenser, *View of the Present State of Ireland* (Dublin: Laurence Flin, 1763), p. 127.

[3] Arthur Young, *Arthur Young's Tour in Ireland (1776–1779)*, ed. Arthur Wollaston (London: George Bell & Sons, 1892), vol. 2, pp. 40, 48.

Irish Materialisms: The Nonhuman and the Making of Colonial Ireland, 1690–1830. Colleen Taylor, Oxford University Press.
© Colleen Taylor 2024. DOI: 10.1093/oso/9780198894834.003.0005

Newbridge even funded the demolition of his tenants' mud cabins and the construction of new mortared stone and slate cottages in their place.[4]

Today, the stereotypical dehumanization of Irish cabin dweller is, thankfully, no longer an acceptable account of Irish life. Nevertheless, the theme of muddy misery—the indescribable 'wretchedness' ascribed to the Irish cabin—remains in historical discussion as an inadvertent refrain of colonial discourse. In 2018, for example, University College Cork erected a replica of a nineteenth-century mud hut or *bothán* as part of the National Famine Commemoration. The replica's pronounced presence on campus was intended to portray 'just how bad the conditions were for these people,' the 'level of deprivation' and desperation among the nineteenth-century Irish.[5] Although the *bothán* has often been associated with *An Gorta Mór* (the Great Famine) mud edifices similar in structure were built and inhabited long before that tragic chapter in Irish history, becoming increasingly common in the second half of the seventeenth century. Still, Marion McGarry, writing a history of mud cabins dating back to the eighteenth century for RTE, characterized the habitations in terms of 'terrible poverty, overcrowding, and filth'—ascribed characteristics not unlike those found in the *Morning Chronicle* two centuries prior.[6]

Classifying the mud cabin in terms of misery alone paradoxically executes a continued effect of the prejudice displayed in Spenser, Young, and Dickens's stereotype: the eclipsed complexity and creative subjectivity of the historical Irish cabin-dweller. Remarks in 1799 from George Cooper in *Letters on the Irish Nation* announce this very discursive effect when he says that the Irish peasant living in muddy conditions becomes 'miserably destitute of fear, reason, and often humanity.'[7] Even when observed with postcolonial pathos, commentators today still characterize the mud cabin as a subhuman mode of domesticity. This insidious bestialization of mud living, therefore, propagates unconsciously in modern discussion, disseminating an uncompromising definition of human relation to nature that originates in English, colonial standards.

This chapter takes Irish mud in a completely new direction. I detach the cabin from centuries of English judgment and recontextualize it—not as a poorly ventilated, filthy hovel that makes no distinction between animal and human, but as an ecosystem of symbiotic and mutually beneficial relationships between dirt and

---

[4] From 1798 until his death, Cobbe renovated the mud cabins without charging higher rent, fixated on 'tenants' improvements' in Ireland. He even sold famous family paintings to fund the renovation. Frances Power Cobbe, 'Irish Tenants Improvements,' Letter to the Editor, *The Spectator*, 27 September 1890.

[5] *Irish Examiner*, 'Simple Mud Hut a Stark Reminder of How the Poorest Lived and Died,' 8 May 2018.

[6] Marion McGarry, 'Room to Improve: The Homes of Ireland's 19th Century Rural Poor,' *RTE Brainstorm*, 8 January 2019.

[7] George Cooper, *Letters on the Irish Nation: Written during a visit to that Kingdom, in the Autumn of the Year 1799*, 2nd ed. (London: Bensley, 1801), p. 212.

Irishman. In what follows, I do not want to romanticize poverty or the painful experiences of colonial subjects. Rather, it is my intention to use new materialism and posthumanism to liberate the mud cabin from colonial, anthropocentric definitions and get closer to the lived domestic details of so many Irish tenants in the eighteenth century. As posthumanist pioneer Rosi Braidotti explains, nature/culture is not a binary, but a continuum where the two concepts and material realities enmesh and interchange, where society is an egalitarian human–environment entanglement.[8] In place of the mud cabin's so-called 'inhuman conditions' posthumanists and new materialists see human–nonhuman cooperation; in place of contamination or filth, we see earthly entanglement.

Contrary to what Spenser, Young, and Dickens would suggest, the mud cabin's composition and natural biology do not always amount to facts of misery. Rereading the cabin through natural science and a more expansive, hybrid definition of human culture, this chapter explores what new characters and narratives emerge from beneath the mud when we recast misery as collaborative survival—when we see what the mud cabin offered the Irish people, rather than what it did not. When read through its biological properties and entangled, earthly relationships, the mud cabin narrates themes of resourcefulness, symbiotic survival, and human connection with the surrounding landscape in the wake of colonial destruction.

Following Kathryn Yusoff's claim that hierarchizing matter 'operationalized' colonialism, I trace how the rhetorical demotion of mud as sub-human matter operationalized colonial power structures predicated on cleaning up all aspects of private Irish life.[9] Arthur Young's *Tour in Ireland*, in particular, used the mud cabin to insinuate a lack of subjectivity and sensibility in the Irish people on the grounds of their 'base' material surroundings. At the end of this chapter, I move to mud in literary fiction by Henry Brooke, Maria Edgeworth, and Sydney Owenson to see how the mud cabin materializes a particular aspect of Irish colonial subjectivity: undisclosed depth. The windowless, smoky cabin with two-foot-thick walls starkly evidences the hidden, illegible interior life of the Irish character, helping to explicate—or at least contextualize—travel writers' aversion to Ireland's unilluminated mud. Reframed as human–nonhuman cooperation, the mud cabin, as it appears in literature, metaphorically insinuates an Irish subjectivity resistant to imperialism's humanist reasoning and hierarchical ordering of matter and people. By trying to understand the mud cabin outside of the unforgiving English pejoratives of filth and misery, we can better understand the inner lives of the poor, tenant Irish in the eighteenth century on their own terms.

[8] Rosi Braidotti, *The Posthuman* (Cambridge: Polity, 2013), pp. 2–3.
[9] Kathryn Yusoff, *A Billion Black Anthropocenes or None* (Minneapolis: University of Minnesota Press, 2018), p. 4.

4.1 The Mud Cabin Ecosystem

Clay, mud houses, known internationally as cob houses, have been a bedrock of human civilization for thousands of years. Even today, 30 percent of the world's habitations are cob—a percentage gaining ground with a recent, environmental interest in returning to vernacular (or locally sourced and inspired) architecture in order to aid terrestrial health, including a small but growing mud architecture movement in Ireland.[10] Although the slander of Irish 'swine-sties' can be traced back as far as Edmund Spenser writing in the sixteenth century, mud cabins were actually not prevalent in Ireland until the seventeenth and eighteenth centuries.[11] Following the Williamite War, mud-walled structures began to proliferate across the Irish landscape, replacing wattle and daub (wood and clay lattice) structures as the main form of rural architecture between the mid-seventeenth century and the Famine (1845–55).[12] By the early nineteenth century, the ubiquity of these mud-walled homes resulted in what Ina Ferris calls the 'veritable cliché' of the Irish cabin.[13] This is why, in his travels, Arthur Young documents that 'more cabbins ar/e building everywhere.'[14] By the 1840s, right before the Famine resulted in the death or emigration of the large majority of the tenant Irish, at least four million people (half the population of Ireland) lived in small mud homes.[15]

The reigning popularity of soil-based structure in the long eighteenth century can be linked historically with both the deforestation of Ireland and a punitive penal law system vindicated by William of Orange's victory over Gaelic Ireland. At the beginning of the seventeenth century, Ireland had about 12 percent woodland on its island, around the same as it was estimated to have at the time of the Norman conquest. Scholars hypothesize that the need for timber as a commodity— especially for building of British naval ships and supplementing London architecture after the fire in 1666—quickly led to the mass extraction and exportation of Irish timber, which then expedited the deforestation of Ireland by the eighteenth

[10] The Heritage Council, for example, has restored an original early eighteenth-century cob and thatch home, the 'Mayglass Farmstead,' as a 'rare survivor' of eighteenth-century Irish lifestyle. Part of the Farmstead's mission is to 'study the technique and maintenance of mud-walled buildings typical of Wexford' and 'increase awareness of the qualities of these buildings.' 'Mayglass Farmstead,' The Heritage Council, Department of Housing, Local Government, and Heritage, 1998–2000, heritage-council.ie. Similarly, in West Cork, the Hollies Centre for Practical Sustainability runs a cob building educational programme and hands-on cob building classes.

[11] Archaeological research indicates that Celtic and Gaelic habitations were primarily constructed out of stone or wood. These habitations could be for individual families or whole communities, and were often composed—at least in part—of oak timber, indicating that the local areas were well-wooded. Wooden houses, in the Gaelic era, it is believed, were common. See William Wilde, *A Descriptive Catalogue of the Antiquities of Stone, Earthen, and Vegetable Materials in the Museum of the Royal Irish Academy* (Dublin: Hodges, Smith, and Co., 1857), pp. 235–7.

[12] Frank McDonald and Peigín Doyle. *Ireland's Earthen Houses* (Dublin: A. & A. Farmar, 1997).

[13] Ina Ferris, *The Romantic National Tale and the Question of Ireland* (Cambridge: Cambridge UP, 2004), p. 35.

[14] Young, *Arthur Young's Tour*, vol. 1, p. 384.

[15] Mark Keenan, 'Mud will Stick, Thank Goodness.' *Sunday Times* [London], 9 January 2005, p. 10.

century.[16] By the start of the nineteenth century, less than 1 percent of the Irish landscape was covered with trees, and even earlier, Irish timber exports had been reduced from 170,000 cubic feet in the seventeenth century to zero in 1770.[17] Seventeenth-century Protestant landowners, seizing ownership and control of Irish woodlands following the victory of William of Orange, harvested their land's timber at rapid speed as a means to quick fortune, outpacing regrowth, and thus resulting in felled landscapes in place of former woodland.[18] In ancient times, timber was widely used in Irish architecture, but by the eighteenth century, Irish poetry documents that timber could not even be obtained for the construction of coffins—a startling and rapid ecological reversal directly resulting from colonial policy and British control of Irish land.[19]

The Gaelic order that had embraced woodland, hunting, and wolves (extinct in Ireland by the eighteenth century) had literally been exported and slowly erased. In its place, the new Protestant Ascendancy took possession of the woodless land and executed a tenant farming system, as the native Irish transitioned from keeping livestock to tilling the treeless ground.[20] Below the felled trees, the exportation of Irish produce and livestock for British consumption damaged the soil too: the sustained cultivation of a single crop, resulting in a lack of plant diversity, David Montgomery explains, rapidly reduces soil fertility.[21] Arthur Young had claimed that Irish soil was not reaching its peak fertility, as it was in England, due to 'inferiority of management' among farmers and tenant laborers. However, the fact that overcultivated soil results in erosion exposes English extraction of Irish harvests as environmental damage.[22]

Building a mud cabin in eighteenth-century Ireland, therefore, was an exercise in creating from dispossession and constructing out of a destroyed landscape. Left without wood, access to resources including building supplies like brick (which was used widely in the homes of the rich and elite in this period) and the right to own land, the impoverished Catholic Irish of the eighteenth century had no choice but to turn to the very soil beneath their feet.[23] The cottier system regulated a hierarchy in which Protestant landowners leased their property to farmers, who grew Ascendancy wealth by cultivating crops as exports, leasing the least

---

[16] Nigel Everett complicates this argument by claiming that a number of other factors in addition to British exportation of timber contributed to Ireland's woodland decline. See Nigel Everett, *The Woods of Ireland, A History, 700–1800* (Dublin: Four Courts, 2015).

[17] Donna Potts, *Contemporary Irish Writing and Environmentalism: The Wearing of the Deep Green* (Basingstoke: Palgrave Macmillan, 2018), p. xxi.

[18] Caoimhín Ó Danachair, 'Materials and Methods in Irish Traditional Building.' *Journal of the Royal Society of Antiquaries of Ireland* 87.1 (1957): p. 71.

[19] Ó Danachair, 'Materials,' p. 70.

[20] Barry O'Reilly and Colm Murray, *Traditional Buildings on Irish Farms.* Built and Natural Heritage, Series 2 (Dublin: Heritage Council and Teagasc, 2007), p. 4.

[21] David Montgomery, *Dirt: The Erosion of Civilizations* (Los Angeles: UCLA Press, 2007), p. 110.

[22] Young, *Arthur Young's Tour*, vol. 2, p. 21.   [23] Ó Danachair, 'Materials,' p. 68.

fruitful patches of land to laborers, often in place of wages.[24] Landlords and their middlemen advocated for very small plot leases in order to keep the majority of lands for crops to supply Britain and its overseas colonies. The smaller the plot the better: this way, laborers would not have the opportunity to put more effort into their own personal tillage than their landlord's farmland.[25] In the first half of the nineteenth century, population increase resulted in even smaller subdivisions of farms and smaller leases.[26]

Irish tenants valued the security of a small plot of land to rent, where they could grow potatoes and erect a small mud cottage despite lack of tools, money, or other building materials, and even keep a pig—one of the most adaptable and intelligent mammals, who had evolved, over time, to coexist with humans in manifold ways and, like the native Irish, thrive on small plots of land, as I discuss in more detail in Chapter 5.[27] Deforestation had eradicated the Irish pig's natural habitat, so they, like their native Irish tenant and laboring keepers, learned to co-evolve with soil and mud.[28] Unlike the urban poor, who had to rely on bought food and rented rooms (both of which rose to increasingly unaffordable prices in the early nineteenth century), a mud cabin, a pig, and a small potato patch, under fruitful conditions, typically meant subsistence for an Irish family.[29]

Irish tenants and laborers constructed their mud cabins themselves, often using only a simple instrument known as a sprong, or digging fork (see Figure 4.1). The project could also be completed with human hands alone; the only prerequisites for building a mud cabin were access to soil, water, straw, and human endurance, as the labor involved in preparing and building mud walls was extensive.[30] The first step involved clearing the topsoil in order to unearth clay for the walls. The clay was dug up with spades, lumps broken, and stones removed to create a smooth texture. Once the clay had been unearthed, it was mixed with water and kneaded with those same pitchforks or sprongs and human hands, in order to obtain a dough-like texture.[31] At this point, the builders would add straw, hay, rushes, twigs, or even animal hair to the kneaded clay as a binding material, then leave it to temper for several days. During this ageing process, the clay would be turned over occasionally and sometimes rekneaded.[32] In many places, builders and tenant farmers would add cow dung or milk to the mud mixture in order to

---

[24] Montgomery, Dirt, p. 108.
[25] Jonathan Bell and Mervyn Watson, A History of Irish Farming, 1750–1850 (Dublin: Four Courts Press, 2008), pp. 46–7.
[26] O'Reilly and Murray, Traditional Buildings, p. 4.
[27] Umberto Albarella, Keith Dobney, Anton Ervynck, and Peter Rowley-Conwy. Pigs and Humans: 10,000 Years of Interaction (Oxford: Oxford UP, 2008), p. 1.
[28] Robert Malcomson and Stephanos Mastoris. The English Pig: A History (London: Bloomsbury, 2001), p. 73.
[29] Montgomery, Dirt, p. 109.　　[30] Ó Danachair, 'Materials,' p. 65.
[31] Ó Danachair, 'Materials,' p. 66.　　[32] Ó Danachair, 'Materials,' p. 66.

Figure 4.1 Arthur Young, *Construction of an Irish Cabin*, 1780, pen and wash drawing, extra-illustrated manuscript copy of *A Tour In Ireland*, 1780. Reproduced courtesy of the National Library of Ireland.

strengthen and fortify the clay as even sturdier building material, practicing an effective method of recycling waste.[33]

When the clay or mud mixture was set, stones were laid on the ground in order to mark the cabin's perimeters. Builders would then pile the clay with pitchforks and shovels layer by layer, topping each layer with rushes or straw to let it set, as seen in Arthur Young's sketch of eighteenth-century cabin assembly (Figure 4.1). Sometimes a child would walk across the surface to make the clay more compact as it dried into a wall.[34] A new layer would be added each day, ultimately amounting to short but very thick walls of two to three feet in width. Finally, the walls would be pared or smoothed out with spades, sometimes whitewashed (painted

---

[33] Ó Danachair, 'Materials,' p 66. Claudia Kinmonth's research has shown that recycling various kinds of waste into new resources was a regular practice in the everyday life of Irish working classes in the eighteenth century, in both rural society and urban Dublin. Working-class peasants recycled linen rags, pieces of silver, lanterns, and horns. The Dublin Society incentivized the Irish working classes to make materials like salt at home, rather than have them imported. See Claudia Kinmonth, 'Rags, Riches, and Recycling: Material and Visual Culture of the Dublin Society, 1731–1781.' *Irish Architectural and Decorative Studies* 21 (2018).

[34] Ó Danachair, 'Materials,' p. 67.

with lime), and the door—and, occasionally, a window—carved out of the structure as a last measure. If windows were included, they would promptly be filled with turf in order to preserve warmth for the inhabitants.[35]

The roof was the next project: cabin's thatched roofs were the result of savvy craftwork, held in place by either a network of ropes and wooden pegs, or they were thrust—that is, sewn onto timbers, with small bundles folded over and knotted.[36] Although structures built up from the ground with human hands would not seem like reliable construction, dried mud architecture offered fortified, load-bearing walls that could support a sizeable and sturdy thatched roof.[37] The roof was designed to hang over the walls, thus providing the mud walls some protection from the rains and wind. Architectural historian Caoimhín Ó Danachair explains that mud-walled cabins remained 'quite sound as long as the roof was maintained' and points to several examples where the original mud walls provided 'good service' to their dwellers for over a century or two.[38] In Waterford, a two-story eighteenth-century mud house known as the Mayglass Farmstead still stands, under conservation by the Heritage Council (Figure 4.2).

Contrary to the stereotypical English opinion in the eighteenth century, the middle and upper classes in rural Ireland also surrounded themselves with mud walls. Cob construction was not merely the refuge of what the English travelers saw as the bestial Irish poor. Ó Danachair explains that 'clay is a facsimile material from which relatively large and complex buildings can be erected.'[39] Two-story, middle-class farmhouses were often constructed from clay mud in eighteenth-century Ireland, as in the Mayglass Farmstead. Ó Danachair also reminds us that the living conditions of the rural and laboring poor in the eighteenth century were not as dire as those of the Famine era, with which the mud cabin has come to be primarily associated, as indicated by UCC's *bothán* replica.[40] Cob homes often accommodated several animals and even larger farming businesses that enabled Catholic families to do relatively well under colonial conditions. In rural Ireland, far from the brick-laid Georgian homes in Dublin, cob structures conveyed and contained what Ó Danachair describes as 'environmental harmony'—that is, the cultivation of vernacular materials for human shelter, comfort, and domesticity without destroying forests, mining stone, or over-cultivating soil.

While architects and scholars can now recognize cob architecture's environmental harmony in the wake of climate change, two centuries ago, the *Irish*

---

[35] Ó Danachair, 'Materials,' pp. 66–7

[36] Finola O'Kane, 'An Irish Cabin on the Commons of Bray.' *British Library: Picturing Places, Town and City*, 17 April 2019, https://www.bl.uk/picturing-places/articles/an-irish-cabin-on-the-commons-of-bray.

[37] Keenan, 'Mud will Stick,' p. 10.   [38] Ó Danachair, Materials,' p. 65.

[39] Ó Danachair, 'Materials,' p. 65.

[40] Caoimhín Ó Danachair, 'Cottier and Landlord in Pre-Famine Ireland.' *Béaloideas* 48/49 (1980): pp. 155–6.

Figure 4.2 *Mayglass Farmstead*, thatch and cob two-storied farm house in Co. Wexford, circa early 1700s. Photograph courtesy of the Heritage Council, Ireland.

Farmer's Journal was one of the few publications to discuss mud cabins in positive terms. In 1814, the journal declared that: 'With a compost of moistened clay and straw, without plumb, square or level, but merely with a...sprong...every man is capable of erecting a house for himself, compact and perpendicular.'[41] What is unwritten but nevertheless poignant in this optimistic account of mud cabin building is a solution to colonial dispossession: even without commodities, land, or resources, the tenant need not be homeless and unsheltered as long as there is soil to dig. It also implies that mud is, in many ways, an ideal building material for the Irishman with few external resources: it easily yielded itself from a deforested landscape, and offered malleable, moldable, quick-drying, and reliable building material.

The cost of building a mud cabin and related rent amounted to two to three pounds whereas the stone and slate cabin deemed superior by so many foreign travelers to Ireland could cost forty pounds, over ten times as much.[42] Slate and brick, popular among the upper classes, required a network of mining, consumerism, construction, laborers, and significantly, some potentially destructive material extraction. Although it may have appeared preferable to English eyes like

---

[41] Qtd. in *Irish Times*, 'Earthen Homes Stuck with Muddy Image.' 23 August 1997.
[42] Young, *Arthur Young's Tour*, vol. 1, p. 186.

those of Arthur Young or Maria Edgeworth, slate, like a wood cabin, involved earthen destruction in its construction. In contrast, mud cabins were assembled in a method of collection—gathering soil, mixing it with straw, and piling it up like sculpture. Tenants were incentivized to remain in mud-walled cabins rather than improving their homes with slate roofs or other materials considered more 'civil' (or English). A finer, slate roof—on top of requiring a network of access to finer consumer materials, perhaps mined in England, and costing a great fee— could also incur increased rents from Anglo-Irish landlords, which tenants feared.[43] Moreover, as I will discuss below in relation to Maria Edgeworth's *Ennui* (1809), a thatch roof built from locally collected straw and potato stalks often proved a better accommodation for the customs of Irish life, such as domestic fires and Ireland's wet, windy climate. Famously in *Ennui*, the slate roof proves no match for the Irish weather.

One very visible and symbolic cabin improvement scheme promoted lime plaster wash, more commonly known as white-washing. Lime plaster was typically made from crushed limestone, which naturally occurs in the south and west of Ireland, mixed with water. White-wash was used as a convenient and efficient paint for the exterior of mud cabins as lime works well with breathable surfaces like mud walls. This pristine-looking finish was encouraged and praised in improving domestic fictions like Mary Leadbeater's *Cottage Dialogues* (1811) and Anna Maria Hall's *Sketches of Irish Character* (1829), discussed in the previous two chapters. As we have seen, these texts mobilized dirt to symbolically connote Irish poverty and laziness, contrasting English industry and prosperity. *Cottage Dialogue's* Rose, for example, who has adopted white-washing and regular laundering practices, tells the less domestic Nancy that the 'English are so cleanly' and their livestock 'thrive much better for it,' whereas 'it is not so in Ireland, where a clean person is wondered at.'[44] Nancy marvels at Rose's clean, 'white-washed' house and Rose encourages her to white-wash her floors with lime.[45]

Both the look and biology of lime wash could civilize the Irish mud cabin in relation to an English definition of human living. Lime wash and plaster were used as far back as Roman times, suggesting some correlation between whitewashing and a classical, more Enlightened and culturally Georgian look, even on a mud cabin. More significantly, lime is an insecticide, meaning it repels bugs in accordance with the humanist imperative to place non-human organisms like insects or pigs outside the interior of the cottage or cabin. Lime wash, therefore, could subtly advance the improvement of the Irish cabin toward English standards by slowly erasing those visible signs of connectedness with the surrounding

[43] O'Reilly and Murray, *Traditional Buildings*, p. 4.
[44] Mary Leadbeater, *Cottage Dialogues among the Irish Peasantry*, with Notes and a Preface by Maria Edgeworth (London: J. Johnson, 1811), p. 185.
[45] Leadbeater, *Cottage Dialogues*, pp. 133, 177.

plant and insect ecosystem: namely, the billions of microscopic bugs of which dirt is composed.[46] Lime held a preservational function for tenants as well: lime wash set the mud walls, further fortifying them against damage and disrepair threatened by the wet climate.

Because white-washing signified an aesthetic choice as well as a structural one, the refinement it connoted might invite those feared increased rents for poor tenants. Tenants avoided windows and chimneys for similar reasons, both of which would also make the cabin more expensive to heat when resources were already limited. Windows, in particular, although considered essential to human domesticity in an Enlightened perspective like Young's, are not energy efficient. Leadbeater and, as we will see, Maria Edgeworth, also considered natural light an essential human need in domestic interiors. However, turf-cutting rights for fire kindling were not always awarded to tenants, so heat conservation was crucial and could be threatened by energy-inefficient windows.[47] Coincidentally, lime wash also brought a brightening effect to the otherwise poorly lit mud cabin, again correlating with that Enlightened British viewpoint that sees light as an essential prerequisite of any comfortable human shelter.

Contrary to eighteenth-century English opinion, the properties and affordances of mud walls, white-washed or not, enabled domestic comforts for the tenant Irish. In 1799, George Cooper wrote in *Letters on the Irish Nation* that the Irish cabins were built of the 'slightest materials' and made 'cold and comfortless habitations.'[48] On the contrary, mud walls are very effective in a wet climate like Ireland's: for one thing, they protect against unhealthy damp and mold growth.[49] Earthen construction actually 'breathes' through the tiny pores in its structure, allowing fresh air to circulate in and keep the airflow inside cleaner, thus helping the Irish to breathe in a cabin where they did not build windows for the sake of heat conservation.[50] In contrast to the so-called 'deadly' smokiness travelers like Young ascribed to the windowless Irish cabin, mud walls permitted oxygen flow and, in a metaphoric sense, life, through their porousness. Furthermore, earthen walls are fire-resistant and hold thermal mass with greater efficacy than other materials, such as stone and slate. Mud walls can maintain a stable temperature throughout the night without fire stoking—a boon to cabin-dwellers with a limited store of kindling. Keeping pigs inside the cabin overnight also ensured further insulation for both the human and animal dweller in the absence of kindling. The mud cabin safeguarded its inhabitants against external exposure from the elements and potentially, imperial voyeurs—a concept I will address in relation to Irish subjectivity later in this chapter.

[46] Montgomery, *Dirt*, p. 17.   [47] Bell and Watson, *History of Irish Farming*, p. 23.
[48] Cooper, *Letters*, p. 61.   [49] 'The Cob Advantage.' cobtherapy.com (updated 2020).
[50] 'The Cob Advantage.'

Earlier in the eighteenth century, some areas followed the Rundale system of landholding and cabin building, which favored temporary earthen habitations built into the natural dips and hills of the landscape. In the Rundale model, a selected leader, known as a *maor* or *rí* (king), would negotiate with the landlord on behalf of the other members of the community in a joint tenancy.[51] At the center of the acreage would be a cluster of houses known as *baile* or *clachán*. At certain times of year, the tenants would move toward the outer circles of the property for livestock grazing and, during those periods, stay in small, earthen shelters or *bothógaí*, often built, for the sake of expedient temporary shelter, onto the side of a hill.[52] Using hillsides as one or two of the walls of the *bothóg* resulted in quicker, less labor-intensive builds than the typical, free-standing mud cabin. These hillside houses accommodated the grazing needs and movement of the tentants' livestock. This temporary, immersive architecture suggests another example of the Irish tenant's architectural adaptability as well as communion with both animal life and his natural landscape. Unsurprisingly, however, it was these kinds of landscape-immersive *bothógaí* that received some of the most caustic commentary in publications like Arthur Young's *Tour in Ireland* and the *Edinburgh Review*, which slandered them as 'ditches' or 'hovels.'[53] Mud homes facilitated the transient and impermanent lifestyles of the tenant Irish and farming laborers who, without the means to own land due to their Catholic background, would often have to move for work or due to increased rent. While landlords may have preferred the permanence of a stone cottage, a mud cabin or *bothóg* cooperated more effectively with the limited civic freedoms of the rural Catholic Irish.

Anglocentric anthropocentrism frames mud cabins and *bothógí* as chaotic, unenlightened spaces that jumble the humanist, speciesist partitions established between humans, animals, and dirt. Such rigid demarcations that wish to see humans and dirt unnaturally distanced from one another obscures the benefits of mud's organic, rich materiality. The soil-based ecosystem of cabin living, from the mud walls to the potato patch to the manure pile safeguarded by the door, enabled a secure life for poor tenants.[54] While, as David Lloyd points out, 'no traveller in Ireland failed to note the ubiquity of the peasant's dunghill and its immediate proximity to the cabin door,' those same travelers failed to see what that pile or mud walls provided, insisting instead on a proscribed lack of civility, from which Ireland has still not recovered. Rob Hopkins, an Irish expert in cob architecture, notes how both academic criticism and modern Irish lifestyle have suffered by this aversion to discussing mud cabins and the backwardness they represent: 'very few people would speak up in praise of [mud cottages], for fear of being

---

[51]   Bell and Watson, *History of Irish Farming*, pp. 25–6.
[52]   Bell and Watson, *History of Irish Farming*, p. 38.
[53]   *Edinburgh Review* 42 (July 1813): 342.
[54]   W. H. A. Williams, *Creating Irish Tourism, the First Century, 1750–1850* (London: Anthem, 2011) p. 180.

accused of wanting to drag Ireland back a hundred years.'[55] There has been cultural reticence, especially within the modern postcolonial context, to acknowledge the benefits of mud walls.

Mud's benefits, therefore, warrant naming here: such as the fact that minerals
in dirt and mud contain anti-inflammatory, anti-infectious properties that emerge
in the cyclical process of soil erosion and production.[56] That abhorrent dunghill
or manure pile outside the Irish cabin, denounced by Young and so many of his
contemporaries, in fact sparks the healing properties of mud and soil. Manure
also served as a natural, available binding agent in the construction of handmade
mud walls in Ireland. In a 1765 publication on farming promoted by the Dublin
Society, the farmer William Ellis heralded hog dung (most commonly used by
tenants) as the preferred 'promoter of growth in all vegetables' and a remarkable
material that 'impregnate[es] the Earth, with its fructuous Qualities.'[57] Animal
manure, gives nitrogen, potassium, phosphorous, and other minerals to soil as it
decomposes, so that soil microbes can absorb more nutrients and reduce the soil's
acidity.[58] Ageing manure exposed to the air over time is able to kill pathogens and
harmful bacteria in soil, which is why the manure pile had to be left outside the
cabin to mature for months on end before being mixed with the dirt in the
ground. Less-exposed dung hidden away in a shed would not prove as fruitful or
effective. The pile's closeness to the cabin was also a protective measure safeguard-
ing vital nutrients for healthy soil, fruitful crops, and, by extension, Irish culture.
The mud cabin could even partially shelter the dung pile from the harsh Irish
climate's destructive winds and rain.[59] Manure plays a vital role in all soil conservation, which is essential for both plant life and a thriving human civilization, and
it was especially invaluable in the west of Ireland with its difficult, otherwise bar-
ren soils.[60] The naturally occurring biological makeup of soil demonstrates that
the English desire to distance dung from the cabin is, in fact, an oxymoron. Soil
contains all kinds of insect and animal feces as well as plant 'litter,' none of which
can be siphoned out.[61] Scottish and Irish soil, for example, is composed primarily
of rocks and earthworm excrement.[62] Thus, the 'humanist' impulse to civilly distance clay or mud-walled cottages from the dung pile is, biologically speaking,
a fool's errand.

In addition to the health benefits of breathable walls, heat preservation, and
protection from outside exposure, mud speaks metaphorically to the crucial,

[55] Qtd. in Keenan. Only one academic book I have come across, the 1997 publication *Ireland's Earthen Houses* by McDonald and Doyle, details the history of mud cabin living with the intention to promote it and portray the lifestyle positively.
[56] Montgomery, *Dirt*, p. 14.
[57] William Ellis, *The Practice of Farming and Husbandry, in all sorts of Soils, according to the latest Improvements, recommended by the Dublin Society*. 2nd ed. (Dublin: James Potts, 1765), pp. 298–9.
[58] Montgomery, *Dirt*, p. 15.   [59] Williams, *Irish Tourism*, p. 180.
[60] Montgomery, *Dirt*, p. 5., Williams, *Irish Tourism*, p. 180.   [61] Montgomery, *Dirt*, p. 21.
[62] Montgomery, *Dirt*, p. 13.

postcolonial theme of regeneration. Soil contains decomposed plant and animal material that has broken down over thousands of years, making dirt itself a living process of history, renewal, and recycling. The biological process of soil decomposition is self-healing and self-animating: the humus in soil stores carbon, which interacts with particles in the soil so that its structure can improve over time. As David Montgomery explains, landscapes are a balance of soil erosion and soil production.[63] Rather than 'dirt' or 'filth,' soil is therefore better understood as a harmonious, collaborative multispecies world in which humans and animals take part. As Susan Signe Morrison explains it, soil 'vibrantly changes itself and provokes change in other actors.'[64] Thus, while Young and Leadbeater observed the Irish people's disinterest in 'improving' actions according to English standards of open windows and slate roofs, the very composition and biology of soil connotes vibrant action. In fact, soil moves, literally, over time, mobilized by earthworms and decomposing plant matter.[65] Morrison sees the interaction of dirt, animal, and human as 'each entity catalyz[ing] the other dynamically to provoke healing and an ecosystem of mutuality.'[66] Indeed, the mud cabin contains an internal ecosystem where soil, oxygen, fire, human, and pig interact, provoking change and contributing toward continued survival and revival.

Mud's biological narrative of regeneration, vibrancy, and protection impels a new reading of the Irish character and his cabin. Rather than a filthy hut devoid of human domesticity and hygiene, mud's self-generating 'vibrant mutuality' with human life signifies creative survival in the wake of imperial destruction. It marks an environmentally friendly form of human sheltering resulting from the collection of local materials, rather than the destruction and exportation of scarce trees or mined stone, as could be said of building materials preferred in eighteenth-century English culture. Moreover, the earthen habitation enabled Irish people's continued connection with their native soil in literal terms, despite being denied nominal ownership of their national land. When we resist and remove humanism's long-entrenched material hierarchies, the image of the impoverished Irish tenant in the so-called 'hovel' regenerates into a new admirable character who, as a means of creative survival, becomes increasingly porous and entangled with the nonhuman in his midst—with mud, thatch, and pig.

4.2   Arthur Young and Colonialism's Racialized Application of Mud

While Irish tenants and laborers worked with mud inventively in the material, co-habitational sense, English writers applied mud cleverly in rhetorical

---

[63] Montgomery, *Dirt*, p. 14.

[64] Susan Signe Morrison, 'Dynamic Dirt: Medieval Holy Dust, Ritual Erosion, and Pilgrimage Ecopoetis.' *Open Library of Humanities* 5.1 (2019): p. 7.

[65] Morrison, 'Dynamic Dirt,' p. 12.   [66] Morrison, 'Dynamic Dirt,' p. 8.

terms—to vindicate British colonial ideology and its cultural supremacy. In fact, the rhetorical application of filth and misery ascribed to mud has been so effective as to remain an ostensibly innate definition today, even escaping thorough scrutiny from Irish postcolonial historians who regret the 'misery' of the *bothán*. Widely read and cited texts like Arthur Young's *Tour in Ireland* and contemporary travel writing on Ireland warrant further analysis in the context of mud's material facts and affordances: for the way these texts invoke a natural, neutral, prehuman material (mud) and give it an ostensibly intrinsic, national definition of bestiality.

Ascribing the connotation of filth or impurity to dirt is a very old and pervasive practice in human thought. Anthropologist Mary Douglas traces the role dirt has played in social ordering across all kinds of cultures for centuries. Complex, varied, and unique social orders, Douglas explains, have emerged from rituals surrounding dirt. Even before the discovery of bacterial transmission of disease in the nineteenth century, even before scientists discovered the process of pollution as we understand it today, beliefs around pollution and purity were used socially in what Douglas calls 'a claim or counter-claim to status.'[67] In Douglas's universal model of social structure, dirt initiates and vindicates the seclusion of certain peoples, practices, and ideas in the service of communal order. 'Where there is dirt,' Douglas explains, 'there is a system,' in which dirt signifies 'matter out of place.'[68] Dirt or the 'uncleanly' becomes 'that which must not be included if a pattern is to be maintained.'[69] In a place like Ireland shortly after the Williamite War, the colonial system was a tenuously held supremacy always in danger of disorder, meaning rituals and ideas around dirt that served to congeal the standing British, Protestant Ascendancy would naturally become all the more imperative. If mud cabins could be othered and eradicated in favor of English cottages, then the British patterns of control across all kinds of other avenues in Irish society could be fortified. Along with dirt, traditional Irish customs and national sentiments might also be gradually excluded from the standard social order.

I see Arthur Young's *Tour in Ireland, 1776–1779* as the most fitting text through which to examine the rhetorical applications of Irish mud under colonialism for two important reasons. First, the *Tour in Ireland* has long been a central document for understanding eighteenth-century Ireland due to its detailed, methodical observations spanning most of the island. It is also a text highly preoccupied with mud cabins. As Finola O'Kane explains, 'It is difficult to overstate the influence of Arthur Young's *A Tour in Ireland* on perceptions of Ireland in the eighteenth century.'[70] Young's widely read text offers detailed accounts of Irish material life, critiques the penal law system, and, at the same time, continues those

---

[67] Mary Douglas, *Purity and Danger: An Analysis of Concepts of Pollution and Taboo* (London: Routledge, 2003), p. 3.

[68] Douglas, *Purity and Danger*, p. 36.   [69] Douglas, *Purity and Danger*, p. 41.

[70] Finola O'Kane, 'Arthur Young's Published and Unpublished Illustrations for "A Tour in Ireland 1776–1779."' *Irish Architectural and Decorative Studies, Journal of the Irish Georgian Society* 19 (2016): p. 118.

damaging imperial stereotypes of the bestialized Irish living in filth propagated by writers like Richard Molesworth, who, in 1723, described the poor Irish as 'shamefully liv[ing] under Hedges, in Ditches and Hutts, worse than Hogsties, from whence you shall often see them creeping out like Vermin.'[71] Although Young's text did not initiate the stereotype of the animal Irish in the mud sty, it did, as O'Kane suggests, powerfully impress that type onto the English mind. Perhaps because of the condemnatory language from commentators like Molesworth, critics have typically seen Arthur Young's *Tour In Ireland* as a more tempered, even at times sympathetic account of Irish life, such as regarding the penal laws, for example. Young's *Tour*, however, requires further new materialist analysis for the ways in which it rhetorically constructs a binary of national and human identity out of the neutral material of mud. Secondly, the *Tour* is worth analyzing because, whereas critiques against Irish cabins by Spenser and Molesworth construct mud as a very legible and visible signifier of Irish character's outward backwardness, Arthur Young's *Tour in Ireland* uses mud to go *inside* the Irish character, to suggest an underdeveloped subjectivity in the mud-dwelling Irish on the basis of bestialized dirt. Young uses mud not just to bifurcate English civility from Irish barbarity, as had been done since the early modern era, but also, crucially, to differentiate English humanist sensibility from a more primitive Irish essentialism. Young's text evinces a key shift in thinking around imperialist stereotyping that moves from the outward typecasting of legible colonial culture to suspicion around the cabin's unseen interior, which then correlates to the interior mind of the Irish native.

Consistently and deliberately, the *Tour* draws distinctions between English civility and Irish barbarity on the basis of mud, ascribing an association with bestial nature to mud walls that opposes the more acceptable English country cottage of greater cultural, human sophistication. To begin with, Young's terminology of cabin (Irish) versus cottage (English), O'Kane explains, was 'highly considered' and uses rhetoric to connote Irish poverty as a primeval form of life in comparison to what one sees among the English working and agricultural classes, where cottagers practice civilized customs like going to a shop and sitting down to tea.[72] Several decades prior, Swift had termed Irish dwellings 'cabbins' in his *Modest Proposal*, discussed in greater detail in the following chapter, where he satirically suggests that Irish children are no different from pork or venison, and might as well be consumed like meat, thereby further connecting the term cabin with the Irish less-than-human, with livestock. The suggestiveness of 'cabin,' therefore, exemplifies Ina Ferris's argument that Young's *Tour in Ireland* is 'openly ideological writing rather than simply a writing operating within an ideology.'[73] The

---

[71] Spenser, *View*, p. 41.   [72] O'Kane, 'Published and Unpublished,' p. 126.
[73] Ina Ferris, 'The Question of Ideological Form: Arthur Young, the Agricultural Tour, and Ireland.' *Ideology and Form in Eighteenth-Century Literature*, ed. David H. Richter (Lubbock, TX: Texas Tech UP, 1999), p. 129.

distinction of the civilized and humanized cottage allowed for clear rhetorical binaries between English human and Irish animal.

Young's occasional classification of mud-walled cabins as 'hovels' is also ideologically tinged. The application of the word hovel to a human dwelling—that is, a 'shed' used for human habitation, or a 'rude' or miserable dwelling place—began in the seventeenth century and rose into more popular usage in the eighteenth century.[74] Previously, 'hovel' had been reserved primarily for animal shelter, most often sheds for cattle, demonstrating ideological intention via etymology. Likewise, although the term and idea of the pigsty dates as far back as the sixteenth century, its application to human habitations only became frequent in the late eighteenth century, right around the time of Young's publication, suggesting potential causality with its popular impact, as people began to demarcate human space more intentionally, as separate from other terrestrial life.[75] Such deliberate denomination and classification of cabin, hovel, and pigsty helps Young associate animality with mud and human civilization with English-style cottages, creating a colonial binary based on the fabricated animalization of mud. Throughout the rest of his writing, Young extends this same nature/culture, animal/human binary to bifurcated comparisons like the repulsive dunghill (Irish) in distinction to fertile, stored manure (English), and, even in terms of diet, freshly dug potatoes (Irish) versus store-bought tea (English).

Although Young's overarching characterization of Irish accommodation is damaging and, as Ina Ferris explains, intentionally ideological, a more complete examination of all mentions of cabins in the *Tour* reveals a discursive complexity in the text that has yet to be fully probed by critics. Between volumes 1 and 2, Young writes himself into a contradiction in which his more instinctual observations on cabins in volume 1 oppose his final design of the cabin as dark, weedy dunghill in the second volume. Ferris was the first to acknowledge formal tension in *A Tour In Ireland* between the 'overarching grand narrative of progress' and what she calls 'microlevel' details throughout—or, for my purposes here, the tension between the ideological platitudes of English improvement culture and the material facts that appear more frequently in Young's first volume.[76]

In volume 1, Young gives a surprisingly complimentary account of mud cabins in Meath, where he says the tenants are 'as well off as most English cottagers.'[77] At this point, he describes the cabin in more objective, architectural terms, describing how their walls are 'two feet thick, and well thatched, which are far warmer than the thin clay walls in England.'[78] He adds that the lack of chimneys and windows 'may be an advantage in warmth,' which, as discussed in the previous section, is biologically factual.[79] In volume 2, however, he transforms this more

---

[74] *Oxford English Dictionary*, s.v. 'hovel' (n.).   [75] *Oxford English Dictionary*, s.v. 'hovel' (n.).
[76] Ferris, 'The Question,' p. 139.   [77] Young, *Arthur Young's Tour*, vol. 1, p. 44.
[78] Young, *Arthur Young's Tour*, vol. 1, p. 44.   [79] Young, *Arthur Young's Tour*, vol. 1, p. 44.

scientific observation on the advantage of thick, windowless walls' into an animalized stereotype, saying that the smoke inside a windowless cabin turns Irish
women into 'a near resemblance to that of a smoked ham,' implying living in dirt
cannot be beneficial for human health.[80] His analogy sees the Irish go into their
cabins and come out as one of the most loathsome and degraded of objects: a
cooked pig. Young's ideological transformation of native colonial substances is
reflective of a wider British imperial instinct. Rajani Sudan has shown how English
travelers to India wrote back home about the miraculous, indigenous technology of
making mortar in a way that transformed an impure colonial substance into pure
wealth while also erasing the native mortar-maker from the process.[81]

As another example of ideological transformation, Young observes in volume 1
that the Irish 'raise dung what they can' to grow potatoes 'as far as their dung will
go,' delineating the common and essential practice of manuring a field.[82] In volume 2, however, he turns the mud cabin itself into an implied pile of dung that
connotes an inhuman mode of sheltering:

> thatched with straw, potatoe stalks, or with heath...sods of turf cut from a grass
> field...weeds sprouting from every part, gives them the appearance of a weedy
> dunghill, especially when the cabbin is not built with regular walls but supported
> on one, or perhaps both sides by the banks of a broad dry ditch, the roof then
> seems a hillock, upon which perhaps the pig grazes.[83]

Whereas in other parts of the *Tour*, Young the agriculturalist praises the potential
fertility of Irish soil, when it comes to habitations, he intentionally dissociates
mud from the nourishing earthforce of soil. These vacillations between praising
Irish material pragmatism to casting the poor Irish as bestial in nature evinces a
contradiction of influences between more scientific or instinctual observations
on an Irish ecosystem and the British humanist ideology of civilizing 'backward'
colonies that live in close harmony with their native environment—a fact that
could threaten British, Protestant ownership of the same soil. Young's *Tour*, like
so much travel writing written through the lens of colonial humanism, records
two kinds of stories unfolding from the Irish cabin: the story told by the mud
itself, about material interconnectedness and terrestrial survival, and the one told
by the colonial ideology that looks at mud and attempts to denaturalize Irish
presence on and within its native soil.[84]

---

[80] Young, *Arthur Young's Tour*, vol. 2, p. 48.
[81] Rajani Sudan, 'Mud, Mortar, and Other Technologies of Empire.' *The Eighteenth Century* 45.2
(2004): pp. 164–5.
[82] Young, *Arthur Young's Tour*, vol. 1, p. 71.   [83] Young, *Arthur Young's Tour*, vol. 2, p. 48.
[84] In fact, the civilizing, ideological response to mud potentially reveals insecurity in the English
mindset around Irish connectedness to their soil. At one point, Young mentions offhandedly that,
despite their misery, the Catholic Irish will not emigrate because they are so historically and emotion-
ally attached to the soil on which their ancestors lived.

Even as the text criticizes and animalizes Irish living conditions, Young paradoxically comments on the good physical health of Irish peasants. He notes that
the 'poor people are as athletic in their form, as robust, and as capable of enduring labour as any upon this earth.'[85] In another passage, Young assesses that the
Irish are less likely to clothe their children than the English, implying a lack of
refinement and bestiality that can be traced back to Spenser's stereotypes of the
naked, bestial Irish in *A View of the Present State of Ireland* (1596). Young also
points out that, despite the absence of shoes, their persons 'so ragged that their
nakedness is scarcely covered' and the 'women among the lower classes in general
in Ireland...ugly,' the Irish are nevertheless 'healthy and active.'[86] Moreover,
absent observation on disease among the cottiers questions and even disproves
the 'fever in the dungheap' stereotype (propagated by Dickens), which had constructed mud walls and dirt floors as images of sickness. Several writers after
Young went on to make the same paradoxical observation on Irish health. In
1799, George Cooper claimed mud cabins were built of the 'slightest materials,'
and yet admits, 'it must be confessed the Irish are naturally an healthy and robust
race of men. Their limbs are well formed, and they possess great strength of
body.'[87] In 1808, Thomas Erlington wrote that the Irish live in 'dirty mire' and yet
'from this nakedness and filth, they grow up to that strength and stature for which
they are admirable.'[88] Each of these writers remarks on Irish physical stature as an
isolated enigma, as if their health must be understood is in spite of their living
conditions, rather than in relation to them.

Young's most conspicuous impressions of the dehumanized cabin appear in his
sketches. O'Kane documents how, as he composed the *Tour*, Young made amateur drawings to use a resource from which to develop his written descriptions
later.[89] One of these sketches became the frontispiece for the publication's second
volume: 'An Irish Cabbin' (Figure 4.3). That this sketch was selected as a featured
image from among thirty or more speaks to the cabin's resonance and centrality
in the text. Moreover, its inclusion as the frontispiece for the second volume,
rather than the first, is significant: the second volume executes the slate/mud,
human/animal, English/Irish binary more explicitly.

As a visual impression, the 'Irish Cabbin' frontispiece is not overtly incriminat-
ing, but when paired with Young's rhetorical description, the image connotes the
desired dehumanization. From an angled viewpoint that underscores the cabin's
three-dimensional depth and dark shadows, Young depicts a heavy cloud of
smoke emitting from the doorway and implies shoddy assemblage through the
dissymmetry of the thatch roof (a hole in one area, weeds protruding on one
side). The text, however, classifies this very cabin as a 'weedy dunghill'—a

---

[85] Young, *Arthur Young's Tour*, vol. 2, pp. 40, 43.
[86] Young, *Arthur Young's Tour*, vol. 1, p. 89, vol. 2, p. 47.   [87] Cooper, *Letters*, p. 64.
[88] Qtd. in Ferris, *Romantic National Tale*, p. 36.   [89] Ferris, 'The Question,' p. 137.

Figure 4.3 Arthur Young, *An Irish Cabbin*, 1780, sketch, engraving on print, Frontispiece, *Tour in Ireland*, vol. 2, 1780. Reproduced courtesy of the National Library of Ireland.

portrayal that invites the reader to see those asymmetrical weeds as, potentially, growing out of excrement.[90] When placed alongside Young's ideologically driven words, the cabin sketch provokes a negative olfactory response to the very idea of the Irish habitation and seems to communicate the impressionable idea that the Irish are living inside filth—or perhaps more accurately, feces. Young's image may be read as a continuation of an earlier topos: Swift's proclivity for the scatological in his characterization of Dublin as filth-laden streets, or Britain's wasteland.[91] However, whereas Swift's pamphlets like *A Modest Proposal* and *An Examination of Certain Abuses, Corruptions and Enormities, in the City of Dublin* (1732) marked excess Irish dung as an allegory for British governmental mistreatment, Young seems to associate living in close proximity to mud and dung as endemic Irish backwardness. Reverend Whitelaw would give an even more egregious

---

[90] Young, *Arthur Young's Tour*, vol. 2, p. 48.
[91] See Sophie Gee, *Making Waste: Leftovers and the Eighteenth-Century Imagination* (Princeton: Princeton University Press, 2010) for a longer discussion of Swift and waste in eighteenth-century England.

Figure 4.4 Arthur Young, *An Irish Cabin*, 1780, pen and wash drawing, extra-illustrated manuscript copy of *A Tour In Ireland*, 1780. Reproduced courtesy of the National Library of Ireland.

description a few years after Young, recounting the 'stench and filth' and crowds of 'wretches' in Ireland 'insensible to the stench, which [he] could scarcely sustain for a few minutes.'[92]

In his original draft of this image (Figure 4.4), Young had depicted a family peeling potatoes and several animals in front of the cabin. Their omission in the final published sketch dehumanizes the Irish cabin by extracting any association with human life that could provoke a sense of kinship in an English reader. Still, even in this original draft, Young may disclose his prejudice: the naked children seem aligned in posture and form with the many animals surrounding the cabin: the rooster, dog, and pig. In direct contrast, a posthumanist, new materialist perspective reframes this symmetry of form as indicating symbiosis between human and animal life within the cabin's ecosystem, a blurring of speciesist hierarchies. The image of naked children playing alongside dogs, roosters, and calves visually articulates the idea that humans are animals too—that humans can form

---

[92] John Warburton, James Whitelaw, and Robert Walsh, *History of the City of Dublin, from the Earliest Accounts to the Present Time*, 2 vols (London: Cadell & Davies, 1818), vol. 1, p. 444.

accommodating relationships with the nonhuman. There is a sense of ease in the human figures in Young's original sketch: the relaxed seated stance of the man and calm working gesture of the wife, alongside the peaceful postures of the animals as well. By excising these human and animal figures in the published sketch, Young ideologically blocks the idea that humans can—and may even benefit from—living closely with animals and other nonhuman earthly organisms.

The most advanced and paradoxical rhetorical effect in Young's *Tour* comes when he uses the three-dimensional features of the mud cabin to cast the Irish people as two-dimensional thinkers, two-dimensional stereotypes. Frequently throughout the *Tour In Ireland*, Young emphasizes the surprising depth of the Irish cabin walls, measuring around 'two feet thick,' and concealing a dark, smokey, windowless interior.[93] The thick walls made such an impression as to become the focal point in his original sketch of the Irish cabin (Figure 4.4). For Young, the impressive thickness of cabin walls contrast with the implied shallowness of the native Irish who live within them. He distills the differentiation between an English cottage decorated with teacups and the sparse, unlit mud cabin into the difference between deep-thinking human sensibility and the absence of it:

> I was in the cabbins of dairymen and farmers, not small ones, whose cabbins were not at all better, nor better furnished than those of the poorest labourer: before, then we can contribute it to absolute poverty, we must take into the account the customs and inclinations of the people. In England a man's cottage will be filled with superfluities before he possesses a cow. I think the comparison much in favor of the Irishman; a hog is a much more valuable piece of goods than a set of tea things; and though his snout in a crock of potatoes is an idea not so poetical as—Broken teacups, wisely kept for shew, Rang'd o'er the chimney, glistened in a row— (vol. 2, p. 49)

Young is ostensibly praising the Irish for their lack of consumer desire, acknowledging their preservation of useful resources, yet the comparison ultimately demotes the Irish character by connoting vulgarity in comparison with the English poor's cultural refinement of sentimentalized consumer goods. Although, as Caoimhín Ó Danachair documents, the vernacular tradition of cob building was varied in eighteenth-century rural Ireland—from laborer's dwellings to two-story farmhouses like the Mayglass Farmstead in Wexford, Young deliberately glosses over these more complex cob structures in the passage above.[94] He suggests the absence of domestic refinement in Ireland is not a matter of poverty, as

---

[93] Young, *Arthur Young's Tour*, vol. 1, p. 44, vol. 2, p. 47.
[94] Caoimhín Ó Danachair, 'Traditional Forms of the Dwelling House in Ireland.' *Journal of the Royal Society of Antiquaries of Ireland* 102.1 (1972): p. 91.

even the Irish middle classes of dairymen and independent farmers neglect to practice the 'civil' English customs of populating domestic interiors with acquired consumer goods.[95] Moreover, the comparison associates the English national character with the sensibility for poetic reflection, thereby implying those lines taken from Oliver Goldsmith's 'The Deserted Village' (1770), the 'broken teacups wisely kept for shew,' hold no resonance for the underdeveloped native Irish sensibility.

In the *Tour's* final passages, Young disqualifies the cabin as a space reflective of or conducive to human thought: 'in Ireland the cabbin is not an object of a moment's consideration; to possess a cow and a pig is an earlier aim; the cabbin begins with a hovel, that is erected with two days' labour.'[96] Young's suggestion that the Irish build these habitations quickly out of their collective disregard for domestic comfort, rather than necessity and lack of alternate resources is ideologically revealing: he paints their method of construction as a fact of Irish unenlightenment, rather than a response to their material surroundings. As we have seen, building a mud cabin—although it could be completed in a few days' time—was labor-intensive and involved creative design, while also accommodating the economic pressures of the sometimes nomadic tenant Irish.

Continuing this typecasting, Young later describes the Irish as 'infinitely more cheerful and lively than anything we commonly see in England, having none of that incivility of sullen silence, with which so many enlightened Englishmen seem to wrap themselves up.'[97] Again, while ostensibly praising the Irish for their good humor, Young simultaneously characterizes the nation as lacking 'enlightenment' and the self-reflective psychological depth of English people, when in fact mud cabin building was both creative and inventive and in tune with the natural landscape. Finally, Young also undermines Irish education by virtue of its outdoor setting: '[hedge schools] might as well be termed ditch ones, for I have seen many a ditch full of scholars.'[98] As with the cabin-turned-dunghill, Young mires hedge schools with implied filth and barbarity that can be linked to Molesworth's tirade about Irish 'vermin' 'shamefully living' in ditches, quoted previously. The *Tour* creates a value system in which a person who lives in continuity with the outside world and the soil around him is less pensive than the one who makes demarcations between outside and inside.

To summarize, the final colonial effect of Young's *Tour* is a new version of the mud cabin pigsty stereotype that dissociates the native Irish from the so-called exclusively 'human' capacity for reflection, rationality, and poetic sensibility. As a

---

[95] Anne McClintock's *Imperial Leather* (London: Routledge, 2013) traces, for example, the rising importance of consumer soap in British racial and colonial politics. One of the most common household commodities in Victorian England, household soap became a racialized pillar of the British Empire's civilizing mission.
[96] Young, *Arthur Young's Tour*, vol. 2, p. 120.   [97] Young, *Arthur Young's Tour*, vol. 2, p. 147.
[98] Young, *Arthur Young's Tour*, vol. 2, p. 147.

corollary, all his binaristic constructions of Irish nature—mud rather than slate, pigs rather than tea, hastily constructed cabins and 'ditch schools'—state that Ireland needs enlightened English education and influence in order to advance into the parameters of 'civil' human habitation and human self-reflection. As expressed so effectively by Kathryn Yusoff's words, discussed previously: the 'categorization of matter enact[s the] racialization' of people.[99] Her logic explains the impact of Young's *Tour*, and all the texts that preempted and echoed its muddy stereotype. When Young categorizes Irish mud and thatch beneath English brick and slate, he creates a binary that consequently racializes the Irish people. The very nomenclature of the 'weedy dunghill' and 'smoked ham' as reclassifications of what are otherwise organic, earthly materials—soil and smoke—denaturalizes and dehumanizes Irish people living in tandem with their native landscape and local materials. The tragic addendum to the racial-animal semiotics of the mud cabin would emerge in the middle of the nineteenth century, when, despite a devastating famine, authority figures in Britain were unwilling, perhaps even unable, to acknowledge Irish humanity and sentience. By 1845, the profound rhetorical work of the eighteenth century had rendered the Irish lifestyle not worth saving in humanist terms.

4.3   Instructive Mud in Eighteenth-Century Literature

Because of its sheer ubiquity in farming and architecture, it makes sense that, over the course of the eighteenth century, mud assembled Irish characters as well as Irish houses. As far back as Jonathan Swift's *Gulliver's Travels* (1724) to Henry Brooke's *Fool of Quality* (1765) to Owenson's *Florence Macarthy* (1818), mud helped writers conceptualize and formulate Irish literary characters. But the approach to mud in Irish literature is varied: Anglo-Irish writer Henry Brooke used mud for surface-level connotations of grit and moral strength while Sydney Owenson used it to go deep within colonial psychology. The depth and dark interior of the mud cabin naturally invites the new materialist critic attuned to the interconnections of matter and discourse to see ulterior, unseen narratives obscured within a text. Mud cabins in Irish literature are not just fixed imagery or tropes that invite comparison with earlier, prejudiced travel writings like Young's, but rather, active textual agents from which Irish subjectivity emerges metaphorically and symbiotically.

Perhaps the most famous Irish text to explore the relationship between mud and colonialism is Jonathan Swift's *Gulliver's Travels* (1724). The fourth and most critical book in *Gulliver's Travels*—and the book famously concerned with

---

[99] Yusoff, *Billion Black Anthropocenes*, p. 20.

racialization—exposes how dirt and mud play a key role in separating animal from human, and, secondarily, colonial subjects from imperial ones. The homo sapiens Yahoos, who 'fall asleep in mud,' are characterized primarily according to their propensity for dirt, what Gulliver describes as 'their strange disposition to nastiness and dirt, whereas there appears to be a natural love of cleanliness in all other animals.'[100] The order of 'nastiness,' implying feces, then 'dirt,' underscores how the latter has been rhetorically employed to connote the former. Furthermore, the origin story of the Yahoos, as it is relayed to Gulliver, involves mud: 'many years ago, two of these brutes appeared together upon a mountain; whether pro-duced by the heat of the sun upon corrupted mud and slime...was never known.'[101] In this origin story, Swift satirizes colonial ideology through literalism: the Yahoos, the base, inhuman homo sapiens and colonial natives of Houyhnhnmland, are 'produced,' quite literally, by 'corrupted mud and slime.' He exposes the material semiotics of colonial stereotype and prejudice—how these ideologies are manufactured and 'produced' out of materiality.

It is very possible to read an Irish theme into Swift's discussion of the Yahoos, who he describes as lying 'in ditches': 'Nature has taught them to dig deep holes with their nails on the side of a rising ground, wherein they lie by themselves.'[102] As we have seen in quotations from Young and Molesworth on hedge schools and Irish people gathering or sheltering in 'ditches,' this was a common refrain with a specifically Irish provenance. Swift's account of Yahoo habitat could also allude to the *bothóg*—the name for temporary Irish shelters built into the side of the hill—which were increasingly common among cottiers in the eighteenth century. Furthermore, the rhetoric exposes colonialism's backstage choreography: he writes that 'nature' taught the Yahoos to make these *bothóg*-like mud dwellings, exposing the binaristic correlation of colony with nature and empire with culture.

In book 4, Swift explores the psychological process by which a human can self-alienate from his own natural species on the basis of cultural beliefs around dirt. Because Gulliver has learned to see the Yahoos' close proximity to dirt as 'filthy' existence, because he has learned to identify himself as a civilized being that lives apart from dirt, his humanist ethos aligns with the more rational, cleanly, and 'human' race, the Houyhnhnms. In a cutting, sardonic irony, these ideologies of dirt and cleanliness see Gulliver identifying with horses rather than humans, and thereby exposing the speciesism inherent in colonial ideology. *Gulliver's Travels* announces the rhetorical effect of imperial English writings on Irish domestic life by literalizing them. It reveals how mud becomes an effective ingredient with which to animalize colonial subjects and thereby categorize them apart from other human and national affiliations.

[100] Jonathan Swift, *Gulliver's Travels* (Oxford: Oxford UP, 2005), p. 245.
[101] Swift, *Gulliver's Travels*, p. 253.   [102] Swift, *Gulliver's Travels*, p. 248.

Forty years after the publication of *Gulliver's Travels*, as the novel was becoming an increasingly more dominant cultural form in England, Anglo-Irish writer and dramatist Henry Brooke approached mud through a more positive valence. Brooke is best known today for *The Fool of Quality* (1765–70), a novel of sensibility influenced by Rousseau as well as Brooke's own Irish surroundings. According to biographer Charles Kingsley, Brooke lived among his tenants later in life and embraced an agricultural lifestyle, practicing botany, farming, and a vegetable diet like his cottiers, whom he viewed as 'family.'[103] Brooke's willingness to embrace communion with the soil seems to have influenced *The Fool of Quality*, where the hero Harry Clinton is distinguished from his foil elder brother by his eagerness to play in the mud as a boy. Harry, a second son sent away to live with foster parents, acquires a 'physical hardiness' his brother lacks by living outside the pampered, aristocratic home.[104] As Clíona Ó Gallchoir has explained, Brooke, following Rousseau, adopts the belief that physical strength is a prerequisite for a strong soul and sense of character.[105] Moreover, Brooke uses Harry's physical hardiness and his experiences with mud and animals to critique the aristocracy's sheltering from the outside world and advocate interaction with nature as the foundation of a strong human character.

Throughout much of the first volume, Brooke uses mud as a moral semiotics of Harry's bildungsroman:

> every member as well as feature exposed to all weathers; [Harry] would run about, mother naked, for near an hour, in a frosty morning; was neither physicked into delicacy, nor flattered into pride, scarce felt the convenience, and much less understood the vanity of clothing; and was daily occupied in playing and wrestling with the pigs and two mongrel spaniels on the Dunghill[106]

From the very outset, the same 'nature' deployed by Molesworth and Young, Cooper as signs of Irish incivility—nakedness, closeness with pigs, exposure to mud, dung, and the elements—marks Harry as the chivalrous, sensible hero of Brooke's novel. Despite the fact that *The Fool of Quality* does not take place in Ireland, a certain Irish resonance emerges in this account of Harry's hero-building, bodily contact with the nonhuman. As Ó Gallchoir argues, 'dunghill' was a very 'localized version of the primitive'—a distinctly Irish term and concept.[107] Whereas travel writers like Young figured Irish robust health as an

[103] Charles Kingsley, Biographical Preface in Henry Brooke, *Fool of Quality*, vol. 1. (New York: Derby & Jackson, 1860), p. xxxix.
[104] Clíona Ó Gallchoir, 'New Beginning or Bearer of Tradition? Early Irish Fiction and the Construction of the Child' in *Irish Literature in Transition, 1700–1780*, ed. Moyra Haslett (Cambridge: Cambridge UP, 2020), p. 354.
[105] Ó Gallchoir, 'New Beginning,' p. 355.
[106] Henry Brooke, *The Fool of Quality*, 5 vols (New York: Derby & Jackson, 1860), vol. 1, p. 51.
[107] Ó Gallchoir, 'New Beginning,' p. 355.

anomaly contrasting their 'filthy' material circumstances, Brooke deliberately correlates nakedness and proximity to mud with Harry's strength in both the physical and moral sense.

Early on, Harry demonstrates compassion for a rooster: 'there was a cock at Harry's nurse's—the lord of the dunghill—between whom and our hero a very particular intimacy and friendship had been contracted.'[108] The language, albeit slightly playful, meaningfully opposes the negative ideology of Spenser and Molesworth around Irish dung, quoted earlier. Harry embraces a genuine, child-like 'intimacy' with dung and its inhabitant, the rooster, demonstrating what critics today might call posthumanism. The text seems to correlate this intimacy with dung and animals as indicative of Harry's compassion for all classes of people, like the naked child he helps or the old gentleman Mr. Fenton, whom he meets on the road and with whom he empathizes. Henry's compassion appears on his face: 'while Mr. Fenton spoke, the muscles of Harry's excessive countenance, like an equally tuned instrument, uttered unisons to every word he heard.'[109] Raised in compassionate encounters with earth and animals, the young hero demonstrates an excessively cultivated and sophisticated sense of sensibility, all visible on his face and symbolically linked with his muddy exterior and, by extension, his moral heroism.

Finally, much like an anti-colonial text, *The Fool of Quality* satirizes the hubris of the upper class. When Harry visits his family home as a child, the family condescendingly remarks that he did not 'appear to be endowed by nature with a single faculty of the *animal rationale*.'[110] Here, Brooke exhibits a different understanding of the human–animal binary than the one predicated on what the elite call the '*animal rationale*,' or reason. Through Harry's superior sensibility and sturdy earthiness, Brooke invites his reader to question who is really human(e) in this novel: Harry, who is empathetically ingratiated in his natural surroundings, or his aristocratic family members, who feign superiority and partition themselves from the surrounding world. The text seems to challenge reason as the foundation of heroism and reattributes it to terrestrial engagement and sensibility with all kinds of living creatures, ultimately undermining the 'reasoning' of social and speciesist hierarchy.

An early example of Anglo-Irish fiction, *The Fool of Quality* is revolutionary by turning to dirt as the origin of Henry's good, moral character. Brooke invokes and inverts the standard English discourse around mud in Ireland by using the dung-hill in positive terms and, even more poignantly, forming an English aristocratic hero out of what would have, in that century, been considered Irish material origins (nakedness, dunghill, pigs). A few years later, his Anglo-Irish contemporary Richard Griffith would showcase a similar line of thinking in his *The Gordian*

---

[108] Brooke, *Fool*, vol. 1, p. 59.   [109] Brooke, *Fool*, vol. 1, p. 142.
[110] Brooke, *Fool*, vol. 1, p. 55.

Knot, appearing in *Two Novels* (1769). The two gentleman characters, upon seeing an old man lying down in the dirt, ask him what he is doing, to which the man replies 'embracing his mother'. The men then engage in a 'philosophic speculation': 'ditchers, gardeners, sextons, and ploughmen, are, therefore said to live longer, than others. It may be possible then, that cottages, because build of sod and turf are more healthy habitations than palaces.'[111] Like Brooke before him, Griffith uses an encounter with dirt—an entanglement between human body and soil—to question (albeit briefly) English cultural standards of domesticity and hierarchies of architectural materials. By speculating, Griffith briefly raises the subversive idea that sod-wall living may, in certain ways, have advantages over a pristine, stone palace. In the developing Anglo-Irish novel, mud and cabins become a site of speculation, where the literary context of symbolic character building allows the novel to undermine the confident conclusions on Irish (bestial) nature by writers like Arthur Young.

At the turn of the century, Maria Edgeworth also used mud as an externalized symbolic code in one of her *Popular Tales*, 'Rosanna' (1800), but under very different terms to her Anglo-Irish literary predecessors. Aimed primarily at children, 'Rosanna' is a moral fable that teaches the value of industry, domestic cleanliness, frugality, and 'fortitude', much like Leadbeater's *Cottage Dialogues*. The start of the tale overwhelms the reader with a sensory deluge: the poor farming family the Grays are 'obliged to go into a poor mud-walled cabin [with]...a dunghill that, reaching to the thatch of the roof, shut out the light, and filled the house with the moist noisome smell.'[112] Edgeworth, continuing Young's dialectic, goes on to critique, in slightly more compassionate terms, the same arguments against the mud cabin, from smokiness, to the resident pig, to the dampness: 'the floor was so damp and soft, that the print of the nails of the brogues was left in it...the smoke was so thick that the pig might have been within a foot of you without your seeing him.'[113] Edgeworth teaches her reader that these kinds of domestic conditions are the 'species of content which leads to beggary' (p. 447). The use of 'species' here is crucial, subtly insinuating only a less-than-human way of life can exist within mud walls.

Edgeworth had a longstanding prejudice against Irish cabins, as Elizabeth Kowaleski-Wallace has documented. When she first arrived in Ireland at 14, she wrote a letter to Fanny Robinson decrying these 'huts' whose 'mudbuilt walls can scarcely support their weather-beaten roofs', evidence of the Irish being 'the laziest civilized nation on the face of the Earth'. Mud cabins ingratiated a clear hierarchical binary and sense of English superiority in Edgeworth in her youth: 'perhaps out of charity you go up to [the Irishman] and tell him he had much better set

---

[111] Richard Griffith, *The Gordian Knot*, in *Two Novels In Letter*, 4 vols (Dublin, 1769), vol. 4, p. 15.
[112] Maria Edgeworth, 'Rosanna' in *Tales and Novels*, vol. 2. *Popular Tales* (London, 1857), p. 442.
[113] Edgeworth, 'Rosanna', p. 443.

about repairing his house.—he would answer you...."when it falls it will be time enough to think of picking it up." '[114] Unlike her early impression, which sees Irish indolence as helpless, the lesson in 'Rosanna' comes when Gray finds a 'solution' to his mud cabin, and implicitly, Ireland's endemic laziness. Edgeworth classifies the mud cabin in 'Rosanna' as a 'necessary evil' that Gray bore with 'patience and fortitude' and remedied with 'industry.'[115] He gets right to work making his cottage more English in structure: 'the rooms were cleared of smoke, for Gray built a chimney, and the kitchen window, which had formerly been stuffed up...was glazed...There was now light in the house. Light! The great friend of cleanliness and order.'[116] Edgeworth's tone draws a clear, legible binary between light and dark, windows and mud, industry and poverty, English civility and Irish boorishness.

The neatly constructed binary of cottage/cabin, however, is the real fiction in Edgeworth's story. Her moral, black-and-white picture that shades Gray's cabin as the inverse of domesticity disregards the practical, material issues tenants faced, such as heat preservation, increased rent, and the question of privacy those 'stuffed-up' windows afforded. Edgeworth uses Gray as a model for segregating and classifying organisms, separating out the components and actors in what we have seen is, in fact, the cabin's intra-acting ecosystem, where mud, smoke, air, animals, and humans cooperate symbiotically. In Edgeworth's clean-up, Gray removes the smoke and places it outside the home along with the pig, removing his manure pile (impractically) out of sight, giving the (false) idea that nonhuman matter has been evicted from the human space. This reorganization of cabin matter enacts a form of humanist hierarchy where humans compartmentalize materials in a scientific, Enlightenment methodology, rather than embracing inter-connected symbiosis across all terrestrial life. On one level, the story becomes a pedagogy in humanist, imperial ideology that operates according to stringent definitions of acceptable human habitations according to English cottage standards and ingratiates hierarchical thinking.

At the conclusion of the story, Edgeworth uses her didactic code of cleanliness versus mud living to vindicate a parallel binary of Englishness over Irishness. When the farmer Gray helps an English soldier and his pregnant wife, and the soldier wishes to thank him, Gray asks for the barracks' horse manure, 'which will make my land and me rich.'[117] Symbolically, this moment is poignant: the Irish tenant Gray uses the excrement of English military horses to enrich his own land. While the allegory could be read from a postcolonial angle of satire— namely, growing life from imperial waste according to mud's regenerative

---

[114] Qtd. in Elizabeth Kowaleski-Wallace, *Their Fathers' Daughters: Hannah More, Maria Edgeworth, and Patriarchal Complicity* (New York: Oxford UP, 1991), p. 142.

[115] Edgeworth, 'Rosanna,' p. 447.   [116] Edgeworth, 'Rosanna,' pp. 447–8.

[117] Edgeworth, 'Rosanna,' p. 457.

thematics—Edgeworth's message about the benefit of English-style industrial work ethic overrides any subversion. Soon after Gray makes uses of the dung, his family move into a cottage in the English style, and an Englishman refers to them as so industrious as to 'almost have been born in England.'[118] The allegorical lesson is unmistakable: with English assistance and nutrients, the Irish can improve themselves—from English dung (specifically, the recycled nutrients of the British army) come better Irishmen. And yet, despite the clear instruction, the tale recognizes the material benefits of manure, of dung, and thereby engages manure's 'vibrant materiality,' as described by Jane Bennett. Ironically, the Gray family's English improvements and furnishings are dependent on manure, on Gray's willingness to recycle and get close to animal dung—a fact that, earlier, Edgeworth had criticized in the cabin's unacceptable proximity to the dung pile.

Edgeworth's lesson about improving Irish domesticity toward English manners is clearest when the titular heroine enamors an English heir, Stafford. Stafford's mother claims that any woman 'having been bred in a mud-walled cabin, could never be expected to turn out at the long run equal to a true-born Englishwoman, bred in a slated house.'[119] But Rosanna, now living in a cottage with her industrious family, increasingly grows to look 'more like an Englishwoman than anything else,' and, after her marriage, she wins over her English mother-in-law with her 'gentle manners and willing obedience.'[120] On one level, Edgeworth challenges the mud cabin stereotype for English readers by showing how the Irish can exhibit manners and earn status beyond their material origins. However, her hierarchy of materiality also implies that eradicating mud is the best means of eradicating native Irishness—a message that seems to reflect Mary Douglas's account of dirt's sociological role. Dirt, like native Irish custom, is matter out of place and therefore disrupts the social order of the Anglo-Irish Ascendancy and Union. Ultimately, the story makes the national and humanist binary Young built from Irish mud even more legible for readers, insisting that good characters should rid themselves of muddy habitations, that the Irish will be at their best (or, most English) when they are cleaned up and rehomed in English-style cottages.

4.4   Inscrutable Depth in Edgeworth's *Ennui*

While Edgeworth's message on mud is, for the most part, straightforward in 'Rosanna,' things become far more complex in her novel, *Ennui* (1809), where mud cabins are a central symbol of native Irish life and Anglo-Irish cultural clash. Lord Glenthorn, the recently restored absentee landlord, builds his former nurse, Ellinor (whom he later discovers is his biological mother), an English-style

---

[118] Edgeworth, 'Rosanna,' p. 511.   [119] Edgeworth, 'Rosanna,' p. 550.
[120] Edgeworth, 'Rosanna,' pp. 512, 550.

cottage to replace her disorderly cabin, but unlike in 'Rosanna,' this English cottage offers no solution to Irish nature. Famously, the cottage collapses in on itself and Ellinor returns to her mud cabin living, suggesting that Glenthorn has failed in his attempt to correct Irish nature. It seems hard to reconcile the fact that the same author could compose such opposing accounts of mud cabins as appear between 'Rosanna' and *Ennui*. But *Ennui* has long proved to be a conundrum for critics. Clíona Ó Gallchoir explains that, unlike the standard English novel of manners at the time, *Ennui* invokes 'popular beliefs about Ireland' and fable-like elements such as babies changed at nurse, which ultimately destabilize any standardized reading of the text.[121] Even Glenthorn the character, changed at nurse with an English lord, originates in a folkloric Irish bull, quoted in Maria and Richard Edgeworth's *Essay on Irish Bulls* (1802): 'I hate that woman for she changed me at nurse.'[122] These native Irish cultural allusions, along with references to 1798, and the Gaelic order of Ireland, Ó Gallchoir argues, enable several subversive and contradictory meanings in the text, resulting in a 'dizzying effect.'[123] Indeed, the mud cabin sits at the center of *Ennui's* 'dizzying' plane.

Although Edgeworth was a key precursor to the novelistic realism of Jane Austen and Sir Walter Scott, her Irish novels are seen as only tangentially associated with the realist style of her English works. In the early twentieth century, Irish writer Frank O'Connor famously cited Irish mud cabins as an obstacle toward realist writing:

> the moment a writer raises his eyes from the slums and cabins, he finds nothing but a vicious and ignorant middle-class, and for aristocracy the remnants of an English garrison, alien in religion and education. From such material he finds it almost impossible to create a picture of life...a realistic literature is clearly impossible[124]

O'Connor recognizes a disconnect between the mud-based reality of Irish cabin life and the alien ideologies of the English ruling class—what he describes as very different 'materials' from which to construct a cohesive fictional world. The distance between these two Irelands disrupts any ideological or cultural coherence that would typically be an essential prerequisite for realism, such as in the fictional world of Jane Austen, for example, which has been long been viewed as the apotheosis of British literary realism. Part of the formal difference can be

---

[121] Clíona Ó Gallchoir, *Maria Edgeworth: Women, Enlightenment, and Nation* (Dublin: UCD Press, 2005), p. 97.
[122] Richard Lovell Edgeworth and Maria Edgeworth, *Essay on Irish Bulls* (London: Johnson, 1802), p. 21.
[123] Ó Gallchoir, *Maria Edgeworth*, p. 97.
[124] Qtd. in James Chandler, 'Edgeworth and Realism' in *Irish Literature in Transition, 1780–1830*, ed. Claire Connolly (Cambridge: Cambridge UP, 2020), p. 190.

explained by the fact that the British realist tradition stems from imperial and Enlightenment ideologies of intellectual reason, individualism, and humanism— the very likes of which, as I have discussed, the inter-species community of the Irish mud cabin living resists and contradicts.

James Chandler, on the other hand, invokes the description of Ellinor's mud cabin, with its litany of animals, dirt floors, and manure pile, as evidence of a semi-realist mode because of its 'grossness of daily life' and its 'flat description of the scene and clinical catalogue of its objects'—what others like George Levine have categorized as the requisite 'ordinary' in realist fiction.[125] *Ennui*, Chandler argues, attempts ethnographic realism, the 'accurate representation' of Ireland as a complex society. For Chandler, the mud cabin enables this kind of realism in the sense that it epitomizes Ireland's ordinary material life.[126] Chandler's assessment therefore invites further probing: where does the realist tradition of the novel and its deep-thinking characters stand in relation to the ecological narrative of the cabin?

When Glenthorn first sees Ellinor's cabin, he rehearses the familiar stereotype: 'a wretched-looking, low, mud-walled cabin'—'a dunghill was before the only window' and 'close to the door, was a puddle of the dirtiest of dirty water,' from which several animals and people emerge upon his arrival.[127] He then gives a satirically exaggerated account of the cabin's many inhabitants: 'At my approach there came out of the cabin a pig, a calf, a lamb, a kid, and two geese... turkeys, cocks, hens, chickens, a dog, a cat, a kitten, a beggar-man, a beggar-woman with a pipe in her mouth, children innumerable, and a stout girl with a pitchfork in her hand.'[128] The final detail in this list—the pitchfork in the hands of a young girl— appears comical from Glenthorn's English point of view, but material knowledge of the cabin's assembly signals a more remarkable fact: that the entire infrastruc- ture, holding such a vast network of animals and people, was most likely built with that single pitchfork or similarly shaped sprong. Instantly, then, the text encompasses two stories, two worlds, two narratives at work: the material and the ideological.

Significantly, the cabin is detailed from within Glenthorn's arrogant first- person narrative, as he literally 'look[s] down upon the roof as I sat on horseback, measuring the superficies with my eye.'[129] The scene engages a skewed optics that underscores and exposes Glenthorn's colonialist perspective: he rhetorically diminishes the cabin at the same time that his list indicates a mysterious, aston- ishing depth to it, capable of holding so many creatures. Glenthorn looks down from his horse 'measuring the superficies with my eye' of the ironically titled

[125] Chandler, 'Edgeworth and Realism,' p. 193.
[126] Chandler, 'Edgeworth and Realism,' p. 201.
[127] Maria Edgeworth, *Ennui*, in *Tales of a Fashionable Life*, vol. 1 (London: Hunter, 1815), p. 101.
[128] Edgeworth, *Ennui*, p. 101.   [129] Edgeworth, *Ennui*, p. 101.

'mansion,' but cannot reason how it was 'capable of containing' so many inhabitants.[130] There is, therefore, an acknowledged mystery and invisible interiority involved in Ellinor's cabin, even when viewed from Glenthorn's superior English purview. Because the text takes such pains to remind us we are in Glenthorn's (limited) cultural, English perspective in this elevated approach to Ellinor's cabin, it necessarily also highlights the ulterior perspective—the one from *inside* the cabin, from the ground below, looking up at Glenthorn. At the same time that Glenthorn rhetorically diminishes the cabin's alleged filthiness and farmyard mayhem, the mud cabin also articulates a narrative for itself—one that he literally cannot measure nor understand.

As Edgeworth's text encourages its reader to see Glenthorn's limits as a narrator, it manifests an omnipresent yet unidentified ulterior narrative voice—one that sees more in Ellinor than Glenthorn does. This other narrative voice and perspective emerges through the material details of the text. Rather than simply a material catalogue that affirms a 'realist,' ordinary picture of Ireland, as Chandler argues, Ellinor's mud cabin becomes a narrative of its own that questions Glenthorn's assumptions about Ireland and Irish people. For example, the unseen depth and extensive network of human and nonhuman inhabitants of Ellinor's mud cabin parallels an unseen depth and network of secrets contained in her very mind. Ellinor harbors the knowledge of Glenthorn's real lineage: that she orchestrated a baby swap many years prior, making him, by birth a disenfranchised Catholic Irishman that her scheme restored to the property rights of an Irish estate. Throughout the first half of the text, Glenthorn is ignorant of the deeper meaning and complexity to all his encounters with Ellinor, much as he is ignorant of the complexity of her cabin's ecosystem. He presumes their meetings are simply that of a nurse and her former foster child, rather than that of a mother and her secret, now powerful son. His response to her home can thereby be read as a direct, material manifestation of his own elitist ideology, as well as his ignorance of the unseen, complex interiority in Ellinor and other native Irish characters, disguised behind a façade of paying homage to her landlord, and indeed, behind the thick mud walls and obscured windows of the cabin.

This subversiveness of the mud cabin's narrative in *Ennui* becomes literal when Irish materiality itself defeats Glenthorn's attempt to replace Ellinor's cabin with an English-style cottage. When Glenthorn decides 'a better house than her present habitation' should be built for Ellinor, he congratulates himself for his 'gratitude to this poor woman.'[131] After the build, he returns to find the materials of the cottage have rebelled against his desire to order and contain Ellinor's Irishness:

---

[130] Edgeworth, *Ennui*, p. 101.   [131] Edgeworth, *Ennui*, p. 104.

I found my old nurse sitting at her wheel, in the midst of the wreck and litter of all sorts of household furniture…Ellinor seemed, alas! To have as little taste for the luxuries with which I had provided her as the pig had for the silver trough. What I called conveniences, were to her encumbrances: she had not been used to them: she was put out of her way; and it was a daily torment to her habits, to keep her house neat and clean.[132]

On the surface level, it seems like Edgeworth is invoking a Youngian ideology. In fact, the particular wording at the end of this passage directly echoes an earlier influence, Spenser's *View of the Present State of Ireland*, which says the Irishman must take more care to 'keep his said House neat and cleanly.'[133] Similarly, when Glenthorn later reflects that 'it must take time to change local and national habits and prejudices, and that it is necessary to raise a taste for comforts, before they can be properly enjoyed,' one might hear Anglo-Irish paternalism and prejudice, often expressed by the Edgeworths, as in 'Rosanna.'[134] After all, Glenthorn's attempt at sanitizing Ellinor's domestic habitat exemplifies Mary Douglas's model of ordering materiality in order to maintain social order.

However, the analogies and arrogant tone, in such dissonance with Ellinor's habits and preferences, underscore the dialogic, double narrative at work in the text. Following the passage quoted above, Glenthorn's reveals that his ostensibly superior slated English cabin had been no match for Irish weather: 'some of the slates were blown off in the night…and Ellinor was forced…to retreat from corner to corner as the rain pursued.'[135] Not only has it rained in the house, but the winds have completely destroyed the interior, and Ellinor has caught cold. The 'wreck and litter' that Glenthorn associates with Irish disorganization is, in fact, the material aftereffects of misapplied English infrastructure and Glenthorn's privileging of English taste over local materials.

In the early nineteenth century, the question of comfort was a central factor in some landlords' decisions to replace their tenants' Irish mud cabins with stone and slate cottages. The slate roof, in particular, was considered by English and Anglo-Irish viewers to be the basic requisite for comfort, and yet this same slate roof in *Ennui* ultimately causes Ellinor extreme *dis*comfort, exposing her to the wind and rain and resulting in rheumatism that keeps her bedridden. In notable irony, this ostensibly superior house made of materials wrought from the earth and perhaps processed in factories experiences its own destruction at the whim of Irish weather. Like the cottage he builds, Glenthorn himself becomes exposed by his presumed superiority and animalized metaphor that figures Ellinor as a pig. His words make him the satiric object of an ulterior narrative stemming from the

---

[132] Edgeworth, *Ennui*, pp. 129–30.   [133] Spenser, *View*, p. 127.
[134] Edgeworth, *Ennui*, p. 133.   [135] Edgeworth, *Ennui*, p. 131.

mud cabin—a perspective that reveals his failure to read the material ecosystem that, as Ellinor later discloses, is his natural birthright. Glenthorn's inability to read the depth of the mud cabin—and read Ellinor's own depth—results in a failed attempt to control Irish matter and an Irish mother, to see an alternative kind of human who can and should live within dirt and cohabit with animals.

Elizabeth Kowaleski-Wallace has read the cottage scenes in *Ennui* as an extended maternal symbolism that aligns with Edgeworth's Anglo-Irish and colonialist sympathies. She argues that as the slate cottage collapses around Ellinor, she collapses back into a 'more natural state' that embraces the 'wild' over the civilized, visualized by these collapsing walls which do not distinguish inside from outside.[136] In other words, the failed English cottage becomes an extended allegory of the nature/culture binary that represents Irish nature versus much-needed English enculturation represented by Glenthorn. However, Kowaleski-Wallace does not read the original cabin for what it is, in spite of Edgeworth's politics: a material reality and common fact of Irish life. Regardless of her ideological background and her didactic plots, Edgeworth records the material details of the Irish cabin life she witnessed: the shared habitats of humans and animals, the manure pile, the smoke, the boarded-up windows and dark interiors. When Glenthorn's cottage falls down around Ellinor in the wind and rain, Edgeworth's text inadvertently points back to the interspecies harmony of the Irish cabin ecosystem—that it works with the Irish environment in ways Glenthorn's English cottage does not.

In each of these encounters with Irish cabin, although inflected with Glenthorn's tone of superiority, there is a clear double, dialogic narrative between the culture of English improvement and the articulating force of mud. Simply put, Edgeworth depicts some cognitive assonance between an acknowledged physical depth to native dwellings like the mud cabin and an acknowledged psychological depth in native characters like Ellinor—between material life and human subjectivity. Ellinor's dialogue, therefore, when read in connection with her ecological complexity as a character inhabiting a thick-walled cabin, intimates more profound and double-edged motives for switching her son with the true heir at birth. Ellinor proclaims herself innocent and ignorant according to English stereotypes of the Irish—'for I was always innocent like, and not worldly given,' she tells Glenthorn, and insists the devil put the thought of changing the babies 'into her head'—but her language suggests otherwise when she mentions she thought it was better for all 'To see my son made a lord of.'[137] Her words, like the dark inside of her cabin, point to some undisclosed interior narrative and nationalist meaning within her world, but they ultimately remain concealed in the same way the reader never sees directly inside Ellinor's cabin.

---

[136] Kowaleski-Wallace, *Fathers' Daughters*, p. 163.   [137] Edgworth, *Ennui*, p. 292.

In the end, Edgeworth's novel tries to return to the idea presented in 'Rosanna' and reflected in her wider *oeuvre*: that Ireland will benefit from English influence in culture and industry. Glenthorn's foster brother Christy, the real heir, proves an incapable leader when his Irish manners and ignorance get the better of him and his inheritance. Meanwhile, Glenthorn's English education, when combined with industry and hard work, ultimately turns him into the ideal landlord, as if an attempt to reconfirm the need for English influence in Ireland. Glenthorn's transition from the wistful, dissipated, and vain aristocrat to the disenfranchised and suddenly competent middle-class lawyer O'Donoghue renders his subjectivity as a protagonist incoherent. The Irish setting crumbles his English-style cottage and, eventually, his own character identity. If the language of novelistic realism is founded on controlled, contained, cohesive narratives and characters, then Glenthorn's sudden industrial work ethic and new character identity appears far less 'real' than the mud cabin. In fact, as Vera Kreilkamp argues, Edgeworth's attempts to didactically control the moral, Enlightened lesson at the end of her novels results in an unsatisfying vision—a contrivance, rather than a probable conclusion.[138] Although the ending of *Ennui* seemingly offers some instructive resolution that landlords must guide and socialize the native Irish, Ellinor and her material world have, in fact, proven enduringly resistant to Glenthorn's Anglicization.

The real story the mud cabin underscores in *Ennui*, therefore, is one of underestimated depth, overlooked assemblages of inter-connected species and organisms, and networks shared between the native Irish and the land they inhabit. The lifestyle Glenthorn first perceives as backward human nature contains within it a 'culture of nature'—that is, relationships between mud, animals, and cottiers that are underestimated by English prejudice, much like the Irish character itself. By recording the material facts of mud cabins' shadowy depth and its thick earthen walls, Edgeworth makes room in her text for a shaded, coded, and deep Irish character (Ellinor) and a plot that, as Ó Gallchoir emphasizes, can be read to challenge paternal order and assert the power of precolonial, Gaelic memory associated with the land.[139] The mud cabin's unlit and unseen interior world points to that same concept within Irish characters, like Ellinor who destabilizes the entire plot and narratorial cohesion with her hidden secret about Glenthorn's birthright. Even at the end, when Glenthorn marries into the same Irish estate he once inherited, his presence, as the biological son of a cottier, is the final, bodily reminder that English culture cannot order and organize Ireland without Irish usurpation. What we see in *Ennui*, through the material narrative of Ellinor's mud cabin, and in contrast to the British realist tradition, is an Irish literary psychology that emerges in dissonance with the overarching master narrative—rather

---

[138] Vera Kreilkamp, *The Anglo-Irish Novel and the Big House* (Syracuse, NY: Syracuse UP, 1998).
[139] Ó Gallchoir, *Maria Edgeworth*, p. 101.

than as naturally cohering with that narrative world. By accurately recording the details of the mud cabin, Edgeworth's text invokes the symbiotic world of native Irish culture and thereby, perhaps unintentionally, reveals the *in*accuracy of her hero's ending as a reformed aristocrat and perfectly English Irishman.

4.5 Owenson's Cabins and Colonial Subjectivity

For centuries, literary critics have been grouping Maria Edgeworth and Sydney Owenson together as contemporary Irish female novelists and founders of the Irish national tale. The conversation, however, has always differentiated them in style: Edgeworth has more often been classified as the realist, Anglo-Irish novelist while Owenson seen as the romantic writer of nationalist sensibility.[140] Their representations of mud cabins, however, provide an opportunity for seeing a formal synchronicity between the two very different writers. Edgeworth and Owenson both seem to intuit the material truth of the mud cabin's ecosystem, and their texts manifest that very real ecology by portraying cottiers with deep subjectivities. As in Edgeworth's *Ennui*, Owenson's mud cabins in *Florence Macarthy* effect a sense of unseen and subversive Irish psychology overlooked by English ideology. The material narrative of the mud cabin, therefore, adds another layer to Owenson's already layered, multi-voiced, and dialogic national tales.

In her romantic descriptions of Irish life, Owenson evokes ecological harmony of human–nonhuman exchange within the space of the mud cabin. In *Patriotic Sketches of Ireland* (1809), a nonfictional account of her travels in Connaught published with political aim to give voice to the 'lower orders of my countrymen,' she describes a boy sleeping in a cabin: 'the head of a calf actually reposing on his arm, and the parent cow quietly slumbering at his feet. A more striking picture of the interior of an Irish cabin could not be given.'[141] This offers a very different definition of domesticity and human relation to nature than the orthodox ideas established by Britain's colonial, Enlightened categorizations of animals and matter. The image so impressed Owenson that she repeated the same bucolic scene in her novel *Florence Macarthy*, demonstrating its resonance for representing Irish character. As opposed to Young and Cooper who balked at the Irish sleeping with their animals, Owenson paints what we might read as a posthumanist vision of the cabin, demonstrating harmonious contact and cohabitation between human, cow, and the earthen floor of the cabin.

---

[140] See Robert Tracy, 'Legality versus Legitimacy' and Joep Leerssen, *Remembrance and Imagination* for instructive comparisons between the national tales of Edgeworth and Owenson.

[141] Sydney Owenson, *Patriotic Sketches of Ireland, written in Connaught* (Baltimore, MD: Dobbin & Murphy, Callendar & Wills, 1809), pp. xiii, 145.

Nevertheless, Owenson ultimately defers to the familiar conscription of 'misery' in an appeal to her reader's sympathy. Rather than align with the Youngian affiliation between cabins and inhumane Irish habits, Owenson, much like postcolonial scholars today, identifies the root of this muddy misery as the colonial, tenant system. She explains, for example, a man she encounters who had to live in a 'wretched' mud cabin rather than build a cottage because of 'fear of a raised rent and his family being turned out, unable to get a lease from the middleman.'[142] She also defers to English and Enlightenment traditions of cleanliness in her defense of the poor Irish. She comes across another cabin that, 'though little better than a mud built hut, it was singularly clean, and we found its mistress busied in preparing dinner for her sons.'[143] Here, Owenson challenges the presumed idea in 'Rosanna' that only cottages can be clean. As opposed to Young who removes the family in his person-less frontispiece of the Irish cabin, Owenson consistently places a loving family inside her mud walls. She attempts to humanize the cabin from within to defend the Irish people on the basis of the familial structure. The corollary is, however, that by humanizing the cabin Irish for an English reader through the tropes of cleanliness and their natural, 'human' desire for better, cottage-style homes, she capitulates on the nonhuman potential of the cabin ecosystem so romantically rendered in her image of the boy sleeping with the cow.

This tension between an appeal for political change, propagandized by affected descriptions of poverty, and an awareness of the mud cabin's internal ecosystem becomes stark in her novel *Florence Macarthy* (1818). Amidst Owenson's *oeuvre*, this novel might qualify as the one that deals most explicitly with the matter of Irish poverty under colonialism, for which mud living becomes a consistent exemplar in the text. For example, in one of her descriptions of the Kerry landscape, Owenson describes how 'the ruins of other castles and monasteries afforded shelter to many wretched families, who had built their perishable huts against the walls of edifices, whose strength had stood the shock of ages.'[144] Her language visualizes the theme of lost civilization, tragically pointing to the reduction of a great, long-lasting Gaelic medieval architecture to 'perishable huts.' However, in the details recorded, mud's material narrative of creativity again articulates outside of this ideological preference for stone. The placement of mud cabins against castle ruins can be read, in a new materialist sense, as demonstrating the Irish peasant's continued architectural and vernacular creativity, implying the Irish people's enduring strength and creative material construction in the wake of colonial destruction, imaged in the ruined castles.

In one of the earlier passages in the novel, the narrative invites the reader to look inside the mud cabin—and inside the native Irish character—with pathos.

[142] Owenson, *Patriotic Sketches*, p. 132.   [143] Owenson, *Patriotic Sketches*, pp. 157–8.
[144] Sydney Owenson, *Florence Macarthy: An Irish Tale*, ed. Jenny McAuley. (London: Routledge, 2015), vol. 3, pp. 255–6.

The scene begins with the typical tropes of the imperial travel narrative as the hero the Commodore and his companion, De Vere, tour the impoverished areas of Ringsend, Dublin, and witness the 'noxious vapors,' 'windows stuffed with straw,' houses in 'ruins,' 'thick smoke of burning straw' and a girl 'half naked, pretty but filthy and emaciated.'[145] Owenson gothicizes Irish poverty in these descriptions, harsher than her earlier accounts of Irish mud cabin living, in what might indicate an increasingly urgent appeal on behalf of her 'countrymen's' lowest classes. Announcing Owenson's political aims, the Commodore denounces the colonialist perspective that looks at mud cabins and focuses on lack of civility and uncleanliness, rather than poverty: 'Who can see such wretchedness as this, with a *man's eye*, and not feel it with a *man's heart*?...Indignation usurps the seat of pity, and spirit rests upon those who have afflicted, not those who suffer.'[146] Owenson uses the Commodore's inner emotion and indignation spurred by the sight of Irish poverty in order to criticize the system that places blame on the Irish people for the ostensibly sub-human standards of mud walled living.

Owenson's Commodore then reflects on the historical meaning of the mud cabin: 'He turned his eyes to the peasant's hut: it was the model of the "*mere Irishman's*" hovel, as it rose amidst scenes of desolation during the civil wars of Elizabeth's reign.'[147] The passage makes a remarkable and deliberate connection between the physical world and internal human consciousness: looking at the Irish peasant's mud cabin, which contains its own hidden and material depth, brings the reader deep into the consciousness of Irish history and imperial violence dating back to 'Elizabeth's reign.' The Commodore, interacting dynamically with the material history of the cabin from within his inner thought, transitions into the depth of the peasant's psychology:

He beheld the tenant of this miserable dwelling working on the roads...laboring in the fields with an expression of lifeless activity marking his exertions...his countenance readily brightening into smiles of gaiety or derision expressed the habitual influence of strong dark passions, the lurking slyness of distrust—the instinctive self-defiance of conscious degradation[148]

In this carefully crafted moment, Owenson invites her reader to see inside the so-called 'miserable hovels' as both a literal and figurative way of looking into the Irish peasant's psyche under colonial conditions. Many of the accounts discussed thus far in this chapter, from Young to Edgeworth, emphasize the darkness inside the mud cabin as a consistent trope and observation, the 'stuffed windows' and

[145] Owenson, *Florence Macarthy*, vol. 1, pp. 38, 42–3.
[146] Owenson, *Florence Macarthy*, vol. 1, p. 44.
[147] Owenson, *Florence Macarthy*, vol. 1, p. 92.
[148] Owenson, *Florence Macarthy*, vol. 1, p. 92.

smoky interior. Interestingly, Owenson describes the interior depth of Irish character in kind: as holding 'strong dark passions.' The text conducts a symbiotic transference from the darkness inside the cabin's thick, windowless mud walls to the obscured interiority of national feeling deep within Irish character. As such, Owenson inverts Young's rhetorical move by using the dark, material depth of the cabin's interior to assert a greater, three-dimensional psychological depth in the tenant Irish, rather than deny them intellectual complexity.

The material narrative of the mud cabin in both *Ennui* and *Florence Macarthy* structures a type of Irish literary character that would, Vera Kreilkamp has argued, become a hallmark of Anglo-Irish Big House novel a century later. The native Irish character who holds quiet resentment against the Ascendancy in *Florence Macarthy* pre-empts the Big House novel's thematic distrust of the peasant cabin dweller. Kreilkamp argues that the Anglo-Irish novels dating back to Maria Edgeworth are 'complex structures of ironic plotting and characterization' as well charting a doubleness between the ideals of Anglo-Irish society and the material realities of Irish life.[149] Similarly, eighteenth-century mud narrates its own ironic doubleness about Irish life and character: that mud cabins were both a means of oppressing and racializing the Irish people at the same time that they afforded a natural, earthly canvas on which Irish people expressed their architectural and literary creativity, as well as their tenacity to survive on the land around them.

That quiet depth of colonial subjectivity described by Owenson in *Florence Macarthy* and insinuated by Edgeworth's *Ennui*—what critics now recognize as a familiar postcolonial reading of the 'other' or the 'subaltern'—emerges through the Irish tradition of mud cabin construction and inhabitation. When reframed as a creative vehicle of survival and expression, eighteenth-century mud cabins highlight a unique creativity within Irish fiction: to represent a character's subjective interiority that both reflects and circumvents the British realist tradition that becomes intimate with its characters' psychological depth. The Irish mud cabin, when it appears in fiction, frankly and unmistakably delineates (if not discloses) the unseen, inner psychology and ulterior narratives of the Irish colonial subject.

*   *   *

This chapter's new materialist history of mud cabins has traced an environmental narrative as well as a colonial one. The effect of colonialism in Ireland was to cut the human off from nature conceptually and physically. Colonial writers sought to intercept the symbiotic relationship between Irish tenant, local soil, and animals like pigs, using powerful metaphors to denaturalize Irish survival and their ability to live creatively in nature. Colonial rule in eighteenth- and nineteenth-century Ireland repressed a way of thinking about the human and his

---

[149] Kreilkamp, *Anglo-Irish Novel*, p. 268.

connection with terrestrial life that may have aided humanity later on, as we now try to relearn our embedded position in an earthly environment that finds itself in crisis. The colonial tragedy in Ireland, therefore, is not just what happened to the native Irish people and their culture, but also the erasure of an entire human–nonhuman ecological system and all its possibilities. Postcolonial rectification must now be found in the pages of literature, where mud still narrates the powerful possibilities of an alternative ecological philosophy.

5

Pigs

Turning to the pig may seem like a strange diversion for a final chapter, given that this book has dealt in materiality, not mammals. Indeed, although they were objectified into consumer items sold at market, pigs are a different kind of object compared to the coins, flax, spinning wheels, and mud that have comprised this study so far. For one thing, pigs are outwardly animated, sentient, and possess a kind of rationale or free will distinct from the vital materiality or 'thing power' of plants, minerals, and other matter described by Jane Bennett.[1] Animal studies, while linked to new materialism, is considered a separate theoretical lens for these very reasons. Although new materialists typically include the animal in their definition of the nonhuman, animal studies and material studies have often been separated as independent posthumanist endeavors in recent scholarship. However, Lynn Festa's recent work on fiction without humanity in the eighteenth century combines the study of animals and objects, arguing that these two theoretical discourses naturally speak to one another, especially in the context of analyzing eighteenth-century humanism.[2]

New materialism, animal studies, and critical posthumanism all work toward the common goal of decentering the human. Each framework scrutinizes the ways in which modern, post-Enlightenment societies divide the exceptional human person from ostensibly passive matter or ostensibly wild, unintelligent animals, and thus they are naturally, polemically linked, as are the objects and animals they study, respectively. For example, Cary Wolfe has argued that speciesism analogizes other human forms of discrimination like sexism, racism, and colonialism.[3] The idea of human exceptionalism—that logical reasoning and the thinking mind distinguish human beings from the rest of the natural world—encodes the logic of speciesism in the same way it objectifies matter as passive. Most powerfully of all, the connections Kathryn Yusoff has drawn between gold mining and the slave trade evince that hierarchizing of materiality naturally lent itself to the hierarchizing of species and races. In short, the human/animal binary

---

[1] Jane Bennett, *Vibrant Matter* (Durham, NC: Duke UP, 2010), p. 18.
[2] Lynn Festa, *Fiction without Humanity: Person, Animal, Thing, in Early Enlightenment Culture* (Philadelphia: University of Pennsylvania, 2021), p. 9.
[3] See Cary Wolfe, *Animal Rites: American Culture, the Discourse of Species, and Posthuman Theory* (Chicago: University of Chicago Press, 2003).

Irish Materialisms: The Nonhuman and the Making of Colonial Ireland, 1690–1830. Colleen Taylor, Oxford University Press.
© Colleen Taylor 2024. DOI: 10.1093/oso/9780198894834.003.0006

helped justify the human/object binary in colonial discourse and vice versa, buttressing the empire's hierarchical hold over its colonies.[4]

In the eighteenth century, the material-semiotic ideology of colonialism was deeply entangled with the ideology of humanist speciesism, especially in Ireland. English discourse regularly invoked pigs as both a beast to racialize the Irish peasantry and a thing of disgust with which to objectify them. In material reality, however, pigs were a crucial and respected part of the eighteenth-century Irish tenantry ecosystem, contributing to rural Ireland's collaborative, creative survival, as in the previous chapter's discussion of the mud cabin ecosystem. Before the pig became an emblem of Irish backwardness in English imagery and rhetoric, it was a real, material mammal actively involved in Irish culture and society.

Pigs have been neglected as primary characters in the history of the Irish nation and indeed the human world at large—a fact which this chapter tries, in a small way, to rectify. Irish character is entangled with the pig: without its historical counterpart, the unique national subjectivity of Ireland would not have emerged or endured. The story of Irish colonial culture and character cannot be fully assessed without the material, evolutionary science of the pig, from the wild Greyhound breed foraging in Irish forests in medieval times to the eighteenth-century mud cabin's domesticized lodger. In the second half of this chapter, I trace how Irish peasants' daily, material interaction with this smart, sentient species provided anti-colonial rhetoric in Irish-language speech and poetry and in the satiric, published work of William Carleton. Irish characters working with pigs in literature subversively resist the speciesist ideology of the imperial system that made Irish peasants and their pigs increasingly co-dependent in the first place.

5.1 A Brief Material History of Pigs in Ireland

The history of the pig in Ireland is, much like that of the native Irish tenant, one of survival and adaptability. From the seventeenth century onward, the pig's physique and habits morphed according to the changed material circumstances of the Irish environment, from a wooded, Gaelic, and feudal system to a colonial and potato tilling society. In fact, the evolutionary story of the pig in Ireland indicates that pigs did not merely adapt to a new human social structure but also helped contribute to certain aspects of tenancy and cabin culture themselves, such as thriving on small plots of land and with very little resources or diversity of crop. In fact, pigs were explicitly associated with small farms in Ireland:

---

[4] A related study is Lucinda Cole's *Imperfect Creatures: Vermin, Literature, and the Sciences of Life, 1600–1740* (Ann Arbor: University of Michigan Press, 2016). Cole traces how undervalued and degraded species like rats, fleas, and frogs helped to both crystallize and challenge early modern England's distinctions between subject and object, human and animal.

paradoxically, farms under 15 acres were likely to have twice as many pigs as those with more land.[5]

The seventeenth-century Irish ancestor of the pig we know today would be unrecognizable next to its modern descendant. The Irish Greyhound pig of Gaelic Ireland was an indigenous, now extinct breed (Figure 5.1). But its genes still endure in the Tamworth pig, with which the Greyhound was bred in the early nineteenth century and which still survives today.[6] Unlike the modern animal, the Greyhound was wiry, narrow, scrappy, with bristles, long head, long legs, and a raised hind that, as William Carleton explains in his *Traits and Stories of the Irish Peasantry,* looked more like a hunting dog than a fat, English pig. In the twelfth century, Giraldus Cambrensis described the Greyhound pig as an 'ill-shaped and cowardly breed, no less degenerate in boldness and ferocity than in their growth and shape.'[7] He is also the first colonial writer to characterize Ireland as a nation of pigs, noting the sheer and extraordinary number of the species on the island: 'In no part of the world are such vast herds of boars and wild pigs to be found.'[8] Although Cambrensis describes the Irish Greyhound pig as 'degenerate,' his account nevertheless documents that the Greyhound pig was a partly domesticated species in twelfth-century Ireland, ostensibly lacking the 'ferocity' he deems characteristic of boars in this period. His account belies the adaptability and resilience of the Irish Greyhound pig, which was both wild and domesticated, herded and hunted in Ireland. It could survive on scraps in both towns and forests, so that even the poorest Irish farmers could afford to keep one well into the twentieth century.[9]

Following the Williamite War and the English and Anglo-Irish aristocracy's increased control in Ireland in the eighteenth century, elite landlords began to experiment with pig breeding to create a so-called 'improved' breed that would rapidly fatten in order to keep up with the demands of the growing international marketplace.[10] Landlords imported these fatter breeds of pigs, such as the Oriental or Neapolitan breeds, into Ireland, and began crossbreeding them with the Greyhound pig in order to enhance their size and caloric intake—which they did successfully within two short generations.[11] By the 1850s, English breeds of pigs surpassed the Greyhound in becoming more populous in Ireland.[12] Still, the Irish

---

[5] Jonathan Bell and Mervyn Watson, *A History of Irish Farming, 1750–1850* (Dublin: Four Courts Press, 2008), p. 263.

[6] Oisin Fitzgerald, 'The Irish "Greyhound" Pig: An Extinct Indigenous Breed of Pig.' *History Ireland: Ireland's History Magazine,* Dublin: History Publications, 2015. https://www.historyireland. com/18th-19th-century-history/the-irish-greyhound-pig-an- extinct-indigenous-breed-of-pig/

[7] Giraldus Cambrensis. *The Topography of Ireland,* tr. Thomas Forester, ed. Thomas Wright (Cambridge, Ontario: In Parantheses, 2000), p. 25.

[8] Giraldus Cambrensis. *Topography of Ireland,* pp. 24–5.

[9] Niall Mac Coitar, *Ireland's Animals: Myths, Legends, and Folklore* (Cork: Collins, 2015).

[10] Fitzgerald, 'Irish Greyhound Pig.'   [11] Fitzgerald, 'Irish Greyhound Pig.'

[12] Bell and Watson, *History of Irish Farming,* p. 265.

48   THE PIG.

over half a ton! An Irish gentleman, Mr. Sherrard, has also brought
the Berkshire swine to great perfection; they are of a white colour,
long-bodied, with very handsome heads, are well skinned, and rapid
growers. I understand that Mr. Sherrard has employed in their
breeding a cross with the Neapolitan, or what is much the same, the
improved Essex.

THE OLD IRISH "GREYHOUND PIG."

These are tall, long-legged, bony, heavy-eared, coarse-haired animals, their throats furnished with pendulous wattles, called in Irish
sluiddeen, and by no means possessing half so much of the appearance
of domesticated swine as they do of the wild boar, the great original of
the race. In Ireland, the old, gaunt race of hogs, has, for many
years past, been gradually wearing away, and is now, perhaps,
wholly confined to the western parts of that country, especially Gal-

THE OLD IRISH "GREYHOUND PIG."

way. These swine are remarkably active, and will clear a five-barred
gate as well as any hunter; on this account they should, if it be
desirable to keep them, be kept in well-fenced inclosures. The breed
of pigs in Ireland has improved greatly of late years, and thus the
old unprofitable stock is rapidly disappearing. The form of the Irish
pig is now so nearly approximated to that of the English, that the two
animals are not readily distinguished from each other. Now, indeed,
I regret to have to state, that there can be little danger of mistake, the

Figure 5.1 W. Oldham and Harrison Weir, *The Old Irish 'Greyhound Pig'*, illustration
on wood. In H. D. Richardson, *Domestic Pigs: Their Origin and Varieties* (London:
Orr & Co., 1852), p. 48. Reproduced courtesy of the National Library of Ireland.

Greyhound pig and its unique, wiry physique endured throughout the nineteenth
century, mostly in the west of Ireland, despite being less profitable for farming
estates.[13]

Pigs, both Greyhound and English 'improver' breeds, are mammals of extraordinary and underestimated capabilities. The pig was domesticated as early as 7000 BC
and for that reason plays a crucial leading role in the history of human civilization
at large.[14] Pigs are one of only fourteen kinds of mammals that have been able to
reorient their natural instincts in order to cohabit and live in peaceful, close proximity with humans. Some researchers believe the pig, rather than the dog, was
man's first domesticated animal.[15] In fact, some zoologists consider pigs to be
even more adaptable to their surroundings than dogs and wolves. As omnivores,
they contain a multitude of possible relationships with humans that are more
complex and varied than most animals.[16] They possess the ability to learn quickly
through observation and problem solve, as well as being friendly, affectionate,
and even emotional animals, as scientific research has proven. A 2016 study, for
instance, demonstrated that pigs' environment impacted their moods, leading
them to what we would call the humanist emotional thought patterns of opti-
mism or pessimism, depending on their positive or negative circumstances,
respectively.[17] Their affection, friendliness, quick adaptability, ability to learn
through observation, and advanced sociability all primed pigs to become the perfect comrades for the native, tenant Irish in the eighteenth century, as both species entered a new and increasingly restricted way of life under the penal laws.

Life for the poor, tenant Irish under the penal laws would not have been sus-
tainable without pigs. The reverse is also partly true: with the destruction of Irish
forests at the hand of colonial exports in the seventeenth century, pigs lost their
natural, wild habitat and had to become increasingly domestic and cohabitable
with humans in order to forage their food. Assimilating to a forestless environment, pigs facilitated a cycle of sustainability and growth in the cabin ecosystem
in spite of extremely limited space. Robert Caras explains that pigs were a 'criti-
cally important, low-cost maintenance meat animal' that contributed to human
subsistence in the face of poverty because they grow fast, have large litters, and eat
constantly without being selective about their diet.[18]

Pigs provided astounding recycling services for the impoverished tenant Irish,
converting the leftovers of farmer's produce—the limited tillage of potatoes—into
income by way of meat sold at market. Pigs convert an astounding 35 percent of

---

[13] Fitzgerald, 'Irish Greyhound Pig.'   [14] See Mac Coitar, *Ireland's Animals.*
[15] Roger A. Caras, *A Perfect Harmony: The Intertwining Lives of Animals and Humans throughout History* (West Lafayette, IN: Purdue University Press, 2002), p. 118.
[16] Umberto Albarella, Keith Dobney, Anton Ervynck, and Peter Rowley-Conwy, eds, *Pigs and
Humans: 10,000 Years of Interaction* (Oxford: Oxford UP, 2008), p. 1.
[17] Mary Friel, Kym Griffin, and Lisa M. Collins. 'Mood and Personality Interact to Determine
Cognitive Biases in Pigs.' *Biology Letters* 12.11 (2016).
[18] Caras, *Perfect Harmony,* p. 111.

the food they eat into meat, whereas, comparatively, sheep only convert 14 percent. Furthermore, as opposed to cows who need to graze year-round, pigs will eat almost anything, including the scraps of a potato-based human diet, and convert it into fat-holding calories. Irish pigs ate everything from potato peels, oats, and even seasonal compost like autumn leaf mast, while their excrement fertilized the soil for the next crop.[19] Crucially, the poor Irish never ate their pigs, selling them instead for annual rental income, which was a more economical option for poor tenants who ate a potato-based vegetarian diet. In fact, for many small-plot farmers in the eighteenth century, the pig was the only steady source of income, its sale at market earning enough rent money for the year—hence, the development of that respectfully wry nickname for Irish pigs: the 'gintleman that pays the rint.'[20] This new conservational economic ecosystem under the penal laws, orbiting around the pig and the potato crop, resulted in salt pork becoming a primary export for Ireland by the late eighteenth century.[21] Irish pork wound up on English dining tables far more frequently than it did on Irish plates. Because of their instinctual adaptability, pigs offered the tenant Irish a way to adapt themselves—both metaphorically and materially—to a new system of colonial rule that had resulted in extreme poverty.

This affinity between Irish human and Irish pig is a material fact not only of history but also of modern science. Today, the pig's anatomy has been proven to contribute to human survival in a medical sense: pig organs are considered immuno-compatible with the human body, which is why pig valves are regularly and effectively used in human heart surgery. Newer research seeks to include pig kidneys, livers, and lungs in human organ replacement.[22] What this bodily transference narrates, materially and symbolically, is the commonality humans share with pigs, rather than their differences, which have been prioritized for centuries, especially in Enlightenment-era Britain when the divide between human and nonhuman was increasingly ratified in service of political power structures. The pig's corporeal physique and habits came to unfairly signify colonial filth and gluttony when, zoologically speaking, the opposite is true. The instinct pigs demonstrate to wallow in mud, or mud bathe—a fact used to racialize the Irish through dirt and proximity to their pigs, as discussed in Chapter 4—marks a sign of good health, even regeneration, in the animal. Pigs are an exceptionally and consciously clean animal by comparison to other mammals.[23]

---

[19] Bell and Watson, *History of Irish Farming*, p. 263.

[20] Margaret Lynch-Brennan, *The Irish Bridget: Irish Immigrant Women in Domestic Service in America, 1840–1930* (Syracuse, NY: Syracuse University Press, 2014), p. 8.

[21] Lynch-Brennan, *Irish Bridget*, p. 8.

[22] Burcin Ekser, James Markmann, and A. Joseph Tector. 'Current Status of Pig Liver Xenotransplantation.' *International Journal of Surgery* 23 (2015): pp. 240–6.

[23] See Roger A. Caras, *A Perfect Harmony: The Intertwining Lives of Animals and Humans throughout History* (West Lafayette, IN: Purdue University Press, 2002).

Despite their own unfair share of misapplied colonial stereotypes, the material fact is that pigs were cultural insurance for the native Irish. The pig offered his Irish keeper a multitude of benefits and services: friendly companionship, heat source, fertilizer, recycling, and of course, essential monetary funds. After the Williamite War, pigs played an absolutely vital role in the survival of Irish laborers and tenants, and thus their language and culture, enabling them to thrive under brutal, otherwise unlivable circumstances. In the context of the pig's impressive symbiotic abilities, married with service to the Irish tenant, that old reproachful English image of the Irish who cohabit with their pigs inside the mud cabin— Dickens's 'pig in the parlour' and Arthur Young's '[pig] snout in a crock of potatoes'—emerges in a new light that connotes natural, mutual affection, much like we have with our pets today.[24] How could the Irish tenant not be endeared to the creature that gifted him survival and comfort when his own landlord did not? As I discuss below, the Irish tenants' affection for their pigs is on display—albeit often filtered through a humanist and modern lens—in writing from the period, including Irish-language poetry and Carleton's *Traits and Stories of the Irish Peasantry.*

5.2 Swinish Rhetoric in English Culture

Although the discursive trope of characterizing Ireland as a nation of pigs can be traced as far back as medieval times in Cambrensis's writings, it developed into more of an ubiquitous cliché in the eighteenth and nineteenth centuries. By then, the Irish body was regularly illustrated as an upright pig in human clothes, as often seen in London's *Punch* Magazine, for example (see Figure 5.2).

This corporeal similitude between Irishman and pig holds taboo prejudicial origins. Giraldus Cambrensis circulated the myth that some ancient Irish tribes were addicted to 'the sin of carnal intercourse with beasts' as a means of deciviliz-ing them.[25] A few centuries later, John Derricke published similar depictions of the Irish people. His *Image of Irelande* (1581) includes a famous image known as the 'MacSweynes Seated at Dinner' (Figure 5.3), an Ulster clan that were infa-mously dubbed the Macke Swine—a pun which Derricke makes use of both rhe-torically and visually. He argues that the Nation of Ulster 'maie bee perceived by their hoggishe fashion.'[26] In the correlating image, the MacSweeneys are depicted

---

[24] Charles Dickens, 'To the Editor of the Morning Chronicle, 25 July 1842' in *The Selected Letters of Charles Dickens*, ed. Jenny Hartley (Oxford: Oxford UP, 2012), p. 107. Arthur Young, *Arthur Young's Tour in Ireland (1776–1779)*, ed. Arthur Wollaston Hutton (London: George Bell & Sons, 1892), vol. 2, p. 49.
[25] Giraldus Cambrensis, *The Topography of Ireland*, tr. Thomas Forester, ed. Thomas Wright (Cambridge, Ontario: In Parantheses, 2000), p. 39.
[26] Qtd in Larissa Tracy, *Heads will Roll: Decapitation in the Medieval and Early Modern Imagination* (Leiden: Brill, 2012), p. 271.

THE PIG AND THE PEER.

PIG. "BEDAD, MELORD, AND IS IT MESELF THAT'S TO BE EVICTED?"
PEER (*tenderly*). "YOU EVICTED! NO, NO. WE'LL TAKE THE GREATEST CARE OF THE 'GENTLEMAN
WHO PAYS THE RENT.'"

Figure 5.2 John Tenniel, *The Pig and the Peer*, *Punch* [London], 7 August 1880.
Punch Cartoon Library/TopFoto.

as barbarously wrestling a hog to the ground, roasting another, while some are
naked in front of the fire—all key signifiers of uncivil, so-called animal behavior.

Eighteenth-century English writers frequently used metaphors to insinuate
swine-like qualities in Irish bodies and behavior, thereby affirming Ireland's need
to be 'kept' and domesticated by British influence and a landlord class system.

Figure 5.3 John Derricke, 'The Mac Sweynes seated at dinner and being entertained by a blind harper,' *Image of Irelande*. Facsimile of 1581 woodcut (printed Edinburgh: A. & C. Black, 1883). Reproduced from the original held by the Department of Special Collections of the Hesburgh Libraries of the University of Notre Dame.

At one point in the *Tour of Ireland,* Arthur Young writes that 'pigs and children bask about, and often resemble one another so much, that it is necessary to look twice before the human face divine is confessed. I believe there are more pigs in Mitchelstown than human beings and yet propagation is the only trade that flourished here for ages.'[27] Young unmistakably associates Irish people with livestock, characterizing them both as herds that do nothing but breed. A poem in 1688 made the comparison between Irish Catholic and pig even more literal, by animalizing a Catholic lawyer from the west of Ireland as a pig. 'An Elegy of the Pig that Followed the Ld Chief Baron Henn and Baron Worth from Connaught to Dublin' mocks this the pig who leaves his sty in Connemara:

> Here a well-travel'd Pig does Lye
> Who did forsake his Native Stye,
> To Waddle in good Company
> With Loss of Sows soft dalliance.[28]

[27] Young, *Arthur Young's Tour*, vol. 1, p. 461.
[28] 'An Elegy of the Pig that Followed the Ld Chief Baron Henn and Braon Worth from Connaught to Dublin' (1688) in *Verse in English from Tudor and Stuart Ireland,* ed. Andrew Carpenter (Cork: Cork University Press, 2003), p. 509.

Crucially, the poem distinguishes the Pale (Dublin) from the rest of native, Gaelic-speaking Ireland, which it paints as the habitat of so different a culture as to be almost a different species. The verse creates an unmistakable hierarchy of Anglo-Irish Ascendancy over the rural west, reasoned, albeit comically, through this animalized personification.

The most (in)famous piece of Irish pig commentary, however, is Jonathan Swift's *A Modest Proposal for preventing the children of poor people from becoming a burthen to their parents or country* (1729). Unlike the images and writings discussed so far, Swift uses the similitude between pig and human to deconstruct (rather than affirm) the pig's function as metaphorical justification for colonial policy. The style is set in the voice of a would-be livestock farmer addressing the overpopulation issue by offering the solution of eating the babies of poor Catholic families like one would eat pig meat. Swift's satirically exaggerated analogy becomes extreme as the conceit progresses: 'butchers we may be assured will not be wanting, although I rather recommend buying the children alive, and dressing them hot from the knife, as we do with roasting pigs.'[29] Swift exploits the imperial rhetoric that compares the Irish native peoples to their pigs as a means of critiquing the cruelty of colonial discourse around improving or controlling certain populations, such as when he refers to the 'collateral advantage' of 'lessening the number of papists among us' and improving all arenas of society.[30] The comparison continues in its absurdity: 'We should soon see an honest emulation among the married women, which of them could bring the fattest child to the market. Men would become as fond of their wives during the time of their pregnancy, as they are now of their mares in the foal, or their sows when they are ready to farrow.'[31] By literalizing the animalized stereotypes of the Irish, as they appeared in English discourse, Swift also exposes other anti-Irish sentiments circulating since the early modern period, such as the belief in Irish female licentiousness or male greed.

James Ward has argued that Swift's 'fictions of madness,' like *A Modest Proposal*, rely on 'shock tactics' and 'visceral imagery' to the point of even risking the destabilization of the satire's message.[32] Ultimately, however, Swift's talent for shock value exposes the texts he imitates: his fictive, ironically titled 'modest' proposal, for example, discredits utopian economic proposals as fictions themselves.[33] Clíona Ó Gallchoir reminds us that *A Modest Proposal* is not a parody, but rather a satiric exaggeration of existing, prejudicial anti-Catholic ideas about fertility

---

[29] Jonathan Swift, *A Modest Proposal and Other Satirical Works* (New York: Dover, 2012), p. 55.
[30] Swift, *Modest Proposal*, p. 54.   [31] Swift, *Modest Proposal*, p. 57.
[32] James Ward, 'Personations: The Political Body in Jonathan Swift's Fiction.' *Irish University Review* 41.1 (2011): p. 48.
[33] Ward, 'Personations,' p. 49.

and the need to control growing colonial populations.[34] In line with this, Swift invokes the corporeal cruelty involved in live roasting pigs in an attempt to expose or exaggerate the cruelty of dehumanizing rhetoric in political writings on Ireland:

> the propagation of swine's flesh, and improvement in the art of making good bacon, so much wanted among us by the great destruction of pigs, too frequent at our table, which are no way comparable in taste or magnificence to a well grown, fat yearling child, which roasted whole will make a considerable figure at a Lord Mayor's feast.[35]

Whereas Cambrensis used the taboo of bestiality to other the Irish, Swift deploys the taboo of gentile cannibalism to critique, through absurdity, a disregard for human life on the grounds of population control. He literalizes the metaphoric descriptions of the swinish Irishman in order to clearly differentiate between human life and livestock. By collapsing the human/animal, pauper/livestock binary, Swift makes a national plea that ultimately defends all human life over animal life.

In *Gulliver's Travels*, Swift again employs cultural degradation of the pig as a critique of colonial prejudice at large. Although readers typically think of the human Yahoos in book 4 as ape-like creatures, Swift employs the sensory-semiotics associated with pigs in order to expose the multi-species animalized mechanics of colonial rhetoric. Swift regularly describes the Yahoos as 'filthy' and loving dirt and slime, categorizing them as the most degraded of all animals: there was a 'violent hatred the Houyhnhnms, as well as all other animals, bore them.'[36] More significantly, he often remarks that the Yahoos have an 'offensive smell' and as a result keeps his nose 'stopt with rue, lavender, and tobacco leaves.'[37] Indeed, as seen in Young's *Tour of Ireland* and other writings like it, the offensive smell was often attributed to the mud cabin cottiers, insinuating a correlation between pigs, filth, smell, and colonial 'nature.' At one point, Gulliver, ruminating on the Yahoo's filth, is reminded of pigs back home, their 'filthy way of feeding, and their custom of wallowing and sleeping in the mud.'[38] Unlike *A Modest Proposal*, which arguably affirms a humanist binary of human/animal, human Gulliver's strong aversion to his fellow human Yahoo's offensive, animal smell—so

---

[34] Clíona Ó Gallchoir, '"Whole Swarms of Bastards": *A Modest Proposal*, the Discourse of Economic Improvement and Protestant Masculinity in Ireland, 1720–1738' in *Ireland and Masculinities in History*, ed. Rebecca Anne Barr, Sean Brady, and Jane McGaughey (London: Palgrave Macmillan, 2019), p. 42.

[35] Swift, *Modest Proposal*, p. 57.

[36] Jonathan Swift, *Gulliver's Travels* (Oxford: Oxford UP, 2005), p. 253.

[37] Swift, *Gulliver's Travels*, p. 276.   [38] Swift, *Gulliver's Travels*, p. 245.

much so that he 'stops' his nose—ridicules the material, semiotic, and sensory logic of colonial ideology's speciesist origins.

Almost as famous as the human/animal inversion of Swift's Yahoos was the appellation from another Anglo-Irish author: Edmund Burke's 'swinish multitude' in his *Reflections on the Revolution in France* (1790). Burke's descriptor, which remains a famous line from the text even today, was very quickly selected as a keynote moment in the *Reflections*, sparking a vibrant literary discourse around classism. Writers disagreeing with Burke saw the phrase as so demeaning that it necessitated a response, inspiring a briefly lived subgenre of satirical but critical retorts, echoing the techniques of Swift's *Modest Proposal* and addressed to Burke from the so-called 'Swinish Multitude' themselves. For example, *Address to the Honourable Edmund Burke from the Swinish Multitude* (1793), attributed to James Parkinson, deploys thick irony to underscore the injustice of Burke's degrading comparison: 'So little, Sir, are you disposed to exceed the plain matter of fact and truth, that for a while we doubted, since you had asserted it, whether we might not have undergone an actual metamorphosis.'[39] The pamphlet reverses Burke's insult, turning the swinish characterization back onto the ruling classes, which it describes as 'the lowest and vilest of mankind that can possibly be': 'whilst you and your friends who are so fond of distinctions, shall be termed Hogs of Quality...We sir, are the poor swine who are exposed to every inclemency of the weather, and ye are the favoured herd who enjoy the shelter and protection of the Stye.'[40] The pamphlet draws its satiric impact from the premise that human and animal are distinctly separate, that there is nothing animal about democracy— that, on the contrary, democracy is the realm of reason and aristocracy the model of the animal world, tucked away in the sty.

With retaliative publications like Parkinson's, Burke's 'swinish multitude' progressed to a discursive life of its own. Even Maria Edgeworth, who was no supporter of the Rebellion of 1798, the French Revolution, or the ideas displayed in *Address to the Hon. Edmund Burke, from the Swinish Multitude*, used her notes for Leadbeater's *Cottage Dialogues* to comically invoke the well-known Burkean sobriquet, recalling that, 'Last winter a pig of the editor's acquaintance devoured or destroyed the entire wardrobe of a poor woman, who had left her clothes in a tub at the mercy of the swinish multitude.'[41] The currency of Burke's phrase indicates its satiric afterlife and the inherent comic element of comparing humans and pigs. Invoking Burke's phrase and his politics, Edgeworth's account seems to challenge the domestic harmony of the 'gentleman that pays the rent,' questioning

[39] James Parkinson, *Address to the Hon. Edmund Burke, from the Swinish Multitude* (London: Ridgway, 1793), p. 6.
[40] Parkinson, *Address*, pp. 10, 15.
[41] Mary Leadbeater, *Cottage Dialogues among the Irish Peasantry.* Introduction by Maria Edgeworth (London: Johnson, 1811), p. 310.

Figure 5.4 James Gillray. *United Irishmen upon Duty,* 1798, etching, hand-colored on paper. © National Portrait Gallery, London

the Irish culture's comingling of human and pig by suggesting a lack of coopera-tion between the Irish and their animals in the home.

Despite the efforts of Parkinson and other republican thinkers to rationalize—and thereby de-animalize—revolution, it would seem the 'swinish multitude' in Burke's original sense outlived its satiric deconstructions. James Gillray's political cartoon depicting the Irish Rebellion of 1798, *United Irishmen on Duty,* published not long after Burke's *Reflections,* would seem to confirm the ethnic implications of Burke's adjective as well as Young's descriptions of the hoggish, uncivil Irish from the previous chapter. In that print, a United Irish soldier carries a pig on his back, followed by several piglets, while all human figures embody a grotesque piggishness: round, pink limbs, states of undress, and in some cases, pig-like facial features (see Figure 5.4). Of course, the print undermines the republican reasoning of the United Irishmen by re-entrenching their efforts as chaotic, ani-mal behavior, and by making the 'swinish multitude' particularly Irish.

At the same time that the debate around the revolutions in France and Ireland circled around the distinction between the human 'reason' at the heart of republi-canism and the so-called 'swinish' behavior of revolution, eighteenth-century popular culture became fascinated with the fad of 'learned pigs.' The first learned pig was an Irish invention, born and purchased in Belfast, becoming popular in the 1780s after being trained by Scotsman Samuel Bisset, who premiered his 'wonderful pig' in Dublin. Bisset was allegedly attacked in Ireland by a zealous policeman who disbelieved the pig's intelligence.[42] Although Bisset died shortly after his pig's premiere, the same pig was adopted by a Mr Nicholson and toured around Britain, generating a growing fascination for performing pigs in eighteenth-century English society. Interestingly, Monica Mattfield argues that, although the pig was Irish, it was quickly adopted as an English novelty after its appearance in London. Commentators were quick to characterize Bisset's learned Belfast pig as signifier of English mirth, English culture, and English exceptionalism.[43] The Belfast pig launched a trend that saw many similarly learned pigs tour around Britain at the turn of the nineteenth century.

Around the time of Bisset's debut, several stories about learned pigs, told from the pig's perspective, were published. The learned pig genre represents an eighteenth-century English literary trend: the personification of animals in novels, fables, and poems, which, Heather Keenleyside argues, brought animals and personhood together in likeness more often than it bifurcated man and animal.[44] For example, the learned pig's satires use the personified voice of the animal to interrogate human nature and human gullibility. In 1817, a one-shilling pamphlet titled *The Life and Adventures of Toby, the Sapient Pig, with his Opinions on Men and Manners*, 'written by himself' appeared in London, distributed by Nicholas Hoare, 'proprietor and teacher of Toby', and likely written by him as well. According to Mark Blackwell, the quasi-it-narrative is an extension of the tongue-in-cheek, deliberately exaggerated advertisements publicizing Toby's performances in London and other English cities.[45] The title to Toby's 'autobiography' also parodies eighteenth-century novels and narratives, perhaps most notably Laurence Sterne's *Tristram Shandy* (1759). Significantly in this narrative, Toby refers to himself as a different 'race', rather than a different species, which may indicate the story was partially and playfully mimicking abolitionist narratives like that of Olaudah Equiano, further indicated by the 'written by himself' epithet that also appears on Equiano's publication. The tale is so thick with sardonic tone it is difficult to distinguish exactly what is being parodied, but clearly human hubris is at the chopping block:

> By the time I was four months old I could read tolerably well: at present I know many boys and girls, at four years old, that can not do anything like it. What a shame that will appear to them, and how angry will they be with themselves,

---

[42] See Monica Mattfield, 'Genus Porcus Sophisticus: The Learned Pig and the Theatrics of National Identity in Late Eighteenth-Century London' in *Performing Animality: Animals in Performance Practices* (Basingstoke: Palgrave Macmillan, 2015), p. 58.

[43] Mattfield, 'Genus Porcus', p. 67.

[44] Heather Keenleyside, *Animals and Other People: Literary Forms and Living Beings in the Long Eighteenth Century* (Philadelphia: University of Pennsylvania Press, 2016), pp. 2–7.

[45] Mark Blackwell, ed., *British It-Narratives, 1750–1830*, vol. 2. *Animals* (London: Pickering & Chatto, 2012), p. 280.

Figure 5.5 'An Elegant Frontispiece, Descriptive of a Literary Pig-sty, with the Author Deep in Study' in Nicholas Hoare, *The Life and Adventures of Toby, the Sapient Pig, with his Opinions on Men and Manners, Written by Himself* (London: Lyon, 1817). © The British Library Board.

when they are able to read this my life, that one of my race should so far surpass them at so tender an age.[46]

The publication is satirically dedicated to the nobility and gentry: 'I have been patronized by the first rank this *vast* empire has to boast of.'[47] The tone seems to chime with the satiric critiques published by the 'swinish multitudes,' and makes humor out of social hierarchy. Finally, the published narrative boasts of its 'elegant frontispiece, descriptive of a literary pig sty, with the author deep in study' (Figure 5.5). This humorous image, which blends the scene of the dirty pigsty with a classical library containing Plutarch, Shakespeare, and Hume, arguably reinforces the pigsty as the bastion of bestiality by highlighting the sheer fantasy of a pig of letters.

An it-narrative titled *The Story of the Learned Pig*, published in 1786 in London, took on the similar task of mocking human nature and reason through the playful voice of the sapient pig. In this text, the human master congratulates himself for training the pig when, in fact, the pig narrator claims superior intelligence to his master—by being a better speller, for instance. As in other it-narratives, this pig

---

[46] Nicholas Hoare, *The Life and Adventures of Toby, the Spaient Pig: with his Opinions on Men and Manners, Written by Himself* (London: Hoare, 1817), p. 13.
[47] Qtd. in Blackwell, *British It-Narratives*, vol. 2, p. 282.

has been reincarnated many times, once living as Brutus in Ancient Rome. This it-narrative clearly criticizes social hierarchy, For example, the pig, after performing for his master's elite social gathering, is enraged to be denied the feast, 'what was not refused even to a hog, the dirtiest brute in whole creation!'—a statement filled with irony because the subject that speaks it literally lives in a hog's body at this point in the narrative. Later, the narrator reflects that as a famous learned pig, he is the 'object of more admiration than I ever was in the monarch, the orator, or the general!' in his human past lives.[48] When he falls in love with a woman at the tale's end, she strokes his nose and calls him a 'filthy creature,' which mortifies the narrator, that he should be denied by a woman from a humble social class when he had been a king.[49] Much like the retaliation penned against Edmund Burke by the 'swinish multitude,' this story takes aim at social elitism by putting a hierarchist thinker inside the body of what was seen as the most lowly earthly being, the pig. The narrative mocks human hubris and pride on the basis of a cultural belief system in which a pig is always an object of mockery. Ironically, at the same time the pig was invoked to affirm colonial hierarchies of English over Irish, it also became a vehicle for challenging social hierarchies themselves, including the objectification of the lower classes.

By the turn of the nineteenth century, some parts of English society held an almost mythic fascination with piggish curiosities, which converged in the myth of the 'Pig-Faced Lady.' A recurring myth in English society since the seventeenth century, the pig-faced lady reflected fears about witchcraft, and perhaps, in those instances of an Irish connection, fear about the infiltration of colonial nature. In 1815, John Fairburn printed a broadside about *The Pig-Faced Lady of Manchester Square, Drawn from the Information of a Female Who Attended on Her,* capitalizing on a rumor that had been spread in other newspapers and pamphlets. Significantly, this broadside mentions that the Pig-Faced Lady of Manchester Square is of 'Irish noble birth,' pointing to some distinctly Irish element to this myth's currency in English society, further correlating the Irish—noble or tenant—with swinish qualities.[50] The broadside also details that his lady eats out of a 'silver trough' and its accompanying image depicts her in a fine, white Regency gown (Figure 5.6)—details that highlight the absurd union of social rank and pig body (and perhaps, secondarily, refinement and Irishness). Maria Edgeworth had used the phrase 'silver trough' in *Ennui* a few years earlier, when Glenthorn demeans Ellinor by saying Ellinor had as much use for a good English cottage as the pig for the 'silver trough.'[51] While the myth of the pig-faced woman

[48] *The Story of the Learned Pig, by an Officer of the Royal Navy* (London: R. Jameson, 1786).
[49] *The Story of the Learned Pig,* p. 114.
[50] John Fairburn, *Fairburn (Senior's) Portrait of the Pig-Faced Lady of Manchester-Square* (London: Fairburn, 1815). Broadside held at the British Library. https://www.bl.uk/collection-items/broadside-on-the-pig-faced-lady.
[51] Maria Edgeworth, *Ennui,* in *Tales of A Fashionable Life,* vol. 1 (London: Hunter, 1815), pp. 129–30.

Figure 5.6 John Fairburn, *The Pig-Faced Lady of Manchester Square*, 1815, broadside, ephemera. © The British Library Board.

in Manchester Square is likely to have been, in reality, a woman with a facial disfiguration, its fascination for English readers nevertheless points to a recurring cultural association that readily blends Irish character with swinish body toward both comic and colonial ends.

In her typical subversive narrative style, Sydney Owenson used the cultural phenomenon around learned pigs in England to make a critique about the treatment of Irish people in English society as similarly exotic curiosities. Describing her experiences in London as the young, celebrated author of *The Wild Irish Girl*, Owenson equates her experience and social position as that of 'the Learned Pig at Exeter,' 'ignorant whether her *keepers* mean to exhibit her for her intelligence or ferocity, like the learned pig at Exeter Change... But whatever part she is destined to play in her cage, it is certain that she will often look forth with delight to those days of her freedom, when untaught and untamed.'[52] In this moment, reminiscent of Gulliver in the courts of Houyhnhnmland, Owenson draws on the long-standing rhetoric that compared Irish people to pigs, while in fact exposing the

---

[52] Sydney Owenson, *Lady Morgan's Memoirs: Autobiography, Diaries and Correspondence,* vol. 1, ed. William Hepworth Dixon (London: William H. Allen, 1862), p. 422.

rude behavior of her English captors. Like the learned pig Toby who mocks his less intelligent master, here Owenson uses the two separate cultural discourses of learned pig and piggish Irishman to make an allegory about her desire for Irish freedom, not just within her social circle, but within her political context. Under the guise of the learned pig, Owenson, it is implied, patiently waits for the moment of Irish independence.

5.3 A Different Kind of Pig in the Irish Language

In contrast to British and Anglo-Irish writing, which presumed the degraded status of the pig, eighteenth-century discourse in the Irish language invoked the pig on a very different register. Irish-speaking and poor farm populations of Ireland engaged a cultural rhetoric that insinuated unracialized, positive connotations in relation to pigs. In Irish rural culture and colloquialism, we can locate a posthumanist scene of democratic alliance between tenant and pig, unlike in the 'swinish multitude' debate. For example, the pig's importance to tenant livelihood was so ingrained that it became a common colloquialism: *Tá tú ar mhuin na muice,* meaning, literally, 'you are on the pig's back,' and figuratively, you are in good spirits.[53] In the eighteenth century, being on the pig's back was also synonymous with doing well financially. The phrase originated among tenants who grew flax, and began to refer to it as the crop that would have you 'on the pig's back'—that is, with enough funds and means to keep a pig.[54] The phrase remains a common idiom among Irish speakers and Irish-born speakers of English today, rhetorically immortalizing the eighteenth-century ecosystem and historical cooperation between land, pig, and human in Ireland and its association with good fortune. Seán Ó Tuama and Thomas Kinsella have recorded another pithy saying about the pig in Irish:

Is maith duine agá mbí muh	It is well for the man with a pig
do bhíodar muca gam féin:	I once had pigs myself.
is fearr an mhuc atá beo,	But your living pig is the best
níl acht ceo san mhuc inné.[55]	yesterday's pig is only vapour

The parable acknowledges that the pig manifests and affords financial security, as well as peace of mind—that, as a result, a living pig at home is better than the sold pig of yesterday. In this Irish worldview, money in comparison to a pig, is as intangible as air.

---

[53] Thanks to Eoin McEvoy for explaining this phrase to me.
[54] Fitzgerald, 'Irish Greyhound Pig.'
[55] Sean Ó Tuama and Thomas Kinsella, eds, *An Duanaire 1600–1900: Poems of the Dispossessed* (Dublin: Dolmen, 1981), p. 66.

Farming historians Jonathan Bell and Mervyn Watson document the fact that some cottiers referred to their pigs as the 'savings bank,' an explicitly clear rhetorical connection that can be linked with the popular, modern piggy bank.[56] The piggy bank dates back to medieval England, when people stored their money in ceramic containers called pygg, a type of orange clay used to make a pitcher or jar.[57] The round style and orange color of this pygg jar bears undeniable physical similarity with the round, fat pig body, and therefore the 'pygg' clay was misused or appropriated as the identical-sounding 'pig' by the nineteenth century.[58] The shift from pygg clay to a coin bank intentionally resembling a pig's body reflects the thinking around farming, markets, and materiality in the eighteenth century, when, in Britain and Ireland, pigs generated economy and self-sufficiency, and when the fatter and heavier the pig, the more coins to gain at market. Thus, the round porcine shape's affiliation with generating income and economy in rural settings in eighteenth-century England and Ireland helps to explicate how the Tudor pygg bank became the animal pig bank a few centuries later. The pygg/piggy bank manifests how matter affords our metaphoric idioms and our cultural practices, so that even a supposedly human idea like a money bank can be traced back to natural, animal origins and the agricultural wealth of pigkeeping. In Irish culture, as in other rural farming communities, pigs signified financial stability and therefore their material resonance at market migrated into the local rhetoric, cultural expression, and the material culture.

Long before eighteenth-century Irish cottiers were on the pig's back in their everyday speech, Irish-language literature encapsulated cultural reverence for the pig—going as far back in documentation as the seventh century. In fact, this old, traditional reverence explains why so many placenames in Ireland have the word *muc* or pig in them.[59] In Irish legend, the boar represented the warrior spirit, while the domesticated pig was associated with fertility and healthy land.[60] Pighunting, for example, appears in many tales of the Fianna, while the Celts and Gaels regularly ate pig in their ritualistic feasts. Over time, the domesticated pig accumulated a number of folkloric ideas, such as the belief that pigs could forecast weather, or that the practice of driving a pig into the house on a May morning meant good luck. The Brehon Laws make special accommodations for pigs, which differentiate between house pigs and trespassing pigs, and insurance for injuries done to humans by pigs, figuring pigs as members of Irish society. Brehon Law also states that runts of a pig's litter would be the pet of the farmer's wife,

---

[56]   Bell and Watson, *History of Irish Farming*, p. 263.
[57]   *Oxford English Dictionary*, s.v. 'pygg' in 'pig' (n.).
[58]   Javanese and Indonesian cultures also used wild boar-shaped ceramics much earlier. In the nineteenth century, more literal pig-shaped banks come into popularity. See Money Box. c.1550–1650, London, British Museum.
[59]   Mac Coitar, *Ireland's Animals*.   [60]   *An Duanaire*, p. 364; Mac Coitar, *Ireland's Animals*.

evidencing that the affectionate relationship between the Irish and their pigs dates back to the seventh century.[61]

Heroic folklore from medieval Ireland not only provides a literary record of ritualistic Gaelic pig feasts but also underscores that, from pre-Christian Ireland to medieval times, pigs were markers of respected status in Irish culture. Most famously, *Scéala Mucce Meic Dathó*, 'The Story of Mac Dathó's Pig' from the Ulster Cycle of Irish legends, involves a competition of masculine honor and ferocity around who will get to carve Mac Dathó's most prized pig. In the legend, Mac Datho invites the clans of Ulster and Connaught to his hall after they both ask for his coveted hound, Ailbe, and slays his best pig for a feast in their honor. The pig's gargantuan, almost mythic size encodes a decidedly masculine, opulent status. According to extant versions of the tale, the animal had been fed on sixty milk cows for seven years and it took sixty oxen to carry its body to the hall.[62] Connacht's warrior Cet mac Matach sits down with his knife to carve the pig, and, as various Ulster warriors challenge him for the right to the honored task, he defeats them verbally with historic accounts of his wins in battle against their clans. Conall of Ulster, however, enters the hall at the last minute with the head of Cet's brother—the only warrior, Cet claims, that can match Conall.

The crux and conflict of the legend then unfolds over the body of Mac Datho's pig.[63] Conall divides the pig, and eats its heavy tail himself—the prized champion's cut or *curadmír*—considered a weight of meat for nine men, as a display of triumph.[64] When he only gives the Connacht warriors a quarter of the pig, the fore-legs, they feel diminished in status by the size and selection of their portion of pig flesh, and a bloody battle breaks out, killing four hundred Connachtmen and Ulstermen. The tale concludes in an arguably sardonic tone by remembering that Ulster and Connacht fell out over a pig.[65]

According to Philip O'Leary, the feast in Mac Datho's hall exemplifies the hierarchical nature of those early Irish feasts, which incite what he calls 'competitive insecurity' and social status resulting from such dramatic displays.[66] Indeed, masculinity and rank become inscribed onto the body of Mac Datho's pig to a fault. In this ancient legend, the pig is elevated as a status symbol, hierarchized above the cows and oxen who must feed and carry it, while, at the same time, its integrity as a mammal is literally dissected in public. The pig's own slaughter proves prophetic of what, the tale can be seen to imply, is a somewhat pointless slaughter of good warriors over a cut of meat. What is most insightful in O'Leary's reading of *Scéala Mucce Meic Dathó* is his assessment that the pig becomes a site of 'struggle' over

---

[61] Mac Coitar, *Ireland's Animals*.
[62] 'The Story Mac Datho's Pig' in *Ancient Irish Tales*, ed. Tom Peete Cross and Clark Harris Slover (New York: Henry Holt, 1936), p. 202.
[63] 'Mac Datho's Pig,' p. 206.   [64] 'Mac Datho's Pig,' p. 206.   [65] 'Mac Datho's Pig,' p. 207.
[66] Philip O'Leary, 'Contention at Feasts in Early Irish Literature.' *Éigse* 20 (1984): p. 122.

which warriors or nations determine their place in the social hierarchy.[67] This idea of the pig as site of hierarchical struggle is applicable to the English mobilizations of the animal in the seventeenth and eighteenth centuries, which inscribed the Irish pig with lowly, slothful status in order to affirm Britain's colonial hegemony over Ireland.

In contrast to the ancient Gaelic legends, where pigs are powerful symbols of Irish ferocity and the triumph of battle, bardic poetry in the wake of the Flight of the Earls in 1607 often employed the pig to articulate national tragedy and loss. For example, Geoffrey Keating, known for his influential history of Ireland, *Foras Feasa Ar Éirinn* (1634), composed a poem titled 'Óm Sceol Ar Ardmhagh Fáil,' in which he laments 'deor níor fágadh i gclár do bhrollaigh mhínghil / nár dheolsad ál gach cránach coigríche.'[68] The lines translate as a metaphor that claims the breast of Irish land is 'drained dry by the litter of every alien sow.'[69] The alien sow, of course, refers to the new Protestant, English reign in Ireland, which secured British control over Irish land and Irish affairs following the Flight of the Earls. Interestingly, Keating uses the otherizing metaphor of the swinish nation against the English 'alien,' characterizing the English as degenerate sows that have drained Ireland dry, reappropriating the piggish imagery wielded by early modern English writers against Gaelic chieftains like the MacSweynes. Significantly, Keating also genders Britain as female sow—a clear contrast to the masculine, revered boar of Gaelic culture and feasts long past, thereby inverting the feminine identity British colonial paternalism had ascribed to Ireland. Keating's metaphor undermines British presence in Ireland through England's own colonial code of bestializing, swinish metaphors.

A century later, Aogán Ó Rathaille, who is considered the last of the Gaelic Bards, similarly used the pig as a tragic symbol in his poem, 'Cabhair Ní Ghairfead.' As one of the last poems he composed, perhaps around 1729, the poem signifies the fall of the Gaelic Order and the Bards. By this time, Ó Rathaille was without a patron, having no Gaelic or Jacobite leaders with the funds to support him, and had become an impoverished tenant on the Protestant Browne estate.[70] He associates the sounds of pigs with a kind of *caoineadh*, or the traditional Irish keen, or wail: 'fonn ní thigeann im ghaire 's mé ag caoi ar bhóithre, / ach foghar na Muice nach gontar le saigheadóireacht.'[71] He laments that 'no music is nigh as I wail about the roads / except for the noise of the Pig no arrows wound.'[72] On the one hand, the pigs join in the *caoineadh*, join in Ó Rathaille's lament for a way of life where he was once respected and patronized, inviting a comparison with the way in which pigs in the Gaelic era freely roamed Ireland's

[67] O'Leary, 'Contention,' p. 119.   [68] Ó Tuama and Kinsella, *An Duanaire*, p. 84.
[69] Ó Tuama and Kinsella, *An Duanaire*, p. 85.
[70] Ó Tuama and Kinsella, *An Duanaire*, p. 165.
[71] Ó Tuama and Kinsella, *An Duanaire*, p. 166.
[72] Ó Tuama and Kinsella, *An Duanaire*, p. 167.

forested land. At the same time, the fact that the only noise left holding any meaning for the poet is the sound of the pig, in place of the once-honored bardic music, also suggests the fall of Irish culture. Ó Rathaille's poem suggests commonality between Irish national emotion and the steadfast companionship of the Irish pig, who helps, literally, to articulate his loss. Instead of the beautiful *spéirbhean* of the *aisling* typical of Ó Rathaille's composition, discussed in Chapter 1, the pig has become the new 'body' that allegorizes Irish national grievance. In the absence of his Gaelic chieftains and reduced to a tenant farmer, Ó Raithaille recognizes a more apt metaphor in the parallel, material experience of the wandering Irish pig, whose noises echo his national pain. From a posthumanist and new materialist perspective, Ó Raithaille's poem recognizes kinship with the pig at the same time it documents Ireland's cultural degradation through that pig's voice.

The pig's poetic affordance also appears in the verse of a less formally educated, oral poet, which was thankfully recorded by a literate acquaintance. A teacher named Amhlaoibh Ó Súilleabháin recorded a diary entry in September of 1828 in which he comes across a 'miserable looking' mud cabin, and a woman 'in her bare feet...tall, thin, and in rags,' who begins to recite a keen, which he titles 'A Widow's Lament.'[73] The widow cries out against everything the rent collector named Devereux has taken from her and her family: 'D'fhág sé an bothán gan doras, an fhuinneog gan gloine, an tinteán gan tine, an deatachán gan deatach, cró san muc gan cráin gan céis gan banbh gan collach gan muc, mór ná mion, meith ná trua.'[74] It translates as: the cabin without a door, the window without glass, the hearth without fire, the chimney without smoke, and significantly, 'the pigsty without piglet or sow, young or old—without a pig or a boar, big or little, fat or lean.'[75] In this remarkable, rhythmic litany—a rare, recorded oration documenting the experience of an Irish-speaking tenant suffering under the penal laws—this woman invokes the absent pig as both a literal manifestation of her national dispossession and a powerful metaphor of loss. That she lingers over the absence of pig, enumerating she has neither pig, boar, sow, nor piglet, emphasizes the importance of the pig as both a central contributor to livelihood in colonial Ireland, as well as a meaning-maker for the cabin Irish who acknowledge their connectedness to this ecosystem of mud, potato, and pig. Significantly, this woman turns to the material absence of the sow and piglet to narrate the depths of her pained, hollow subjectivity. The pigless sty analogizes her grief-stricken family—their home and inner feeling empty without her late husband.

This remarkable piece of folk poetry confirms the material narrative of the native Irish I have been tracing throughout this book: how things like flax, mud, and pigs offered the Irish people survival as well as creative, metaphoric languages

[73] Ó Tuama and Kinsella, *An Duanaire*, p. 255.
[74] Ó Tuama and Kinsella, *An Duanaire*, p. 256.
[75] Ó Tuama and Kinsella, *An Duanaire*, p. 257.

of national resistance and national loss. For this keening widow, the pig is not a
bestialized representation of the inhumane English, as in Keating's writing, but
rather, the core of her most deeply felt, human emotions: of anger, loss, injustice,
and grief, which she expresses on the personal and national level, referencing her
own family and the wider system of a prejudiced, colonial tenancy system. In
contrast to the easily recognized pig metaphors in Britain's satiric cartoons and
colonial ideology, the pig's narrative presence in native Irish colloquialism, folklore, bardic poetry, and keens reflects a range of complicated material-semiotic
ideas, from colonial resistance to humor, to profound loss. In a text like this widow's keen (an otherwise lost verbal expression of colonial experience), there is
nothing mocking or degrading about the pig at all, confirming an alternative,
native Irish imagination around the mammal, rooted in its central role as
co-survivor in rural life under colonialism.

5.4 Anti-Colonial Satire in Carleton's 'Phil Purcel, the Pig Driver'

Perhaps one of the most famous characterizations of pigs in Irish literature in the
English language is that of William Carleton's 'Phil Purcel, the Pig Driver,' which
celebrates the subversive potentials of the hoggish Irish stereotype. In Carleton's
early nineteenth-century writing, the Swiftian absurdism undermining the speciesist foundation of colonial ideology merges with the Irish-language tradition
that recognizes the pig's contribution to Irish culture and survival. Carleton has
long been deemed important to the history and development of modern Irish literature, beginning with W. B. Yeats who edited and republished *Stories from
Carleton* in 1889. Likewise, contemporary critics have figured Carleton as a key
precursor to literary giants like Yeats himself and James Joyce. Seamus Deane, for
example, locates the 'beginning of the Joycean complex' in Carleton's writings,
while Declan Kiberd praises Carleton for his authentic depiction of 'peasant
types.'[76] For Terry Eagleton, Carleton is the 'finest nineteenth-century novelist of
all' in the Irish canon.[77] Writing in the wake of the heyday Irish national tale,
Carleton had a novelistic legacy on which to draw, but he remains uniquely placed
in Irish criticism for depicting a more 'authentic' peasant class, pointing to the
dawning of 'ethnographic modernism' in the Irish novel.[78] Roy Foster, for
example, awards Carleton the title of the 'finest-ever delineator of Irish rural

[76] Seamus Deane, *A Short History of Irish Literature* (South Bend, IN: University of Notre Dame
Press, 1994), p. 112; Declan Kiberd, *Irish Classics* (Cambridge, MA: Harvard University Press,
2001), p. 274.
[77] Terry Eagleton, *Heathcliff and the Great Hunger: Studies in Irish Culture* (London: Verso,
1995), p. 207.
[78] Marjorie Howes, *Colonial Crossings: Figures in Literary History* (Dublin: Field Day, 2006), p. 35.

life.'[79] If Carleton, through his own rural background, authentically delineates Irish rural life in literature, reading his work through the deeper material knowledge of the Irish pig will only enhance a study of his Irish literary authenticity.

The learned pig narratives, along with the piggish semiotics of the Anglo-Irish satiric tradition initiated by Swift contextualize the tone of Carleton's picaresque-like story, 'Phil Purcel, the Pig Driver,' published in the second series of *Traits and Stories of the Irish Peasantry* in 1833. Although Carleton's pig does not speak or write, she takes on a deliberately nationalist project that, as with the learned pig it-narrative and Toby the Sapient Pig, outsmarts her English onlookers. The preface to the second series of *Traits and Stories,* published in 1833 engages Carleton's comic approach and his aim to accurately depict the Irish peasant class: 'This preface...was to have given a touching dissertation on the Irish character...all within the compass of four pages!'[80] Carleton acknowledges the complexity of the Irish character via his own self-referential sarcasm. As I will demonstrate, what is distinct about 'Phil Purcel, the Pig Driver,' among Carleton's other stories, is that its comedy emerges from the unique Irish context of human–animal confluence between peasant and his pig—a collaboration that carries national significance both within and outside of the fictional text.

'Purcel' begins by literalizing the very stereotype it seeks to challenge: that of the uncivilized, unintelligent, piggish Irishman. Parodying other national literature of this time, the story mourns the loss of Gaelic Ireland by anthropomorphizing the Irish Greyhound pig like the Irish chieftains of the early modern period: 'There were a tall, loose species, with legs of an unusual length, with no flesh, short ears, as if they had been cropped for sedition, and with long faces of a highly intellectual cast.'[81] The description about seditious cropped ears alludes to the Gaels who wore glibbes (hair cropped at the front of the head), which had been forbidden under Poynings Law in the fifteenth century. Carleton's use of 'cast' and 'species' is tactically employed, referring to both a formerly high-class Gaelic culture and education, while also exposing the ways the Irish have been more recently characterized as a different species through their association with pigs.

Carleton continues this elongated comic analogy by parodying another theme in eighteenth-century writing about Ireland, from antiquarians to national tale writers like Owenson, who praise the lost, elevated culture of ancient Gaelic Ireland. Carleton anthropomorphizes the old Greyhound pig against the modern-day English improver breed:

---

[79] R. F. Foster, *Modern Ireland, 1660–1972* (London: Penguin, 1989), p. 370.

[80] William Carleton, *Traits and Stories of the Irish Peasantry* (London: Routledge & Sons, 1856), p. vii.

[81] Carleton, *Traits and Stories*, p. 180.

The pigs, however, of the present day are a fat, gross, and degenerate breed; and more like the well-fed alderman than Irish pigs of the old school. They are in fact a proud, lazy, carnal race, that we do not eat, but ship them out of the country... we should repine a little on thinking of the good old times of sixty years since, when every Irishman could kill his own pig, eat it when he pleased.[82]

The 'Irish pigs of the old school' are a comic allusion to the former Gaelic chieftains, compared to a harsh characterization of eighteenth-century landlords of the Anglo-Irish class as a 'fat, gross, and degenerate breed.' Like Geoffrey Keating before him, Carleton inverts the stereotype by animalizing the Ascendancy as the piggish 'breed' in Ireland, rather than the Catholic, peasant Irish. Carleton also highlights economic inequality when he points out that Irish pigs are shipped out of the country, rather than eaten at home, which both recognizes the colonial economic system in which the Irish could not afford to keep their pigs, as well as alludes to the pattern of absentee landlords and a parliament housed in London, rather than Dublin. Carleton weaves a complex patois of national and economic critique, parodied colonial metaphors, and the narrative voice of an absurdist colonial thinker, all through the material body of the pig, which he uses to undermine multiple colonial and national discourses about Ireland.

His more explicit satiric critique emerges when Carleton ironically frames pig-driving as a modern technique of early-nineteenth-century 'improvement culture,' as discussed in Chapters 2 and 4. He refers to his main character, Phil Purcel, for example, as the 'Professor of Pig Driving.' In Phil's era, the narrator explains, 'pig-driving was not so general, nor had it made such rapid advances as in modern times. It was then simply pig-driving, unaccompanied by the improvements of poverty, sickness, and famine.'[83] The unmistakable irony of Carleton's critique of British improvement ideology invites the English reader directly into the depth of Irish antipathy against colonial attempts to 'improve Ireland' while in fact impoverishing its people. Later, Carleton draws comparisons between the Arab and his horse and the Irishman and his pig to further expose the universal tactics of British colonialism, arguing that 'had our English neighbours known as much of Ireland as they did of Arabia, they would have found as signal instances of attachment subsisting between [the Irishman and his pig].'[84] By deflecting his ideas through the burlesque of this mock-treatise on Irish affairs, thinly veiled through the wider cultural mockery of pigs, Carleton can effectively critique of British rule in Ireland and British accounts of Irish character without censorship.

Despite its many layers of irony, 'Phil Purcel, the Pig Driver' offers a genuine critique of a colonial system that exploits the Irishman as much as it does the pig. The satire is complex in both defending the cohabitation and cooperation of the

---

[82] Carleton, *Traits and Stories*, p. 181.   [83] Carleton, *Traits and Stories*, p. 179.
[84] Carleton, *Traits and Stories*, p. 181.

Irishman and his pig, forced into co-survival under such unjust colonial strains, while also critiquing a colonial economy where the metropole will not bestow its colonial subjects with a proper meat diet. For example, Carleton writes, 'In Ireland swine are not kept in sties as they are among English feeders, but permitted to go at liberty through pasture fields, where they make up as well as they can for the scanty pittance allowed them at home during meal-times.'[85] While his tone is lighthearted, his message about poverty and national injustice is severe.

Later in the story, Phil's Irish pig becomes a central character in the plot. The narrator introduces Phil's pig by discussing her residence in Irish cabins, noting that the *bothán*'s placement against the slopes of the hill meant that it was easy for pigs to enter the cabin through the chimney. Such an entrance 'was usually received by the cottager and his family with a degree of mirth and good humour that were not lost upon the sagacity of the pig.'[86] When the visiting landlord expresses disgust at his tenants for letting the pig in the finest room in the house, the woman of the house replies by saying that there isn't 'a claner or dacenter pig in the kingdom.'[87] Phil adds that 'nobody has a better right to the run of the house, whether upstairs or downstairs, than him that *pays the rint*.'[88] By invoking that famous Hiberno-English appellation, Carleton both acknowledges the unjust reality of peasant living, but also points to a genuine, charming sympathy that Irish peasants held for their pigs as welcome members of the household. The subversive corollary of Phil's response that 'nobody has a better right to the run of the house' implies that the pig should sooner enter the cabin than the landlord.

Although his descriptions of Irish pigs are undoubtedly in jest, Carleton nevertheless presents them as characters with thinking minds open to the humor of colonial opposition. He insinuates the pig's resistance to English interference in Irish habitats and natural life by saying Irish pigs held 'utter scorn' for 'all attempts to fatten them.' The material narrative of the pig's colonial experience, when English and Anglo-Irish landlords cross-bred Greyhounds with the more corporeal English breeds to increase pork exports, enables a collaborative human–nonhuman satiric critique in Carleton's rhetoric. He implies a rebellious recalcitrance in the Irish pig, that they 'gloried in maceration and liberty,' opposing endeavors to fatten them for slaughter.[89]

What is most significant for this study of Irish materiality and expression, however, is the conclusion to 'Phil Pucel, the Pig Driver,' which points to a shift in the relationship between the workings of an Irish mind and the (presumably English) reader. Phil Purcel tries to sell his sow in England by marketing her like an Irish servant girl: 'She is like a Christyeen, yer haner, an' no trouble, Sir, if you'd be seein' company or any thing...a clane an' dacent crathur, sir!' The personification

---

[85] Carleton, *Traits and Stories*, p. 185.   [86] Carleton, *Traits and Stories*, p. 183.
[87] Carleton, *Traits and Stories*, p. 184.   [88] Carleton, *Traits and Stories*, p. 184.
[89] Carleton, *Traits and Stories*, p. 184.

of the Irish pig highlights the unjust animalization of poor Irish people in English culture. Phil's good humor here, however, becomes cutting when he promises his English customer that he can 'in no time put a knife in her whin you plazed'—a line that intimates subtextual nationalist critique of ruthless English violence against Ireland, based in the longstanding equation of Irish native with the pig ripe for slaughter, dating back to Swift's *Modest Proposal*.[90] In his speech, Phil plays the role of ignorant Irish stereotype, driving his pig up to the house of an Englishman who has no interest in buying her, but he nevertheless begs to show the sow to the 'mistress.' The Englishman's wife and several other ladies come out to view Phil, rather than the pig, as an 'Irish specimen.' In front of Phil, the women discuss that he is 'actually not ill-looking' and his 'eyes are good' and 'were it not that his nose is rather short and turned up, he would be human.'[91] This scene enacts creative empathy with pigs, imagining what it is like to be within their own interior mind and sensibility, to be sized up and objectified—as the English women do to Phil with his 'inhuman' pig's nose. In placing the reader inside the colonial subject's body and perspective, inside the stereotype of the Irishman illustrated as a pig, Carleton's text inhabits the pig's inner subjectivity as well. This moment, blending Phil and his pig in facial features and in colonial/anthropomorphic objectification, exerts a deliberate message about the cruelty of prejudice—both nationalist and, by default, speciesist.

While the mistresses and the Englishman discuss the Irish specimens, the mistress remarks, 'he is like most Irishmen of his class that I have seen; indeed, scarcely so intelligent, for he appears quite a simpleton, except, perhaps, a lurking kind of expression, which is a sign of their good humour.'[92] This assessment self-consciously invokes the hidden, interior Irish mind I have addressed in the other Irish texts, like Owenson's *Wild Irish Girl* and Edgeworth's *Ennui*, where the detail of certain expressions on the native Irish face point to a concealed and unreadable depth residing within the Irish subject. Carleton uses this blatant underestimation exhibited by the English party to subtly invite his readers into the idea that Phil possesses a deeper intelligence than the prejudiced English allow. Phil goes on to charm the lady of the house and her friends with flattery and discussions of Anglo-Irish gentlemen, and eventually the Englishman pays him for the pig, to which Phil replies 'Sir, this'll come so handy for the landlord at home, in regard o' the rint for the bit o' phatie ground.'[93] Phil mentions his poor wife at home in Ireland and convinces the Englishman to pay him more money. The group takes pity upon Phil and express amazement at his affection for his family despite living in a 'half-savage state' and being supremely ignorant.

---

[90] Carleton, *Traits and Stories*, p. 188.
[91] Carleton, *Traits and Stories*, pp. 189–90.
[92] Carleton, *Traits and Stories*, p. 190.
[93] Carleton, *Traits and Stories*, p. 192.

At the conclusion to the pig-driving episode, the narrative suddenly shifts from Phil's façade of the ignorant Irishman to someone with a greater scheme hidden underneath his stereotypical disguise. When an English servant and Phil disagree, Carleton finally acknowledges and identifies Phil's disguised antipathy: 'It is impossible to express [the Englishman's] contempt for the sense and intellect of Phil; nothing could surpass it but the contempt which Phil entertained for him.'[94] Suddenly, Carleton alerts his reader to the fact that his protagonist, Phil Purcel, holds contempt toward the English, rather than being a mere doting simpleton. In the morning, the servant attends the barn to find Phil and his pig have escaped, with full payment for that same pig jingling in Phil's pocket:

> Phil and the pig had actually travelled fifteen miles that morning...Phil going at a dog's trot, and the pig following at such a respectful distance as might not appear to identify them to fellow travels. In this manner Phil sold the pig to upwards of two dozen intelligent English gentleman and farmers[95]

What is unique about this mirthful usurpation is Carleton's detail that the cunning, financially advantageous escape is a combined effort between Phil and his pig, who follows him at a 'respectful distance' so as not to attract attention. The story underscores greater depth to both the native, Hiberno-English talking Irishman and the scrappy pig than they are perceived to have by the several 'intelligent Englishmen' that they have outwitted together. The word 'intelligent' is tactically placed, inviting the reader to question and laugh at the relative 'intelligence' of the 'specimens' of pig, Irishman, and Englishman. Carleton's wording speaks to the pig's material narrative traced above: that biologically and anatomically pigs are intelligent, emotive creatures with an astounding ability to cooperate with humans. In Phil, Carleton creates a character who uses the material reality of a pig's overlooked capabilities to his financial advantage. Critics like Cathal Ó Háinle have argued that Carleton intended his Irish characters to be 'perceived by his readers as equally quaint or barbarous.'[96] However, 'Phil Purcel, the Pig Driver' goes further to unravel the reader's initial impression of the Irish native co-living with the pig as barbarous by slowly unveiling Phil's subversive mind—both his cunning plan and his contempt for the English people at the estate. Carleton establishes the stereotype of the quaint Irishman in Phil only to later upend that impression and invite the reader inside the secret of Irish intelligence, which emerges through material symbiosis with the pig.

The wry satisfaction of this story's conclusion, after all the unsavory prejudice against Phil for his national background, denotes a progression in Irish character

---

[94] Carleton, *Traits and Stories*, p. 194.   [95] Carleton, *Traits and Stories*, p. 195.
[96] Cathal G. Ó Háinle, 'The Gaelic Background of Carleton's Traits and Stories.' *Éire-Ireland* 18.1 (1983): p. 11.

development from previous national tales. Unlike Owenson's works that imply the anti-colonial thoughts of an Irish peasant, signaled through material contexts, Carleton's writing encourages his reader to experience the colonial perspective directly and enjoy the humor as a pointedly postcolonial coup. What was previously intimated by material textuality, as in Florence Macarthy's spinning wheel or Ellinor's mud cabin, becomes the textual reality itself in 'Phil Purcel, the Pig Driver' through the posthuman image of the Irishman and pig jointly choreographing their escape. In laughing at the prejudiced English gullibility, the reader enjoys Phil outsmarting the English characters—characters who would more likely be protagonists in most English-language writing at this time. Thus, the reader is intentionally positioned to celebrate Carleton's undoing of the typical national stereotypes attributed to Irish pigs and so-called simpleton Irishmen.

Carleton concludes the tale by addressing his reader: 'This slight sketch of Phil Purcel we have presented to our readers as a specimen of the low, cunning Connaughtman.'[97] Carleton uses the word 'specimen' deliberately as a satiric postscript to a story that has added depth to the Irish peasant character and his relationship with pigs. The final line of the story 'Never *trust* a Connaughtman,' while comic, is also a reminder of Irish national subversion: that the Irishman from the west of Ireland, much like the pig, has more underneath the surface than the English reader might otherwise have thought. Phil, who appreciates his sow as a partner and co-conspirator, rather than object of purchase like the Englishman, reveals himself as open to more social and economic possibilities than those blinded by national and speciesist prejudice. The nonverbal but clever, sentient pig puts pressure on the eighteenth century's overarching colonial discourse about Irish animal nature and humane British civility by challenging its logistical roots in the hierarchizing of species.

5.5 Conclusion

This tour through Irish matter began with a talking coin, and it will now conclude with a coin that prompted a lot of talk. In 1926, William Butler Yeats was elected Chairman of the Commission on Coinage, which heralded the important task of choosing new coin designs for the Irish Free State. Ireland had not had its own unique coinage since 1822, when minting separate, Hibernia-impressed coins for Ireland was discontinued. The decision around the new Free State currency was a momentous and symbolically nationalist one, answering two hundred years of absent economic freedom and inaugurating the symbology of a new, independent Ireland. Standing before the new Irish Senate, Yeats announced that these coins

---

[97] Carleton, *Traits and Stories*, p. 199.

would be 'silent ambassadors of national taste.' Rather than resurrecting the classical, beautiful figure of Hibernia, which Yeats claimed would grow 'empty and academic,' the poet found inspiration in ancient Greek coinage, specifically the animal-impressed Sicilian coins of the Greek colonies, which he deemed the most beautiful classical coins and saw as analogous to Ireland's own historical and mythological culture.[98]

Yeats proposed that the animals of Ireland adorn the tails of the coins, such as the horse, hare, bull, wolfhound, woodcock, pig or ram, and salmon, aligning with what scholars consider his anti-modernist and anti-materialist ethos.[99] The Committee approved the theme, along with the signature Brian Boru harp as the uniting insignia on the obverse side of each coin. Yeats and the Committee then announced a design competition for the new coins and provided images of the Sicilian-Greek coins as models for the participating artists. They judged the submissions in 1927, and by 1928, the artwork of unanimous winner Percy Metcalfe was minted in copper and silver (Figure 5.7). While the Committee had agreed on the imagery and the winner, public opinion quickly divided when the coins appeared in circulation. Some Irish citizens admired the beauty of the animal design and homage to ancient Greek coinage, while others cried out for more distinctly Irish symbols or Christian imagery, criticizing the provincial nature of barnyard animals. Of all the animals depicted, the pig adorning the halfpenny proved most controversial.

Two hundred years after Wood's halfpence inspired Jonathan Swift to express national opposition to British-controlled currency, the same halfpenny incited a debate about how Irish identity should be presented to the world. Even before the pig's image was approved for the tails of the Irish Free State's halfpenny, the Committee anticipated that, out of all the animals, the pig would invite the most criticism and potentially, a certain amount of mockery, rooted in the Irish pigsty stereotype examined throughout this final chapter. In fact, Percy Metcalfe had submitted two designs for halfpenny: one of a ram and one of a sow. Leo McCauley, secretary to the Committee, recalled the time and consideration the committee gave to the choice of the pig over the ram:

We had at first some hesitation in deciding to recommend the pig as a type for one of the coins, because of the ridicule with which it is associated in connection with this country; but further consideration has convinced us that the idea underlying the series of designs makes the inclusion of the pig inevitable. As a valuable product of the country we believe that it merits a place in the series,

[98] William Butler Yeats, 'What we Did or Tried to Do' in *W. B. Yeats and the Designing of Ireland's Coinage*, ed. Brian Cleeve (Dublin: Dolmen, 1972), p. 10.

[99] For more on Yeats and his involvement in the Free State coin designs, see *W. B. Yeats and Ireland's Coinage*, ed. Cleeve, and Jack Quin, 'Some Master of Design: W.B. Yeats and the Free State Coinage.' *Modernist Cultures* 15.4 (2020): pp. 464–87.

Figure 5.7 Percy Metcalfe, *Halfpenny, Leath Phingin*, bronze, 1928. Irish Free State coin. Reproduced with the kind permission of the National Museum of Ireland. Photograph by Paul and Bente Withers, Galata Print Ltd, Llanfyllin, Wales.

and that the objections to it are unworthy of serious consideration. Moreover, the artist employed to prepare the design may well elect to depict a boar, as it appears in the crests of several old Irish families.[100]

While ostensibly vindicating the choice of the pig, McCauley betrays his own trepidation around the contentious idea, even suggesting that the wild boar would be a preferred substitute for the sow's historically damning symbolism. Other members of the committee, such as Thomas Bodkin, were more bravely invested in the pig. At a lecture delivered in the Metropolitan School of Art in November 1928, Bodkin mentioned the 'unfair ridicule with which this noble and useful animal is often associated.'[101] The pig, Bodkin argued, was better suited to the halfpenny than the ram or boar and, as McCauley predicted, its inclusion in the series was 'inevitable.'[102] In a later instance, Bodkin's defense became even more impassioned: 'If I am asked to defend the pig, I do so with the sharp answer St. Peter himself got: "What God hath made clean, do not thou call common."'[103]

[100] Leo T. McCauley, 'Summary of the Proceedings of the Committee' in *W. B. Yeats and Ireland's Coinage*, ed. Cleeve, pp. 32–3.
[101] Thomas Bodkin, 'The Irish Coinage Designs.' Lecture at the Metropolitan School of Art, 30 November 1928, in *W. B. Yeats and Ireland's Coinage*, ed. Cleeve, p. 47.
[102] McCauley, 'Summary,' p. 47.
[103] Thomas Bodkin, 'Thomas Bodkin's Postscript to "Coinage of Saorstat Eireann"' in *W. B. Yeats and Ireland's Coinage*, ed. Cleeve, p. 58.

In honoring the natural integrity of the mammal and its active role in Irish culture, trade, and history, Yeats, Bodkin, and the Committee on Coinage also underestimated the impact of its long-lasting, caustic signification in colonial ideology, as a symbol used to racialize and demean the native Irish people since the seventeenth century. Even in 1928, the residual impact of colonial ideology's animalizing rhetoric maintained its own symbolic currency in the psychology of the Irish people. Even if colonialism in the Republic of Ireland had come to end, colonialist thinking had not.

In August 1927, Mr Duffy of the National League in Galway challenged the choice of pig in the Dáil, asking,

> whether the design of a pig and her litter and other farmyard animals is calculated to inspire the public as to the standard of Gaelic culture that national Ireland is striving for to-day; whether something more in keeping with the Christian glories of Ireland should not be substituted for a series of designs which are regarded by many people as a travesty on our country[104]

Duffy's words convey clear criticism—that the pig, especially, is 'calculated' by the Committee to undermine Gaelic culture in a modern, free Ireland. As Duffy and others contend, a free Ireland should not propagate the same stereotyped symbols used by the British Empire to belittle Irish character. The *Catholic Bulletin* made similar comments, describing the animal designs as 'beast coinage'—another pointed choice of words that consciously objects to iconography associated with Britain's historic work of bestializing the Irish people in cultural representation, from political cartoons to literary texts. To the *Catholic Bulletin*, the pig signified nothing more than 'petty peasant nationality.'[105] These objections to the pig, to the 'beast' of the old Irish character, reveal that in the minds of the complainants, the racialized, hierarchical ideology rhetorically ascribed to pigs by English colonialist writers had overtaken the collective memory of a lived, Irish material experience. In short, rhetorical conscription had silenced the material fact of pig and human cooperation in Ireland, demonstrating continuing colonial ideological control even after the Irish War of Independence.

One of the most impassioned objections to the pig halfpenny appeared in a small opinion piece published in the *Irish Times* in December 1928, shortly after Bodkin's lecture defending the 'noble and useful animal.' This writer claims: 'There cannot be much humour left in Ireland, or why this pig... "The gintleman— or lady—that pays the rint." True, but why rub it in? Especially in a country where that obnoxious exaction is extinct.'[106] In asking 'why rub it in?' this critic

---

[104] *Irish Times*, 'Free State Coins: Farmyard Animals Used in Designs.' 3 August 1927, p. 7.
[105] Qtd. in Bernard McKenna, '"The Silent Ambassadors": Yeats, Irish Coinage, and the Aesthetics of a National Material Culture.' *Yeats Eliot Review* 31.3/4 (2015): p. 10.
[106] *Irish Times*. 'The Free State Coins: Importance of the Pig.' 4 December 1928, p. 7.

questions the cultural act of remembering Irish economy under colonial rule, when pigs—as sources of indoor heating and rent money—facilitated native Irish survival during the penal laws. By saying the 'obnoxious exaction' of the 'gentleman that pays the rent' is 'extinct' in Ireland, he or she insists that eighteenth-century Irish thinking, which viewed the pig in more democratic, non-speciesist terms as a collaborator in Irish survival and rural economy, should be exterminated from national memory. Furthermore, the critic's claim that 'there cannot be much humour left in Ireland' underestimates the complexity of Irish satire in the long eighteenth century, which recognized the intellectual capacity and subversive potential in the pig, seized on by Jonathan Swift and William Carleton. For this anonymous *Irish Times* critic operating within a modern, humanist, and speciesist ideology, Ireland's history of cohabiting with pigs should be forgotten in place of a new, modern character, who never sees a pig as a gentleman, but as a grotesque manifestation of colonial *in*humanity.

This pig-stamped halfpenny, then, makes a fitting conclusion to this book's study of Irish matter and character. It distills centuries of clashing narratives—about British colonial ideology, Irish materiality, and Irish national character—onto its small veneer. It also signifies a key change in Irish subjectivity: when native Ireland's cultural narrative, embedded in material experience and human–nonhuman interaction for centuries, was overwritten by humanist Irish nationalism and anthropocentric ideologies that, coincidentally, had also supported imperialism for at least the past two centuries. When Yeats chose the animals for the Free State coinage, he instructed his committee and the contributing artists that he wanted to see 'emblems or symbols, not pictures.' Indeed, as a symbol, the pig was contentious: it had been used to symbolize two very different ideas of Irish character dating back to the early modern period: both the swinish Irishman and the gentleman that pays the rent. The 1928 objection that asks, 'why this pig?', 'why rub it in?', encapsulates the many vectors of material and rhetorical narrative that come into conflict on the surface of this pig-stamped coin.

Despite the controversy surrounding its national significations, the Irish pig halfpenny was minted and used from 1928 until 1967. It was demonetized in December of 1969, when Ireland adopted a decimal system in accordance with international trends of monetization, rather than following the British standard. From the 1970s until the introduction of the Euro in 2002, the sow and her litter were replaced with a Celtic knot resembling a bird. Gabriel Hayes, a female, Dublin-born sculptor and medalist, adapted the new halfpenny coin design from a Celtic manuscript held at Cologne Cathedral.[107] At last, a woman was designing Irish coins, rather than emblematizing them. But this Celtic knot is not unproblematic in terms of the narrative it circulates. By seeking inspiration in the

---

[107] Oliver O'Hanlon, 'A Woman Who Made her Mark: An Irishman's Diary on Sculptor Gabriel Hayes.' *Irish Times*, 6 July 2020.

elite culture of a much more distant Celtic past, rather than the everyday, material life of eighteenth- and nineteenth-century colonial Ireland, this new Celtic half-penny seemed to answer the complaints of the critics of the unpopular pig half-penny in 1928. However, replacing the pig with abstract Celtic art adorning the margins of rare medieval manuscripts not even held in Ireland omits a narrative about the modern Irish character's origins in colonial survival. Contrary to what Yeats claimed in the Irish Senate, the pig halfpenny was not a 'silent ambassador' but an articulate historical impression rooted in a material narrative of colonial survival and resistance.

From a new materialist perspective, the pig halfpenny in 1928 engineered its own omission. The problem with Yeats's and Metcalfe's halfpenny arises not from what it depicts—the pig and her litter—but what it leaves out: her Irish keeper or driver. Although celebrating Irish materiality and Irish animal, the coin design ultimately served to partition Irish human life from Irish animal life. In the wake of several centuries of colonial ideology and prejudiced characterizations of native Irish peoples founded in Anglocentric and anthropocentric hierarchies, it was probably inevitable that citizens would be more inclined to view the pig half-penny as a depiction of base, inhuman nature, rather a complex ecosystem of material networks, relations, and, historically, creative co-survival or creative lit-erary coup, as in Carleton's imagination. In the pig's halfpenny, critics saw the familiar colonial degradation of the Irish who are *like* devalued pigs, rather than the accurate historic image of the Irish who survived *with* pigs under centuries of colonial oppression and who expressed their national loss in harmony with the pig's material experience, as in Aogán Ó Rathaille's 'Cabhair Ní Ghairfead' and the anonymous widow's keen. The pig on the Irish state's halfpenny left the wrong impression, literally, without her human counterpart, failing to fully represent the complete image of material cooperation and creative survival under colonialism. Ultimately, in the iconography of modern Ireland, colonial prejudice became more visible than the national material memory.

As discussed at the very beginning of this book, coins in Ireland signified national contracts as much as they represented material wealth. The tension between the external impression of a coin and its deeper subjective meanings helped writers to encapsulate the complexity of Irish character under colonial rule at the turn of the nineteenth century. Like the bad shilling protagonist of Chapter 1 explains: to melt, remold, and rebrand a material object is to change and sometimes obscure the national narrative. Still, as the enduring consciousness of the coin narrator—who moved from the bodily forms of Celtic statue to Catholic chalice to forged British penny—colonial experience and subjectivity endures deep within materiality despite the dominant narratives written over it. To read matter in detail—the inside of a flax stalk, the movement of the spinning wheel, the biology of mud, and the complex intelligence and anatomy of a pig—is to retrieve parts of the character and consciousness of colonial Ireland that have not always been overtly documented in written texts. In this new materialist, methodological transition from the outward impression of an object to the deeper, subversive meanings of its material, contextual details, I have found a new portrait of Irish character that is both material and semiotic, whose unique, sometimes concealed subjectivity finds expression in resilient matter.

There are many more unstudied narratives waiting in Ireland's material archive—and in so many other national, colonial histories. Today, the historical loss and silence of the average eighteenth-century Irish tenant need not be total: he has left his material imprint for us to continue deciphering. Materiality will always supply the supplementary narratives that canonical discourse omits. Like flax, spinning wheels, mud, and pigs, a coin *can* speak its own narrative, if we are willing, like the man walking through Dublin in *The Adventures of a Bad Shilling in the Kingdom of Ireland,* to stop, suspend prejudices, and listen.

*   *   *

Bibliography

Alaimo, Stacy, 'Trans-Corporeal Feminisms and the Ethical Space of Nature' in *Material Feminisms*, ed. Stacy Alaimo and Susan Hekman (Bloomington: Indiana University Press, 2008).

Albarella, Umberto, Keith Dobney, Anton Ervynck, and Peter Rowley-Conwy, *Pigs and Humans: 10,000 Years of Interaction* (Oxford: Oxford University Press, 2008).

Amory, Thomas, *The Life of John Buncle, Esq.* (London: Johnson, 1766).

An Abstract of the Acts of Parliament now in Force, Relating to the Linen Manufacture. Published by order of the Commissioners and Trustees appointed by his Majesty for Improving the Linen Manufacture of Scotland (Edinburgh, 1751).

'An Elegy of the Pig that Followed the Ld Chief Baron Henn and Baron Worth from Connaught to Dublin' (1688) in *Verse in English from Tudor and Stuart Ireland*, ed. Andrew Carpenter (Cork: Cork University Press, 2003).

Armstrong, Charles I., 'Poetic Industry: The Modernity of the Rhyming Weavers.' *Review of Irish Studies in Europe* 2.1 (2018): 139–48.

Austen, Jane, *Jane Austen's Letters*, ed. Deirdre Le Faye, 4th edition (Oxford: Oxford University Press, 2011).

A View of the Present State of Ireland (Anon.) (London: Faulder, 1780).

Baker, Henry, 'The Spinning-Wheel.' *Original Poems: Serious and Humorous* (London: Roberts, 1725).

Baltes-Ellerman, Sabine, ed., *Jonathan Swift's Allies: The Wood's Halfpence Controversy in Ireland* (Oxford: Peter Lang, 2017).

Banim, John and Michael, *Tales of the O'Hara Family* (Duffy, 1865).

Banim, John and Michael, *The Croppy; A Tale of 1798*, 3 vols (London: Colburn, 1828).

Barad, Karen, *Meeting the Universe Halfway: Quantum Physics and the Entanglement of Matter and Meaning* (Durham, NC: Duke University Press, 2007).

Barad, Karen, 'Posthumanist Performativity: Toward an Understanding of How Matter Comes to Matter.' *Signs* 28.3 (2003): 801–31.

Barbour's Prize Needlework Series: A Treatise on Lace Making, Embroidery, and Needlework with Irish Flax Threads (New York: Barbour, 1894)

Barnard, Toby, *Improving Ireland? Projectors, Prophets, and Profiteers 1641–1786* (Dublin: Four Courts Press, 2008).

Bell, Jonathan, and Mervyn Watson, *A History of Irish Farming, 1750–1850* (Dublin: Four Courts Press, 2008).

Bellamy, Liz, 'It-Narrators and Circulation: Defining a Subgenre' in *The Secret Life of Things*, ed. Mark Blackwell (Lewisburg: Bucknell University Press, 2007).

Benedict, Barbara, 'The Moral in the Material: Numismatics and Identity in Evelyn, Addison, and Pope.' In *Queen Anne and the Arts*, ed. Cedric D. Reverand II (Lanham, MD: Bucknell, 2015), pp. 65–83.

Bennett, Jane, *Vibrant Matter* (Durham, NC: Duke University Press, 2010).

Biscoglio, Frances, '"Unspun" Heroes: Iconography of the Spinning Woman in the Middle Ages.' *Journal of Medieval and Renaissance Studies* 25.2 (1995): 163–76.

Blackwell, Bonnie, 'Corkscrews and Courtesans: Death and Sex in Circulation Novels' in *The Secret Life of Things: Animals, Objects, and It-Narratives in Eighteenth-Century England*, ed. Mark Blackwell (Lewisburg, PA: Bucknell University Press, 2007).

Blackwell, Mark, ed., *British It-Narratives, 1750–1830*, 2 vols (London: Pickering & Chatto, 2012).

Bodkin, Thomas, 'The Irish Coinage Designs.' Lecture at the Metropolitan School of Art, 30 November 1928, in *W. B. Yeats and the Designing of Ireland's Coinage*, ed. Brian Cleeve (Dublin: Dolmen, 1972).

Bodkin, Thomas, 'Thomas Bodkin's Postscript to "Coinage of Saorstat Eireann"' in *W. B. Yeats and the Designing of Ireland's Coinage*, ed. Brian Cleeve (Dublin: Dolmen, 1972).

Braidotti, Rosi, *The Posthuman* (Cambridge: Polity, 2013).

Breakey, James, 'Process and Affidavit, as also his Remarks' in *To the Right Honourable and Honourable Trustees of the Linen and Hempen Manufacture* (Dublin, 1783).

Brooke, Henry, *The Fool of Quality*, 5 vols (New York: Derby & Jackson, 1860).

Burke, Mary, 'The Cottage, the Castle, and the Couture Cloak: "Traditional" Irish Fabrics and "Modern" Irish America, 1952–1969.' *Journal of Design History* 31.4 (2018): 364–82.

Butler, Marilyn, *Maria Edgeworth: A Literary Biography* (Oxford: Clarendon, 1972).

Cambrensis, Giraldus, *The Topography of Ireland*, tr. Thomas Forester, ed. Thomas Wright (Cambridge, Ontario: In Parantheses, 2000).

Campbell, Mary, *Lady Morgan: The Life and Times of Sydney Owenson* (London: Pandora, 1988).

Caras, Roger A., *A Perfect Harmony: The Intertwining Lives of Animals and Humans throughout History* (West Lafayette, IN: Purdue University Press, 2002).

Carleton, William, *Traits and Stories of the Irish Peasantry* (London: Routledge & Sons, 1856).

Chaigneau, William, 'Three Letters to the Fool' in *History of Jack Connor*, 2nd edition (Dublin: Hulton Bradley, 1766).

Chakrabarty, Diphesh, 'The Climate of History: Four Theses.' *Critical Inquiry* 35.2 (2009): 197–222.

Chandler, James, 'Edgeworth and Realism.' *Irish Literature in Transition, 1780–1830*, ed. Claire Connolly (Cambridge: Cambridge University Press, 2020).

Clark, Timothy, *The Cambridge Introduction to Literature and the Environment* (Cambridge: Cambridge University Press, 2011).

Cobbe, Frances Power, 'Irish Tenants Improvements.' Letter to the Editor, *The Spectator*, 27 September 1890.

Cole, Lucinda, *Imperfect Creatures: Vermin, Literature, and the Sciences of Life, 1600–1740* (Ann Arbor: University of Michigan Press, 2016).

Collins, Brenda, *From Flax to Fabric: The Story of Irish Linen* (Lisburn: Lisburn Museum Publication, 1994).

Connolly, Claire, *A Cultural History of the Irish Novel: 1790–1829* (Cambridge: Cambridge University Press, 2012).

Connolly, Claire, '"I accuse Miss Owenson": The Wild Irish Girl as Media Event.' *Colby Quarterly* 36.3 (2000): 98–115.

Cooper, George, *Letters on the Irish Nation: Written during a visit to that Kingdom, in the Autumn of the Year 1799*, 2nd edition (London: Bensley, 1801).

Corbett, Mary Jean, 'Allegories of Prescription: Gendering Union in *The Wild Irish Girl*.' *Eighteenth-Century Life* 22.3 (1998): 92–102.

Corkery, Daniel, *The Hidden Ireland: A Study of Gaelic Munster in the Eighteenth Century*, 2nd edition (Dublin: Gill, 1956).

Costello, Eileen, *Amhráin Mhuighe Seóla* (Dublin, 1923).

Crawford, W. H., *The Impact of the Domestic Linen Industry in Ulster* (Belfast: Ulster Historical Foundation, 2005).

Crommelin, Samuel-Louis, *An Essay Towards the Improving of the Hempen and Flaxen Manufactures in the Kingdom of Ireland* (Dublin: R. Owen, 1734) [originally printed Dublin, 1705].

Davies, Geoffrey, 'Swift's "The Story of the Injured Lady."' *Huntington Library Quarterly* 6.4 (1943): 388–92.

Deane, Seamus, *A Short History of Irish Literature* (South Bend, IN: University of Notre Dame Press, 1994).

Deane, Seamus, 'Classic Swift' in *The Cambridge Companion to Jonathan Swift*, ed. Christopher Fox (Cambridge: Cambridge University Press, 2003).

Deane, Seamus, *Strange Country: Modernity and Nationhood in Irish Writing since 1790* (Oxford: Oxford University Press, 1997).

Defoe, Daniel, *The Female Manufacturer's Complaint, Being the Humble Petition of Dorothy Distaff, Abigail Spinning-Wheel, and Eleanore Reel, &c, Spinsters, to Lady Rebecca Woollpack* (London: Boreham, 1720).

Derricke, John, 'The Mac Sweynes Seated at Dinner and Being Entertained by a Blind Harper.' *Image of Ireland*, 1581.

Dickens, Charles, 'To the Editor of the Morning Chronicle, 25 July 1842' in *The Selected Letters of Charles Dickens*, ed. Jenny Hartley (Oxford: Oxford University Press, 2012), 107.

Douglas, Aileen, 'Britannia's Rule and the It-Narrator.' *Eighteenth-Century Fiction* 6.1 (1993): 65–82.

Douglas, Mary, *Purity and Danger: An Analysis of Concepts of Pollution and Taboo* (London: Routledge, 2003).

Dyer, Serena, and Chloe Wigston Smith, eds, *Material Literacy in Eighteenth-Century Britain: A Nation of Makers* (London: Bloomsbury, 2020).

Eagleton, Terry, *Heathcliff and the Great Hunger: Studies in Irish Culture* (London: Verso, 1995).

Edgeworth, Maria, *Castle Rackrent*, ed. George Watson (Oxford: Oxford University Press, 2008).

Edgeworth, Maria, *Ennui*, in *Tales of A Fashionable Life*, vol. 1 (London: Hunter, 1815).

Edgeworth, Maria, 'Rosanna' in *Tales and Novels*, vol. 2. *Popular Tales* (London: Simpkin, Marshall & Company, 1857). projectgutenberg.org.

Edgeworth, Richard Lovell and Maria, *Essay on Irish Bulls* (London: Johnson, 1802), *Edinburgh Review* 42 (July 1813).

Egenolf, Susan, 'Maria Edgeworth in Blackface: *Castle Rackrent* and the Irish Rebellion of 1798.' *ELH* 72.4 (2005): 845–69.

Ehrenpreis, Irvin, *Swift: The Man, his Works, and the Age*, vol. 3. *Dean Swift* (Ann Arbor: University of Michigan, 1962).

Ekser, Burcin, James Markmann, and A. Joseph Tector, 'Current Status of Pig Liver Xenotransplantation.' *International Journal of Surgery* 23 (2015): 240–46.

Ellis, William, *The Practice of Farming and Husbandry, in all sorts of Soils, according to the latest Improvements, recommended by the Dublin Society*. 2nd edition (Dublin: James Potts, 1765).

Essays by the Dublin Society (London, reprinted 1740).

Everett, Nigel, *The Woods of Ireland: A History, 700–1800* (Dublin: Four Courts, 2015).

Fabricant, Carole, 'Speaking for the Irish Nation: The Drapier, the Bishop, and the Problems of Colonial Representation.' *ELH* 66.2 (1999): 337–72.

Fairburn, John, *Fairburn (Senior's) Portrait of the Pig-Faced Lady of Manchester-Square* (London: Fairburn, 1815). Broadside held at the British Library.

Ferguson, Frank, 'We wove our ain wab: The Ulster Weaver Poets' Working Lives, Myths and Afterlives' in *A History of Irish Working Class Writing*, ed. Michael Pierse (Cambridge: Cambridge University Press, 2017).

Ferris, Ina, 'The Question of Ideological Form: Arthur Young, the Agricultural Tour, and Ireland' in *Ideology and Form in Eighteenth-Century Literature*, ed. David H. Richter (Lubbock, TX: Texas Tech University Press, 1999).

Ferris, Ina, *The Romantic National Tale and the Question of Ireland* (Cambridge: Cambridge University Press, 2004).

Festa, Lynn, *Fiction without Humanity: Person, Animal, Thing, in Early Enlightenment Culture* (Philadelphia: University of Pennsylvania, 2021).

Fitzgerald, Oisin, 'The Irish "Greyhound" Pig: An Extinct Indigenous Breed of Pig.' *History Ireland: Ireland's History Magazine* (Dublin: History Publications, 2015). https://www.historyireland.com/18th-19th-century-history/the-irish-greyhound-pig-an-extinct-indigenous-breed-of-pig/

Foster, R. F., *Modern Ireland 1600–1972* (New York: Penguin, 1989).

Fox, Christopher. Introduction to *The Cambridge Companion to Jonathan Swift* (Cambridge: Cambridge University Press, 2003).

Friel, Mary, Kym Griffin, and Lisa M. Collins. 'Mood and Personality Interact to Determine Cognitive Biases in Pigs.' *Biology Letters* 12.11 (2016): 20160402.

Gee, Sophie, *Making Waste: Leftovers and the Eighteenth-Century Imagination* (Princeton: Princeton University Press, 2010).

Gibson, James J., *The Ecological Approach to Visual Perception* (Hillsdale, NJ: Lawrence Erlbaum, 1986).

Gillray, James, *United Irishmen upon Duty*, 1798. Etching, hand-colored on paper, printed by Hannah Humphrey.

'Glorviniana' in *The Port Folio*, vol. 7., ed. Joseph Dennie (Philadelphia: Dennick & Dickins, 1812), 227, 230.

Gray, Andrew, *A Treatise on Spinning Machinery* (Edinburgh: Constable, 1819).

Gray, David, ' "Stemmed from the Scots"? The Ulsters-Scots Literary "Baird" and the Pastoral Tradition.' *Eighteenth-Century Ireland* 32 (2017): 28–43.

Gray, Jane, *Spinning the Threads of Uneven Development: Gender and Industrialization in Ireland during the Long Eighteenth Century* (Lanham, MD: Lexington, 2005).

Griffith, Richard, *The Gordian Knot*, in *Two Novels In Letter*, 4 vols (Dublin, 1769).

Hall, Anna Maria, *Sketches of Irish Character* (London: How & Parsons, 1842).

Haraway, Donna, 'Otherworldly Conversations: Terran Topics, Local Terms' in *Material Feminisms*, ed. Stacy Alaimo and Susan Hekman (Bloomington, IN: Indiana University Press, 2008).

Haraway, Donna, 'Situated Knowledges: The Science Question in Feminism and the Privilege of Patrial Perspective.' *Feminist Studies* 14.3 (1988): 575–99.

Haslett, Moyra, 'Experimentalism in the Irish Novel, 1750–1770.' *Irish University Review* 41.1 (2011): 63–79.

Haslett, Moyra, 'Fictions of Sisterhood in Eighteenth-Century Irish Writing' in *Irish Literature in Transition, 1700–1780*, ed. Moyra Haslett (Cambridge: Cambridge University Press, 2021).

Hawes, Clement, Introduction and 'Three Times Round the Globe: Gulliver and Colonial Discourse' in *Jonathan Swift: Gulliver's Travels and Other Writings*, ed. Clement Hawes (Boston: Houghton Mifflin, 2004).

Hayton, David W., and Adam Rounce, eds, *Irish Political Writings After 1725: A Modest Proposal and Other Works*. In The Cambridge Edition of the Works of Jonathan Swift, vol. 14 (Cambridge: Cambridge University Press, 2018).

Helland, Janice, ' "A Delightful Change of Fashion": Fair Trade, Cottage Craft and Tweed in Late Nineteenth-Century Ireland.' *Canadian Journal of Irish Studies* 36.2 (2010): 34–55.

Helland, Janice, *British and Irish Home Arts and Industries, 1880–1914: Marketing Craft, Making Fashion* (Dublin: Irish Academic Press, 2007).

Helland, Janice, 'Caprices of Fashion: Handmade Lace in Ireland 1883–1907.' *Textile History* 39.2 (2008): 193–222.

Hibernia's Triumph, A Masque of Two Interludes and written in Honor of King William III and performed at the Theatre Royal in Dublin, on the anniversary day of his birth (Dublin: Nelson, 1748).

Higgins, Padhraig, *A Nation of Politicians: Gender, Patriotism, and Political Culture in Late Eighteenth-Century Ireland* (Madison, WI: University of Wisconsin Press, 2010).

Hincks, William, *The Irish Linen Industry*, twelve plates (London, 1791).

Hinton, Peta Tara Mehrabi, and Josef Barla, 'New Materialisms/New Colonialisms.' *newmaterialisms.eu*. https://newmaterialism.eu/content/5-workingU-groups/2-working-group-2/position-papers/subgroup-position-paper-_-new-materialisms_new-colonialisms.pdf

Hoare, Nicholas, *The Life and Adventures of Toby, the Sapient Pig, with his Opinions on Men and Manners, Written by Himself* (London: Lyon, 1817).

Howes, Marjorie, *Colonial Crossings: Figures in Literary History* (Dublin: Field Day, 2006).

Hume, A., 'Historical Notices of Spinning and Weaving.' *Ulster Journal of Archaeology* 5.1 (1857).

Hume, A., 'Spinning and Weaving: Their Influence on Popular Language and Literature,' *Ulster Journal of Archaeology* 5.1 (1857).

Iovino, Serenella, and Serpil Opperman, *Material Ecocriticism* (Bloomington, IN: Indiana University Press, 2015).

Irish Examiner, 'Simple Mud Hut a Stark Reminder of How the Poorest Lived and Died.' 8 May 2018.

Irish Times, 'Earthen Homes Stuck with Muddy Image.' 23 August 1997.

Irish Times, 'Free State Coins: Farmyard Animals Used in Designs.' 3 August 1927.

Irish Times, 'The Free State Coins: Importance of the Pig.' 4 December 1928.

Isdell, Sarah, *The Irish Recluse*, 3 vols (London: J. Booth, 1809).

Johnson, Mary, *Madam Johnson's Present; or Every Young Woman's Companion in Useful and Universal Knowledge* (Dublin: Williams, 1770).

Johnston, Joseph, 'Irish Currency in the Eighteenth Century.' *Hermanthena* 27.52 (1938): 3–26.

Johnstone, Charles, *Chrysal; Or the Adventures Of a Guinea*, 2 vols (London: T. Beckett, 1760).

Jones, Ann Rosalind, and Peter Stallybrass, *Renaissance Clothing and the Materials of Memory* (Cambridge: Cambridge University Press, 2000).

Kvande, Marta, and Emily Gilliland Grover, 'The Mediation is the Messsage: Charles Johnstone's *Chrysal.*' *Eighteenth-Century Fiction* 32.4 (2020): 535–57.

Keenan, Mark, 'Mud will Stick, Thank Goodness.' *Sunday Times* [London], 9 January 2005.

Keenleyside, Heather, *Animals and Other People: Literary Forms and Living Beings in the Long Eighteenth Century* (Philadelphia: University of Pennsylvania Press, 2016).

Kelly, James, and Ciarán Mac Murchaidh, eds, *Irish and English: Essays on the Irish Linguistic and Cultural Frontier 1600–1900* (Dublin: Four Courts Press, 2012).

Kiberd, Declan, *Inventing Ireland: The Literature of the Modern Nation* (Cambridge, MA: Harvard University Press, 1996).

Kiberd, Declan, *Irish Classics* (Cambridge, MA: Harvard University Press, 2001).

Kingsley, Charles, Biographical Preface in Henry Brooke, *Fool of Quality*, vol. 1 (New York: Derby & Jackson, 1860).

Kinmonth, Claudia, 'Rags, Riches, and Recycling: Material and Visual Culture of the Dublin Society, 1731–1781.' *Irish Architectural and Decorative Studies* 21 (2018).

Kirby, Vicky, 'Natural Convers(at)ions: Or, What if Culture was Really Nature All Along' in *Material Feminisms*, ed. Stacy Alaimo and Susan Hekman (Bloomington, IN: Indiana University Press, 2008).

Kowaleski-Wallace, Elizabeth, *Consuming Subjects: Women, Shopping and Business in the Eighteenth Century* (Columbia: Columbia University Press, 1997).

Kowaleski-Wallace, Elizabeth, *Their Fathers' Daughters: Hannah More, Maria Edgeworth, and Patriarchal Complicity* (New York: Oxford University Press, 1991).

Kreilkamp, Vera, *The Anglo-Irish Novel and the Big House* (Syracuse, NY: Syracuse University Press, 1998).

Lake, Crystal B., *Artifacts: How we Think and Write about Found Objects* (Baltimore, MD: Johns Hopkins University Press, 2020).

Leadbeater, Mary, *Cottage Dialogues among the Irish Peasantry*, Introduction and notes by Maria Edgeworth (London: Johnson, 1811).

Leadbeater, Mary, and Elizabeth Shackleton, *Tales for Cottagers, accommodated to the present condition of the Irish Peasantry* (Dublin: Cumming, 1814).

LeCain, Timothy, *The Matter of History: How Things Create the Past* (Cambridge: Cambridge University Press, 2017).

Leech, Sarah, *Poems on Various Subjects, by Sarah Leech, a Peasant Girl. With a Biographical Memoir* (Dublin: J. Charles, 1828).

Leerssen, Joep, *Mere Irish and Fíor-Ghael: Studies in the Idea of Irish Nationality, its Development, and Literary Expression Prior to the Nineteenth Century* (South Bend, IN: University of Notre Dame Press, 1997).

Leerssen, Joep, *Remembrance and Imagination: Patterns in the Historical and Literary Representation of Ireland in the Nineteenth Century* (South Bend, IN: University of Notre Dame Press, 1997).

Lemire, Beverly, 'An Education in Comfort: Indian Textiles and the Remaking of English Homes of the Long Eighteenth Century' in *Selling Textiles in the Long Eighteenth Century: Comparative Perspectives from Western Europe*, ed. Jon Stobart and B. Blondé (London: Palgrave Macmillan, 2014).

Lines, Joe, *The Rogue Narrative and Irish Fiction, 1660–1790* (Syracuse, NY: Syracuse University Press, 2021).

Longfield, Ada K., 'Notes on the Linen and Cotton Printing Industry in Northern Ireland in the Eighteenth Century.' *Belfast Natural History and Philosophy Society* 4.2 (1950–5).

Lynch-Brennan, Margaret, *The Irish Bridget: Irish Immigrant Women in Domestic Service in America, 1840–1930* (Syracuse, NY: Syracuse University Press, 2014).

McCauley, Leo T., 'Summary of the Proceedings of the Committee' in *W. B. Yeats and the Designing of Ireland's Coinage*, ed. Brian Cleeve (Dublin: Dolmen, 1972).

McClintock, Anne, *Imperial Leather* (London: Routledge, 2013).

Mac Coitar, Niall, *Ireland's Animals: Myths, Legends, and Folklore* (Cork: Collins, 2015).

McDonald, Frank, and Peigín Doyle, *Ireland's Earthen Houses* (Dublin: A. & A. Farmar, 1997).

McGarry, Marion, 'Room to Improve: The Homes of Ireland's 19th Century Rural Poor.' *RTE Brainstorm*, 8 January 2019.

McKenna, Bernard, '"The Silent Ambassadors": Yeats, Irish Coinage, and the Aesthetics of a National Material Culture.' *Yeats Eliot Review* 31.3/4 (2015).

McKernan, Anne, 'War, Gender, and Industrial Innovation: Recruiting Women Weavers in Early Nineteenth Century Ireland.' *Journal of Social History* 28.1 (1994).

Malcomson, Robert, and Stephanos Mastoris. *The English Pig: A History* (London: Bloomsbury, 2001).

Mattfield, Monica, '"Genus Porcus Sophisticus: The Learned Pig and the Theatrics of National Identity in Late Eighteenth-Century London' in *Performing Animality: Animals in Performance Practices* (Basingstoke: Palgrave Macmillan, 2015).

Montgomery, David, *Dirt: The Erosion of Civilizations* (Los Angeles: UCLA Press, 2007).

Moore, Sean, *Swift, the Book, and the Irish Financial Revolution* (Baltimore, MD: Johns Hopkins, 2010).

Moore, Thomas, *Memoirs of Captain Rock* (London: Longman, Hurst, Rees, Orme, Brown, & Green, 1824).

Morley, Vincent, *The Popular Mind in Eighteenth-Century Ireland* (Cork: Cork University Press, 2017).

Morrison, Susan Signe, 'Dynamic Dirt: Medieval Holy Dust, Ritual Erosion, and Pilgrimage Ecopoetis.' *Open Library of Humanities* 5.1 (2019): 1–30.

Nic Lochlainn, Sorcha, '"Out of a Reverie, and as if Giving Unconscious Expression to a Deep Internal Feeling": Women's Clothmaking Songs in the Gaelic Tradition' in *Oxford Handbook of Irish Song, 1100–1850*, ed. Conor Caldwell. (Oxford: Oxford University Press, 2021).

O'Connell, Helen, *Ireland and the Fiction of Improvement* (Oxford: Oxford University Press, 2006).

O'Connor, Roderick, 'Esquire's Letter and Observations on Ashes and James Breakey's Process and Affidavit, as also his Remarks' in *To the Right Honourable and Honourable Trustees of the Linen and Hempen Manufacture* (Dublin, 1783).

Ó Danachair, Caoimhín, 'Cottier and Landlord in Pre-Famine Ireland.' *Béaloideas* 48/49 (1980): 154–65.

Ó Danachair, Caoimhín, 'Materials and Methods in Irish Traditional Building.' *Journal of the Royal Society of Antiquaries of Ireland*. 87.1 (1957): 61–74.

Ó Danachair, Caoimhín, 'Traditional Forms of the Dwelling House in Ireland.' *Journal of the Royal Society of Antiquaries of Ireland* 102.1 (1972): 77–96.

O'Donnell, Mary Louise, 'A Driving Image of Revolution: The Harp and its Utopian Space in the Eighteenth Century.' *Utopian Studies* 21.2 (2010): 252–73.

O' Dowd, Mary, *A History of Women in Ireland, 1500–1800* (London: Pearson, 2005).

Ó Gallchoir, Clíona, *Maria Edgeworth: Women, Enlightenment, and Nation* (Dublin: UCD Press, 2005).

Ó Gallchoir, Clíona, 'New Beginning or Bearer of Tradition? Early Irish Fiction and the Construction of the Child' in *Irish Literature in Transition, 1700–1780*, ed. Moyra Haslett (Cambridge: Cambridge University Press, 2020).

Ó Gallchoir, Clíona, '"Whole Swarms of Bastards": A Modest Proposal, the discourse of Economic Improvement and Protestant Masculinity in Ireland, 1720–1738' in *Ireland and Masculinities in History*, ed. Rebecca Anne Barr, Sean Brady, and Jane McGaughey (London: Palgrave Macmillan, 2019).

Ó Háinle, Cathal G. 'The Gaelic Background of Carleton's Traits and Stories.' *Éire-Ireland* 18.1 (1983): 6–19.

O'Halloran, Clare, 'From Antiquarian Text to Fiction's Subtext: The Extended Afterlife of Spenser's "View of the Present State of Ireland".' *Spenser Studies* 31–32 (2018): 511–30.

O'Halloran, Clare, *Golden Ages and Barbarous Nations: Antiquarian Debate and Cultural Politics in Ireland, c.1750–1800* (Cork: Cork University Press in association with Field Day, 2004).

O'Hanlon, Oliver, 'A Woman Who Made her Mark: An Irishman's Diary on Sculptor Gabriel Hayes.' *Irish Times*, 6 July 2020.

Ohlmeyer, Jane, 'Colonization within Britain and Ireland, 1580s–1640s' in *The Oxford History of the British Empire*, vol. 1, ed. Nicholas Canny and Alaine Low (Oxford University Press, 1998).

O'Kane, Finola, 'An Irish Cabin on the Commons of Bray.' *British Library: Picturing Places, Town and City*, 17 April 2019, https://www.bl.uk/picturing-places/articles/an-irish-cabin-on-the-commons-of-bray.

O'Kane, Finola, 'Arthur Young's Published and Unpublished Illustrations for "A Tour in Ireland 1776–1779".' *Irish Architectural and Decorative Studies, Journal of the Irish Georgian Society* 19 (2016).

O'Leary, Philip, 'Contention at Feasts in Early Irish Literature.' *Éigse* 20 (1984).

Ó Madagáin, Breandán, 'The Functions of Irish Song in the Nineteenth Century.' *Béaloideas* 53 (1985): 130–216.

O'Reilly, Barry, and Colm Murray, *Traditional Buildings on Irish Farms*. Built and Natural Heritage, Series 2 (Dublin: Heritage Council and Teagasc, 2007).

Orr, Jennifer, ' "No John Clare": Minute Observations from the Ulster Cottage Door.' *John Clare Society Journal* 29 (2010): 51.

Ó Tuama, Sean and Thomas Kinsella, *An Duanaire, Poems of the Dispossessed 1600–1900* (Dublin: Dolmen, 1981).

Owenson, Sydney, *Florence Macarthy: An Irish Tale*, ed. Jenny McAuley (London: Routledge, 2015).

Owenson, Sydney, *Lady Morgan's Memoirs: Autobiography, Diaries and Correspondence*, vol. 1, ed. William Hepworth Dixon (London: William H. Allen, 1862).

Owenson, Sydney, *Patriotic Sketches of Ireland, written in Connaught* (Baltimore, MD: Dobbin & Murphy, Callendar & Wills, 1809).

Owenson, Sydney, *The Wild Irish Girl*, ed. Kathryn Kirkpatrick (Oxford: Oxford University Press, 1999),

Parkinson, James, *Address to the Hon. Edmund Burke, from the Swinish Multitude* (London: Ridgway, 1793).

Pasanek, Brad, *Metaphors of Mind: An Eighteenth-Century Dictionary* (Baltimore, MD: Johns Hopkins University Press, 2015).

Pennell, Sara, 'Making the Bed in Later Stuart and Georgian England' in *Selling Textiles in the Long Eighteenth Century: Comparative Perspectives from Western Europe*, ed. Jon Stobart and B. Blondé (London: Palgrave Macmillan, 2014).

Petty, William, 'Of Making Cloth with Sheep's Wool' (1661) in *The History of the Royal Society of London For Improving of Natural Knowledge, from its Rise* (London: A. Millar, 1756).

Plumwood, Val, 'Journey to the Heart of Stone' in *Culture, Creativity, and Environment: New Environmentalist Criticism*, ed. Fiona Becket and Terry Gifford (New York: Rodopi, 2007).

Potts, Donna, *Contemporary Irish Writing and Environmentalism: The Wearing of the Deep Green* (London: Palgrave Macmillan, 2018).

Prescott, Sarah, 'Ellen Taylor (years unknown; one extant publication, 1792)' in *Irish Women Poets Rediscovered*, ed. Maria Johnston and Conor Linnie (Cork: Cork University Press, 2021).

Proceedings of the Dublin Society 10 (Dublin: S. Powell: 1773–4), 27 January 1774.

Quin, Jack, 'Some Master of Design: W. B. Yeats and the Free State Coinage.' *Modernist Cultures* 15.4 (2020): 464–87.

Ramsay, David, *The Weaver and Housewife's Pocket Book, containing the Rules for the right Making of Linen Cloth* (Edinburgh: Ramsay, 1750).

Richardson, D., *Domestic Pigs: Their Origin and Varieties* (London: Orr & Co., 1852).

Rivera, Maya, *Poetics of the Flesh* (Durham, NC: Duke University Press, 2015).

Roberts, Daniel, 'A "Teague" and a "True Briton": Charles Johnstone, Ireland, and Empire.' *Irish University Review* 41.1 (2011): 133–50.

Roberts, Daniel Sanjiv, Introduction to Charles Johnston, *The History of Arsaces* (Dublin: Four Courts, 2014).

Robertson, Emma, Michael Pickering, and Marke Korczynski, '"And Spinning so with Voices Meet, like Nightingales they Sung Full Sweet": Unraveling Representations of Singing in Pre-Industrial Textile Production.' *Cultural and Social History* 5.1 (2008): 11–31.

Rosenthal, Angela, 'Visceral Culture: Blushing and the Legibility of Whiteness in Eighteenth-Century British Culture.' *Art History* 27.4 (2004): 563–92.

Rosiek, Jerry Lee, Jimmy Snider, and Scott Pratt, 'The New Materialisms and Indigenous Theories of Non-Human Agency.' *Qualitative Inquiry* 26.3–4 (2020): 331–46.

Ross, Ian Campbell, 'Thomas Amory, John Buncle, and the Origins of Irish Fiction.' *Eire-Ireland* 18.3 (1983): 71–85.

Ross, Robert, *Some Considerations on the Improvement of the Linen Manufacture in Ireland, Particularly with Relation to the Raising and Dressing of Flax and Flax-Seed* (Dublin: printed by R. Reilly, 1735).

Sen, Malcolm, ed., *A History of Irish Literature and the Environment* (Cambridge: Cambridge University Press, 2022).

Sharma, H. S. Shekhar, and C. F. van Sumere, *The Biology and Processing of Flax* (Belfast: M Publications, 1992).

Shelley, Percy Bysshe, *The Poetical Works of Percy Bysshe Shelley*, ed. Mary Shelley (London: Moxon, 1840).

Silver, Sean, 'Production and Practice' in *A Cultural History of Hair in the Age of Enlightenment*, ed. Margaret Powell and Joseph Roche (London: Bloomsbury, 2021).

Silver, Sean, *The Mind is a Collection: Case Studies in Eighteenth-Century Thought* (Philadelphia: UPenn Press, 2015).

Simon, James, *An Essay Towards an Historical Account of Irish Coins* (Dublin: Proctor, 1810).

Smith, Chloe Wigston, *Women, Work, and Clothes in the Eighteenth-Century Novel* (Cambridge: Cambridge University Press, 2013).

Smith, Kate, *Material Goods, Moving Hands: Perceiving Production in England, 1700–1830* (Manchester: Manchester University Press, 2014).

Spenser, Edmund, *View of the Present State of Ireland* (Dublin: Laurence Flin, 1763).

Spenser, Edmund, *A View of the Present State of Ireland*, ed. W. L. Renwick (Oxford: Clarendon, 1970).

Stephenson, Robert, *A Letter to the Right Honourable and Honourable the Trustees of the Linen Manufacture* (Dublin: James Hunter, 1759).

Stephenson, Robert, 'Considerations on the Present State of the Linen Manufacture, Humbly Addressed to the Trustees of the Linen Board, 1754' in *An Inquiry into the State and Progress of the Linen Manufacture in Ireland* (Dublin: Powell, 1757).

Stephenson, Robert, *Observations on the Present State of the Linen Trade of Ireland: in a series of letters addressed to the Right Honourable trustees of the Linen Manufacture. In which the Reports, Libel, and British Examination of Mr. John Arbuthnot, Inspector General of Leinster, Munster, and Connaught, are considered and refuted* (Dublin, 1784).

Stephenson, Robert, 'Report of the State of the linen Manufacture of Ireland for 1765,' *The Reports and Observations of Robert Stephenson made to the Right Honourable and Honourable Trustees of the Linen Manufacture for 1764 and 1765* (Dublin: Printed by the order of the Linen Board, 1766).

Stephenson, S. M. M. D., *On the Processes and Utensils Employed in the Preparation of Flax, and in the Manufacture of Linen in Ireland* (Belfast: Transactions of Belfast Literary Society, 1811).

Sudan, Rajani, 'Mud, Mortar, and Other Technologies of Empire.' *The Eighteenth Century* 45.2 (2004): 147–69.

Sudan, Rajani, *The Alchemy of Empire: Abject Materials and the Technologies of Colonialism* (New York: Fordham University Press, 2016).

Swift, Jonathan, *A Modest Proposal and Other Satirical Works* (New York: Dover, 2012).

Swift, Jonathan, *A Proposal for the Universal Use of Irish Manufacture in Cloaths and Furniture of Houses, etc. Utterly Rejecting and Renouncing Every Thing wearable that comes from England* (Dublin: E. Waters, 1720).

Swift, Jonathan, 'Drapier's Letters' in *Major Works*, ed. David Woolley (Oxford: Oxford University Press, 2003).

Swift, Jonathan, *Gulliver's Travels* (Oxford: Oxford University Press, 2005).

Swift, Jonathan, *The Story of the Injured Lady. Being a true picture of Scotch perfidy, Irish poverty, and English partiality. With letters and poems never before printed. By the Rev. Dr. Swift* (London: M. Cooper, 1746).

Synge, J. M., *My Wallet of Photographs* (Dublin: Dolmen, 1971).

Taylor, Ellen, *Poems by Ellen Taylor, the Irish Cottager* (Dublin: Grafton, 1792).

Temple, Sir William, 'An Essay Upon the Advancement of Trade in Ireland, written to the Earl of Essex, Lord Lieutenant of that Kingdom. July 22, 1673' in *Miscellanea in Two Parts* (London: Tonson, 1697).

Tenniel, John, 'The Pig and the Peer, 1880.' *Punch* [London], 7 August 1880.

The Adventures of a Bad Shilling in the Kingdom of Ireland, in *British It-Narratives, 1750–1830*, ed. Mark Blackwell, vol. 1 (London: Pickering & Chatto, 2012).

The Adventures of a Bad Shilling in the Kingdom of Ireland, in *Ireland's Mirror, or The Masonic Magazine* [Dublin] 3 (Jan. 1806).

The Bridgeport Telegram, 'Michael Delohery Dies in Danbury: Hat Manufacturer, Once an Immigrant Boy, Won Wide Success,' 16 April 1927, p. 8.

The Observer, classified ads, 1808, p. 1.

The Spinning Wheel's Garland, Containing Five Excellent New Songs (London, 1775).

'The Story Mac Datho's Pig' in *Ancient Irish Tales*, ed. Tom Peete Cross and Clark Harris Slover (New York: Henry Holt, 1936).

The Story of the Learned Pig, by an Officer of the Royal Navy (London: R. Jameson, 1786).

Thompson, James, *Models of Value: Eighteenth Century Political Economy and the Novel* (Durham, NC: Duke University Press, 1996).

Tracy, Larissa, *Heads will Roll: Decapitation in the Medieval and Early Modern Imagination* (Leiden: Brill, 2012).

Tracy, Robert, '"Maria Edgeworth and Lady Morgan: Legality versus Legitimacy.' *Nineteenth-Century Fiction* 40.1 (1985): 1–22.

Trustees for Promoting the Linen and Hempen Manufactures of Ireland, Broadside (Dublin: Williamson, 2 March 1790).

Wakefield, Edward, *An Account of Ireland, Statistical and Political*, vol. 1 (London: Longman, Hurst, Rees, Orme, & Browne, 1812).

Walsh, Claire, 'Shop Design and the Display of Goods in Eighteenth-Century London.' *Journal of Design History* 8.3 (1995): 157–76.

Warburton, John, James Whitelaw, and Robert Walsh, *History of the City of Dublin, from the Earliest Accounts to the Present Time*, 2 vols (London: Cadell & Davies, 1818).

Ward, James, 'Pamphlets into Rags: Swift on Paper' in *Reading Swift: Papers from the Sixth Munster Symposium on Jonathan Swift*, ed. Kirsten Juhas, Hermann J. Real, and Sandra Simon (Munich: Wilhelm Fink, 2013).

Ward, James, 'Personations: The Political Body in Jonathan Swift's Fiction.' *Irish University Review* 41.1 (2011): 40–53.

Ward, James, 'The Political Body in Jonathan Swift's Fiction.' *Irish University Review* 41.1 (2011): 40–53.

Went, Arthur E. J., 'The Coinage of Ireland, 1000 A.D. to the Present Day' in *W. B. Yeats and the Designing of Ireland's Coinage*, ed. Brian Cleeve (Dublin: Dolmen Press, 1972).

Wheeler, Wendy, 'Natural Play, Natural Metaphor, and Natural Stories: Biosemetic Realism' in *Material Ecocriticism*, ed. Serenella Iovino and Serpil Opperman (Bloomington, IN: Indiana University Press, 2015).

Williams, W. H. A., *Creating Irish Tourism, the First Century, 1750–1850* (London: Anthem, 2011).

Wilson, Augusta Evans, *Vashi* (New York, 1869).

Wilson, Kathleen Curtis, *Irish People, Irish Linen* (Athens, OH: Ohio University Press, 2011).

Wolfe, Cary, *Animal Rites: American Culture, the Discourse of Species, and Posthuman Theory* (Chicago: University of Chicago Press, 2003).

Wright, Julia, *Representing the National Landscape in Irish Romanticism* (Syracuse, NY: Syracuse University Press, 2014).

Yeats, William Butler, 'What we Did or Tried to Do' in *W. B. Yeats and the Designing of Ireland's Coinage*, ed. Brian Cleeve (Dublin: Dolmen, 1972).

Young, Arthur, *Tour in Ireland* (1776–1779), 2 vols, ed. Arthur Wollaston Hutton (London: George Bell & Sons, 1892).

Yusoff, Kathryn, *A Billion Black Anthropocenes or None* (Minneapolis: University of Minnesota Press, 2018).

Index